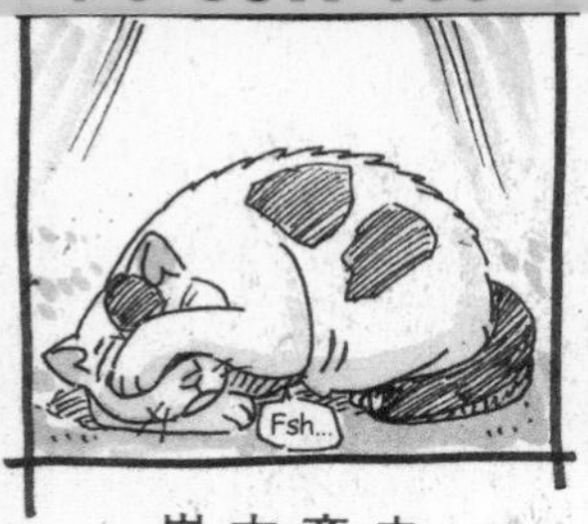
Fsh...

岸本斉史

One member of my family is our pet cat Shû-san. He's quite elderly, so he can't get around much. In fact, he sleeps most of the time. He's always asleep, even during the daytime, but it must get too bright, because he'll cleverly cover both eyes with his arm. That gesture is just so cool.

—*Masashi Kishimoto, 2010*

Author/artist Masashi Kishimoto was born in 1974 in rural Okayama Prefecture, Japan. After spending time in art college, he won the Hop Step Award for new manga artists with his manga **Karakuri** (Mechanism). Kishimoto decided to base his next story on traditional Japanese culture. His first version of **Naruto**, drawn in 1997, was a one-shot story about fox spirits; his final version, which debuted in **Weekly Shonen Jump** in 1999, quickly became the most popular ninja manga in Japan.

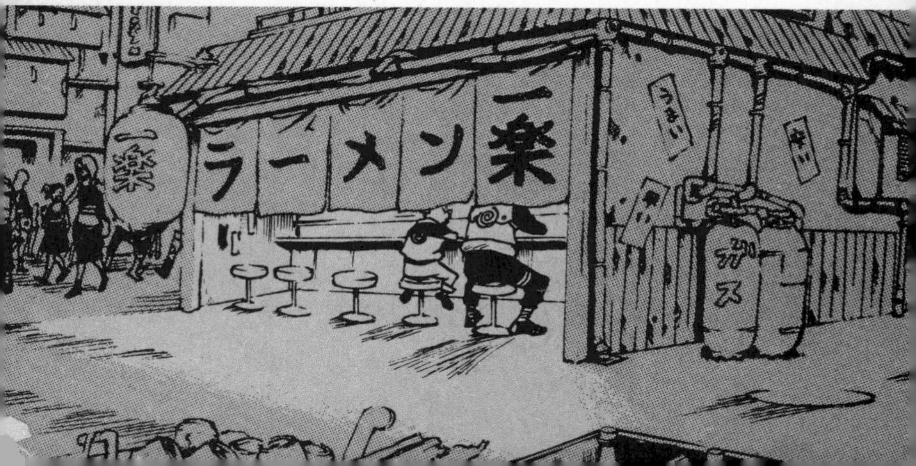
一楽
ラーメン一楽

NARUTO VOL. 52
SHONEN JUMP Manga Edition

This graphic novel contains material that was originally published in English in SHONEN JUMP #95–98. Artwork in the magazine may have been slightly altered from that presented here.

STORY AND ART BY MASASHI KISHIMOTO

Translation/Mari Morimoto
Touch-up Art & Lettering/Inori Fukuda Trant
Design/Sam Elzway
Series Editor/Joel Enos
Graphic Novel Editor/Megan Bates

Printed in the U.S.A.

Published by VIZ Media, LLC
P.O. Box 77010
San Francisco, CA 94107

10 9 8 7 6 5 4 3 2 1
First printing, September 2011

www.viz.com

PARENTAL ADVISORY
NARUTO is rated T for Teen and is recommended for ages 13 and up. This volume contains realistic and fantasy violence.
ratings.viz.com

THE WORLD'S
MOST POPULAR MANGA
SHONEN JUMP
www.shonenjump.com

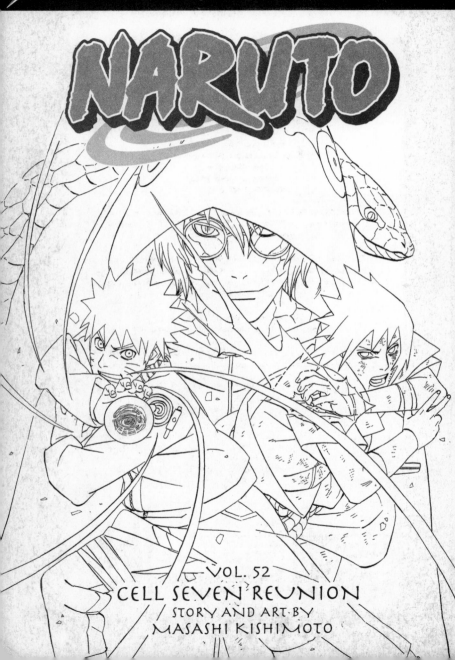

SHONEN JUMP MANGA EDITION

VOL. 52
CELL SEVEN REUNION
STORY AND ART BY
MASASHI KISHIMOTO

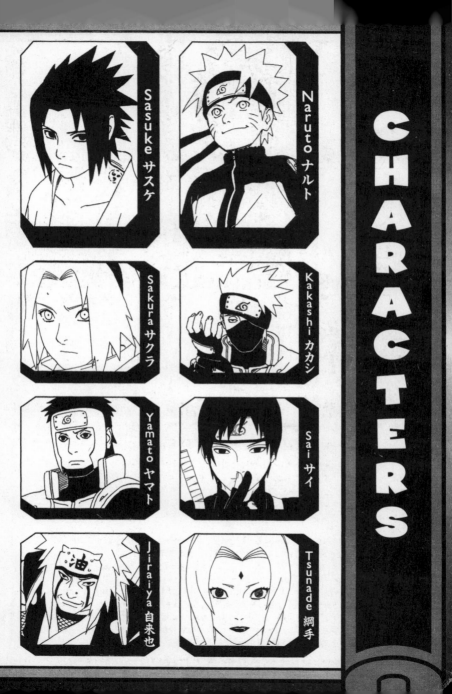

CHARACTERS

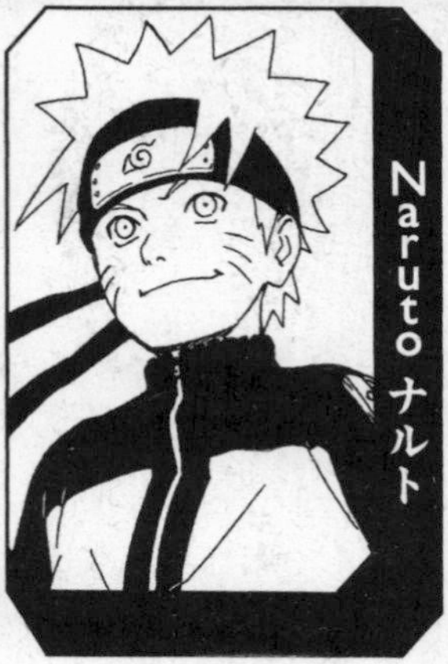
Naruto ナルト

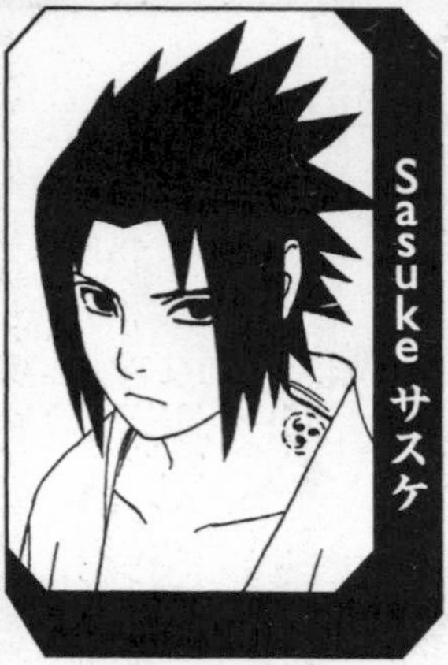
Sasuke サスケ

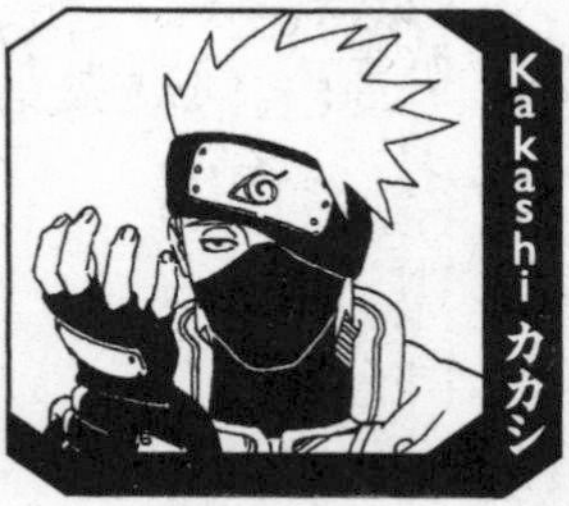
Kakashi カカシ

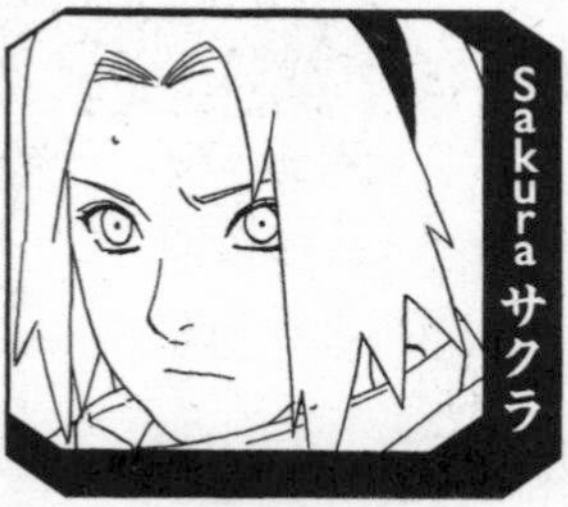
Sakura サクラ

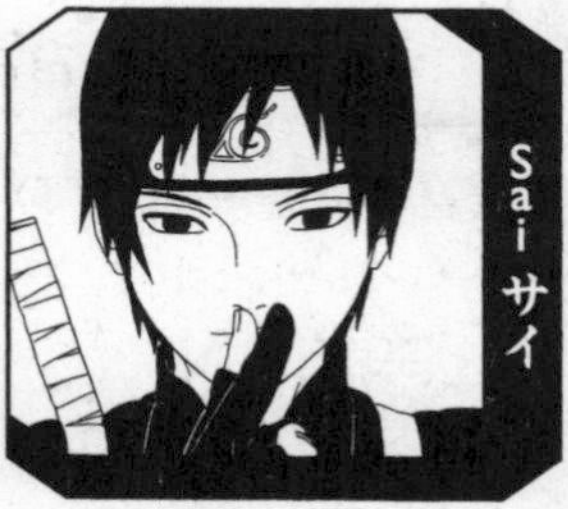
Sai サイ

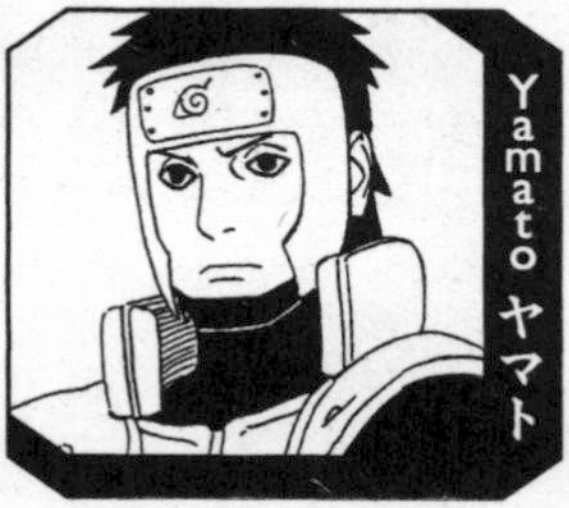
Yamato ヤマト

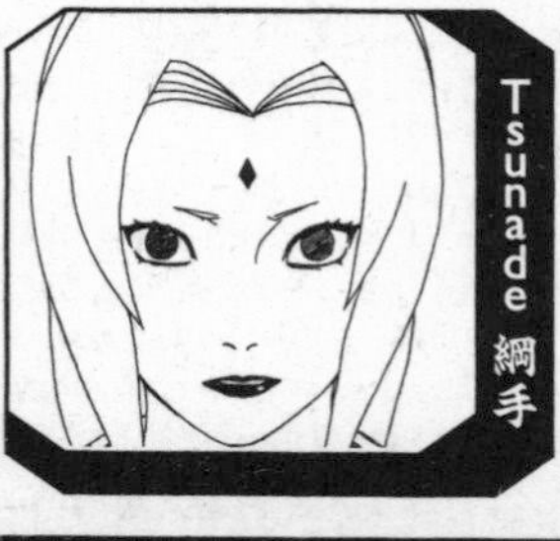
Tsunade 綱手

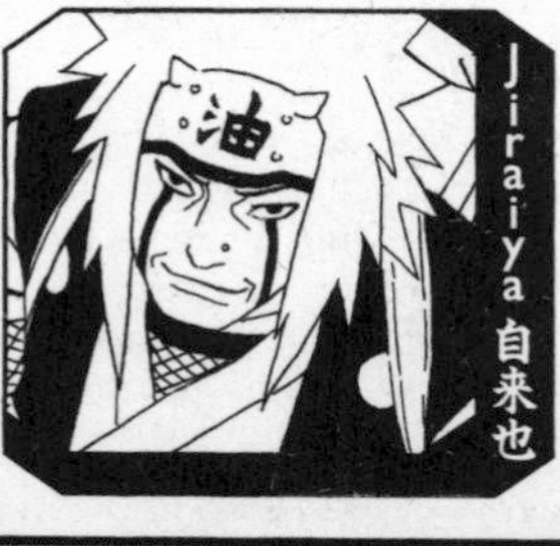
Jiraiya 自来也

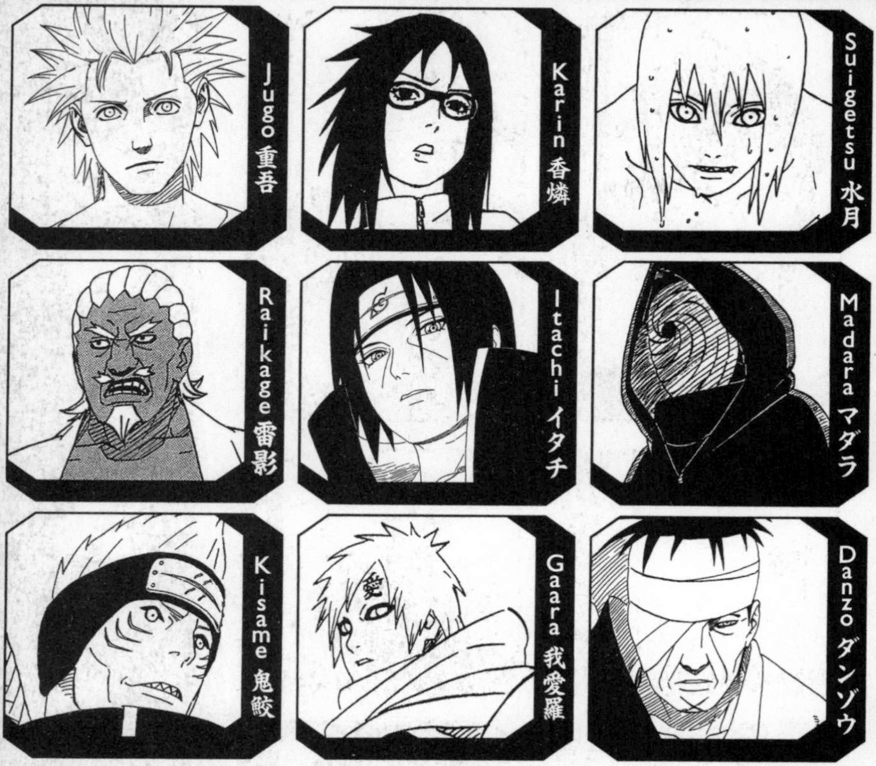
Suigetsu 水月
Karin 香燐
Jugo 重吾
Madara マダラ
Itachi イタチ
Raikage 雷影
Danzo ダンゾウ
Gaara 我愛羅
Kisame 鬼鮫

THE STORY SO FAR...

Naruto, the biggest troublemaker at the Ninja Academy in the Village of Konohagakure, finally becomes a ninja. Along with his classmates Sasuke and Sakura, he grows and matures during countless trials and battles. Sasuke, unable to give up his quest for vengeance, leaves Konohagakure to seek the renegade ninja Orochimaru, from whom he hopes to gain immense power.

In the years that pass, Naruto engages in fierce battles against the Tailed Beast-targeting Akatsuki. Elsewhere, after winning the heroic battle against Itachi and learning his older brother's true intentions, Sasuke allies with the Akatsuki organization and sets out to destroy Konoha.

Upon Madara's declaration of war, each shinobi village leader prepares to form an Allied Shinobi Force. Meanwhile, Sasuke finally gets to defeat one of his enemies; Danzo falls at his hands. Sakura tries to stop the vengeance-obsessed Sasuke, but he turns his murderous intentions on her... Just then, Kakashi comes to the rescue!

NARUTO

VOL. 52
CELL SEVEN REUNION

CONTENTS

Number 484: Cell Seven Reunion!!

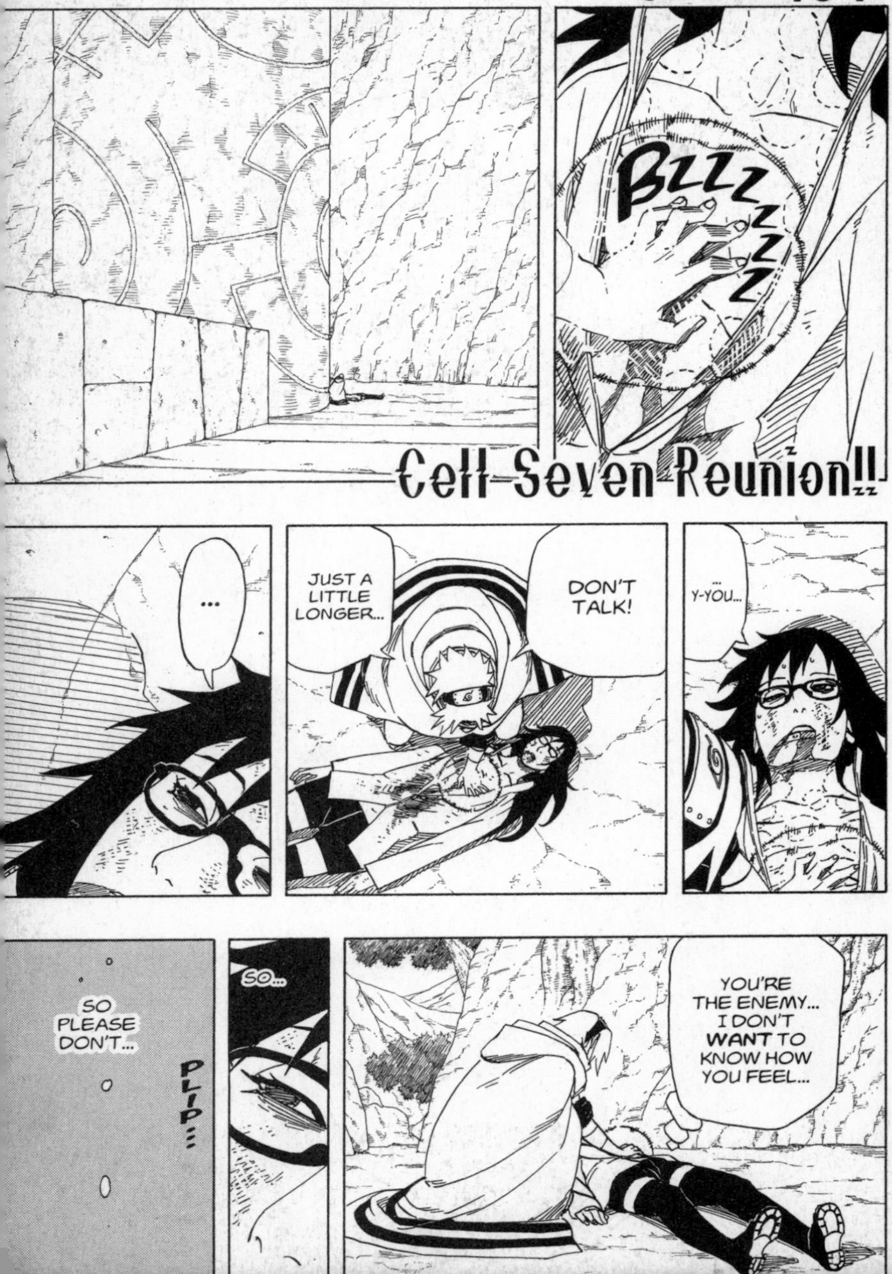
BZZZZZ
... Y-YOU...
DON'T TALK!
JUST A LITTLE LONGER...
...
YOU'RE THE ENEMY... I DON'T **WANT** TO KNOW HOW YOU FEEL...
SO...
PLIP
SO PLEASE DON'T...

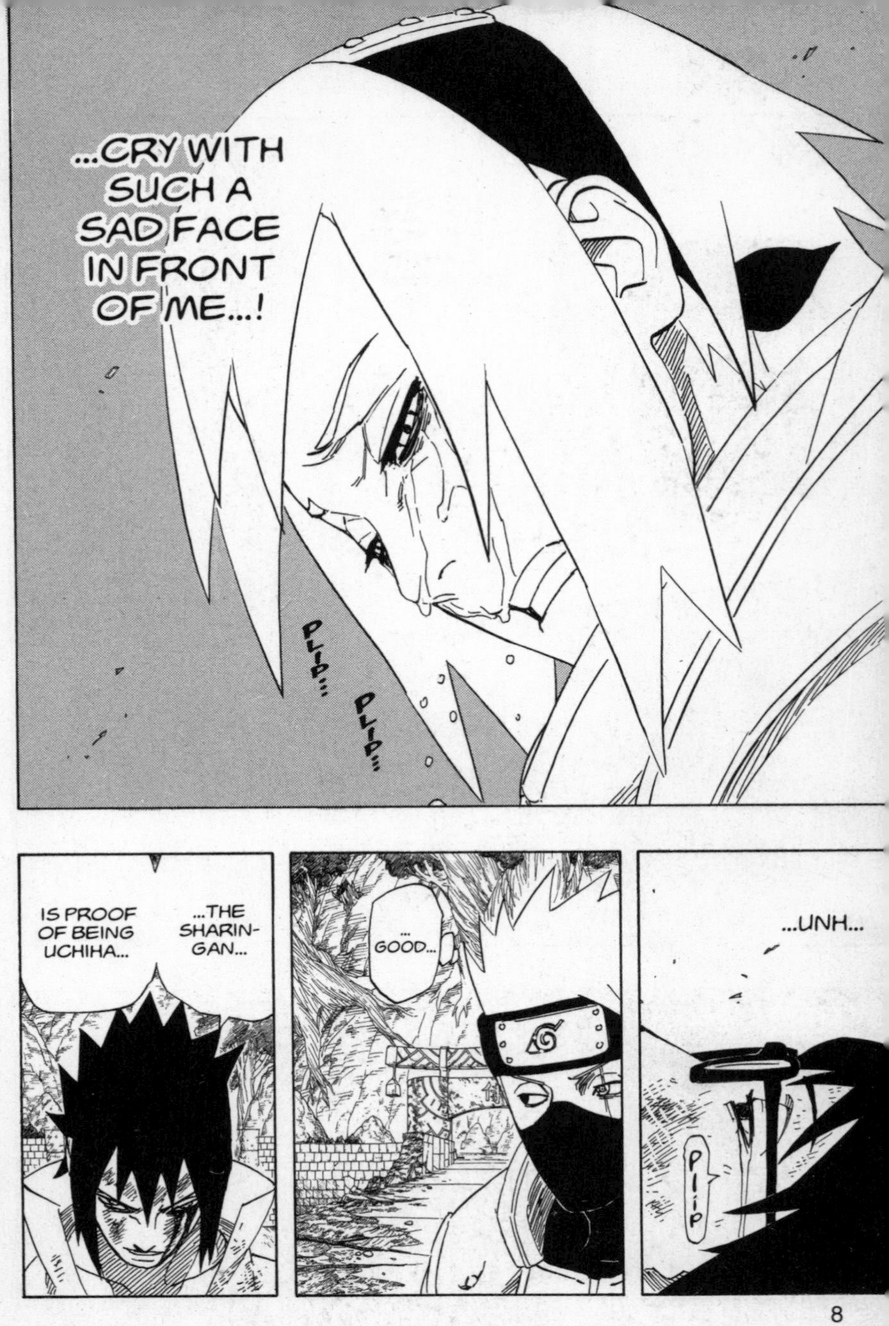
...CRY WITH SUCH A SAD FACE IN FRONT OF ME...!
PLIP... PLIP...
...UNH...
PLIP
...GOOD...
...THE SHARIN-GAN...
IS PROOF OF BEING UCHIHA...

READ THIS WAY

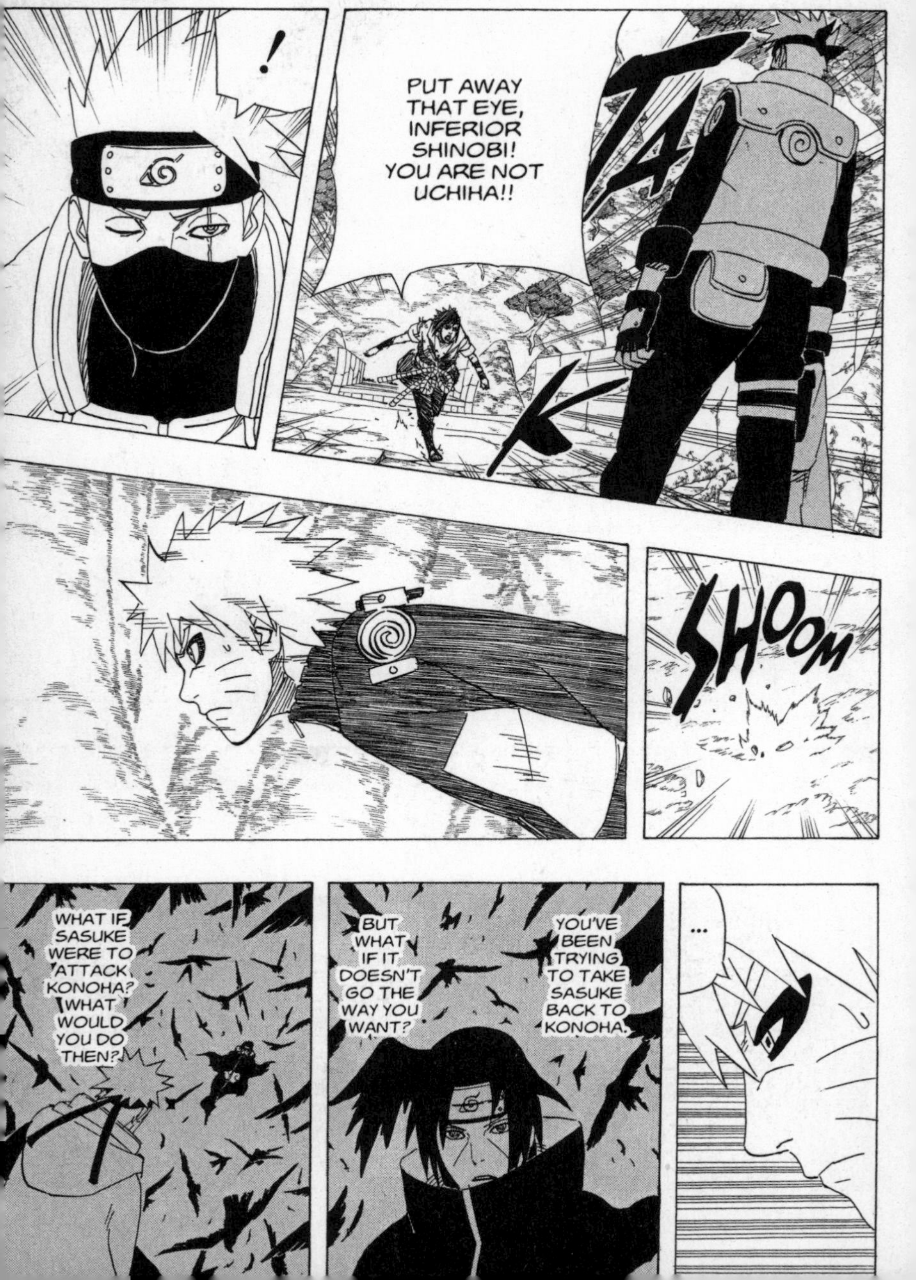
PUT AWAY THAT EYE, INFERIOR SHINOBI! YOU ARE NOT UCHIHA!!
!
SHOOM
...
YOU'VE BEEN TRYING TO TAKE SASUKE BACK TO KONOHA.
BUT WHAT IF IT DOESN'T GO THE WAY YOU WANT?
WHAT IF SASUKE WERE TO ATTACK KONOHA? WHAT WOULD YOU DO THEN?

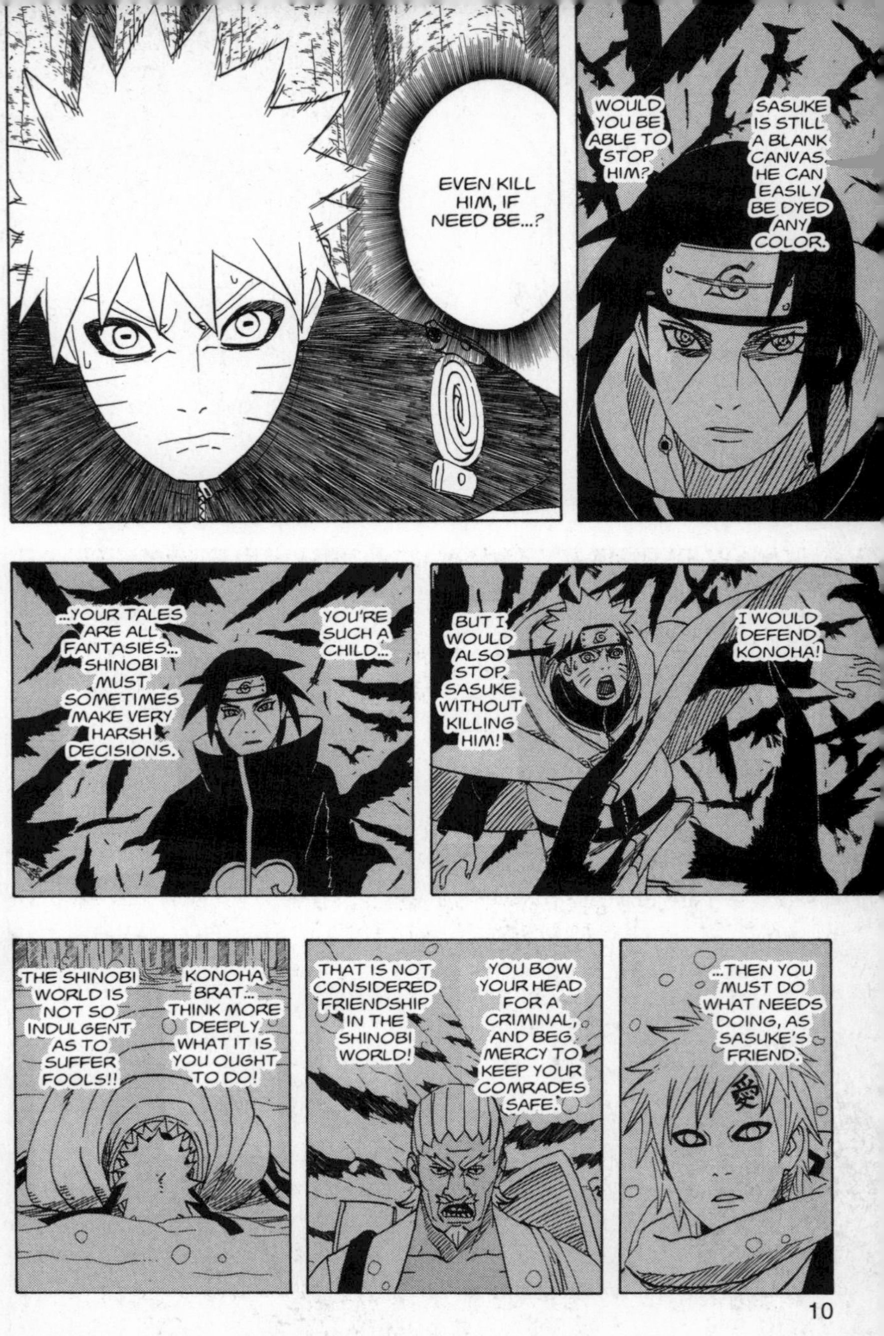
SASUKE IS STILL A BLANK CANVAS. HE CAN EASILY BE DYED ANY COLOR.
WOULD YOU BE ABLE TO STOP HIM?
EVEN KILL HIM, IF NEED BE...?
I WOULD DEFEND KONOHA!
BUT I WOULD ALSO STOP SASUKE WITHOUT KILLING HIM!
YOU'RE SUCH A CHILD...
...YOUR TALES ARE ALL FANTASIES... SHINOBI MUST SOMETIMES MAKE VERY HARSH DECISIONS.
...THEN YOU MUST DO WHAT NEEDS DOING, AS SASUKE'S FRIEND.
YOU BOW YOUR HEAD FOR A CRIMINAL, AND BEG MERCY TO KEEP YOUR COMRADES SAFE.
THAT IS NOT CONSIDERED FRIENDSHIP IN THE SHINOBI WORLD!
KONOHA BRAT... THINK MORE DEEPLY WHAT IT IS YOU OUGHT TO DO!
THE SHINOBI WORLD IS NOT SO INDULGENT AS TO SUFFER FOOLS!!

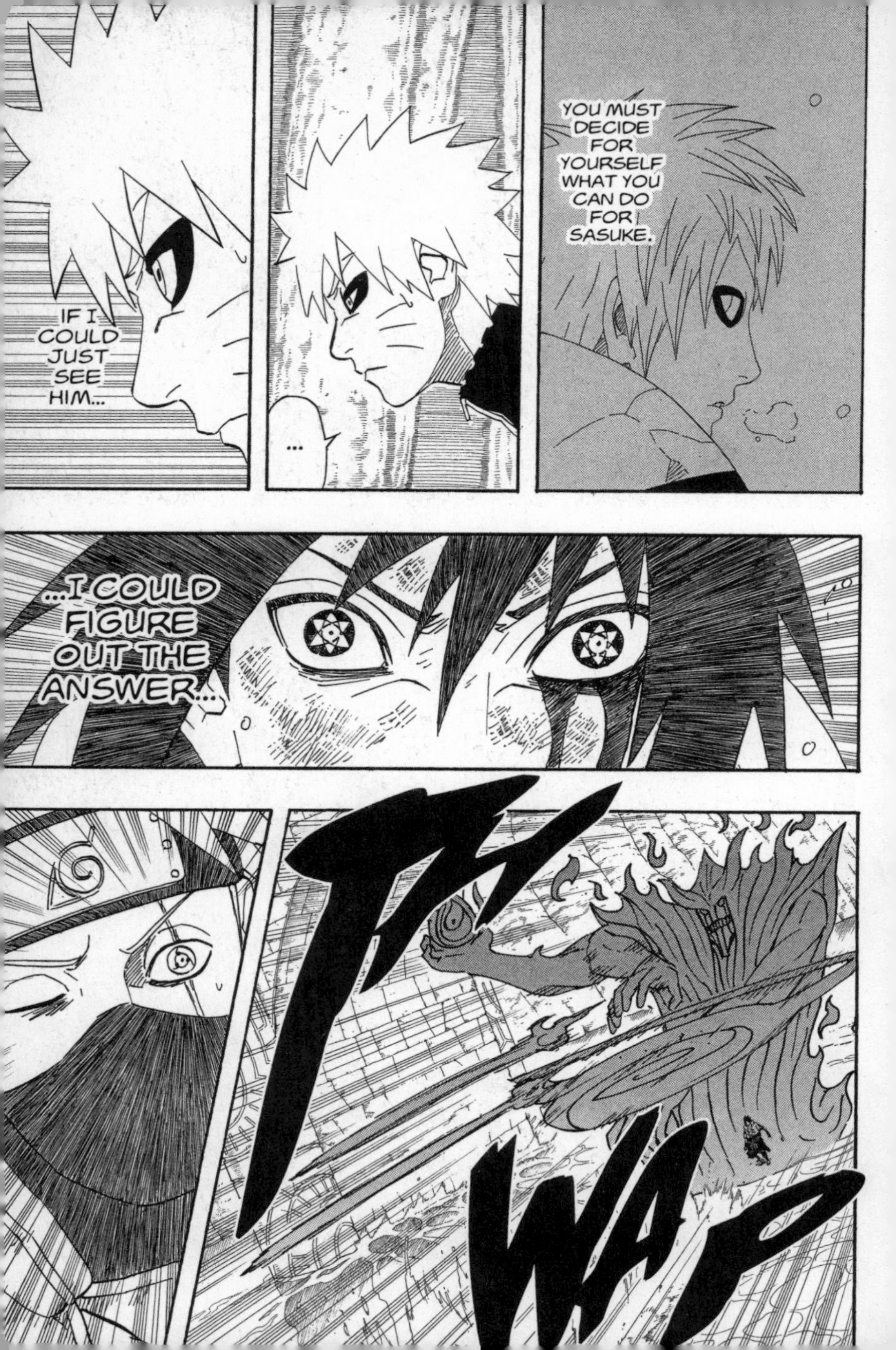
YOU MUST DECIDE FOR YOURSELF WHAT YOU CAN DO FOR SASUKE.
...
IF I COULD JUST SEE HIM...
...I COULD FIGURE OUT THE ANSWER...
FWAP

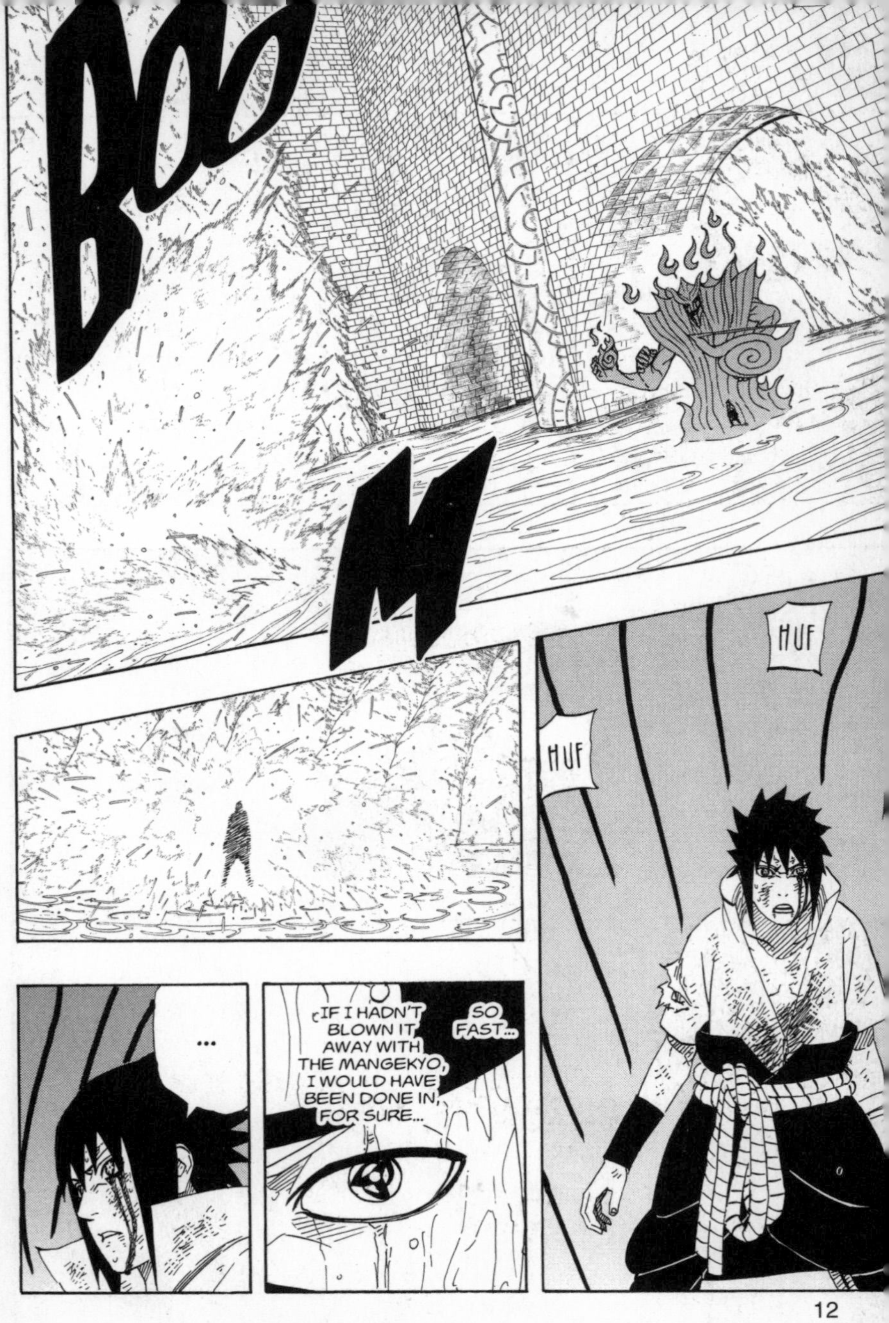

BOOM
HUF
HUF
SO FAST...
IF I HADN'T BLOWN IT AWAY WITH THE MANGEKYO, I WOULD HAVE BEEN DONE IN, FOR SURE...
...

READ THIS WAY

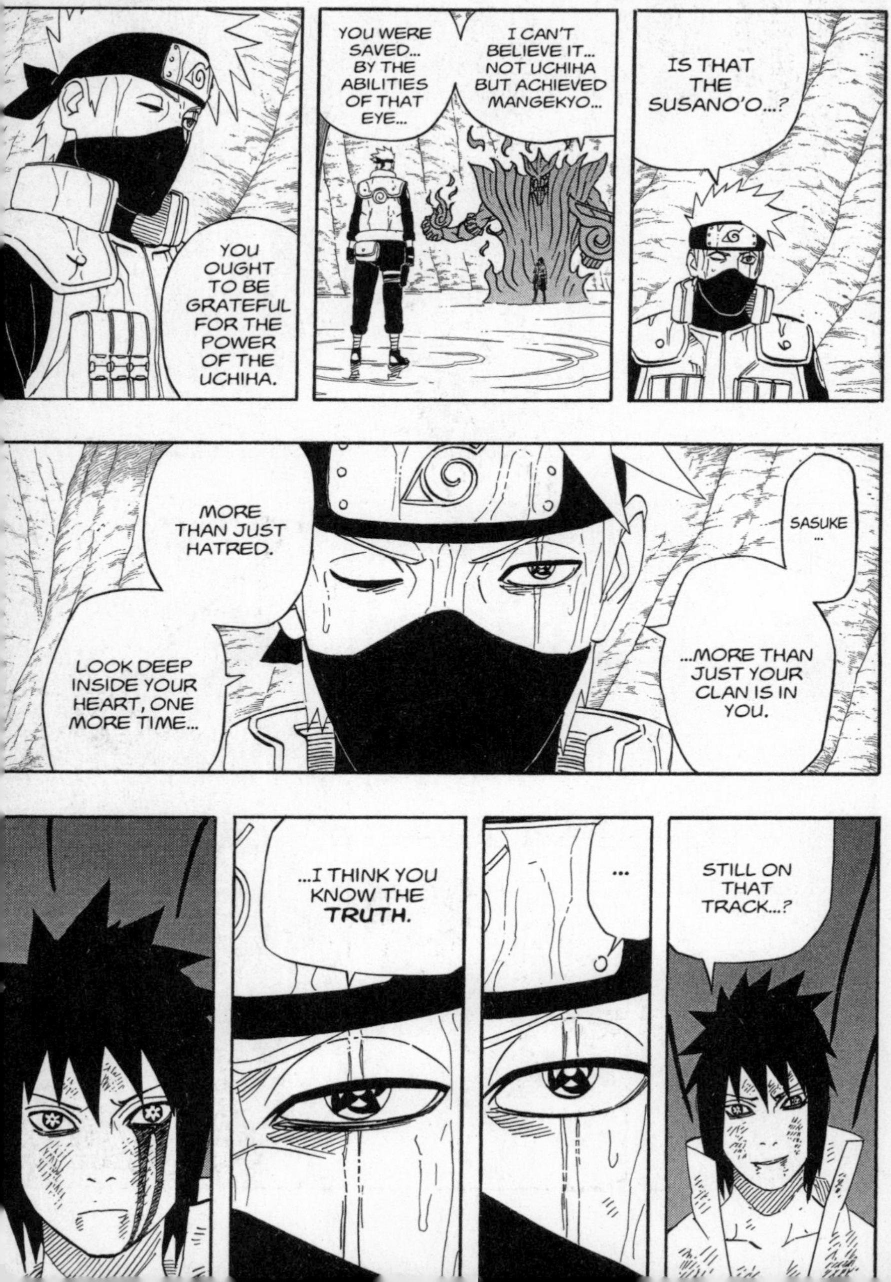
IS THAT THE SUSANO'O...?
I CAN'T BELIEVE IT... NOT UCHIHA BUT ACHIEVED MANGEKYO...
YOU WERE SAVED... BY THE ABILITIES OF THAT EYE...
YOU OUGHT TO BE GRATEFUL FOR THE POWER OF THE UCHIHA.
SASUKE...
...MORE THAN JUST YOUR CLAN IS IN YOU.
MORE THAN JUST HATRED.
LOOK DEEP INSIDE YOUR HEART, ONE MORE TIME...
STILL ON THAT TRACK...?
...
...I THINK YOU KNOW THE TRUTH.

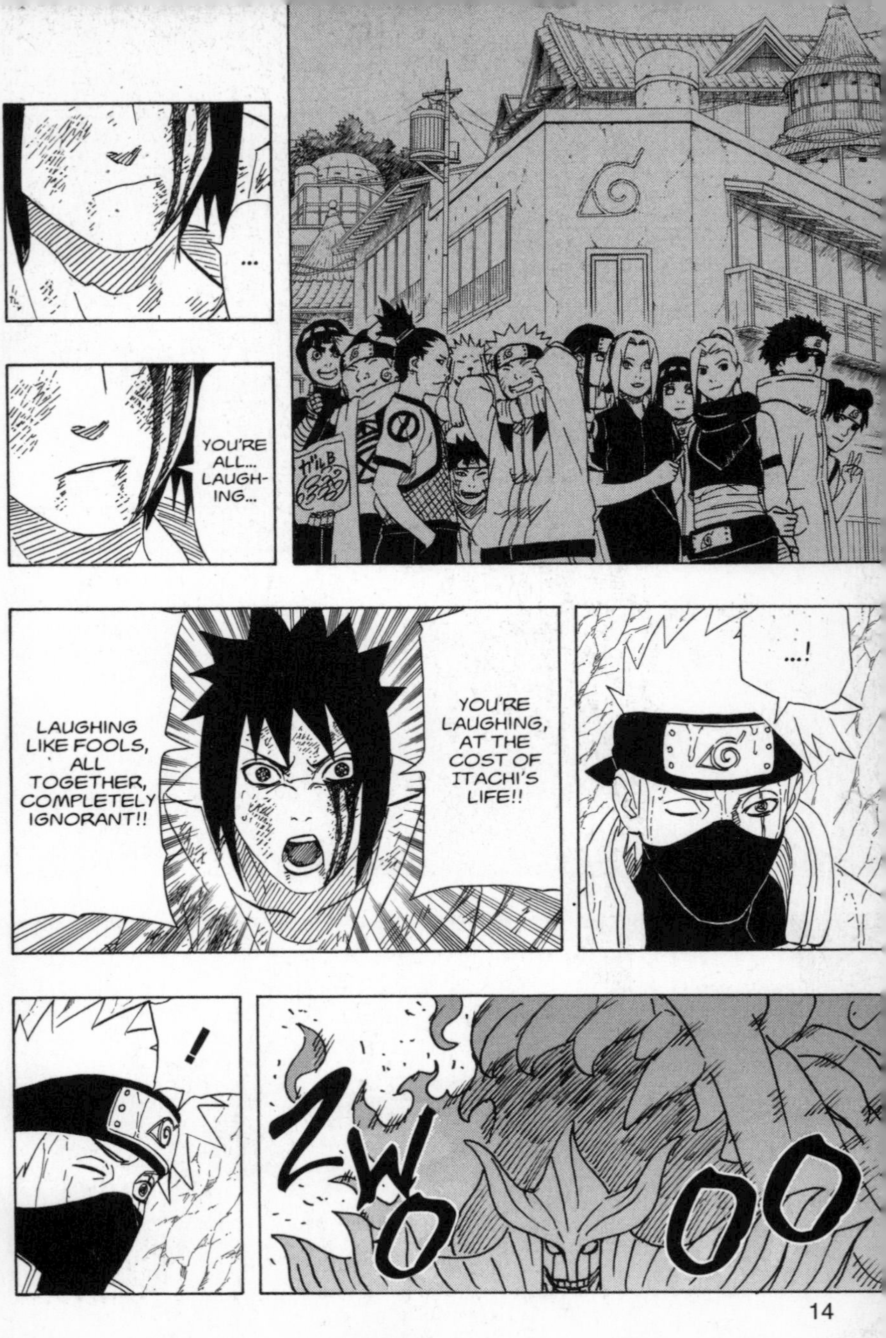
...
YOU'RE ALL... LAUGHING...
...!
YOU'RE LAUGHING, AT THE COST OF ITACHI'S LIFE!!
LAUGHING LIKE FOOLS, ALL TOGETHER, COMPLETELY IGNORANT!!
ZWOOO
!

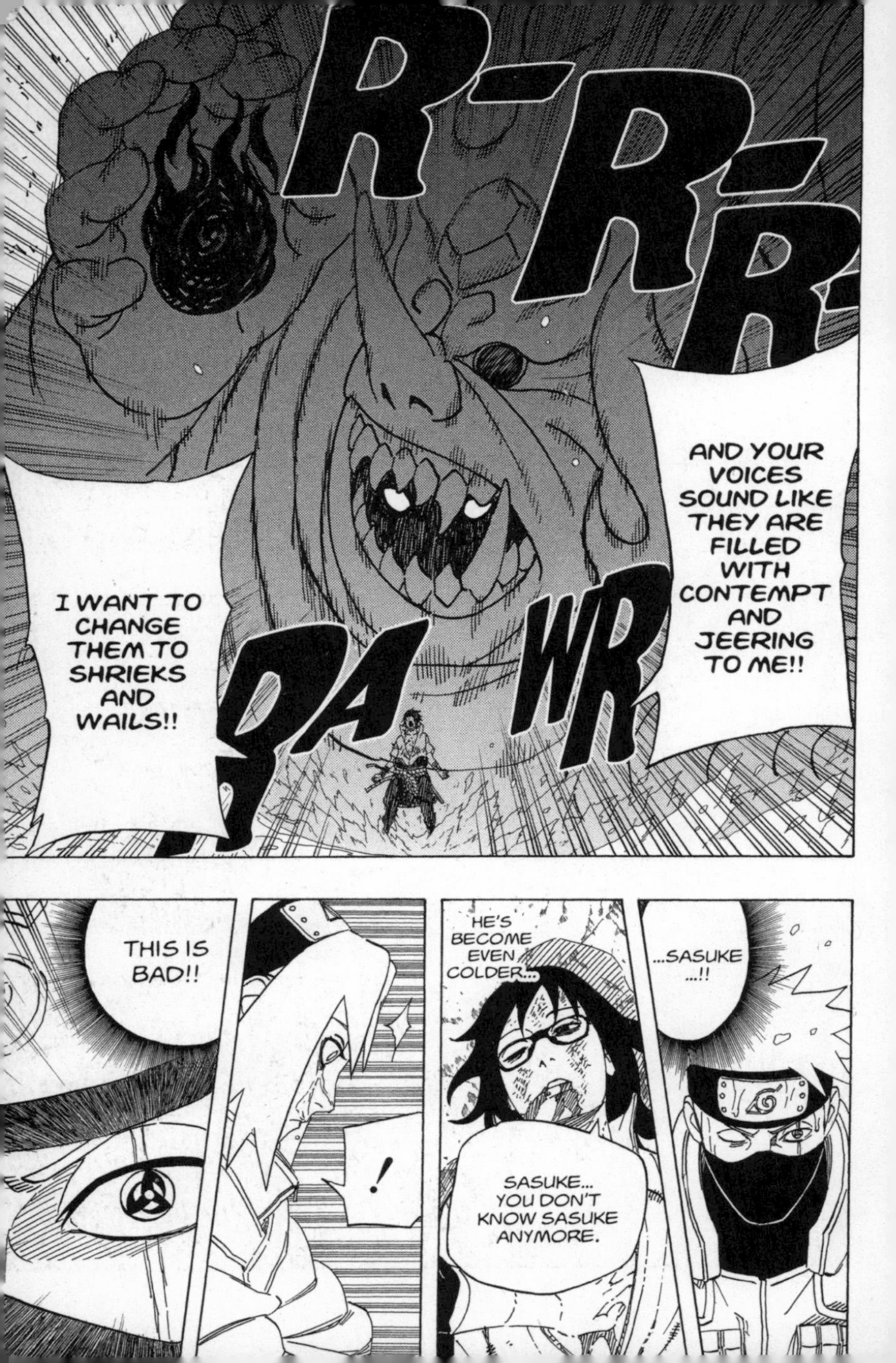
R-R-R-R
AND YOUR VOICES SOUND LIKE THEY ARE FILLED WITH CONTEMPT AND JEERING TO ME!!
DA WR
I WANT TO CHANGE THEM TO SHRIEKS AND WAILS!!
...SASUKE ...!!
HE'S BECOME EVEN COLDER...
SASUKE... YOU DON'T KNOW SASUKE ANYMORE.
!
THIS IS BAD!!

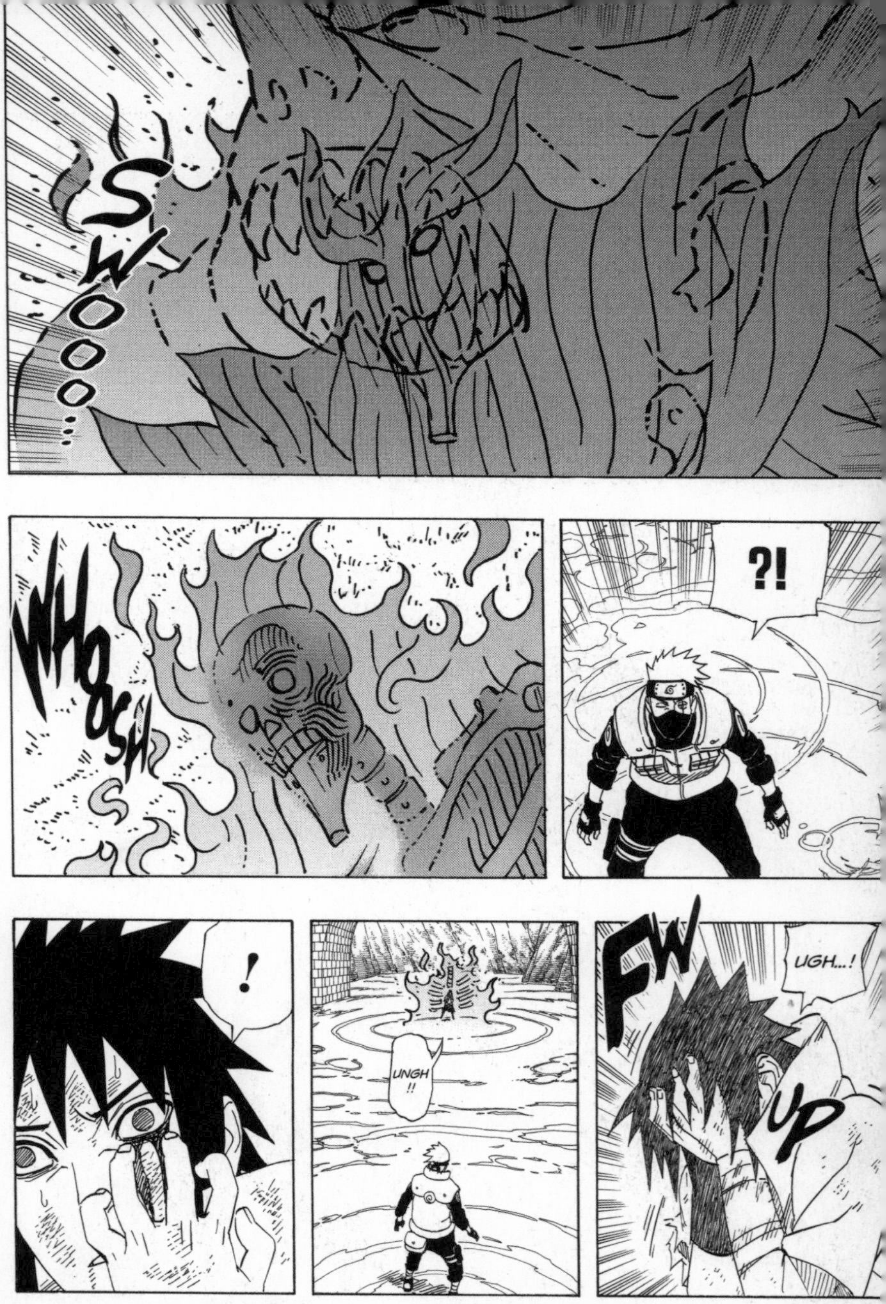
SWOOOOO...
?!
WHOOSH
UGH...!
FWUP
UNGH !!
!

READ THIS WAY

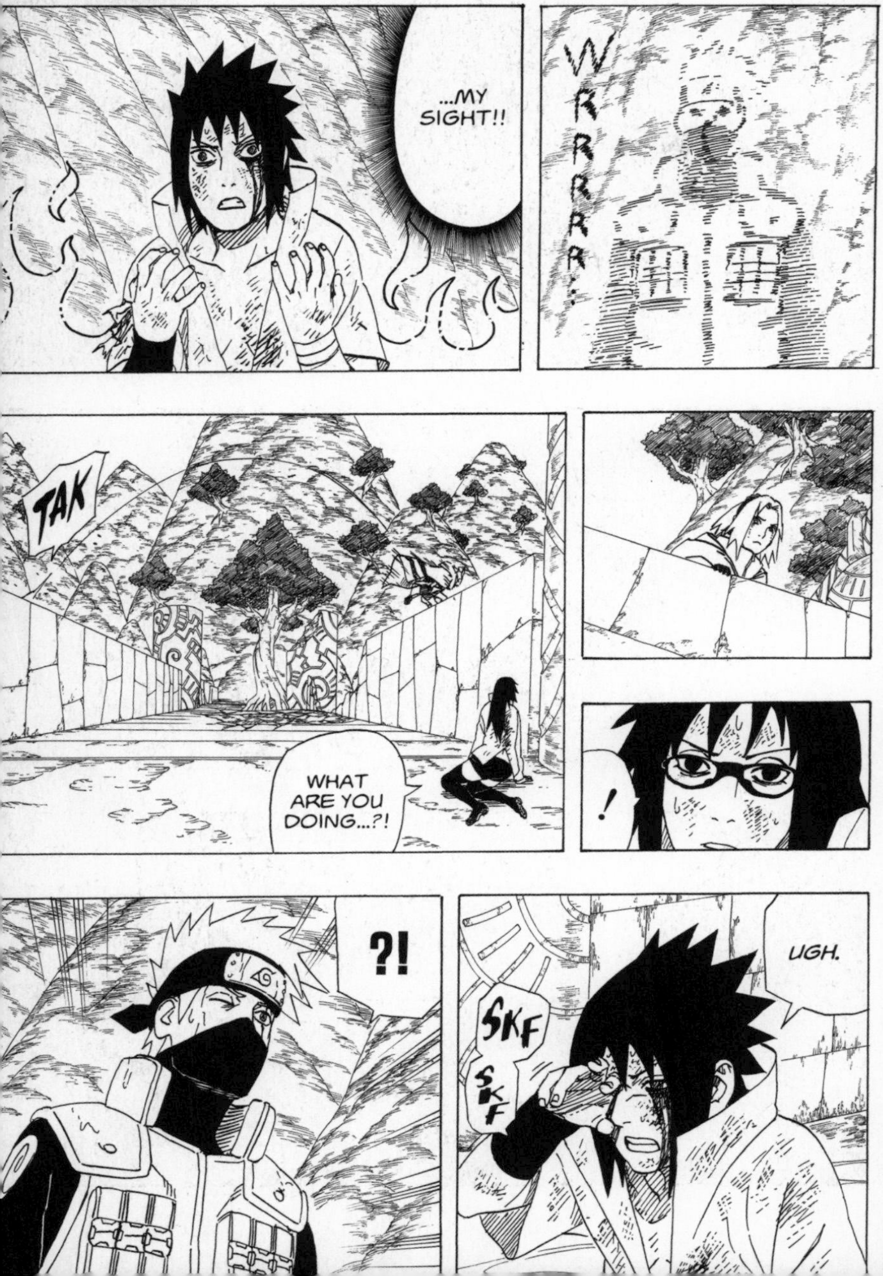
WRRRR...
...MY SIGHT!!
!
TAK
WHAT ARE YOU DOING...?!
UGH.
SKF
SKF
?!

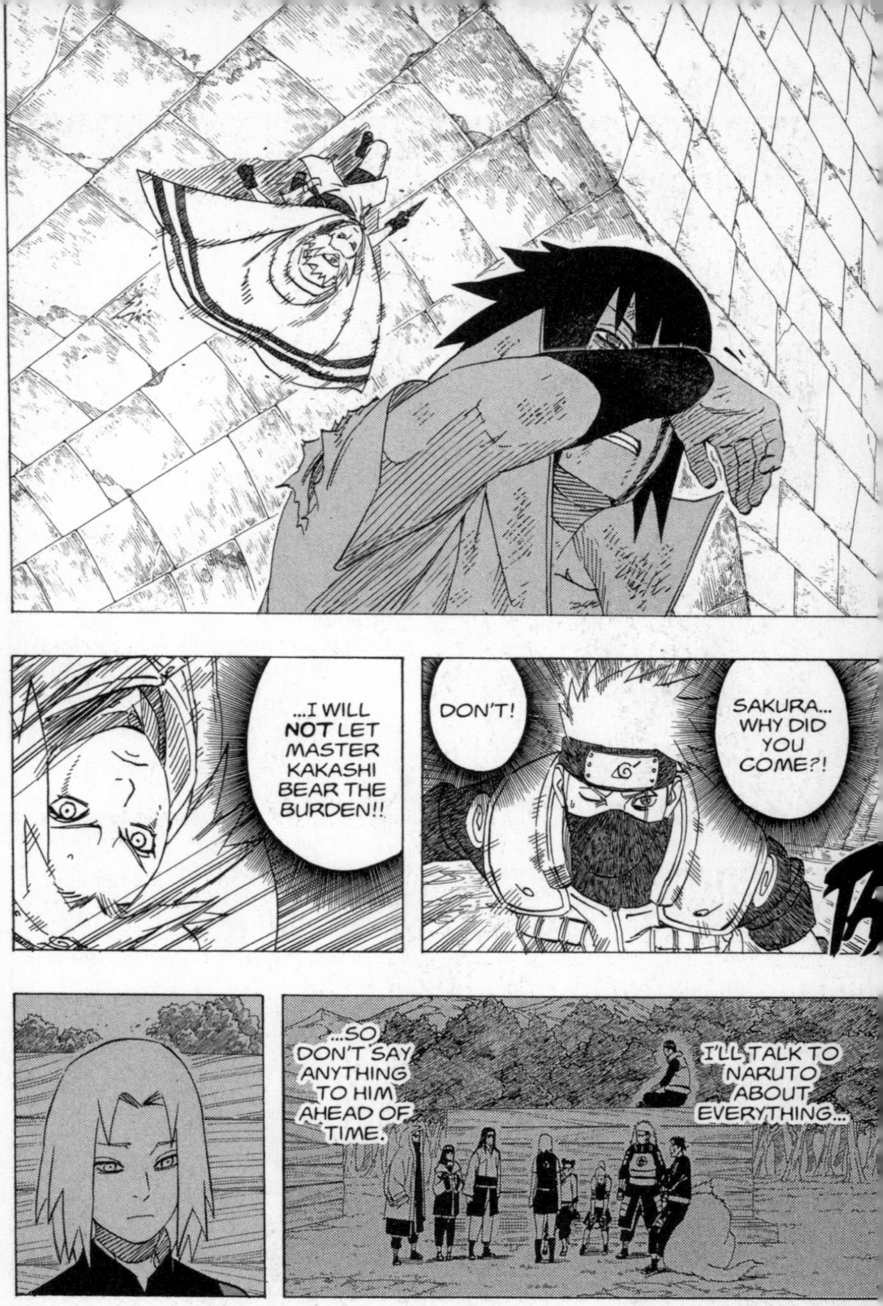
SAKURA... WHY DID YOU COME?!
DON'T!
...I WILL NOT LET MASTER KAKASHI BEAR THE BURDEN!!
I'LL TALK TO NARUTO ABOUT EVERYTHING...
...SO DON'T SAY ANYTHING TO HIM AHEAD OF TIME.

READ THIS WAY

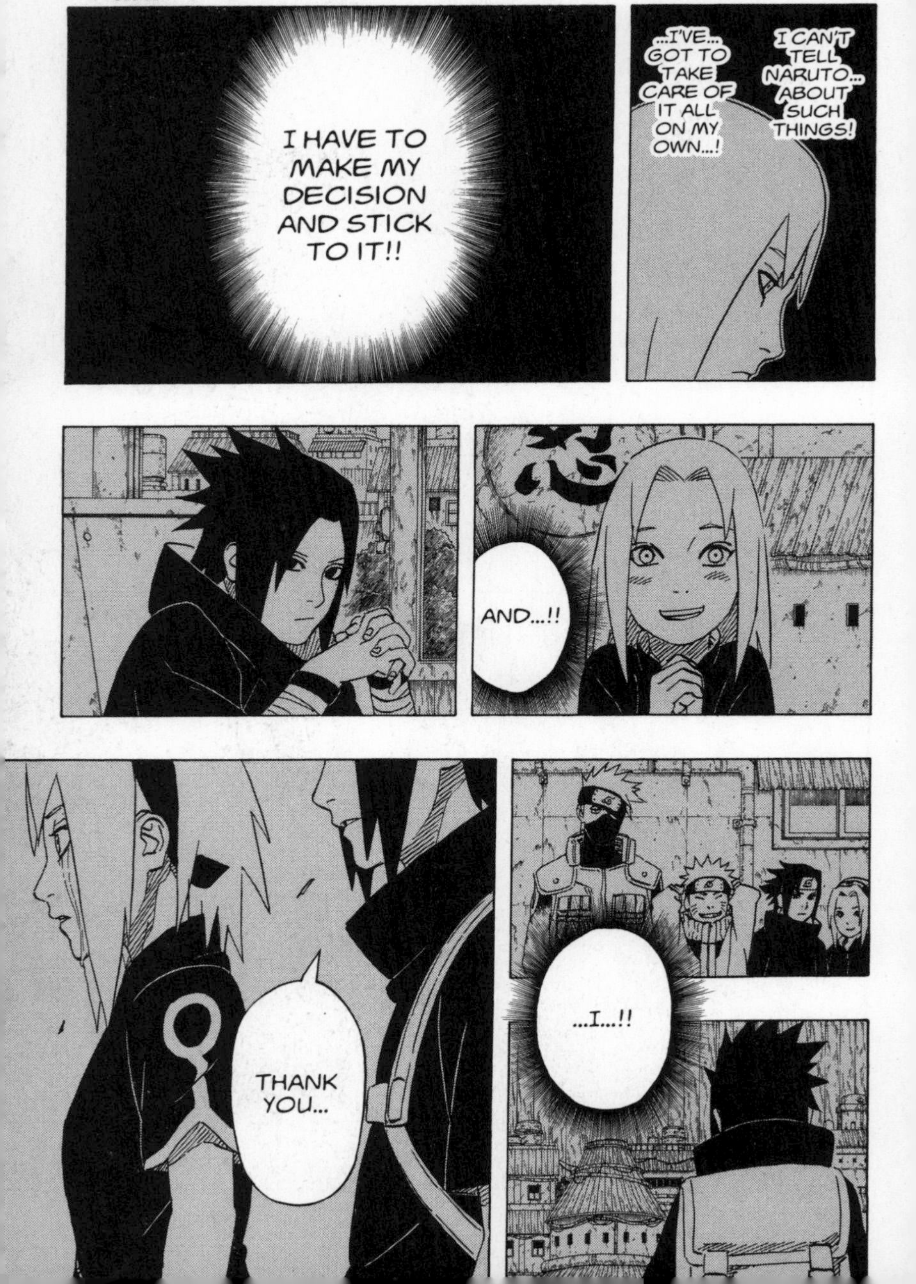
I CAN'T TELL NARUTO... ABOUT SUCH THINGS!
...I'VE... GOT TO TAKE CARE OF IT ALL ON MY OWN...!
I HAVE TO MAKE MY DECISION AND STICK TO IT!!
AND...!!
...I...!!
THANK YOU...

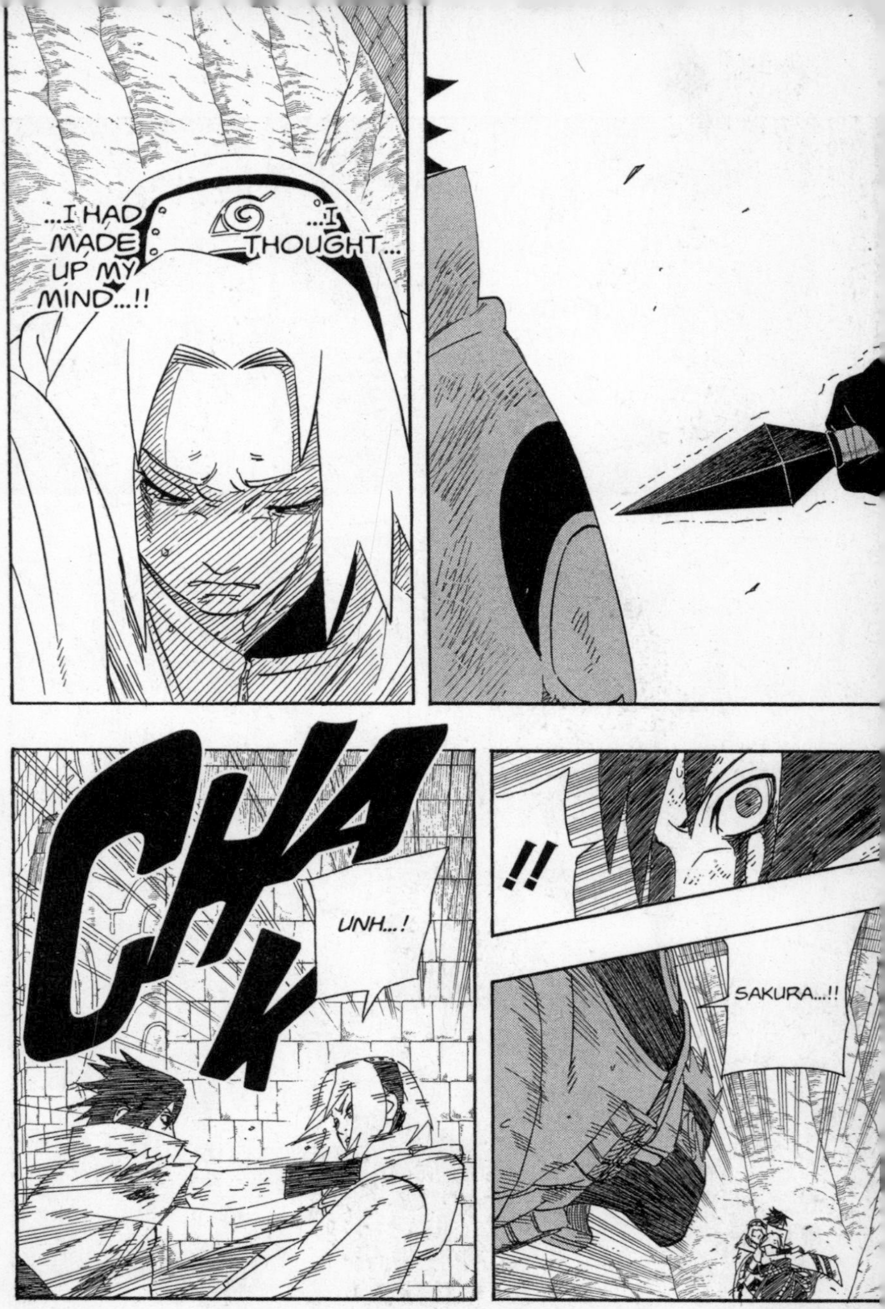
...I THOUGHT...
...I HAD MADE UP MY MIND...!!
!!
SAKURA...!!
CHAK
UNH...!

READ THIS WAY

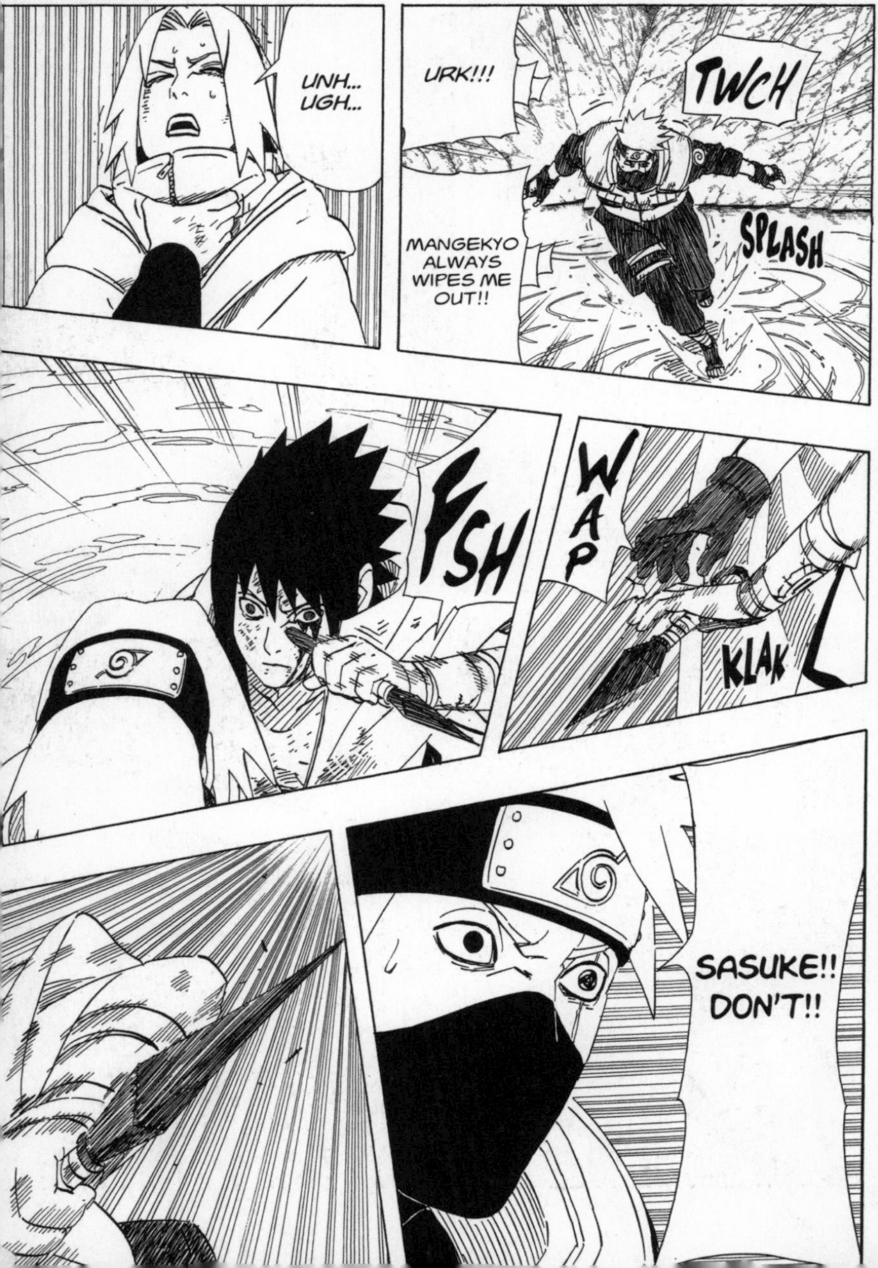

TWCH
URK!!!
SPLASH
MANGEKYO ALWAYS WIPES ME OUT!!
UNH... UGH...
WAP
KLAK
FSH
SASUKE!! DON'T!!

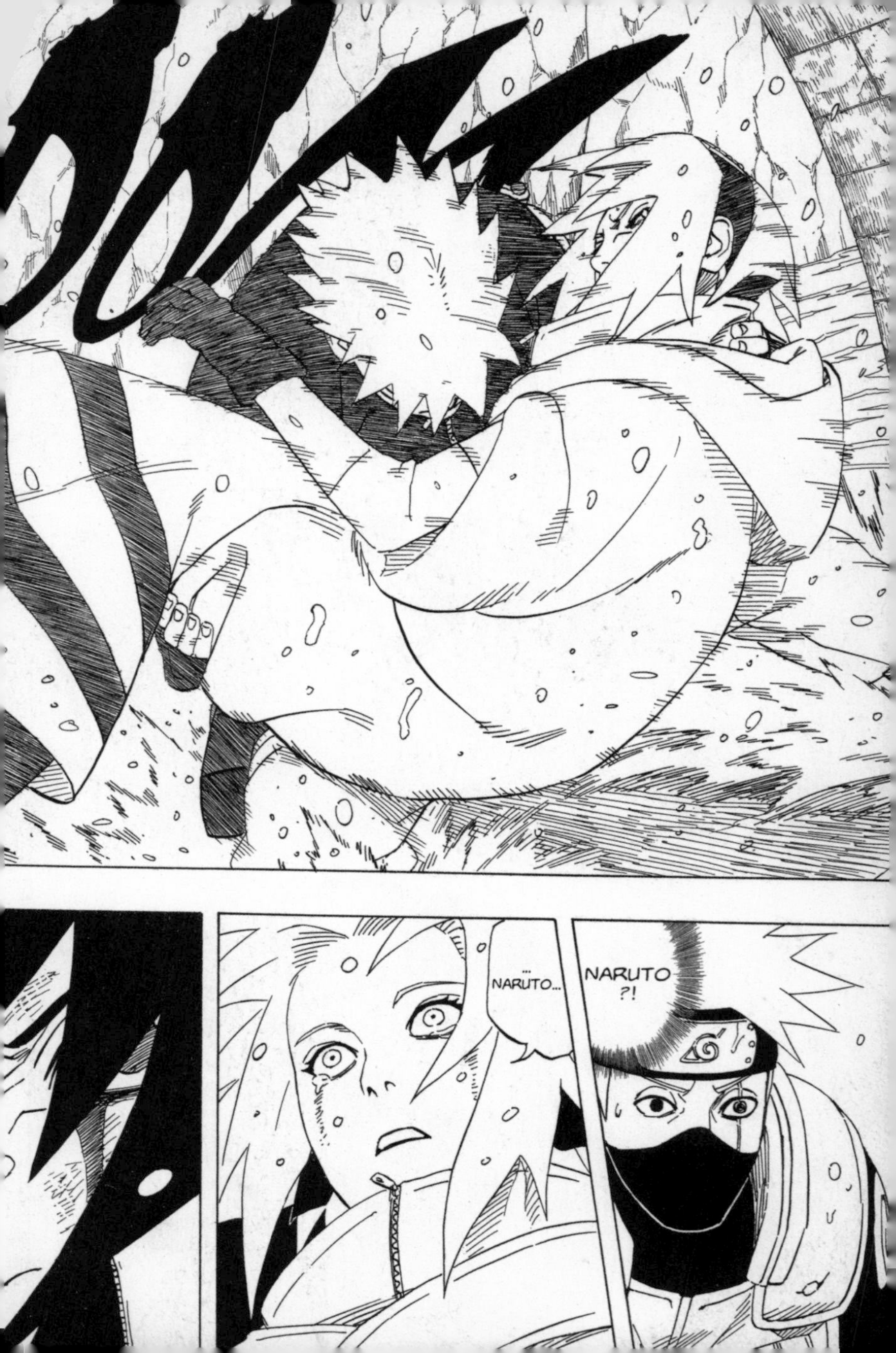
NARUTO ?!
... NARUTO...

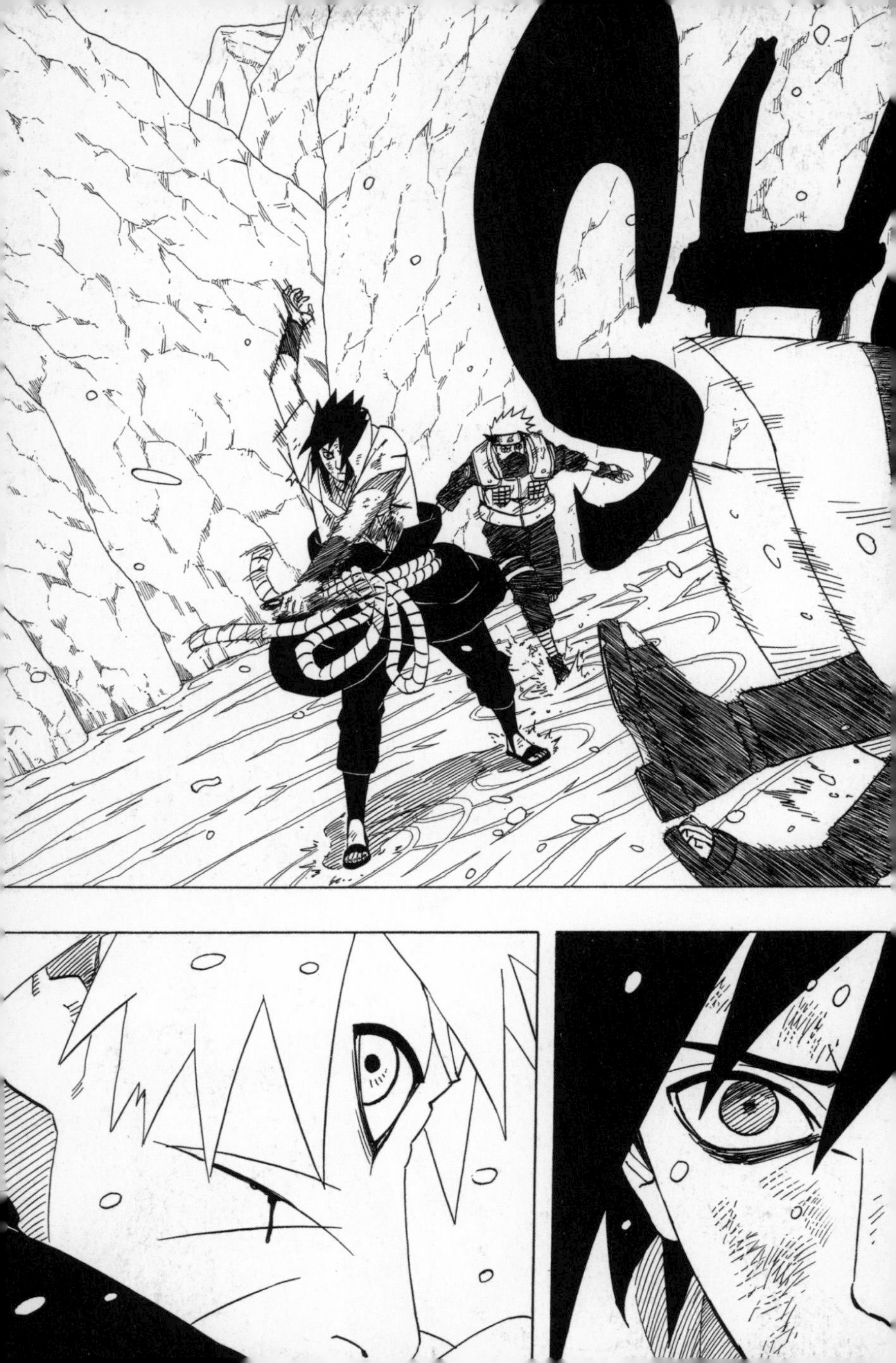
SH

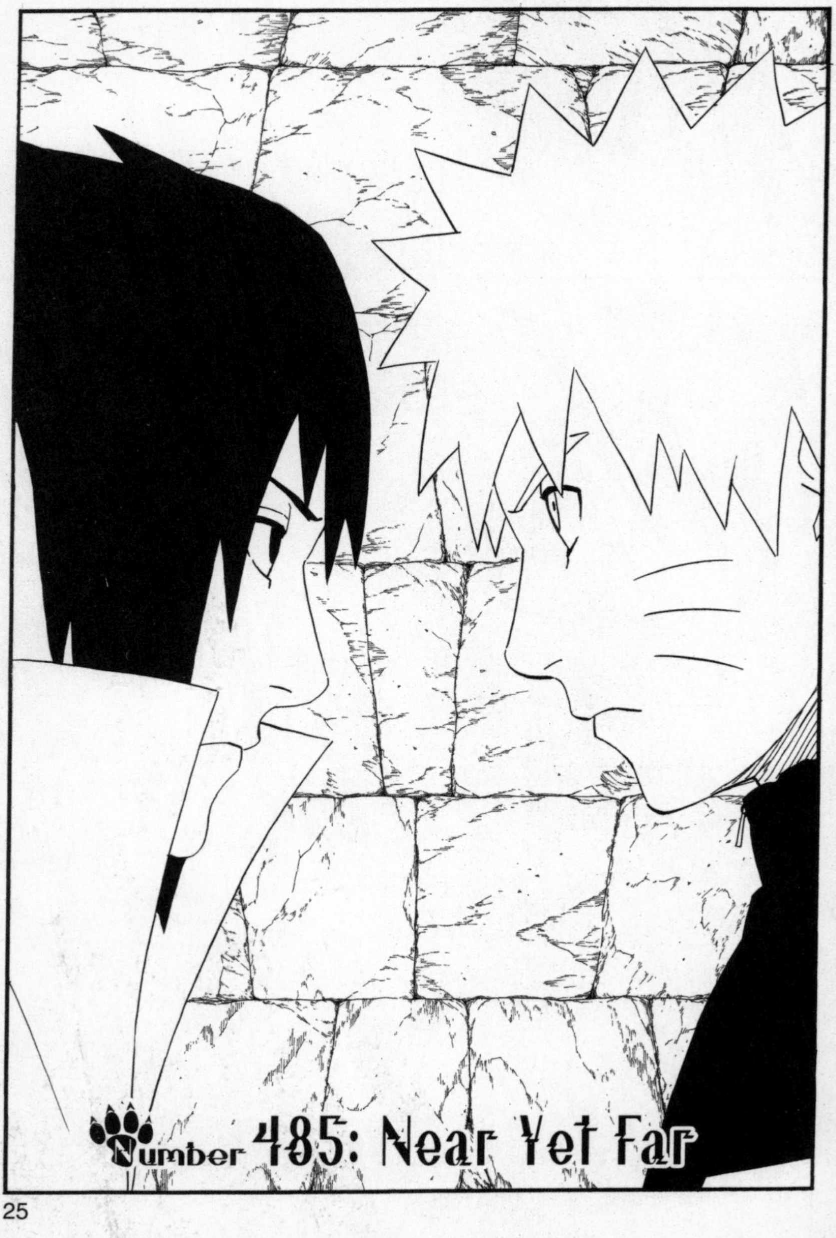
Number 485: Near Yet Far

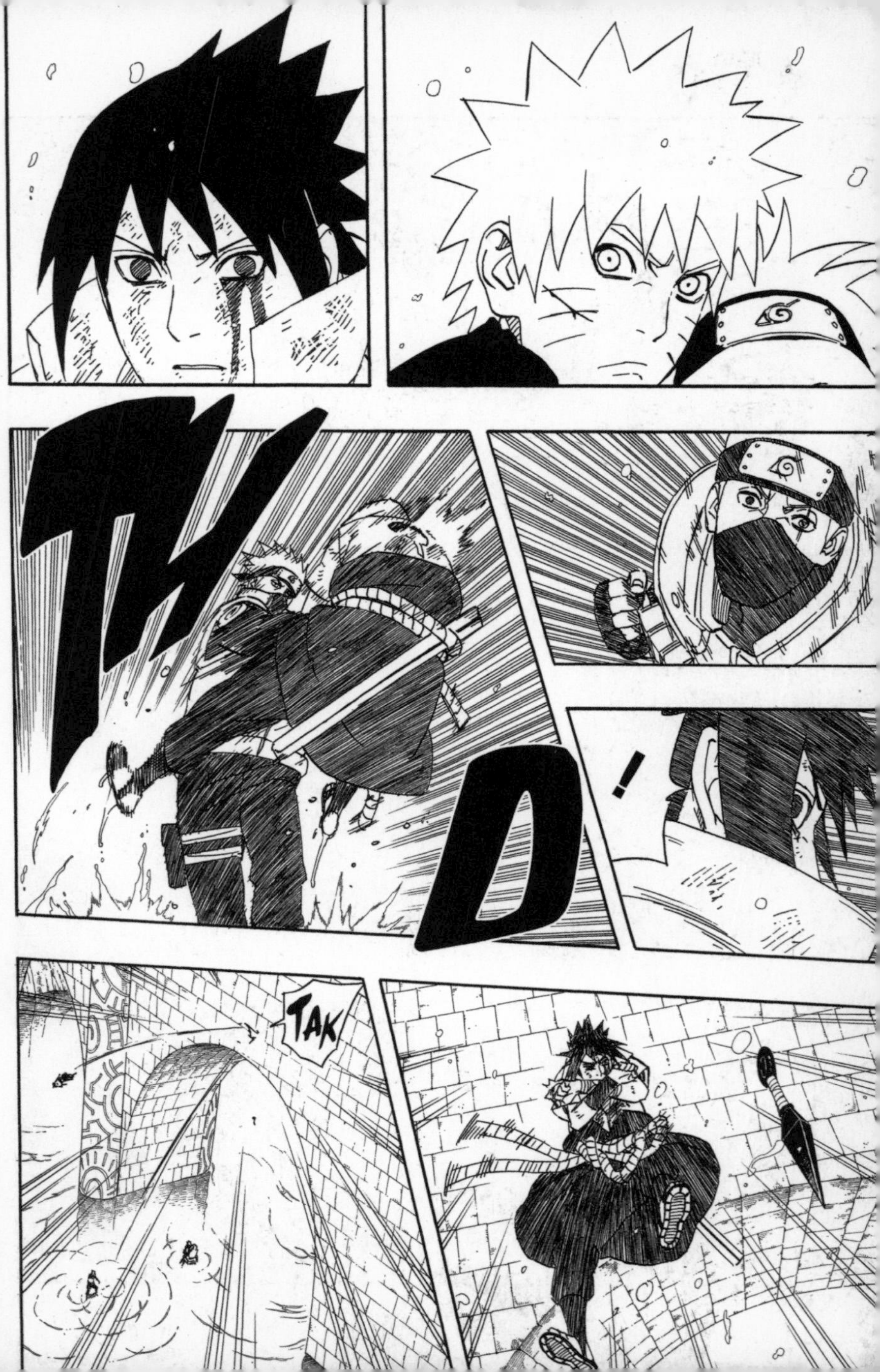
!
THUD
TAK

READ THIS WAY

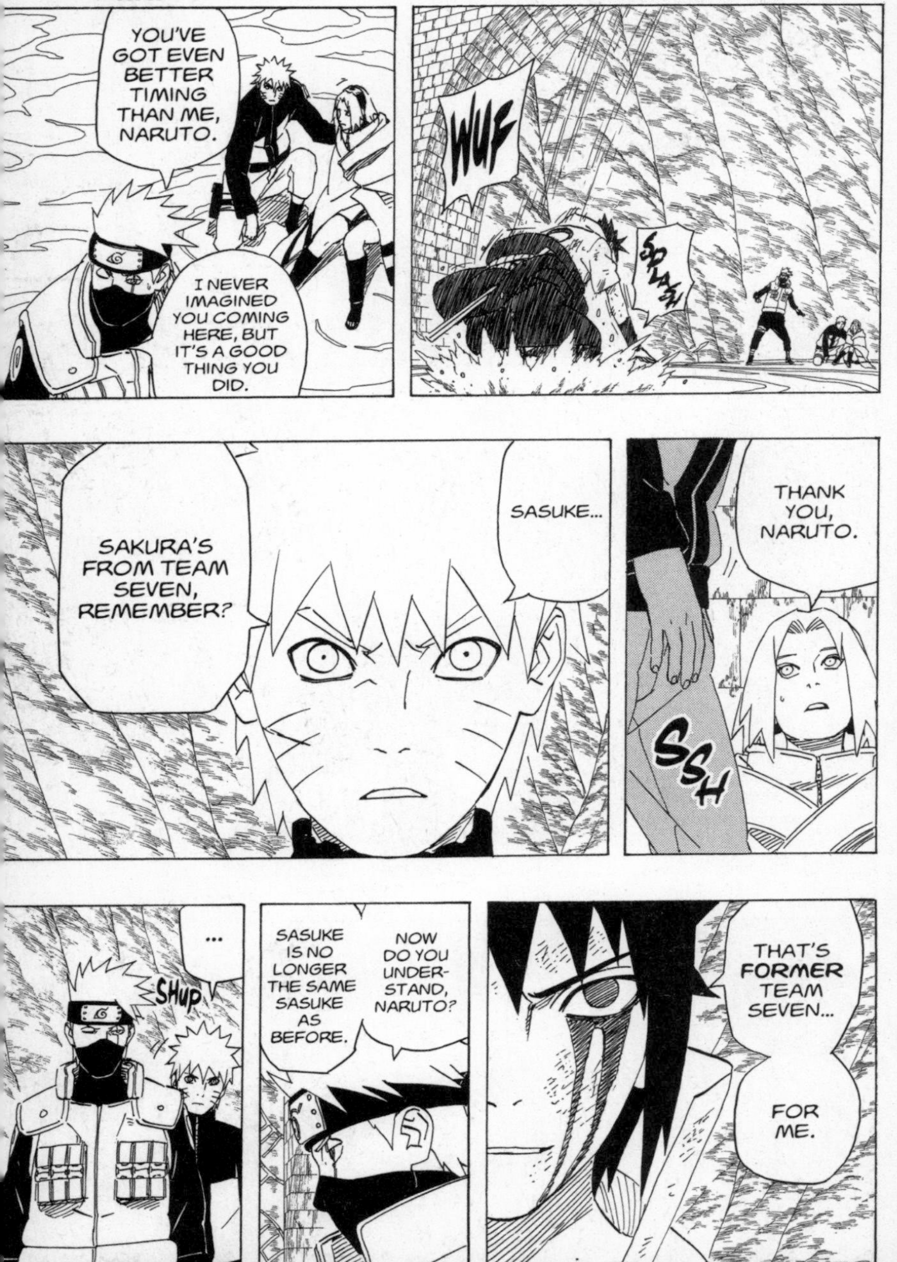
WUF
SPLASH
YOU'VE GOT EVEN BETTER TIMING THAN ME, NARUTO.
I NEVER IMAGINED YOU COMING HERE, BUT IT'S A GOOD THING YOU DID.
THANK YOU, NARUTO.
SSH
SASUKE...
SAKURA'S FROM TEAM SEVEN, REMEMBER?
THAT'S FORMER TEAM SEVEN...
FOR ME.
NOW DO YOU UNDERSTAND, NARUTO?
SASUKE IS NO LONGER THE SAME SASUKE AS BEFORE.
...
SHUP

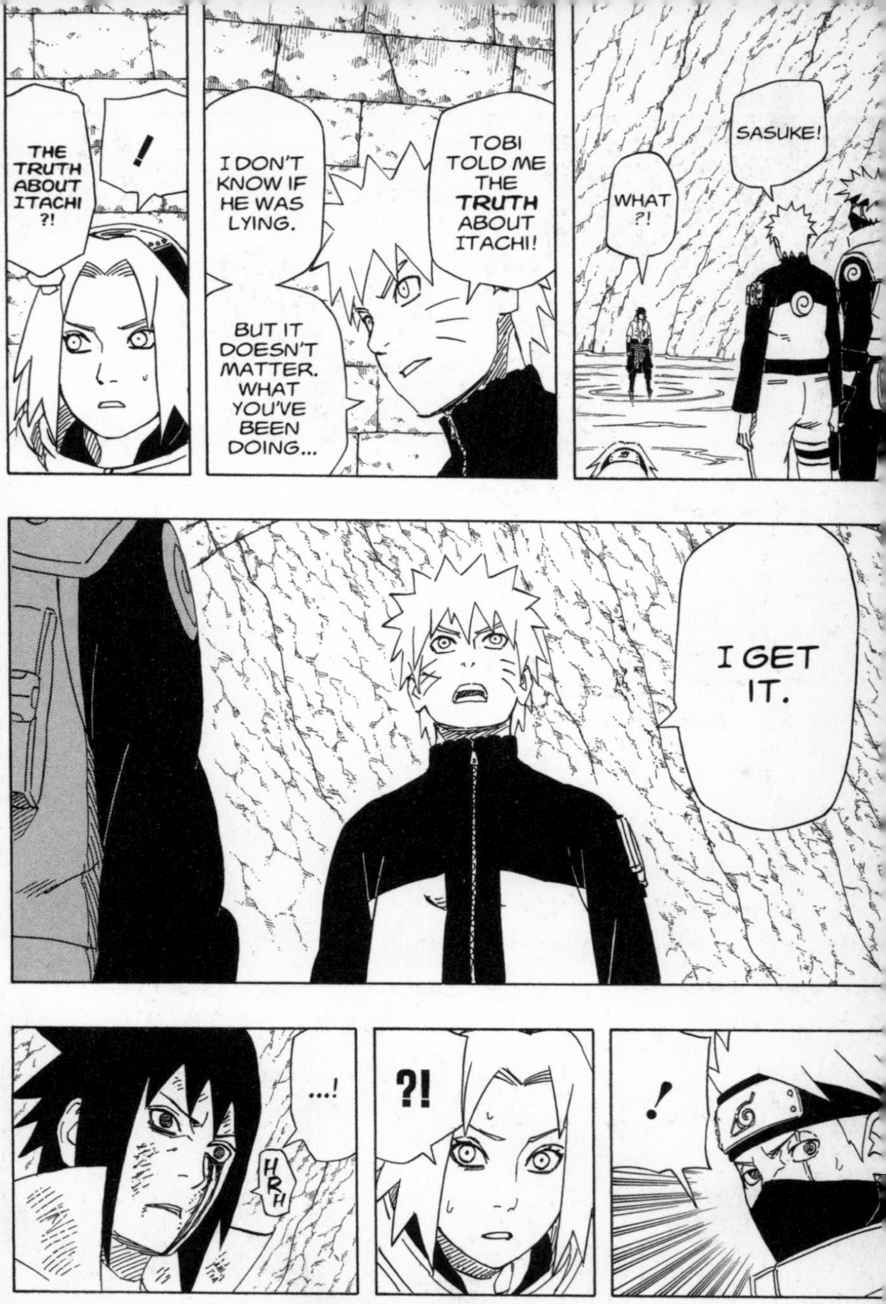

SASUKE!
WHAT?!
TOBI TOLD ME THE TRUTH ABOUT ITACHI!
I DON'T KNOW IF HE WAS LYING.
BUT IT DOESN'T MATTER. WHAT YOU'VE BEEN DOING...
!
THE TRUTH ABOUT ITACHI?!
I GET IT.
!
?!
...!
HRH

READ THIS WAY

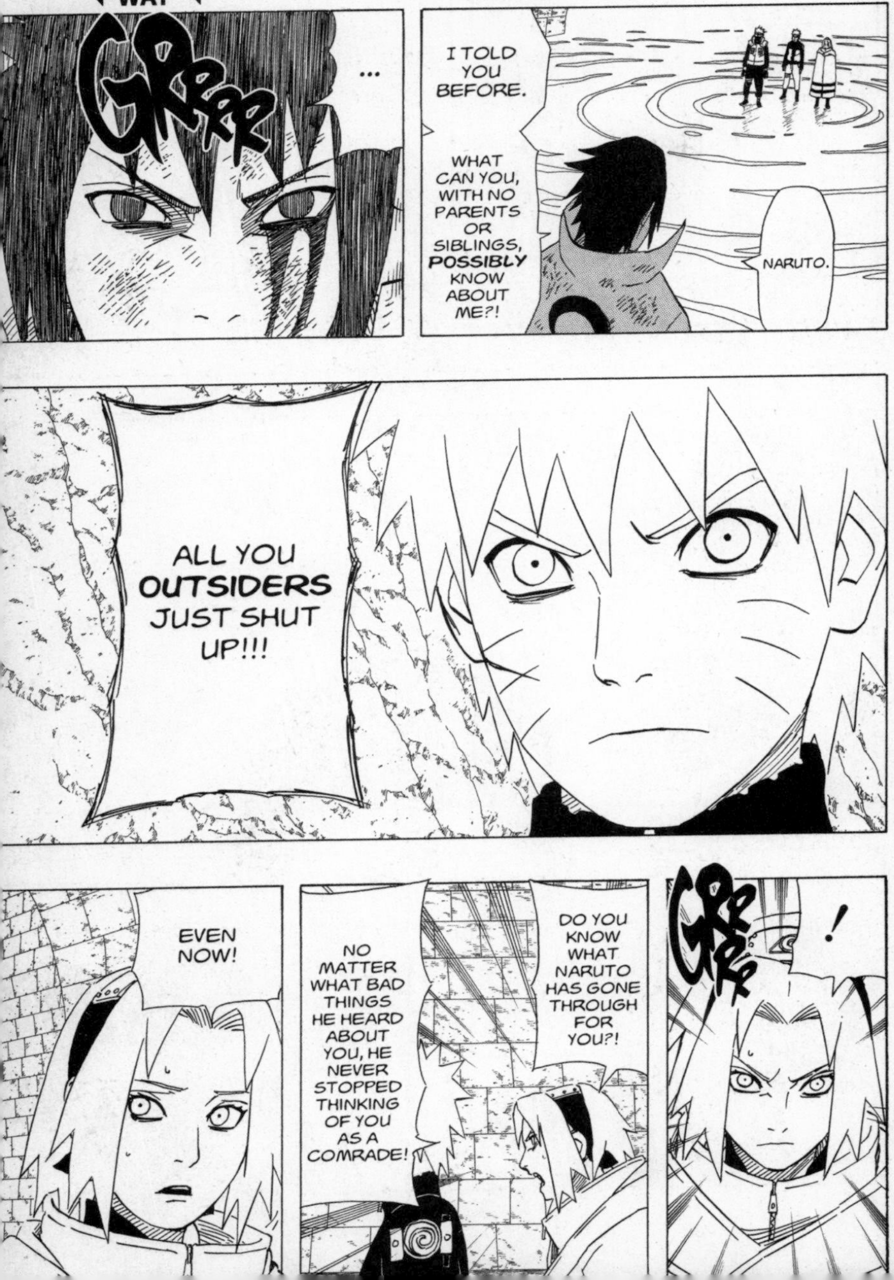
NARUTO.
I TOLD YOU BEFORE.
WHAT CAN YOU, WITH NO PARENTS OR SIBLINGS, **POSSIBLY** KNOW ABOUT ME?!
GRRR
...
ALL YOU **OUTSIDERS** JUST SHUT UP!!!
GRRR
!
DO YOU KNOW WHAT NARUTO HAS GONE THROUGH FOR YOU?!
NO MATTER WHAT BAD THINGS HE HEARD ABOUT YOU, HE NEVER STOPPED THINKING OF YOU AS A COMRADE!
EVEN NOW!

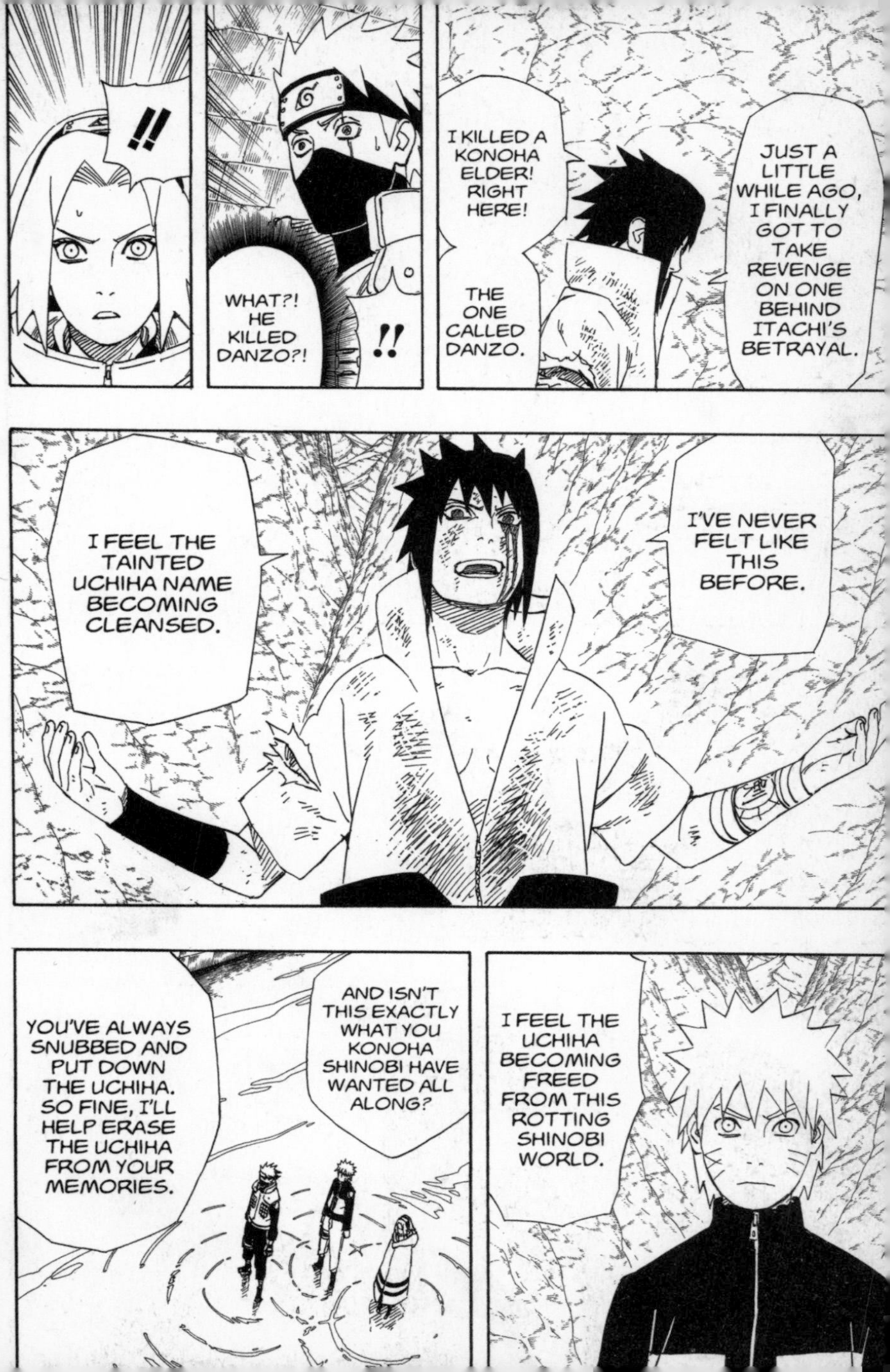

JUST A LITTLE WHILE AGO, I FINALLY GOT TO TAKE REVENGE ON ONE BEHIND ITACHI'S BETRAYAL.
I KILLED A KONOHA ELDER! RIGHT HERE!
THE ONE CALLED DANZO.
WHAT?! HE KILLED DANZO?!
!!
!!
I'VE NEVER FELT LIKE THIS BEFORE.
I FEEL THE TAINTED UCHIHA NAME BECOMING CLEANSED.
I FEEL THE UCHIHA BECOMING FREED FROM THIS ROTTING SHINOBI WORLD.
AND ISN'T THIS EXACTLY WHAT YOU KONOHA SHINOBI HAVE WANTED ALL ALONG?
YOU'VE ALWAYS SNUBBED AND PUT DOWN THE UCHIHA. SO FINE, I'LL HELP ERASE THE UCHIHA FROM YOUR MEMORIES.

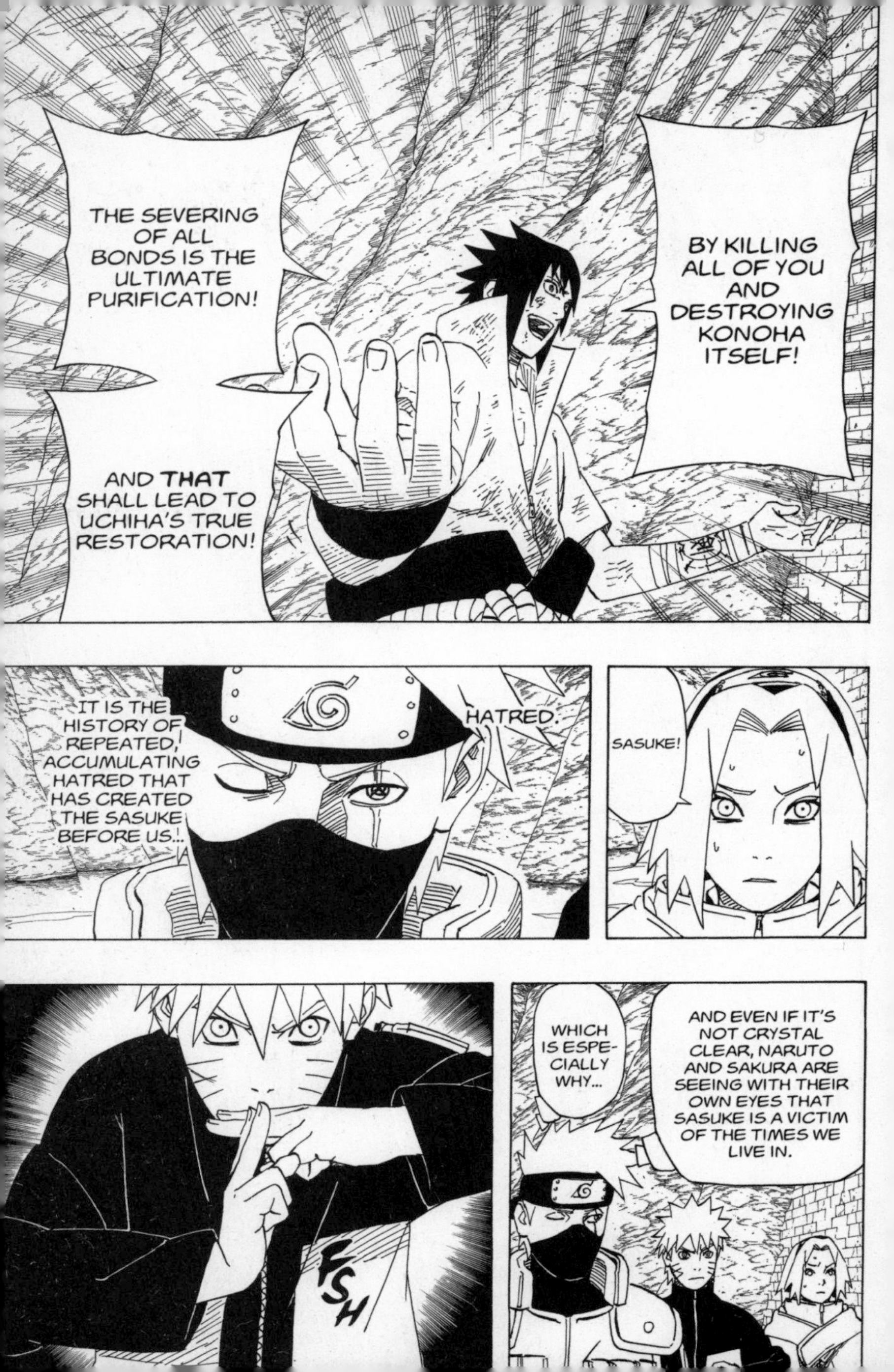
BY KILLING ALL OF YOU AND DESTROYING KONOHA ITSELF!
THE SEVERING OF ALL BONDS IS THE ULTIMATE PURIFICATION!
AND **THAT** SHALL LEAD TO UCHIHA'S TRUE RESTORATION!
SASUKE!
HATRED.
IT IS THE HISTORY OF REPEATED, ACCUMULATING HATRED THAT HAS CREATED THE SASUKE BEFORE US...
AND EVEN IF IT'S NOT CRYSTAL CLEAR, NARUTO AND SAKURA ARE SEEING WITH THEIR OWN EYES THAT SASUKE IS A VICTIM OF THE TIMES WE LIVE IN.
WHICH IS ESPE-CIALLY WHY...
FSH

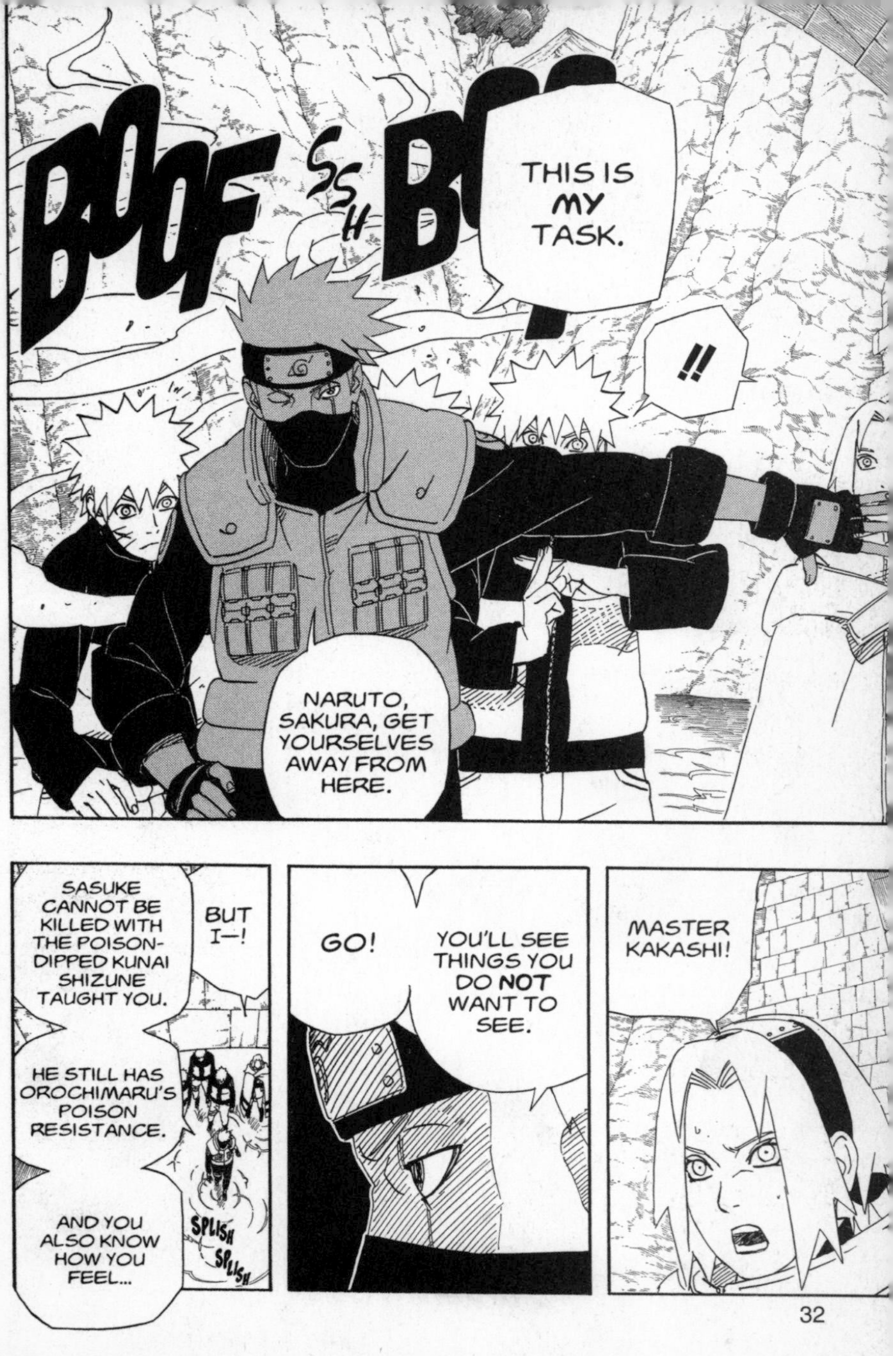
THIS IS MY TASK.
!!
BOOF
SSH
NARUTO, SAKURA, GET YOURSELVES AWAY FROM HERE.
MASTER KAKASHI!
YOU'LL SEE THINGS YOU DO NOT WANT TO SEE.
GO!
BUT I—!
SASUKE CANNOT BE KILLED WITH THE POISON-DIPPED KUNAI SHIZUNE TAUGHT YOU.
HE STILL HAS OROCHIMARU'S POISON RESISTANCE.
SPLISH
SPLISH
AND YOU ALSO KNOW HOW YOU FEEL...

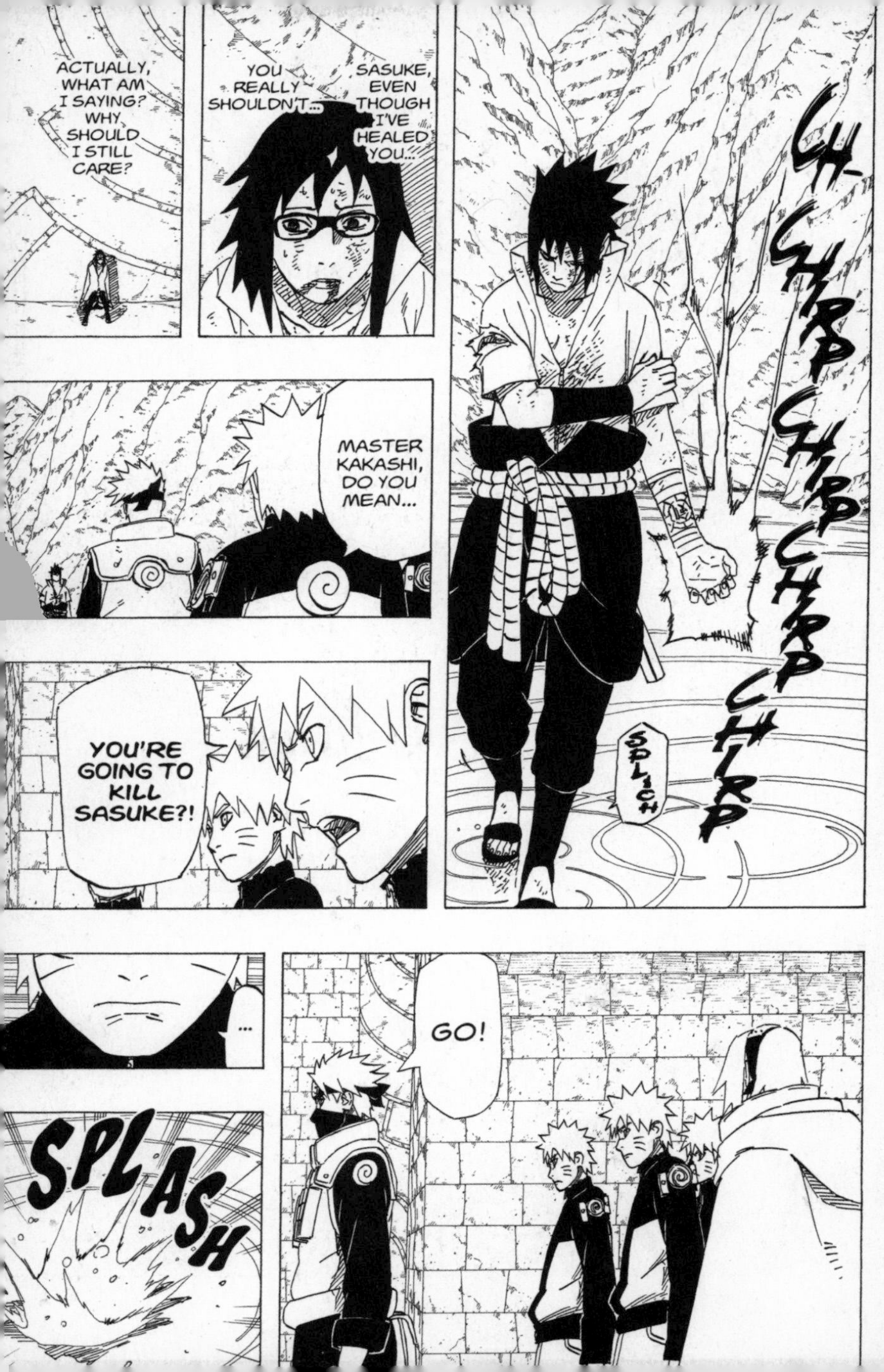
CH-CHIRP CHIRP CHIRP CHIRP
SPLISH
SASUKE, EVEN THOUGH I'VE HEALED YOU...
YOU REALLY SHOULDN'T...
ACTUALLY, WHAT AM I SAYING? WHY SHOULD I STILL CARE?
MASTER KAKASHI, DO YOU MEAN...
YOU'RE GOING TO KILL SASUKE?!
GO!
...
SPLASH

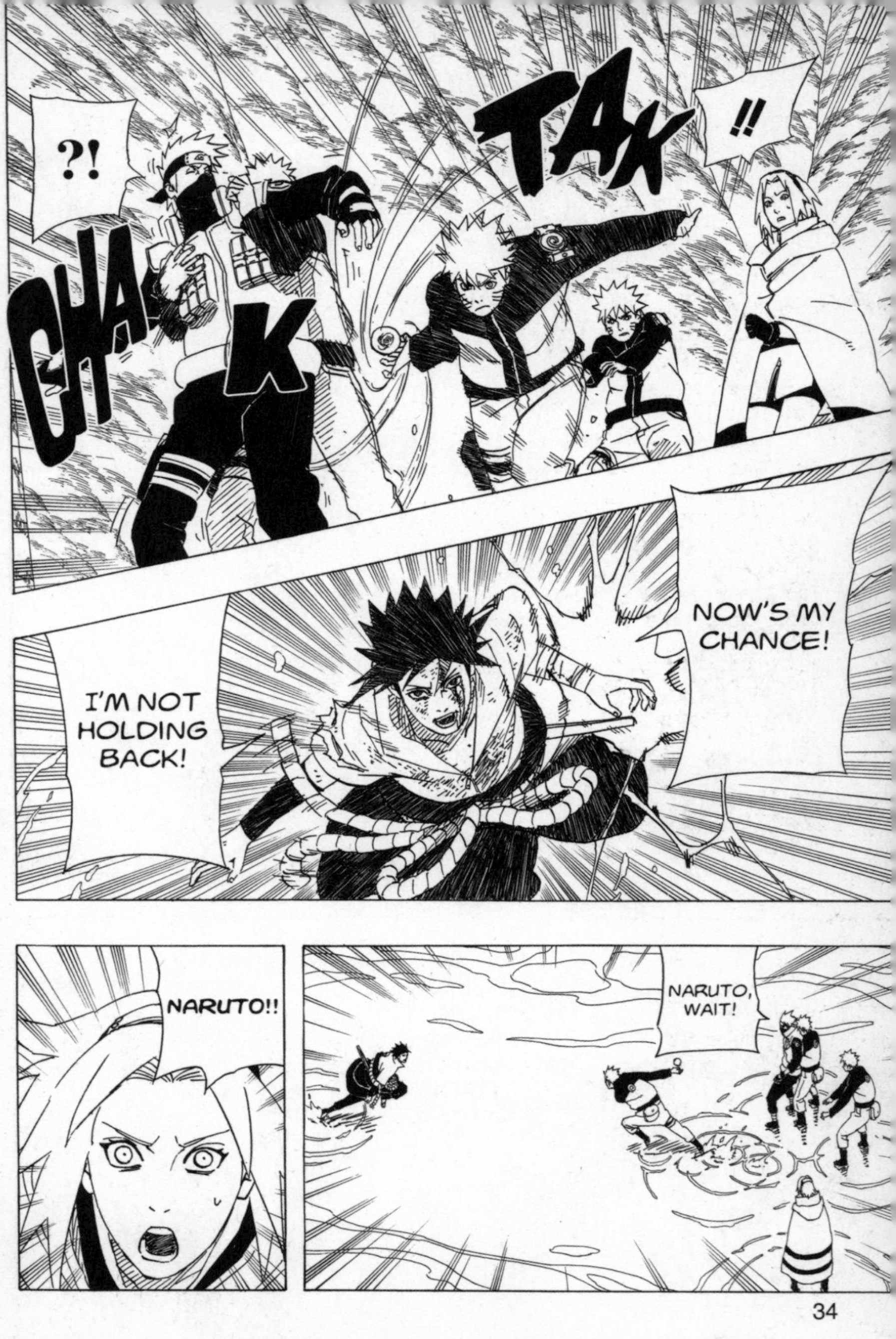
!!
TAK
?!
CHAK
NOW'S MY CHANCE!
I'M NOT HOLDING BACK!
NARUTO, WAIT!
NARUTO!!

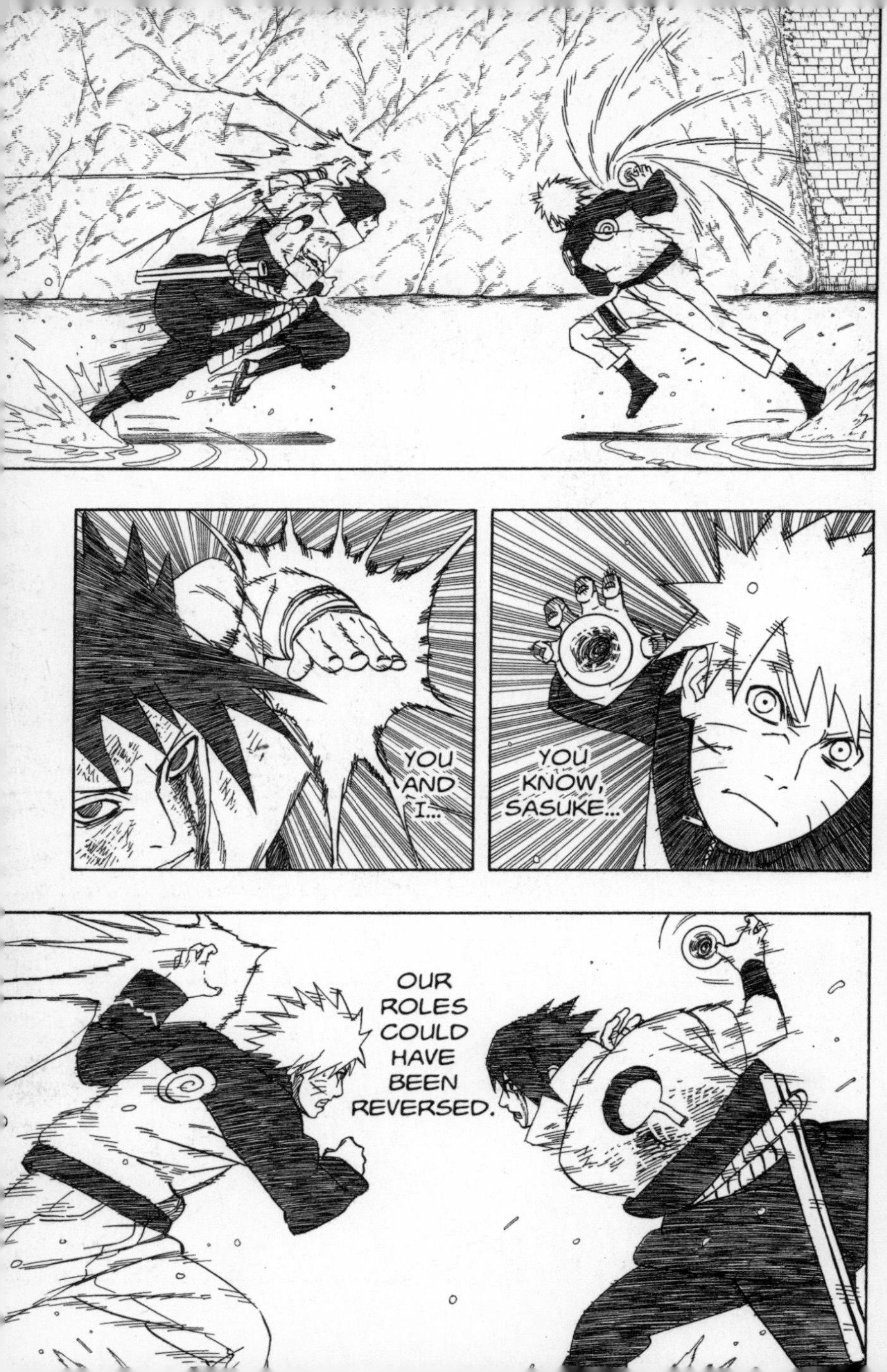
YOU KNOW, SASUKE...
YOU AND I...
OUR ROLES COULD HAVE BEEN REVERSED.

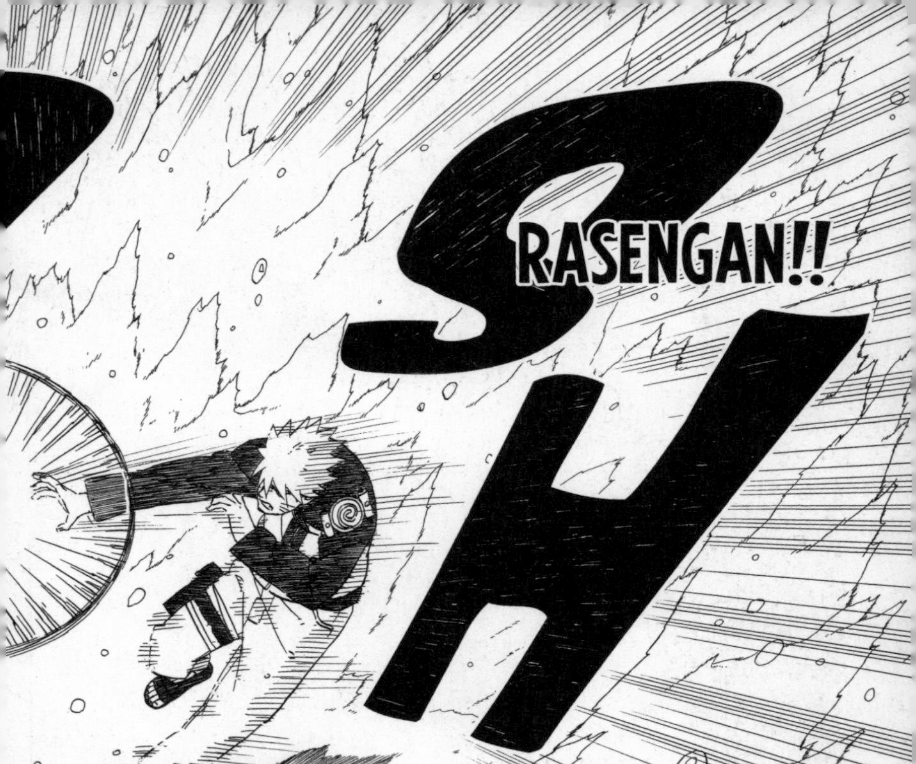
SH
RASENGAN!!
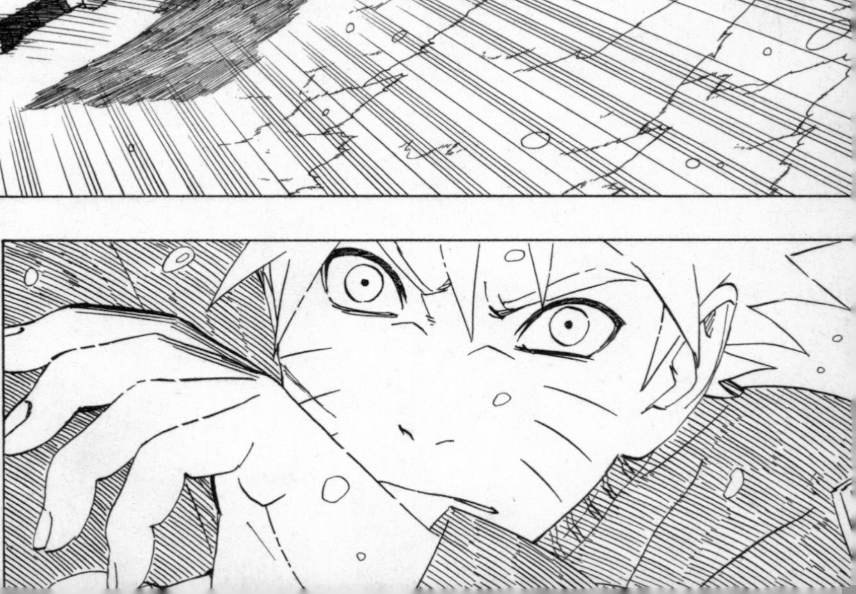

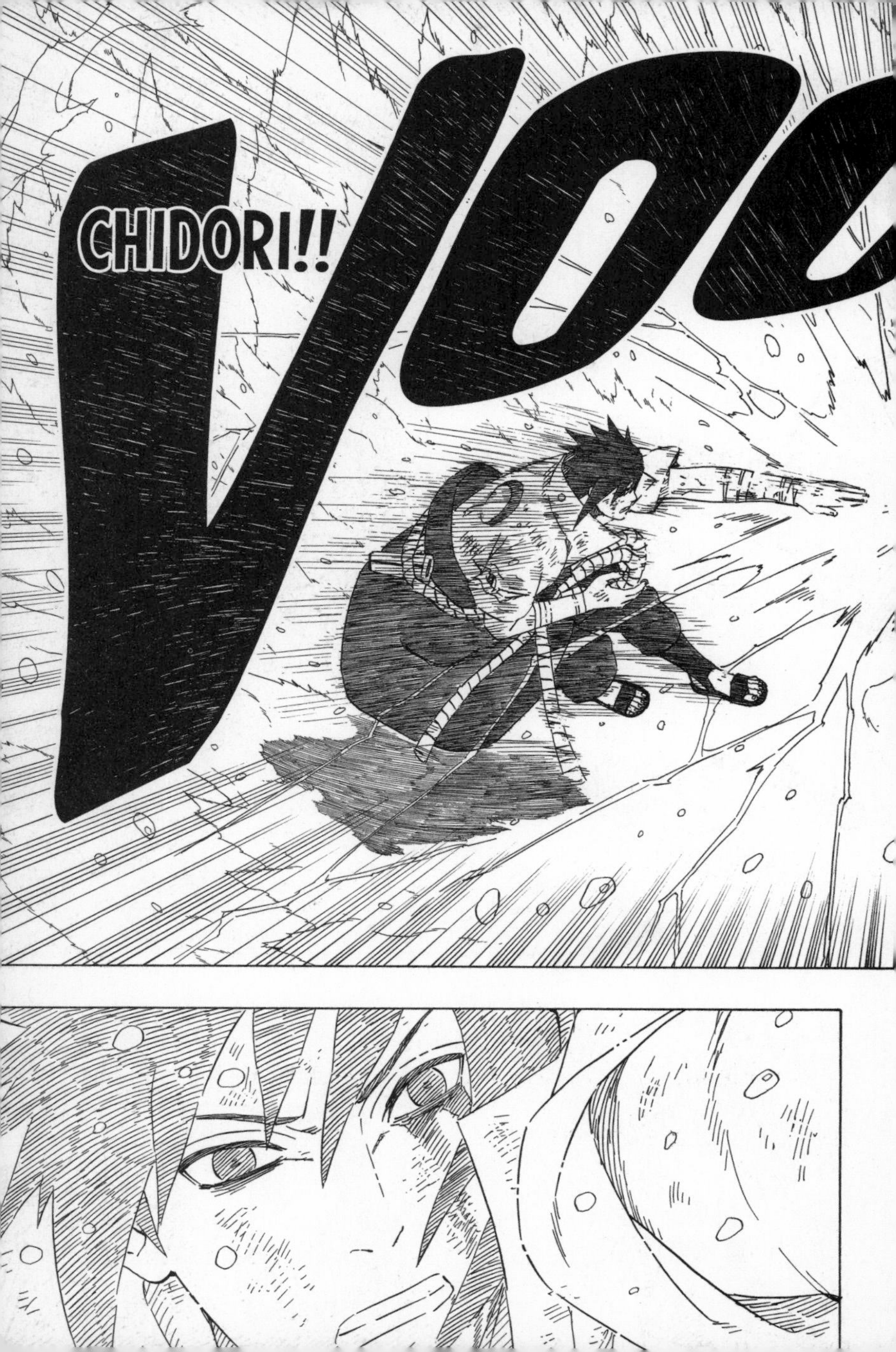
VOO
CHIDORI!!

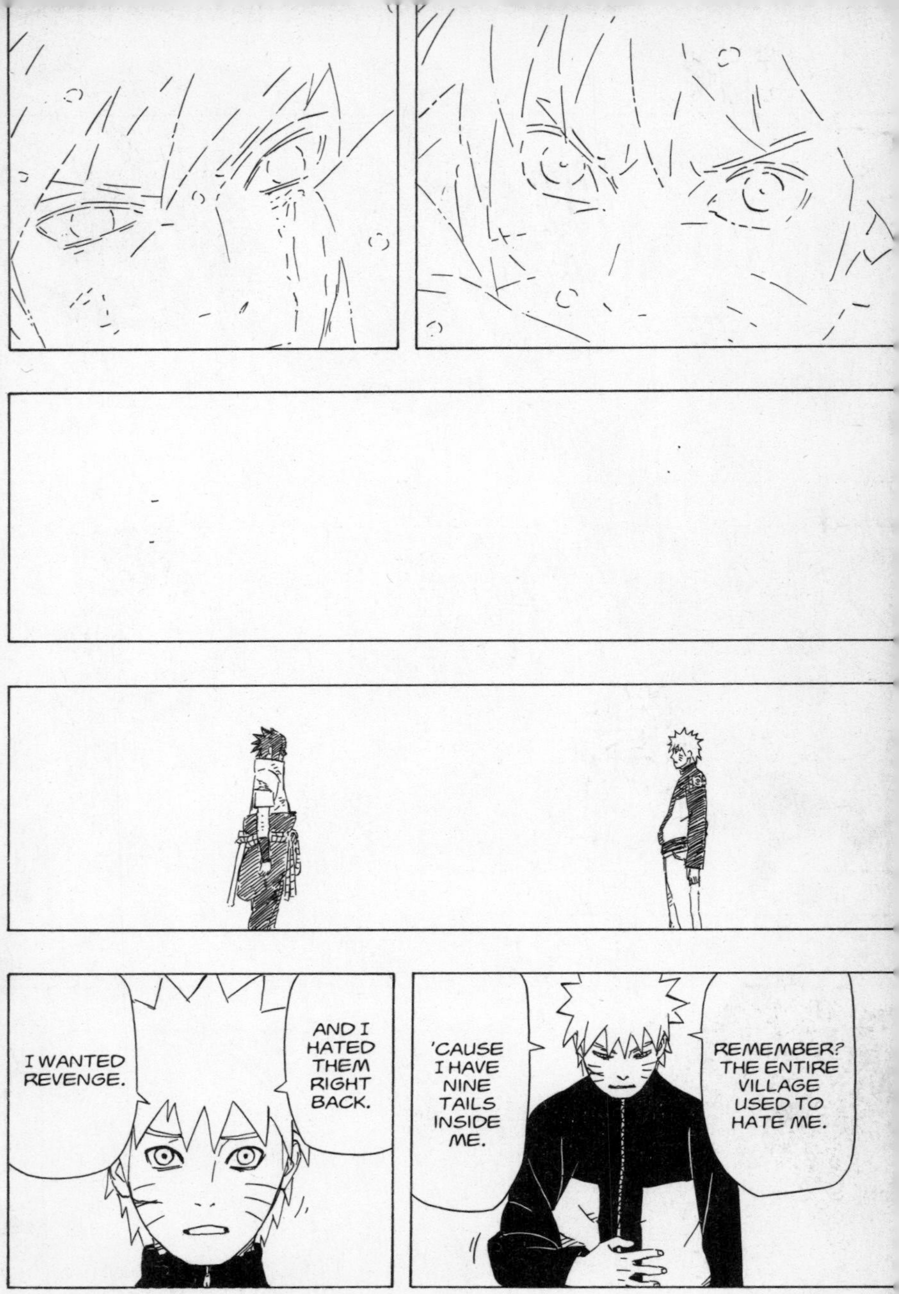
REMEMBER? THE ENTIRE VILLAGE USED TO HATE ME.
'CAUSE I HAVE NINE TAILS INSIDE ME.
AND I HATED THEM RIGHT BACK.
I WANTED REVENGE.

READ THIS WAY

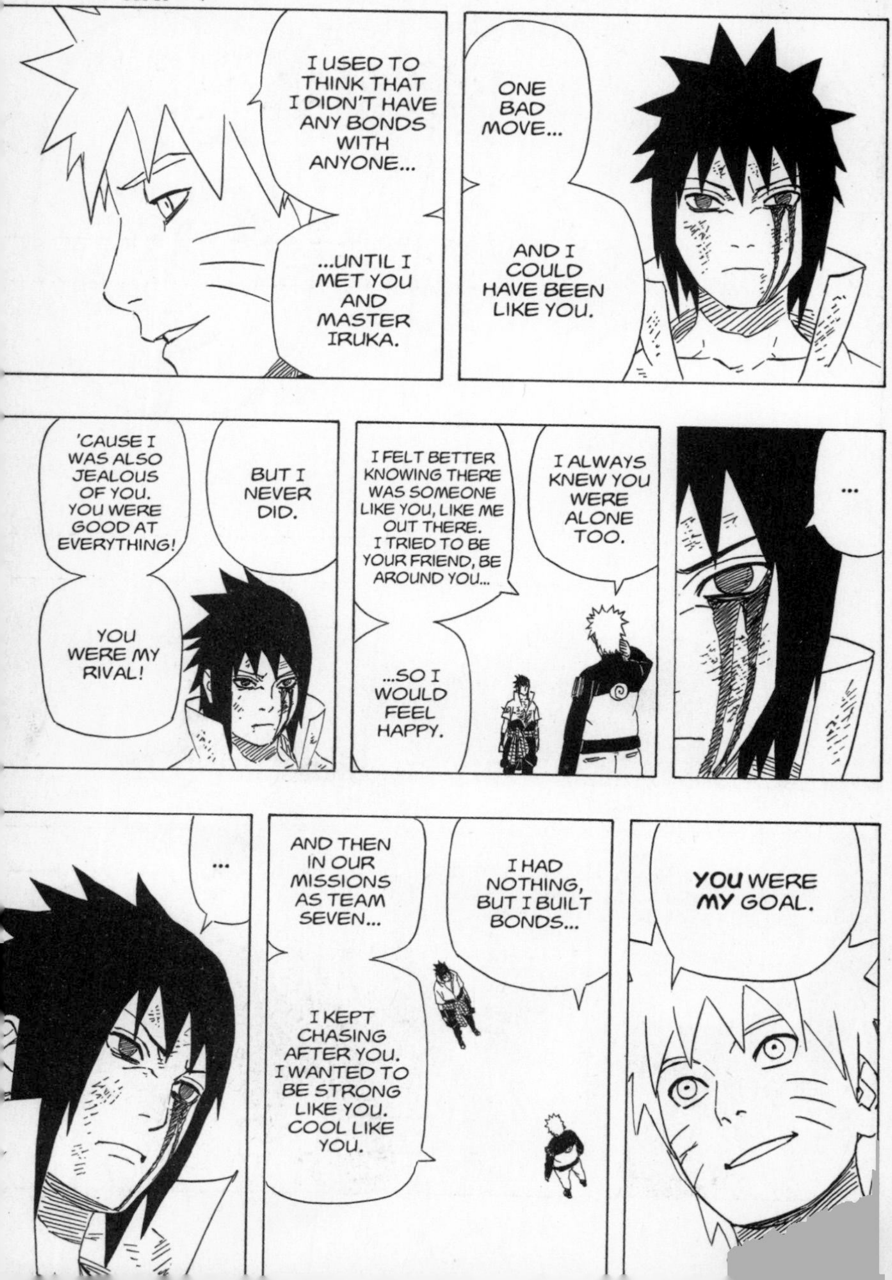
ONE BAD MOVE...
AND I COULD HAVE BEEN LIKE YOU.
I USED TO THINK THAT I DIDN'T HAVE ANY BONDS WITH ANYONE...
...UNTIL I MET YOU AND MASTER IRUKA.
...
I ALWAYS KNEW YOU WERE ALONE TOO.
I FELT BETTER KNOWING THERE WAS SOMEONE LIKE YOU, LIKE ME OUT THERE. I TRIED TO BE YOUR FRIEND, BE AROUND YOU...
...SO I WOULD FEEL HAPPY.
BUT I NEVER DID.
'CAUSE I WAS ALSO JEALOUS OF YOU. YOU WERE GOOD AT EVERYTHING!
YOU WERE MY RIVAL!
YOU WERE MY GOAL.
I HAD NOTHING, BUT I BUILT BONDS...
AND THEN IN OUR MISSIONS AS TEAM SEVEN...
I KEPT CHASING AFTER YOU. I WANTED TO BE STRONG LIKE YOU. COOL LIKE YOU.
...

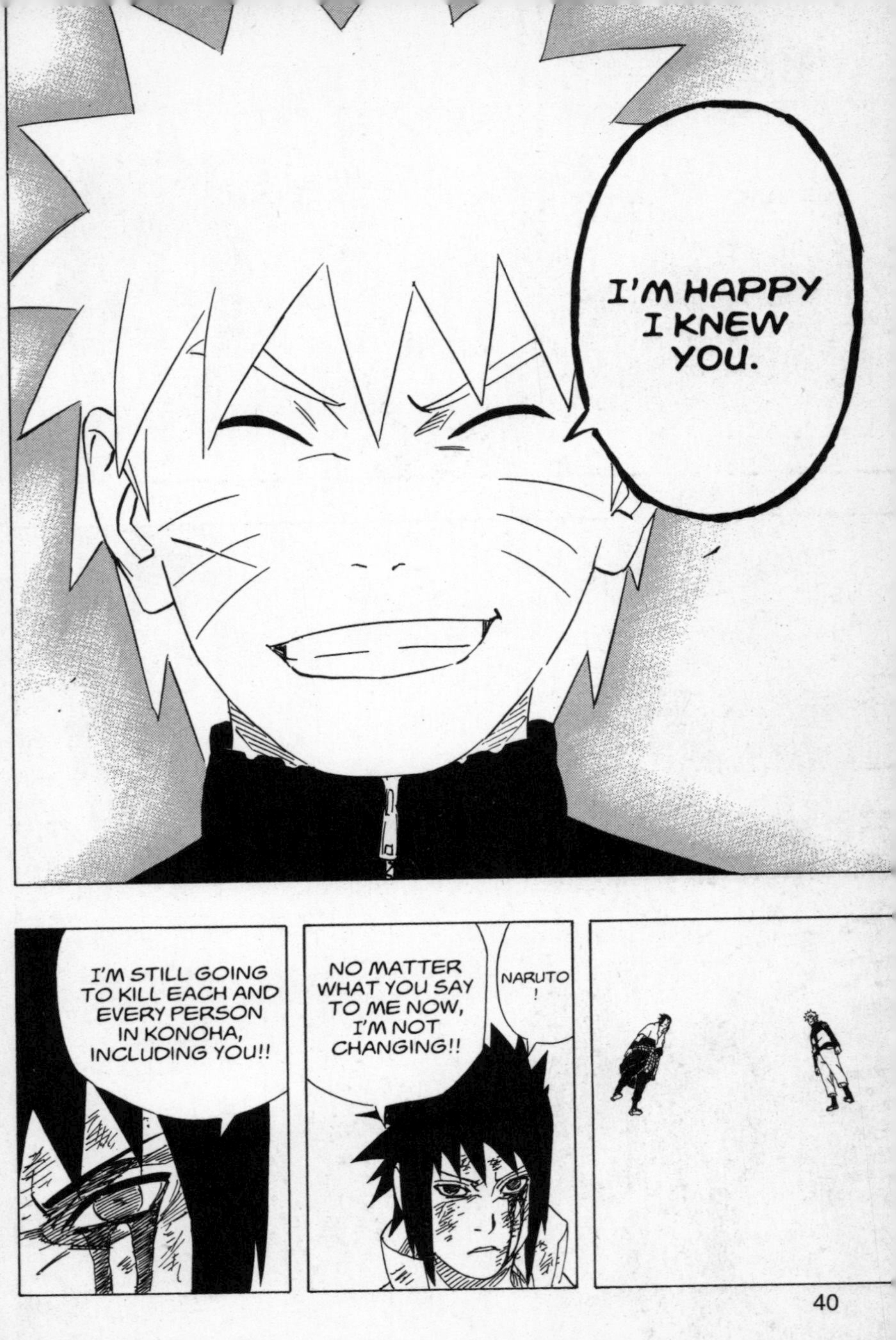
I'M HAPPY I KNEW YOU.
NARUTO!
NO MATTER WHAT YOU SAY TO ME NOW, I'M NOT CHANGING!!
I'M STILL GOING TO KILL EACH AND EVERY PERSON IN KONOHA, INCLUDING YOU!!

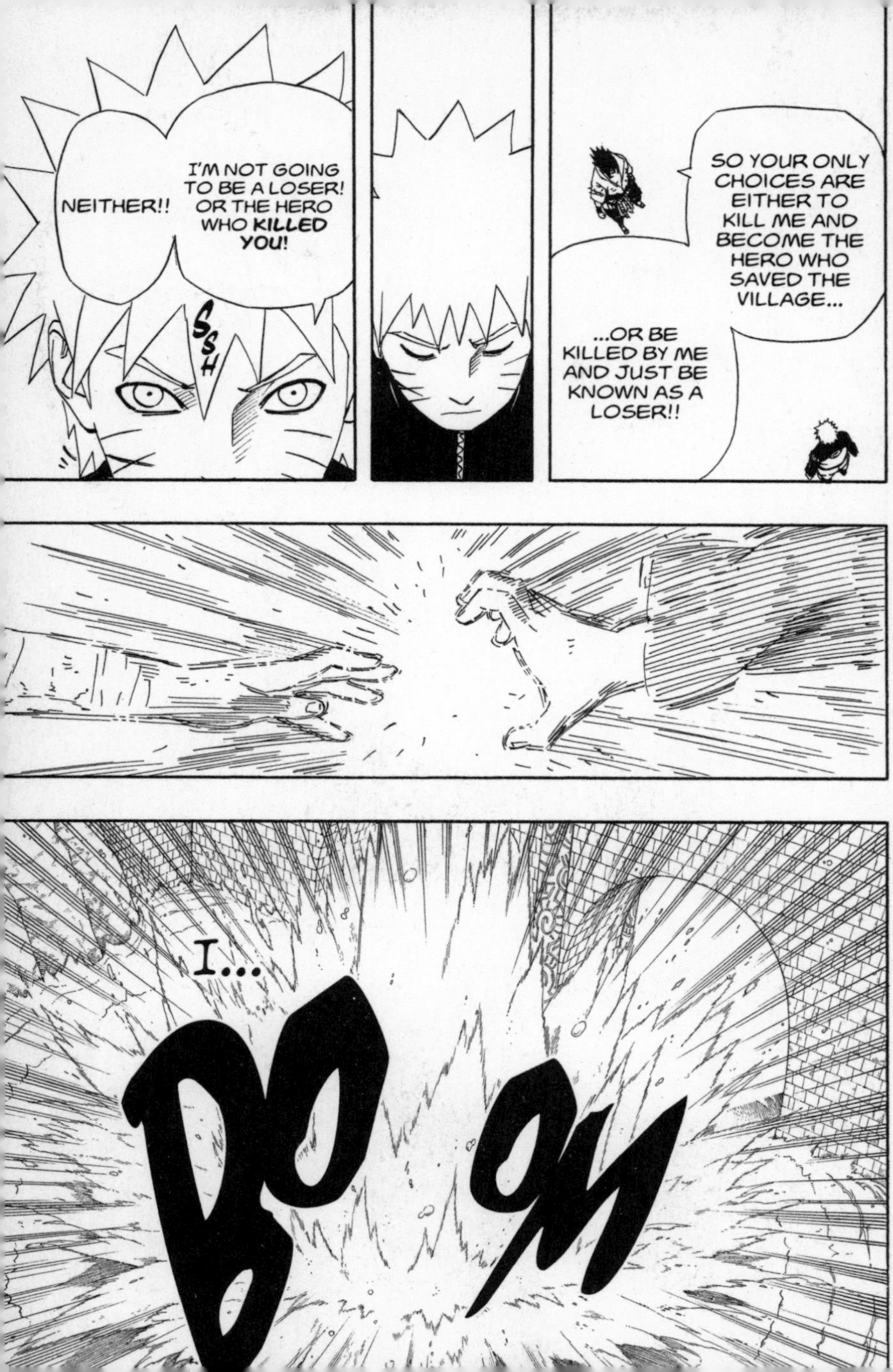
SO YOUR ONLY CHOICES ARE EITHER TO KILL ME AND BECOME THE HERO WHO SAVED THE VILLAGE...
...OR BE KILLED BY ME AND JUST BE KNOWN AS A LOSER!!
I'M NOT GOING TO BE A LOSER! OR THE HERO WHO **KILLED YOU**!
NEITHER!!
SSH
I...
BOOM

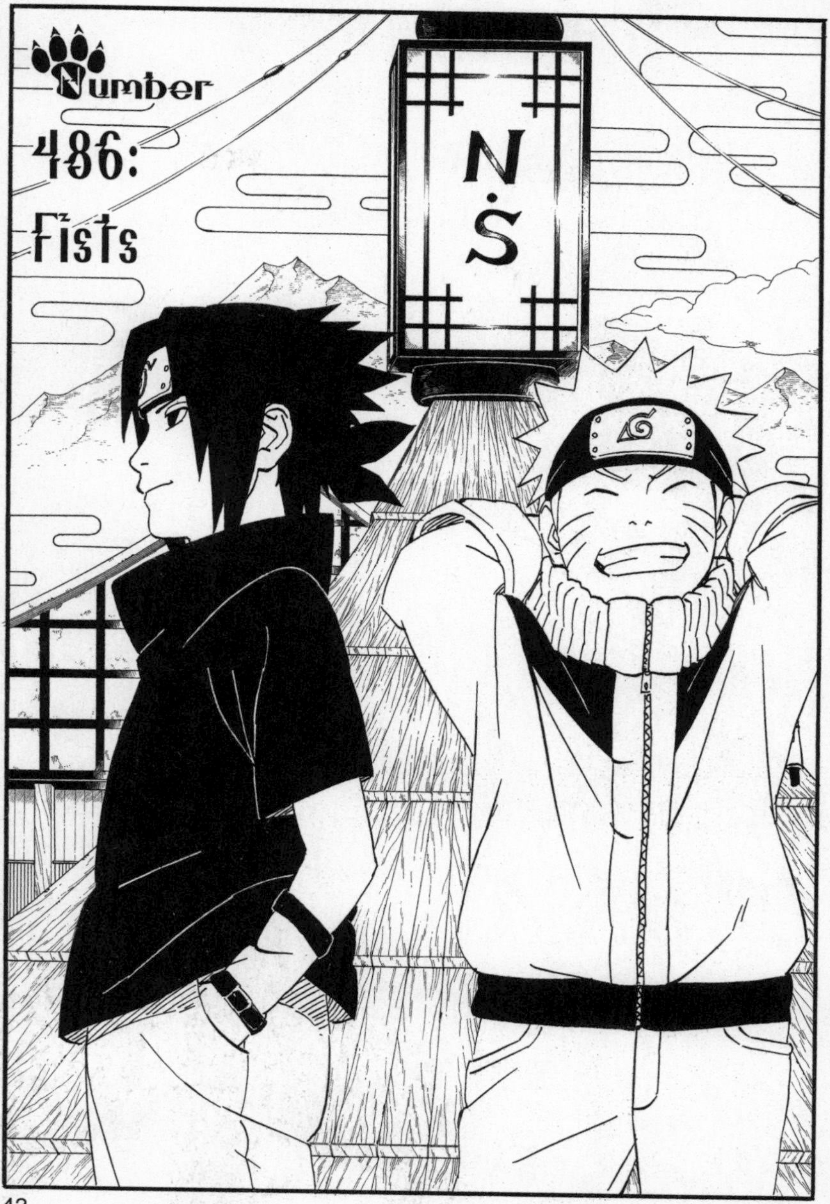
Number 486: Fists
N·S

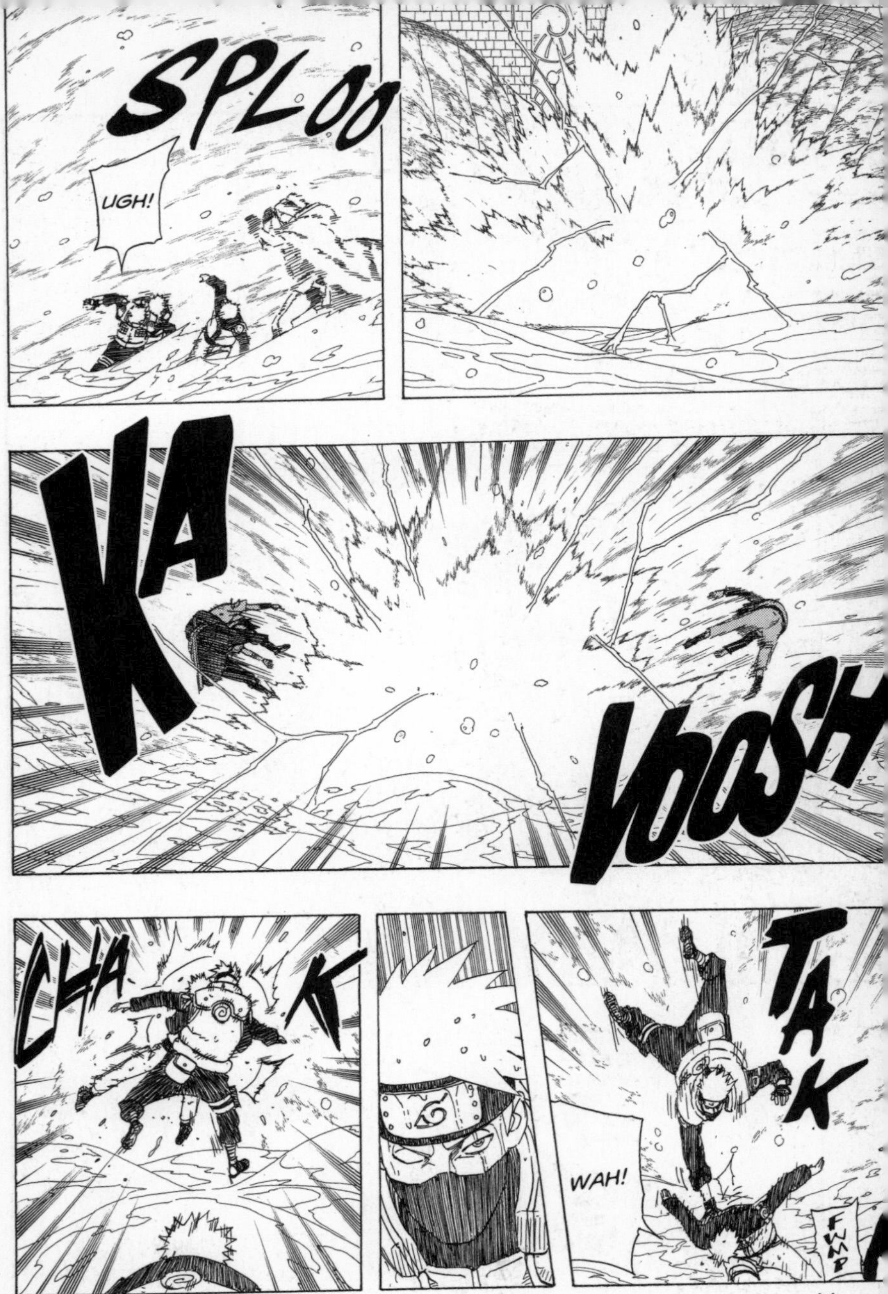
SPLOO
UGH!
KA
VOOSH
TAK
WAH!
FWMP
CHAK

READ THIS WAY

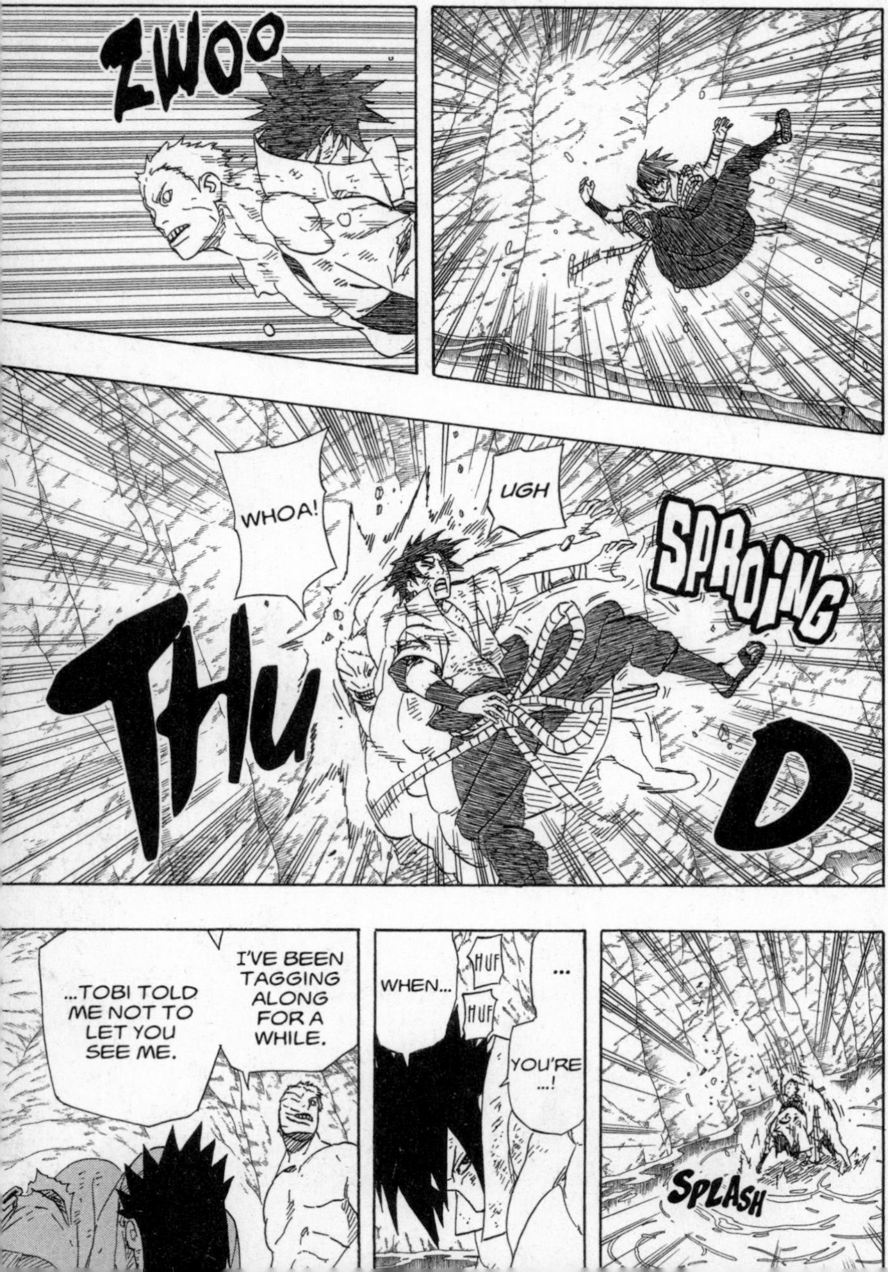

ZWOO
SPROING
UGH
WHOA!
THU
D
SPLASH
...
HUF
HUF
WHEN...
YOU'RE ...!
I'VE BEEN TAGGING ALONG FOR A WHILE.
...TOBI TOLD ME NOT TO LET YOU SEE ME.

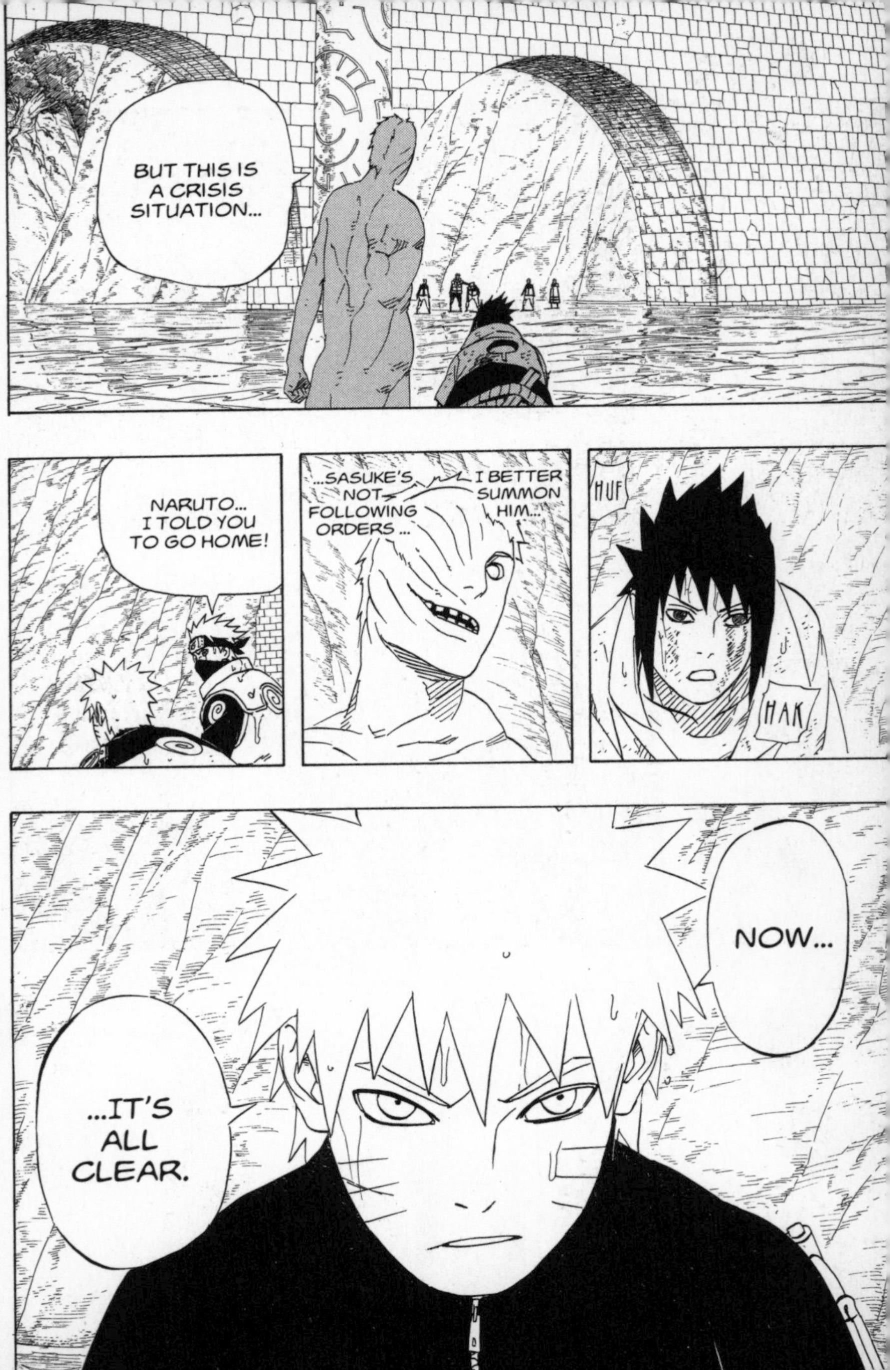
BUT THIS IS A CRISIS SITUATION...
HUF
HAK
...SASUKE'S NOT FOLLOWING ORDERS ...
I BETTER SUMMON HIM...
NARUTO... I TOLD YOU TO GO HOME!
NOW...
...IT'S ALL CLEAR.

READ THIS WAY

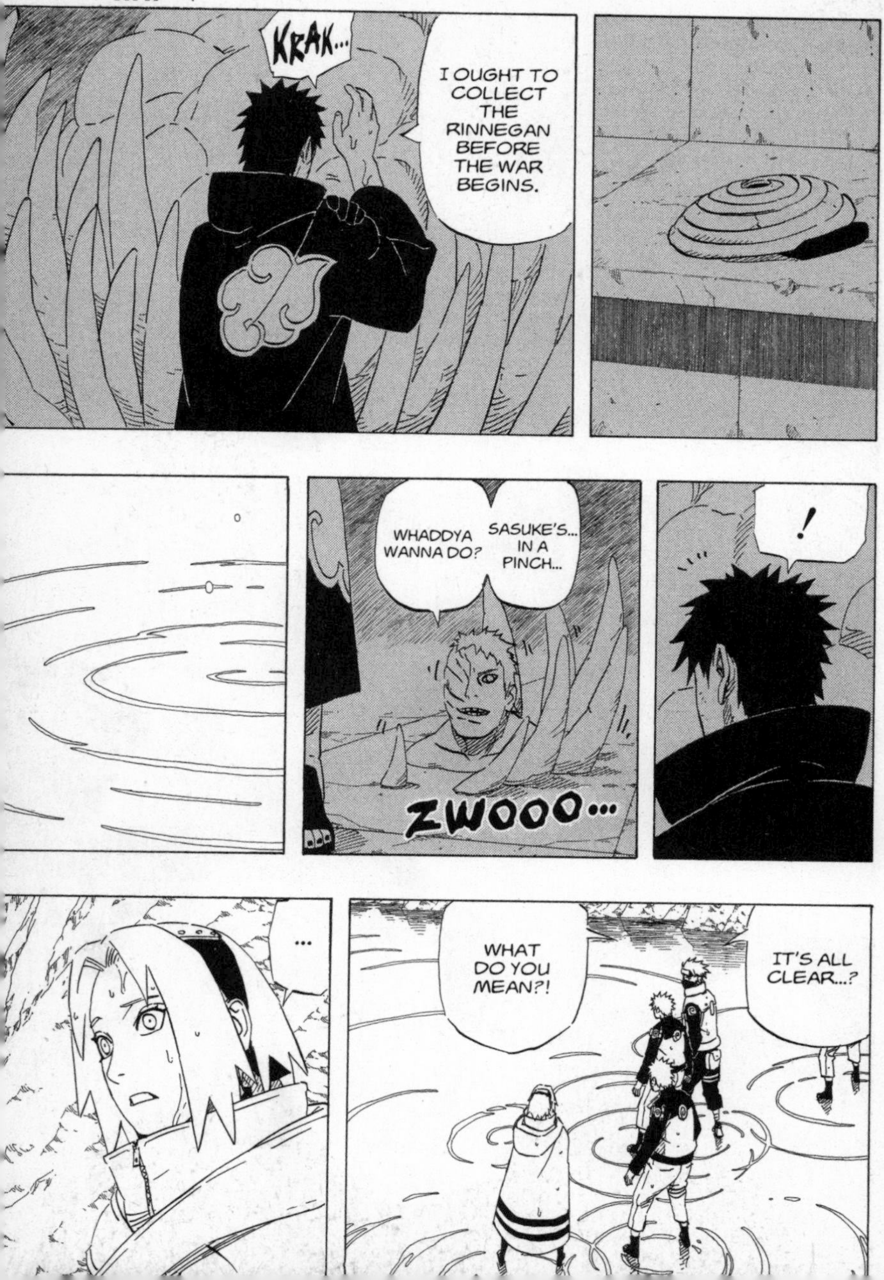
I OUGHT TO COLLECT THE RINNEGAN BEFORE THE WAR BEGINS.
KRAK...
!
SASUKE'S... IN A PINCH...
WHADDYA WANNA DO?
ZWOOO...
IT'S ALL CLEAR...?
WHAT DO YOU MEAN?!
...

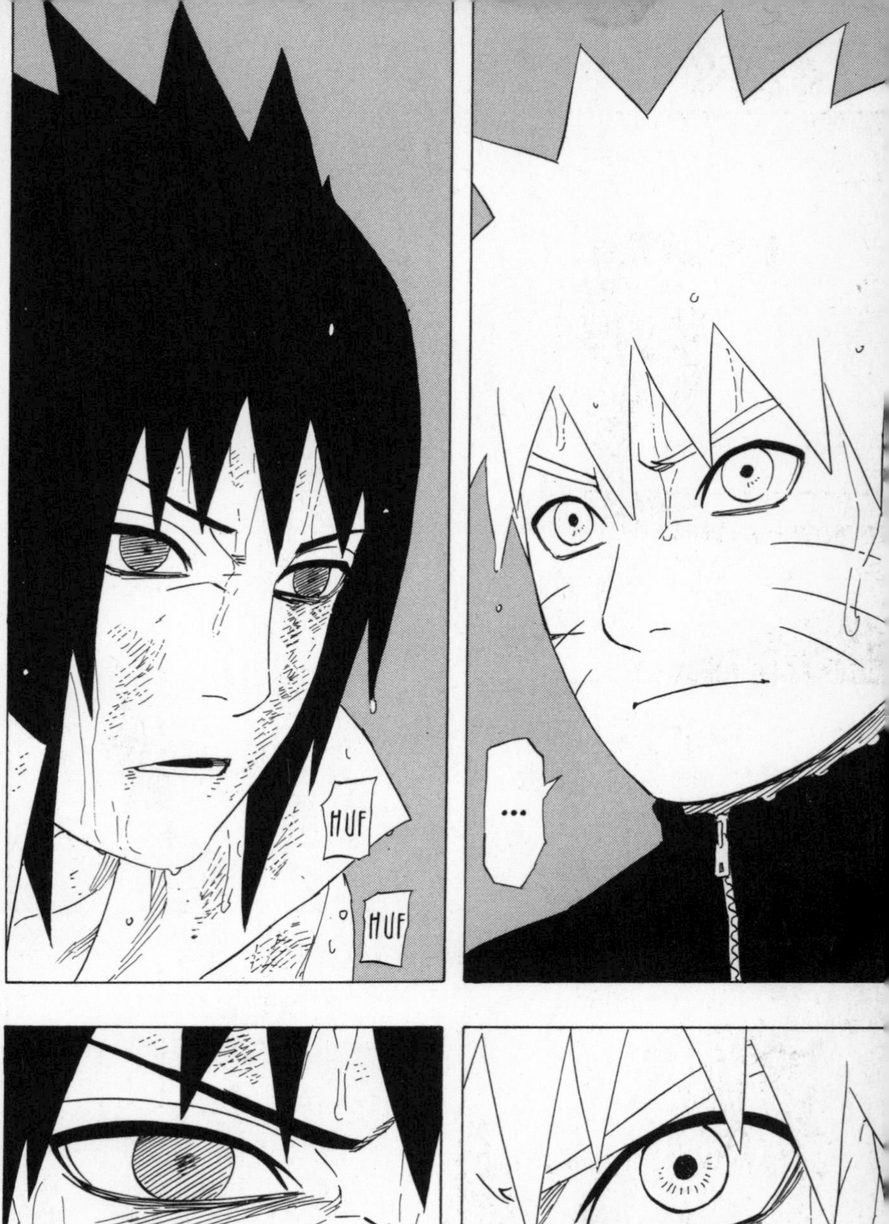
...
HUF
HUF

READ THIS WAY

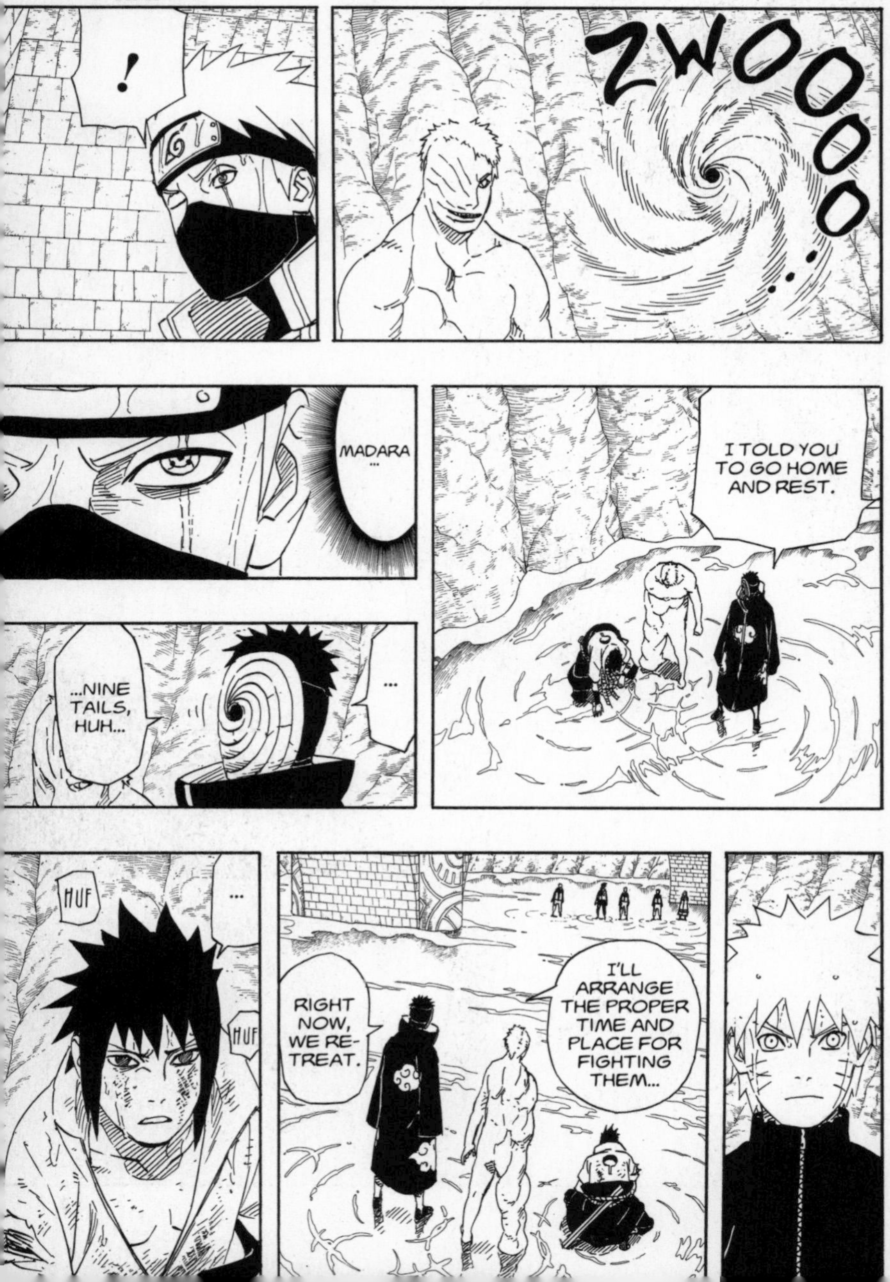

ZWOOOO...
!
I TOLD YOU TO GO HOME AND REST.
MADARA...
...
...NINE TAILS, HUH...
I'LL ARRANGE THE PROPER TIME AND PLACE FOR FIGHTING THEM...
RIGHT NOW, WE RETREAT.
...
HUF
HUF

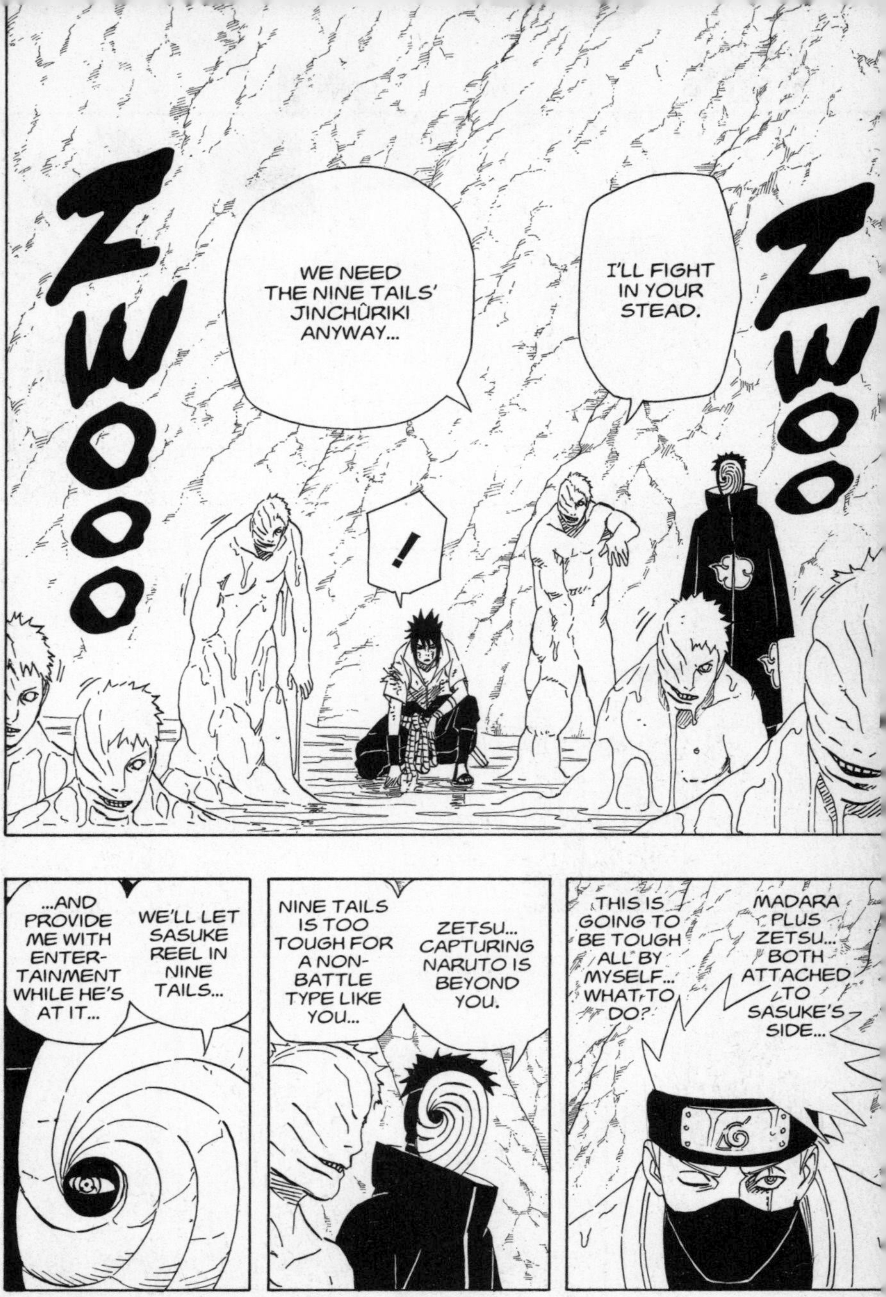
ZWOOO
I'LL FIGHT IN YOUR STEAD.
WE NEED THE NINE TAILS' JINCHÛRIKI ANYWAY...
ZWOOOO
!
MADARA PLUS ZETSU... BOTH ATTACHED TO SASUKE'S SIDE...
THIS IS GOING TO BE TOUGH ALL BY MYSELF... WHAT TO DO?
ZETSU... CAPTURING NARUTO IS BEYOND YOU.
NINE TAILS IS TOO TOUGH FOR A NON-BATTLE TYPE LIKE YOU...
WE'LL LET SASUKE REEL IN NINE TAILS...
...AND PROVIDE ME WITH ENTER-TAINMENT WHILE HE'S AT IT...

READ THIS WAY

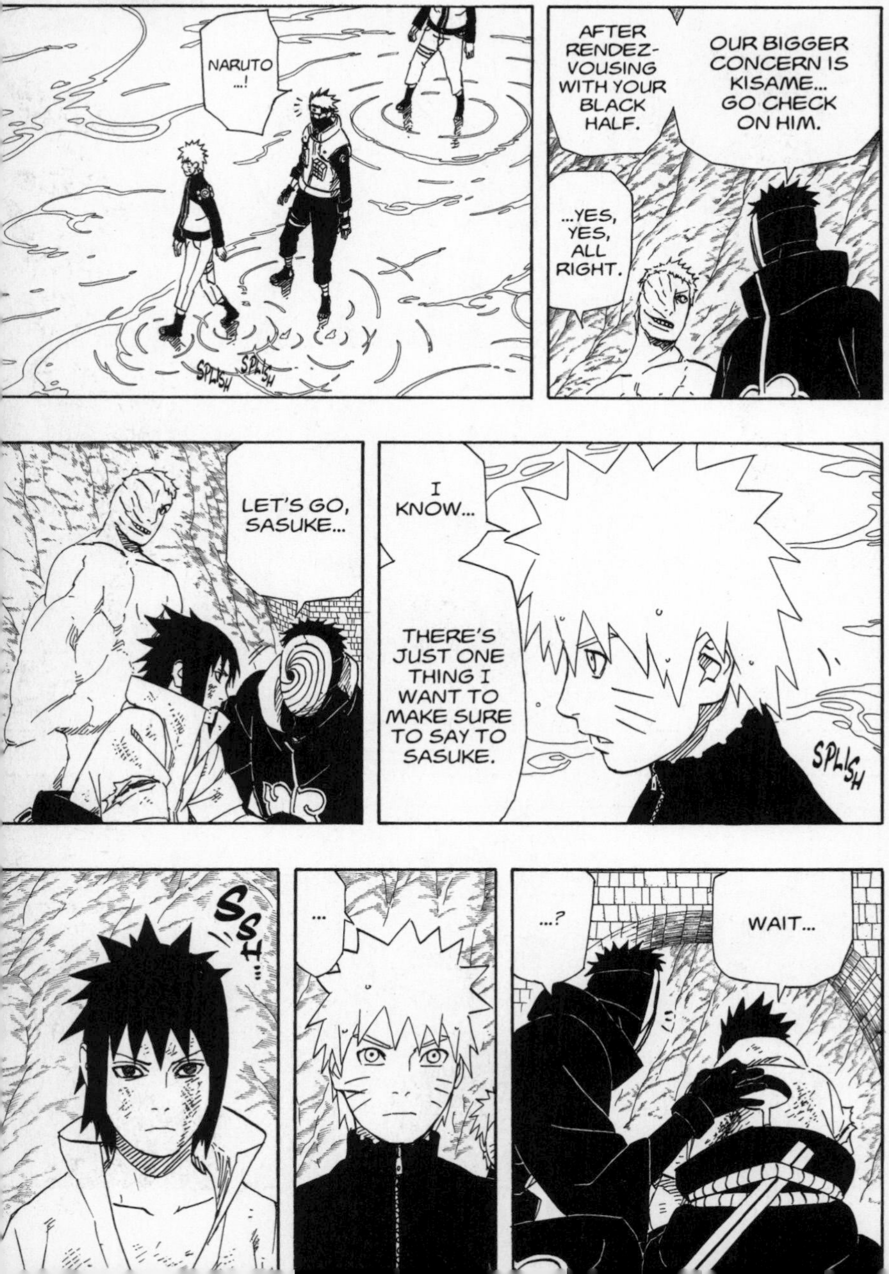
OUR BIGGER CONCERN IS KISAME... GO CHECK ON HIM.
AFTER RENDEZ-VOUSING WITH YOUR BLACK HALF.
...YES, YES, ALL RIGHT.
NARUTO ...!
SPLISH
SPLISH
I KNOW...
THERE'S JUST ONE THING I WANT TO MAKE SURE TO SAY TO SASUKE.
SPLISH
LET'S GO, SASUKE...
WAIT...
...?
...
SSH...

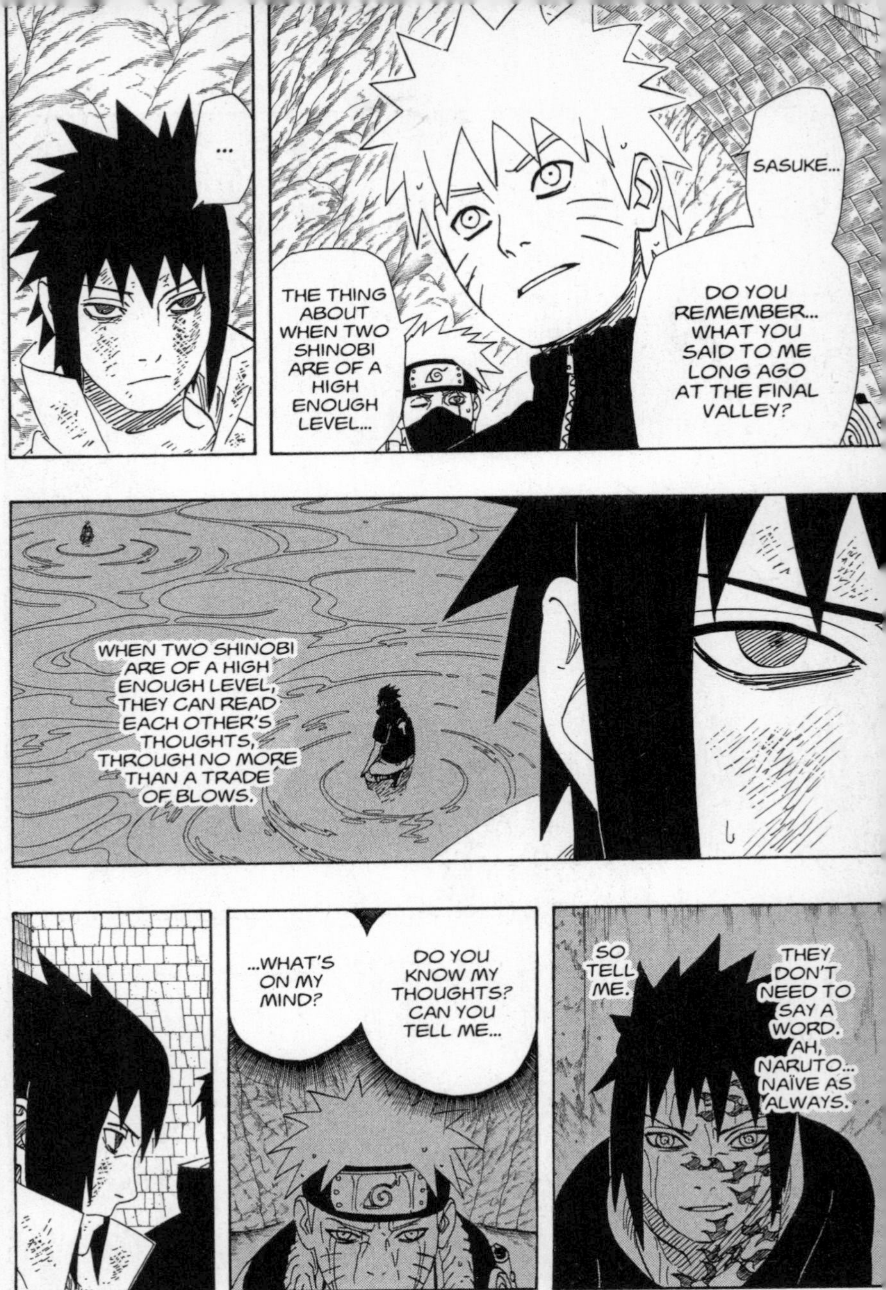
SASUKE...
DO YOU REMEMBER... WHAT YOU SAID TO ME LONG AGO AT THE FINAL VALLEY?
THE THING ABOUT WHEN TWO SHINOBI ARE OF A HIGH ENOUGH LEVEL...
...
WHEN TWO SHINOBI ARE OF A HIGH ENOUGH LEVEL, THEY CAN READ EACH OTHER'S THOUGHTS, THROUGH NO MORE THAN A TRADE OF BLOWS.
THEY DON'T NEED TO SAY A WORD. AH, NARUTO... NAÏVE AS ALWAYS.
SO TELL ME.
DO YOU KNOW MY THOUGHTS? CAN YOU TELL ME...
...WHAT'S ON MY MIND?

READ THIS WAY

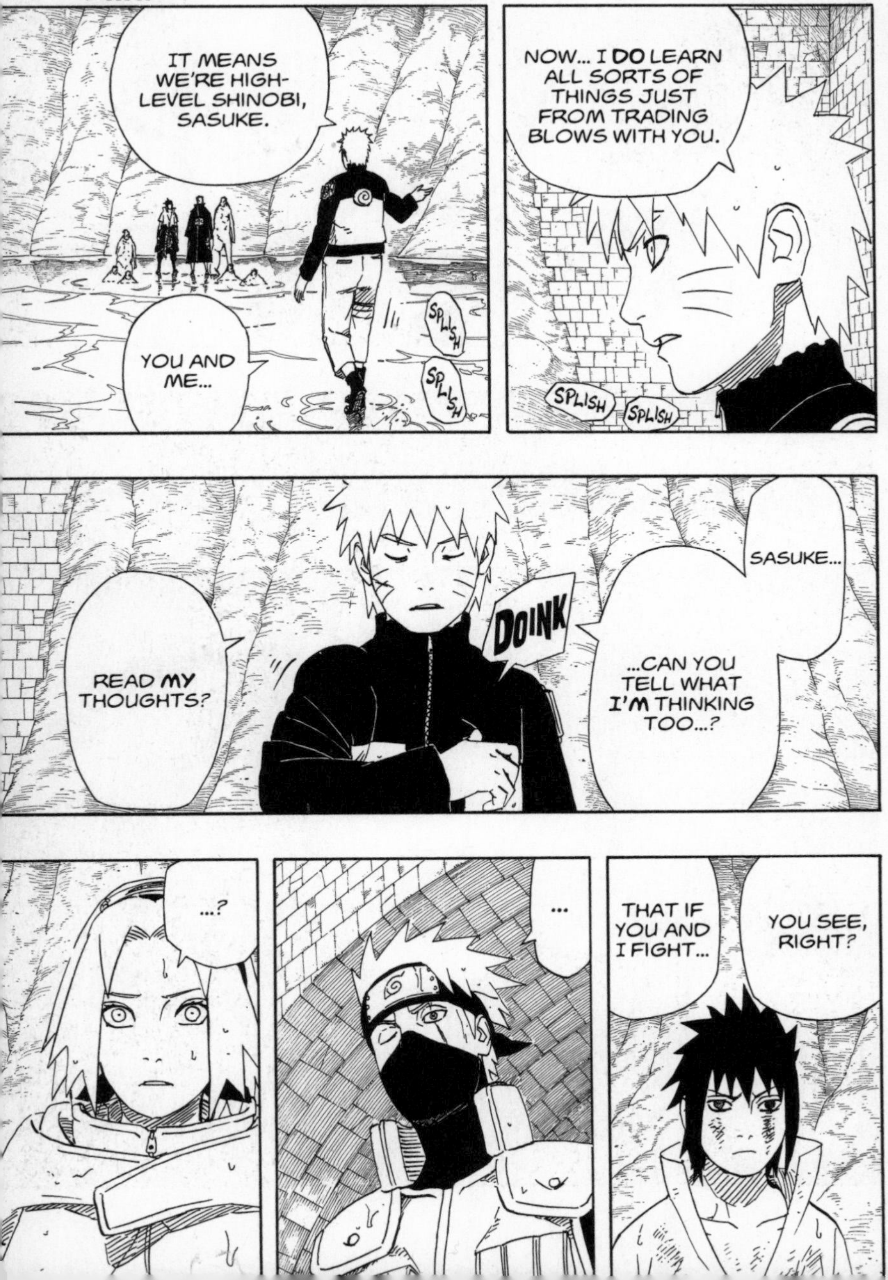
NOW... I DO LEARN ALL SORTS OF THINGS JUST FROM TRADING BLOWS WITH YOU.
SPLISH
SPLISH
IT MEANS WE'RE HIGH-LEVEL SHINOBI, SASUKE.
YOU AND ME...
SPLISH
SPLISH
SASUKE...
...CAN YOU TELL WHAT I'M THINKING TOO...?
DOINK
READ MY THOUGHTS?
YOU SEE, RIGHT?
THAT IF YOU AND I FIGHT...
...
...?

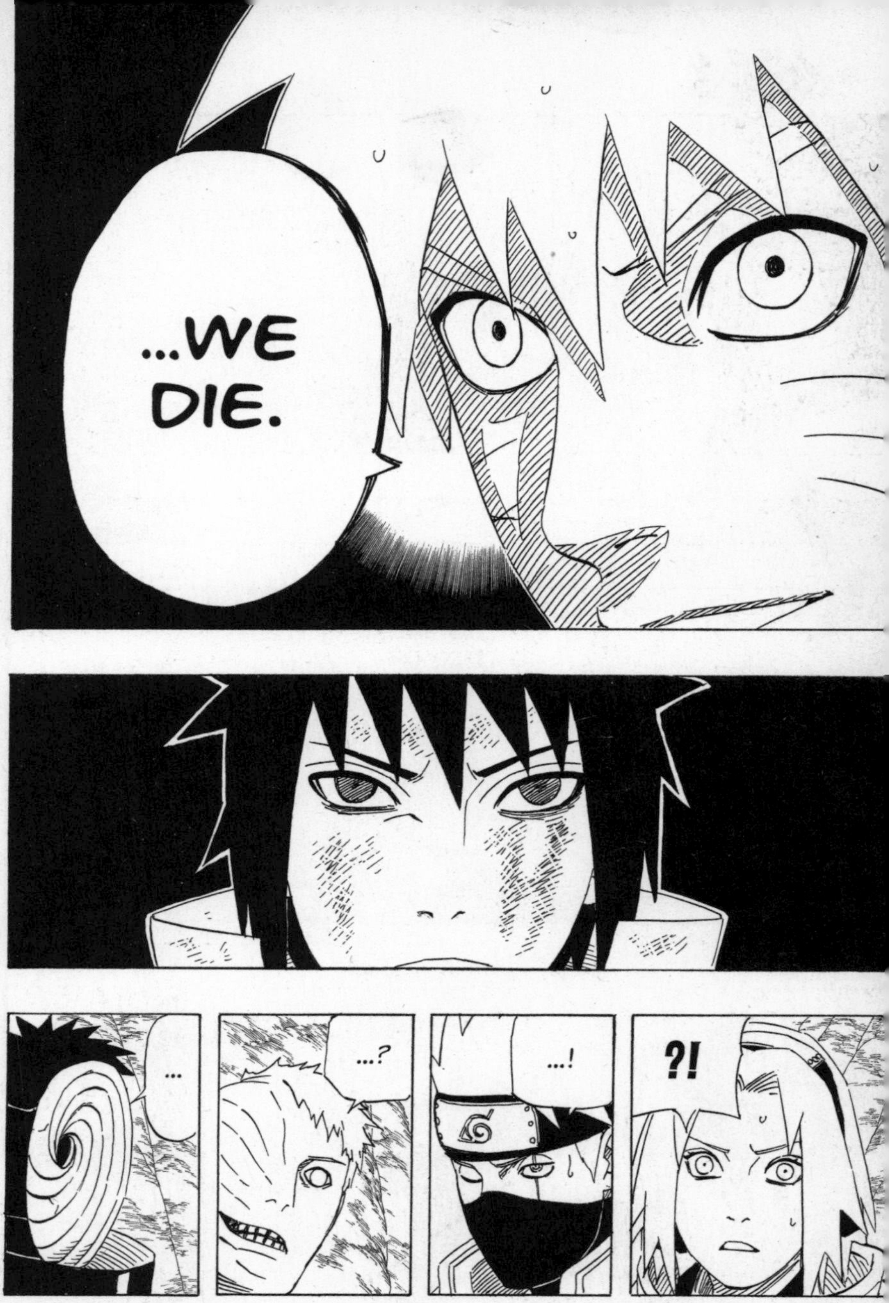
...WE DIE.
?!
...!
...?
...

READ THIS WAY

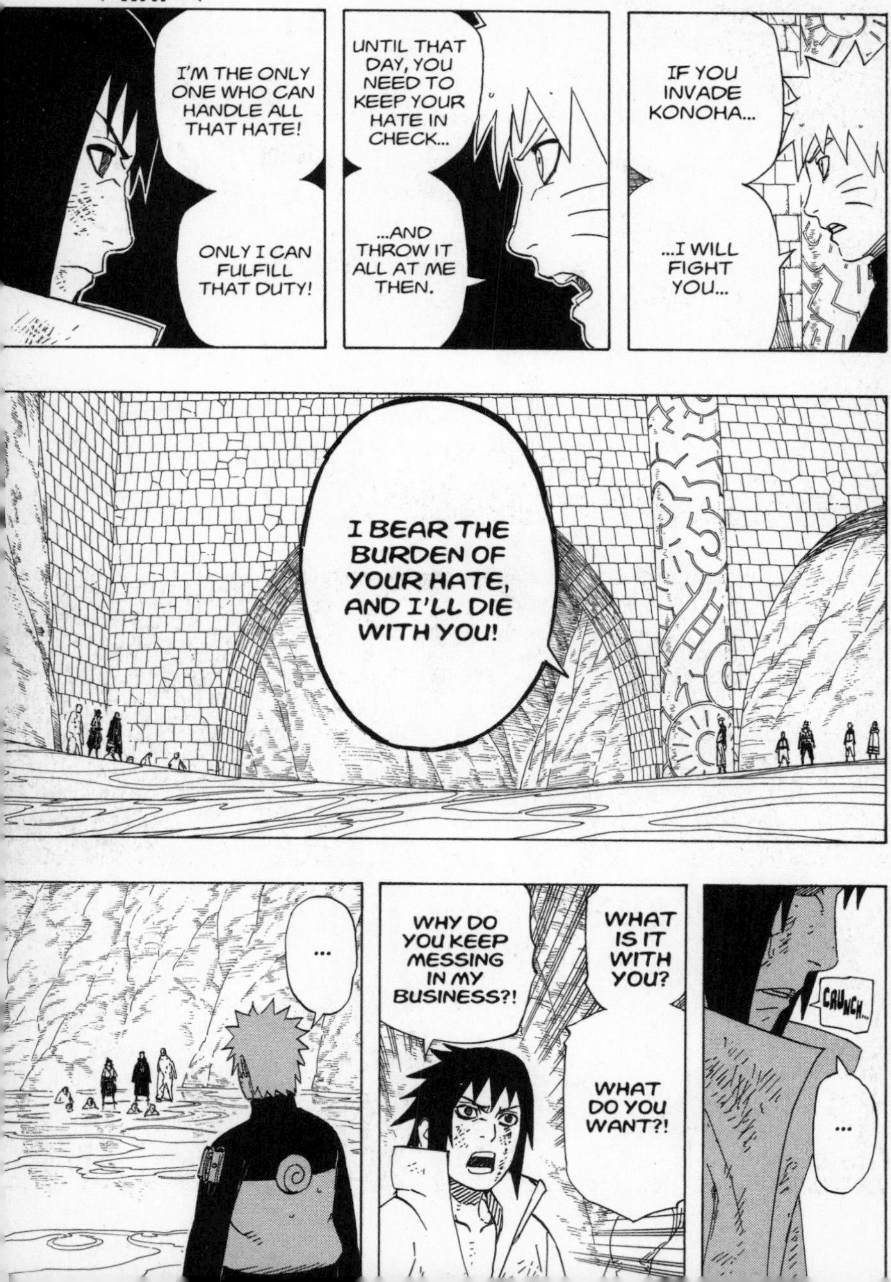
IF YOU INVADE KONOHA...
...I WILL FIGHT YOU...
UNTIL THAT DAY, YOU NEED TO KEEP YOUR HATE IN CHECK...
...AND THROW IT ALL AT ME THEN.
I'M THE ONLY ONE WHO CAN HANDLE ALL THAT HATE!
ONLY I CAN FULFILL THAT DUTY!
I BEAR THE BURDEN OF YOUR HATE, AND I'LL DIE WITH YOU!
CRUNCH...
...
WHAT IS IT WITH YOU?
WHAT DO YOU WANT?!
WHY DO YOU KEEP MESSING IN MY BUSINESS?!
...

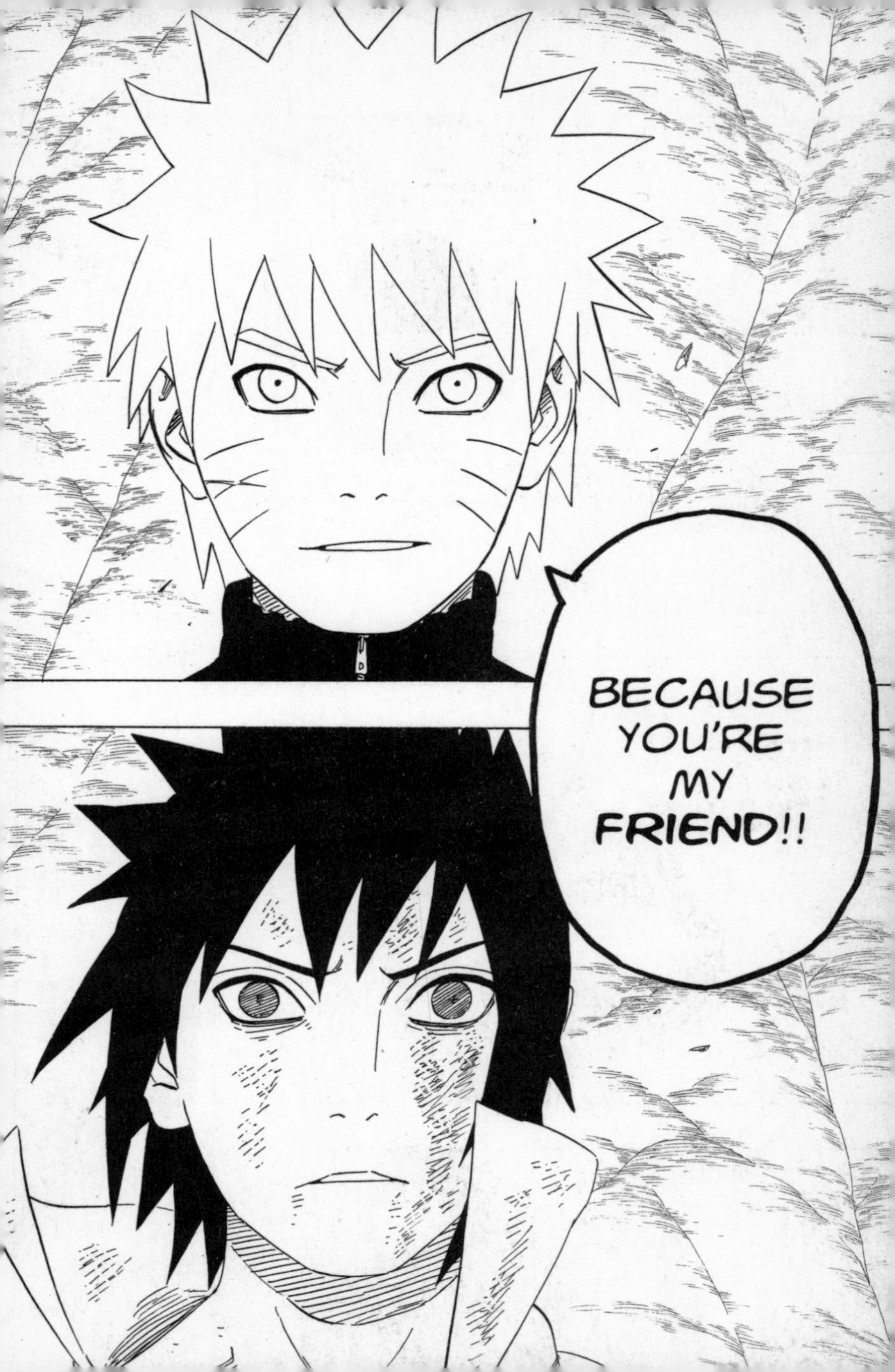
BECAUSE YOU'RE MY FRIEND!!

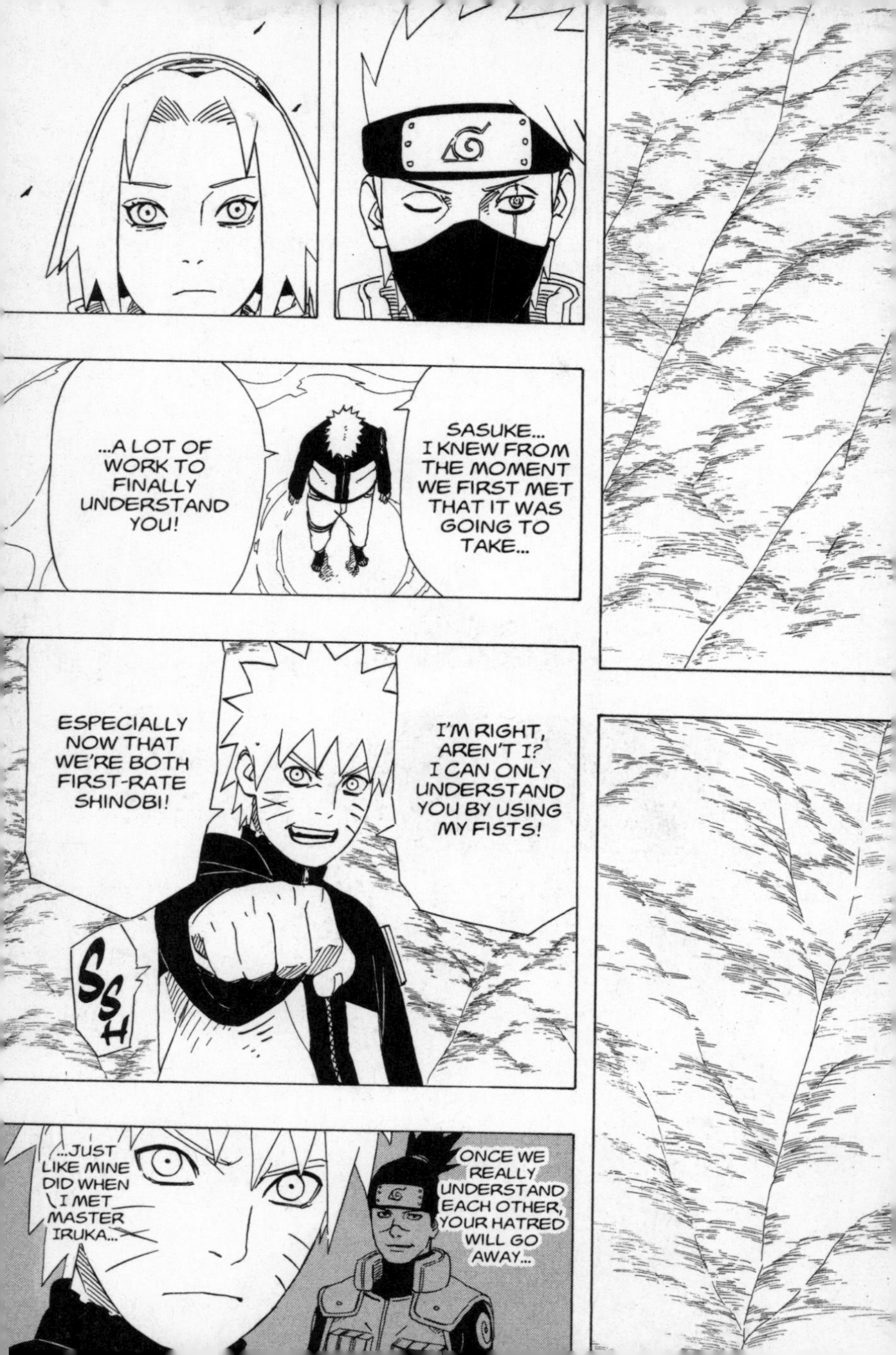
SASUKE... I KNEW FROM THE MOMENT WE FIRST MET THAT IT WAS GOING TO TAKE...
...A LOT OF WORK TO FINALLY UNDERSTAND YOU!
I'M RIGHT, AREN'T I? I CAN ONLY UNDERSTAND YOU BY USING MY FISTS!
ESPECIALLY NOW THAT WE'RE BOTH FIRST-RATE SHINOBI!
SSH
ONCE WE REALLY UNDERSTAND EACH OTHER, YOUR HATRED WILL GO AWAY...
...JUST LIKE MINE DID WHEN I MET MASTER IRUKA...

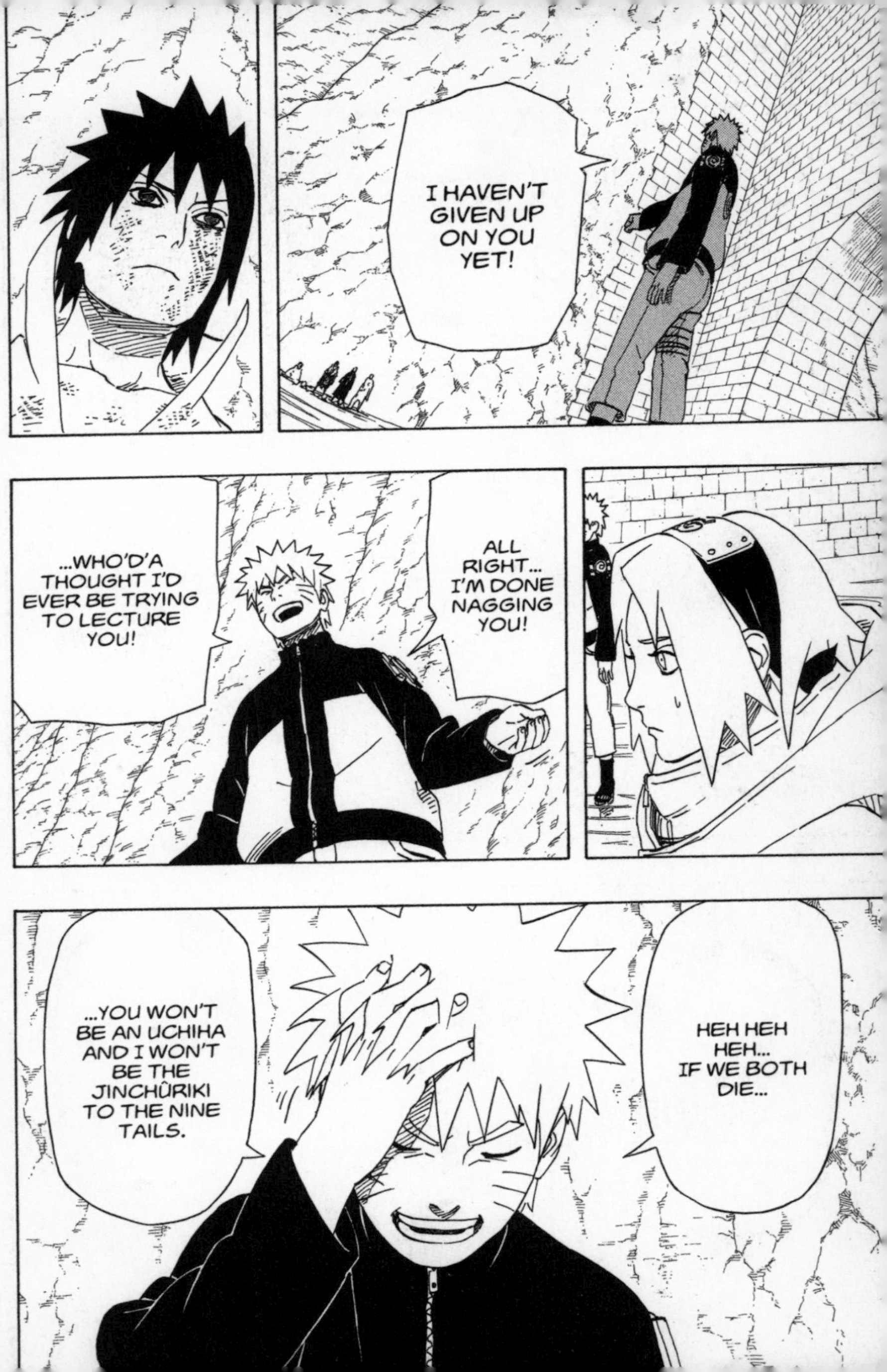
I HAVEN'T GIVEN UP ON YOU YET!
ALL RIGHT... I'M DONE NAGGING YOU!
...WHO'D'A THOUGHT I'D EVER BE TRYING TO LECTURE YOU!
HEH HEH HEH... IF WE BOTH DIE...
...YOU WON'T BE AN UCHIHA AND I WON'T BE THE JINCHÛRIKI TO THE NINE TAILS.

READ THIS WAY

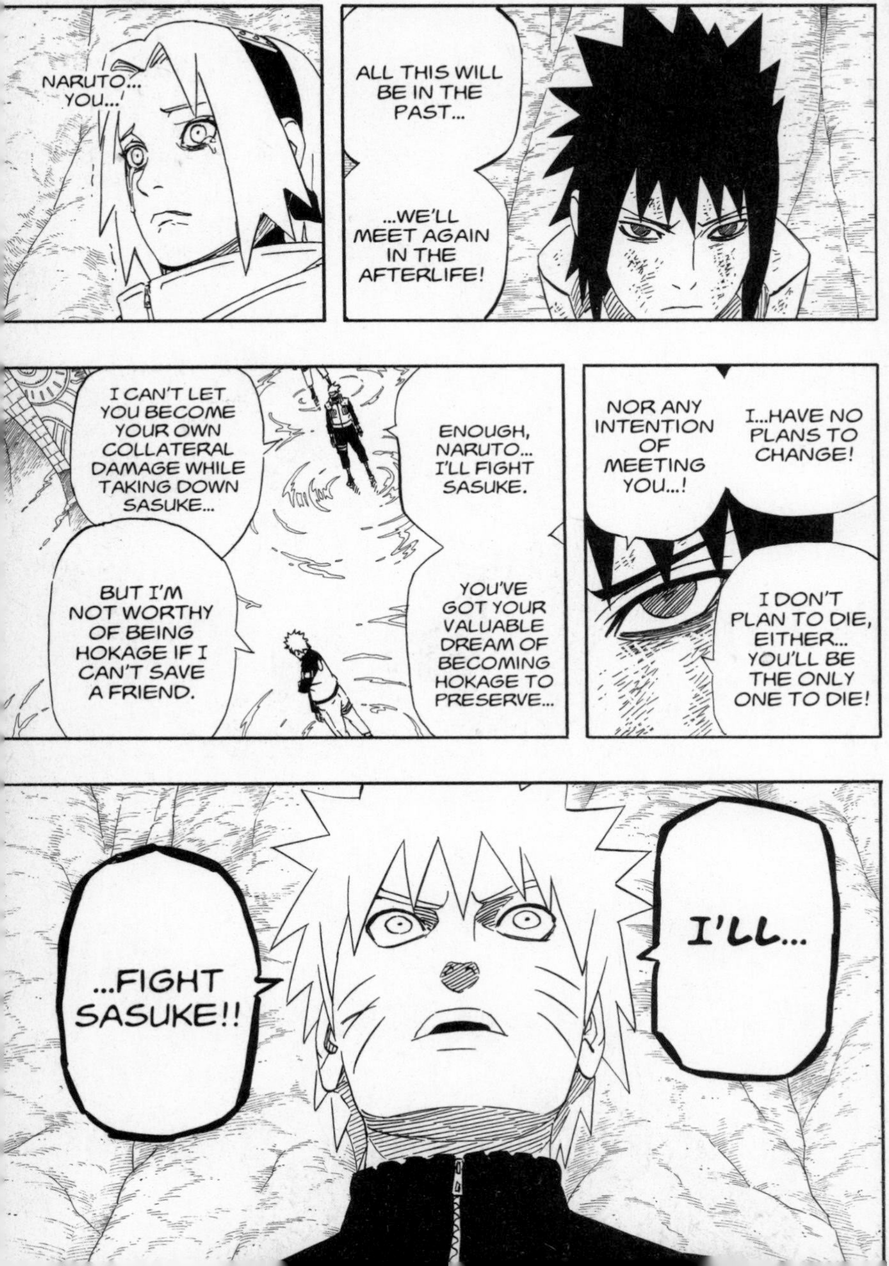
ALL THIS WILL BE IN THE PAST...
...WE'LL MEET AGAIN IN THE AFTERLIFE!
NARUTO... YOU...
I...HAVE NO PLANS TO CHANGE!
NOR ANY INTENTION OF MEETING YOU...!
I DON'T PLAN TO DIE, EITHER... YOU'LL BE THE ONLY ONE TO DIE!
ENOUGH, NARUTO... I'LL FIGHT SASUKE.
YOU'VE GOT YOUR VALUABLE DREAM OF BECOMING HOKAGE TO PRESERVE...
I CAN'T LET YOU BECOME YOUR OWN COLLATERAL DAMAGE WHILE TAKING DOWN SASUKE...
BUT I'M NOT WORTHY OF BEING HOKAGE IF I CAN'T SAVE A FRIEND.
I'LL...
...FIGHT SASUKE!!

NARUTO

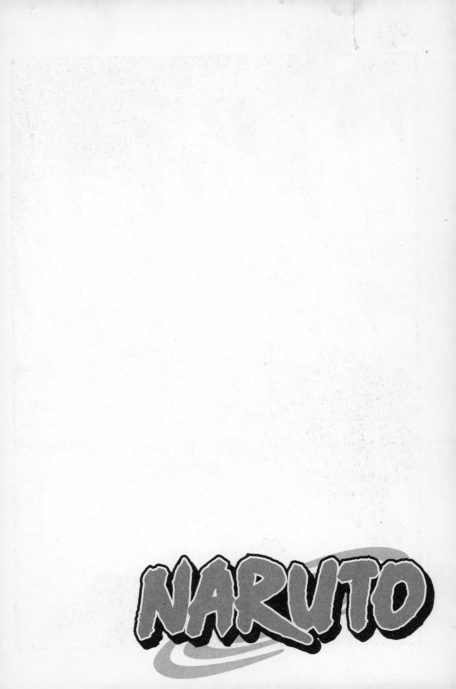

Number 487: The Battle Begins...!!

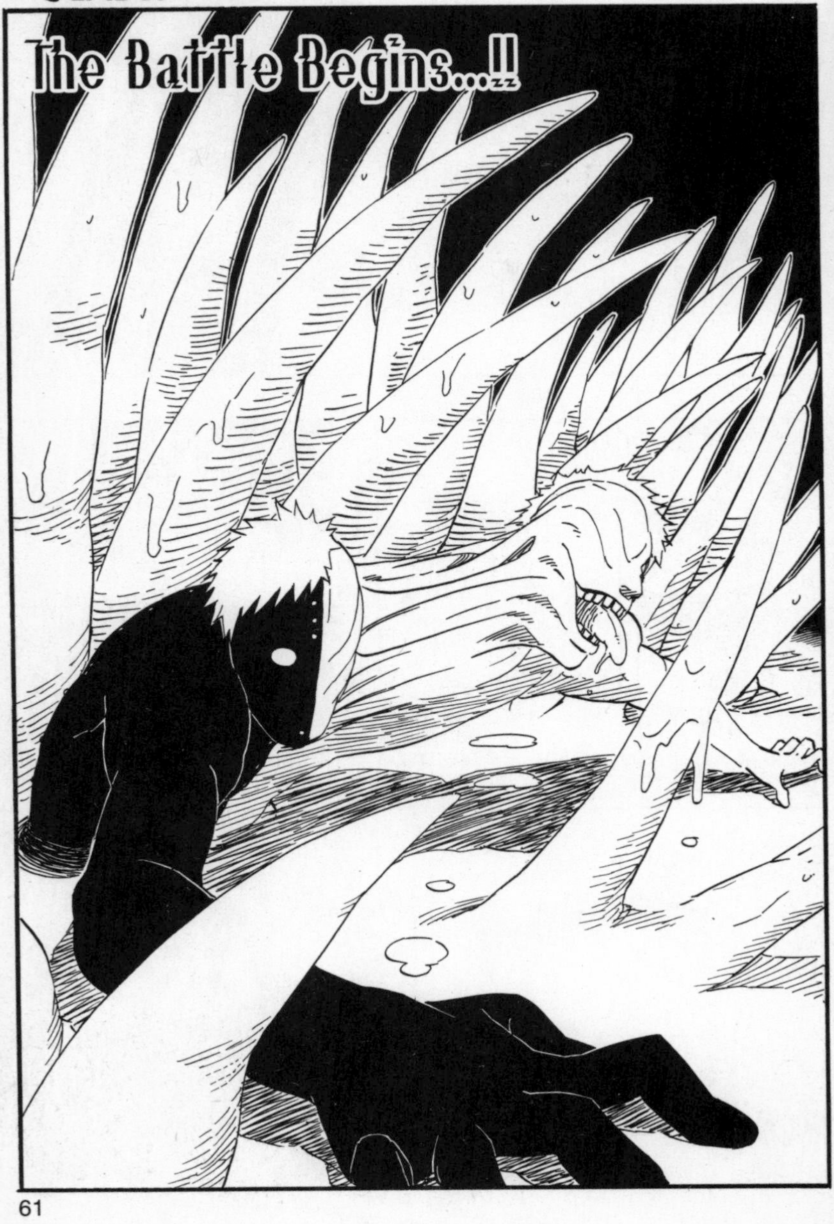

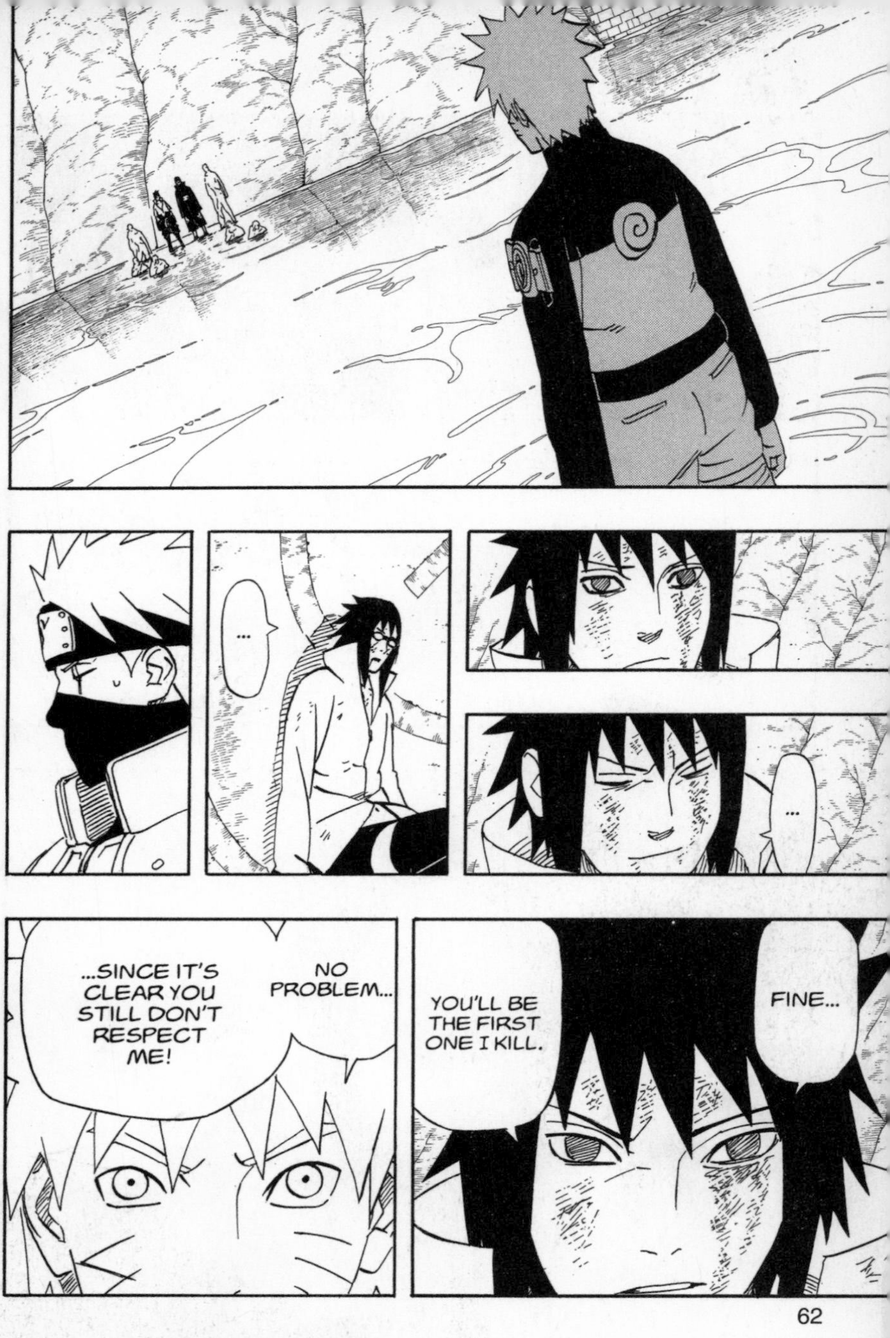
...
...
FINE...
YOU'LL BE THE FIRST ONE I KILL.
NO PROBLEM...
...SINCE IT'S CLEAR YOU STILL DON'T RESPECT ME!

READ THIS WAY

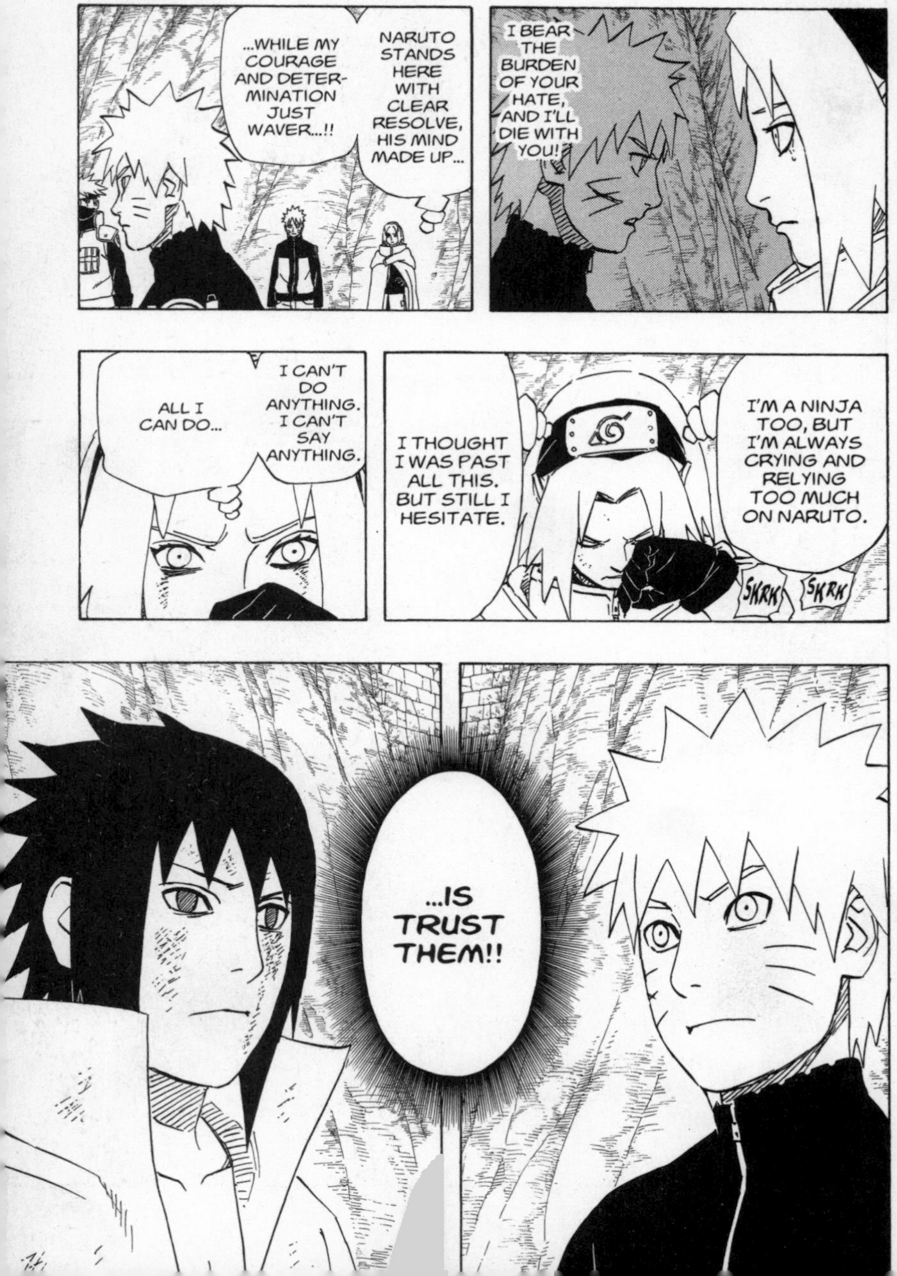

I BEAR THE BURDEN OF YOUR HATE, AND I'LL DIE WITH YOU!!
NARUTO STANDS HERE WITH CLEAR RESOLVE, HIS MIND MADE UP...
...WHILE MY COURAGE AND DETERMINATION JUST WAVER...!!
I'M A NINJA TOO, BUT I'M ALWAYS CRYING AND RELYING TOO MUCH ON NARUTO.
SKRK
SKRK
I THOUGHT I WAS PAST ALL THIS. BUT STILL I HESITATE.
I CAN'T DO ANYTHING. I CAN'T SAY ANYTHING.
ALL I CAN DO...
...IS TRUST THEM!!

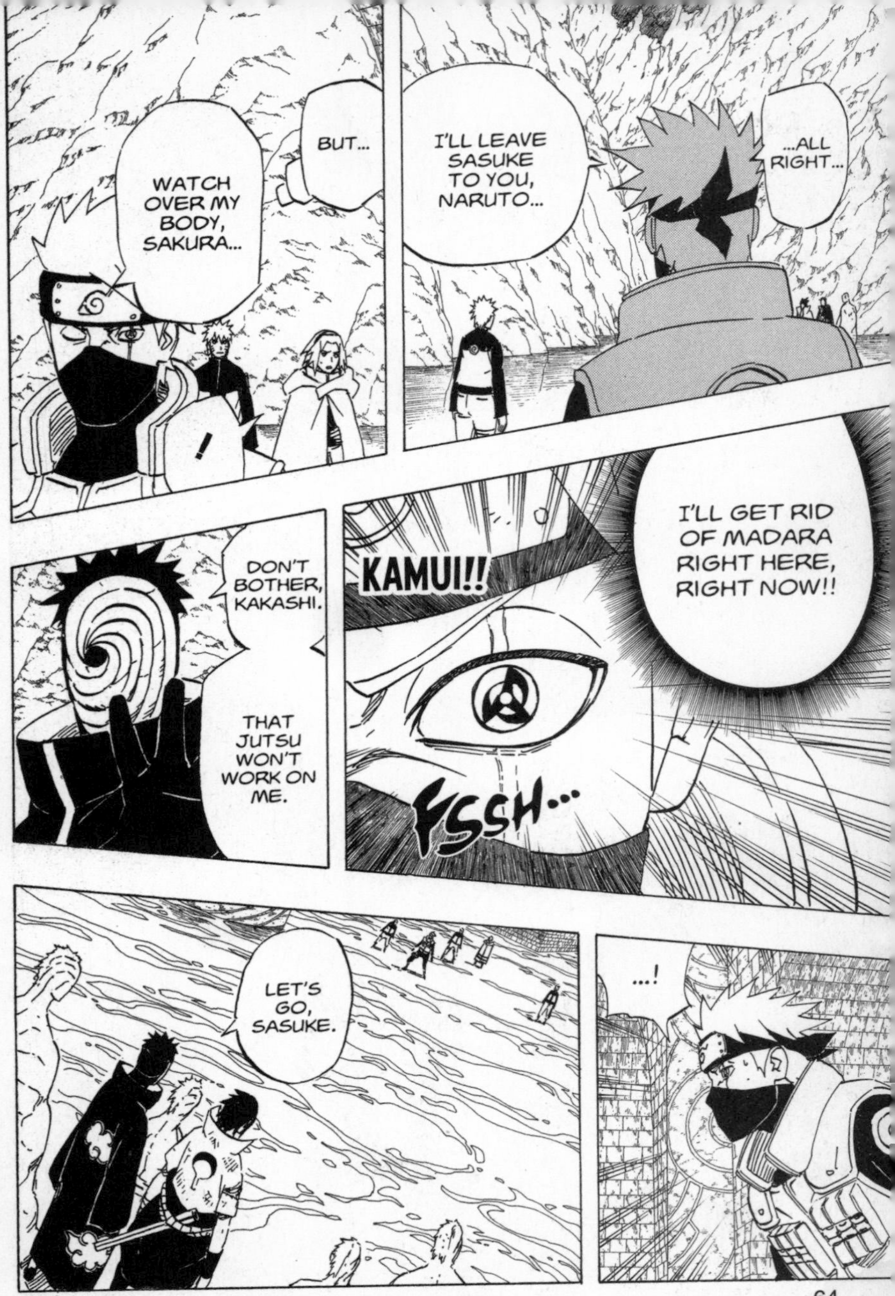
I'LL LEAVE SASUKE TO YOU, NARUTO...
...ALL RIGHT...
WATCH OVER MY BODY, SAKURA...
BUT...
!
I'LL GET RID OF MADARA RIGHT HERE, RIGHT NOW!!
KAMUI!!
FSSH...
DON'T BOTHER, KAKASHI.
THAT JUTSU WON'T WORK ON ME.
...!
LET'S GO, SASUKE.

READ THIS WAY

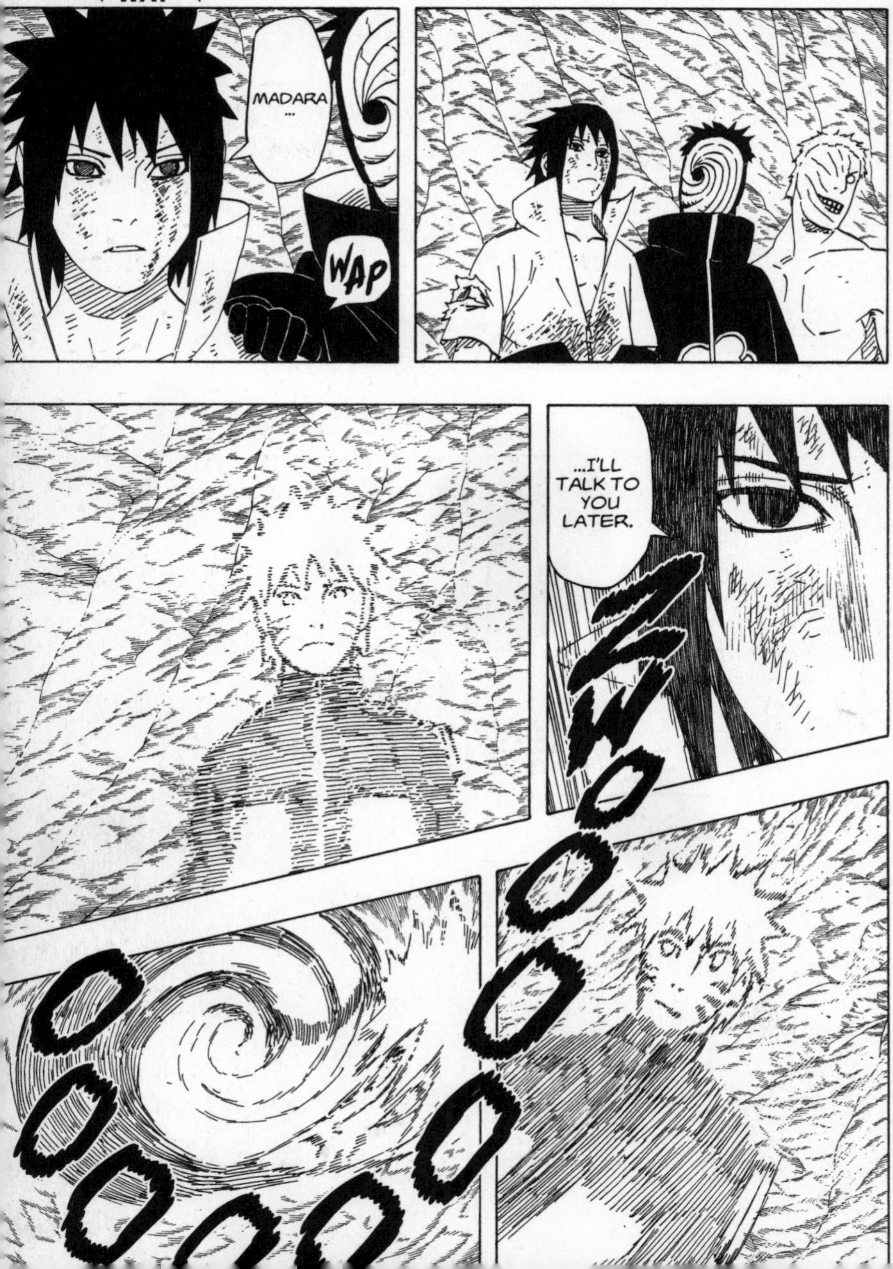
MADARA ...
WAP
...I'LL TALK TO YOU LATER.
ZWOOOOOOOO

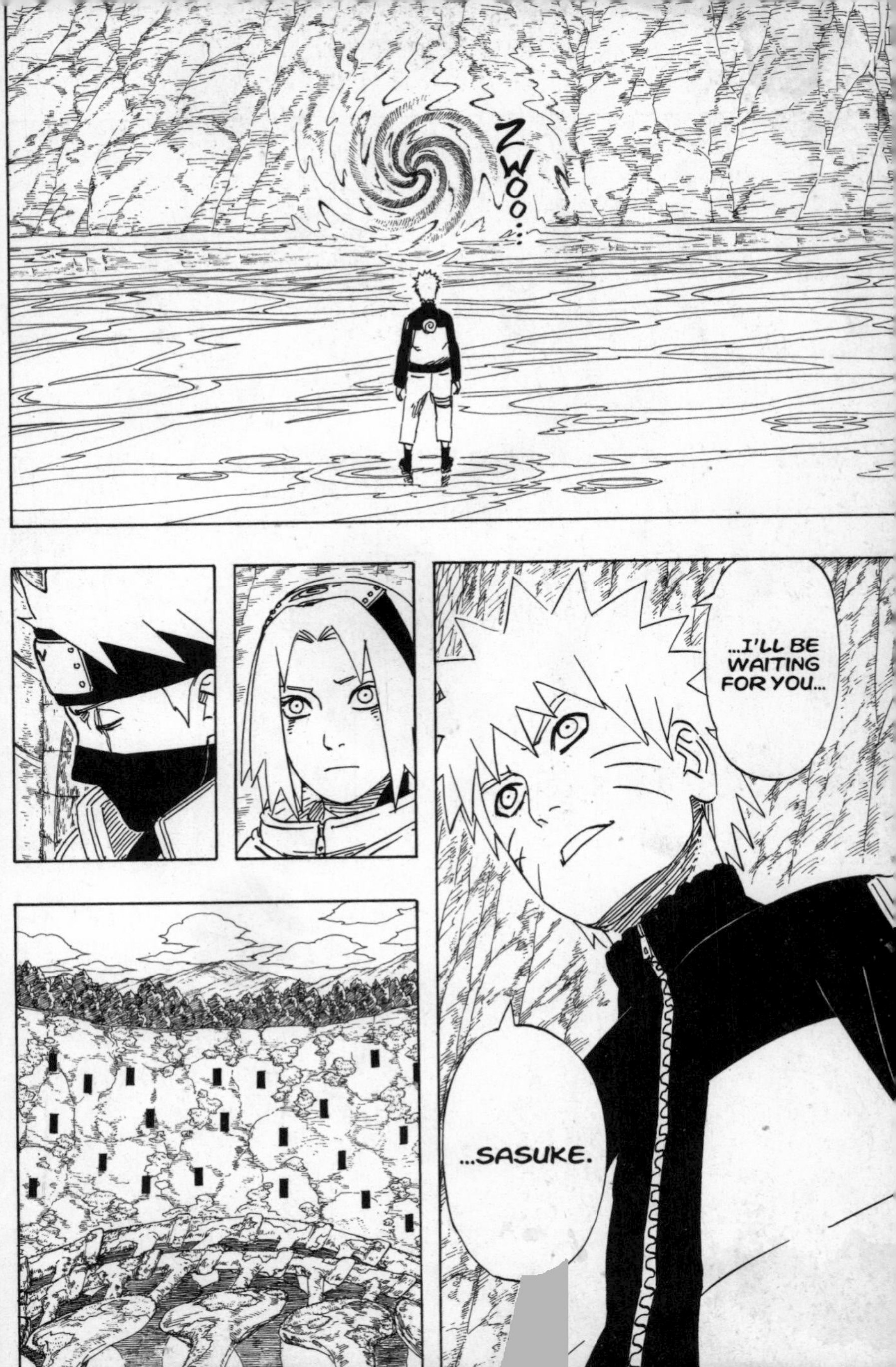
ZWOO...
...I'LL BE WAITING FOR YOU...
...SASUKE.

READ THIS WAY

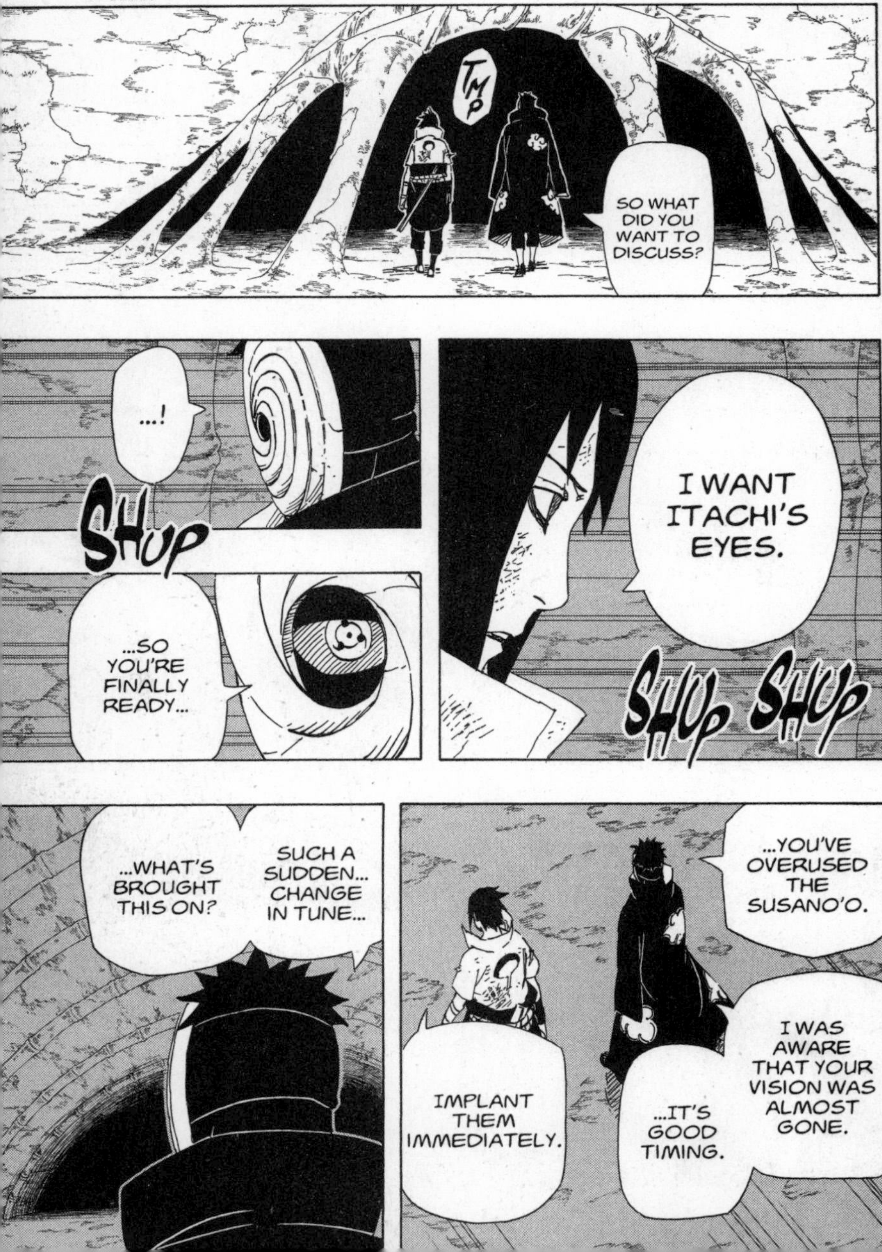
TMP
SO WHAT DID YOU WANT TO DISCUSS?
I WANT ITACHI'S EYES.
SHUP SHUP
...!
SHUP
...SO YOU'RE FINALLY READY...
...YOU'VE OVERUSED THE SUSANO'O.
I WAS AWARE THAT YOUR VISION WAS ALMOST GONE.
...IT'S GOOD TIMING.
IMPLANT THEM IMMEDIATELY.
SUCH A SUDDEN... CHANGE IN TUNE...
...WHAT'S BROUGHT THIS ON?

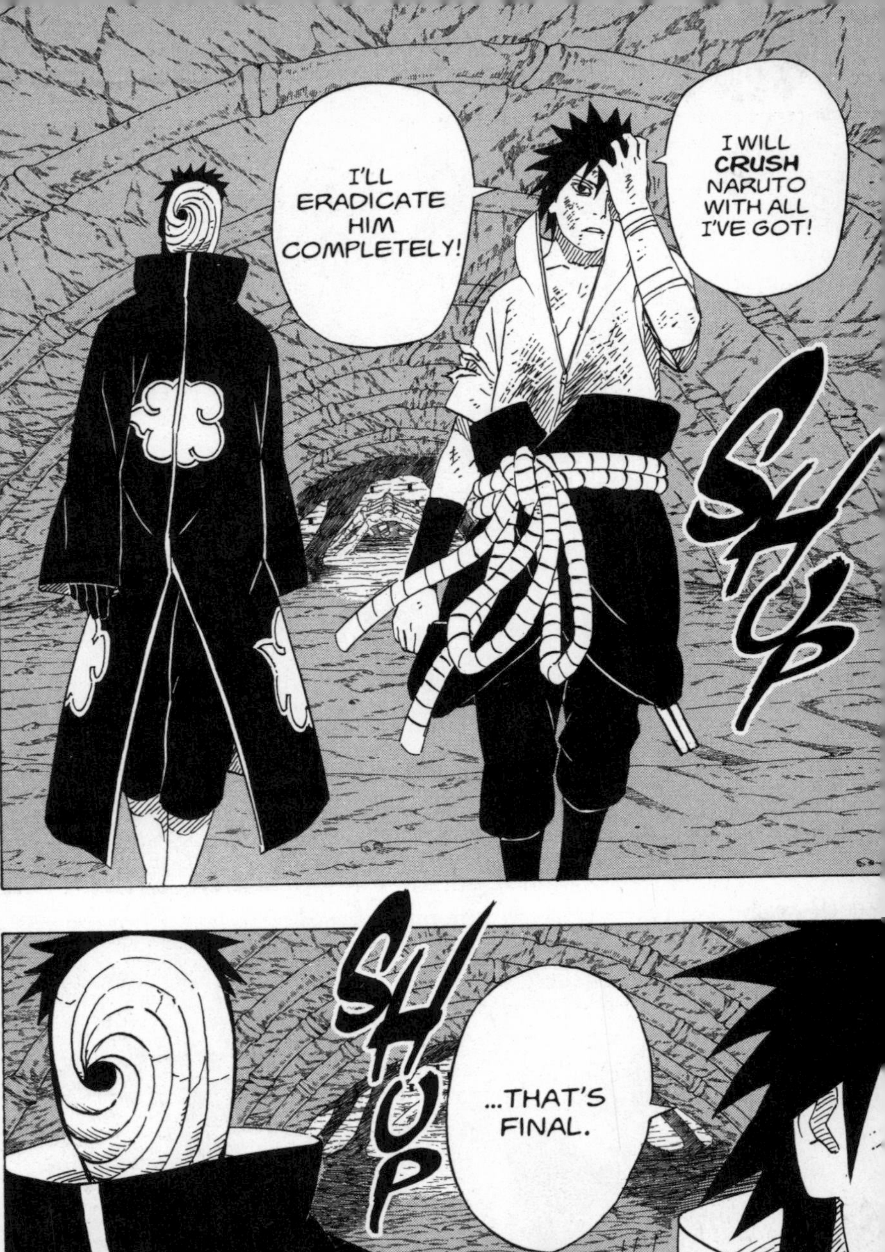
I WILL **CRUSH** NARUTO WITH ALL I'VE GOT!
SHUP
I'LL ERADICATE HIM COMPLETELY!
...THAT'S FINAL.
SHUP

READ THIS WAY

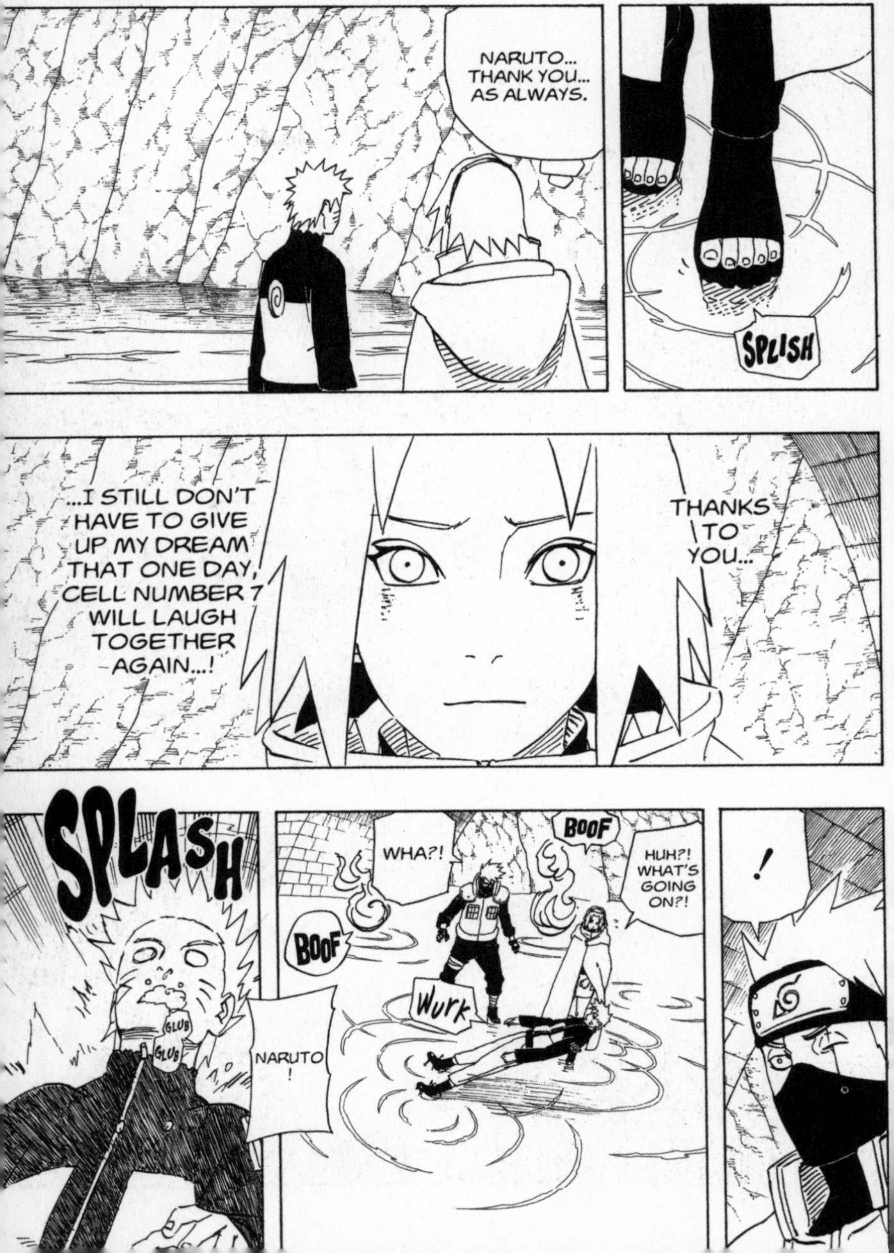
SPLISH
NARUTO... THANK YOU... AS ALWAYS.
THANKS TO YOU...
...I STILL DON'T HAVE TO GIVE UP MY DREAM THAT ONE DAY, CELL NUMBER 7 WILL LAUGH TOGETHER AGAIN...!
!
BOOF
HUH?! WHAT'S GOING ON?!
WHA?!
BOOF
Wurk
SPLASH
GLUB
GLUB
NARUTO!

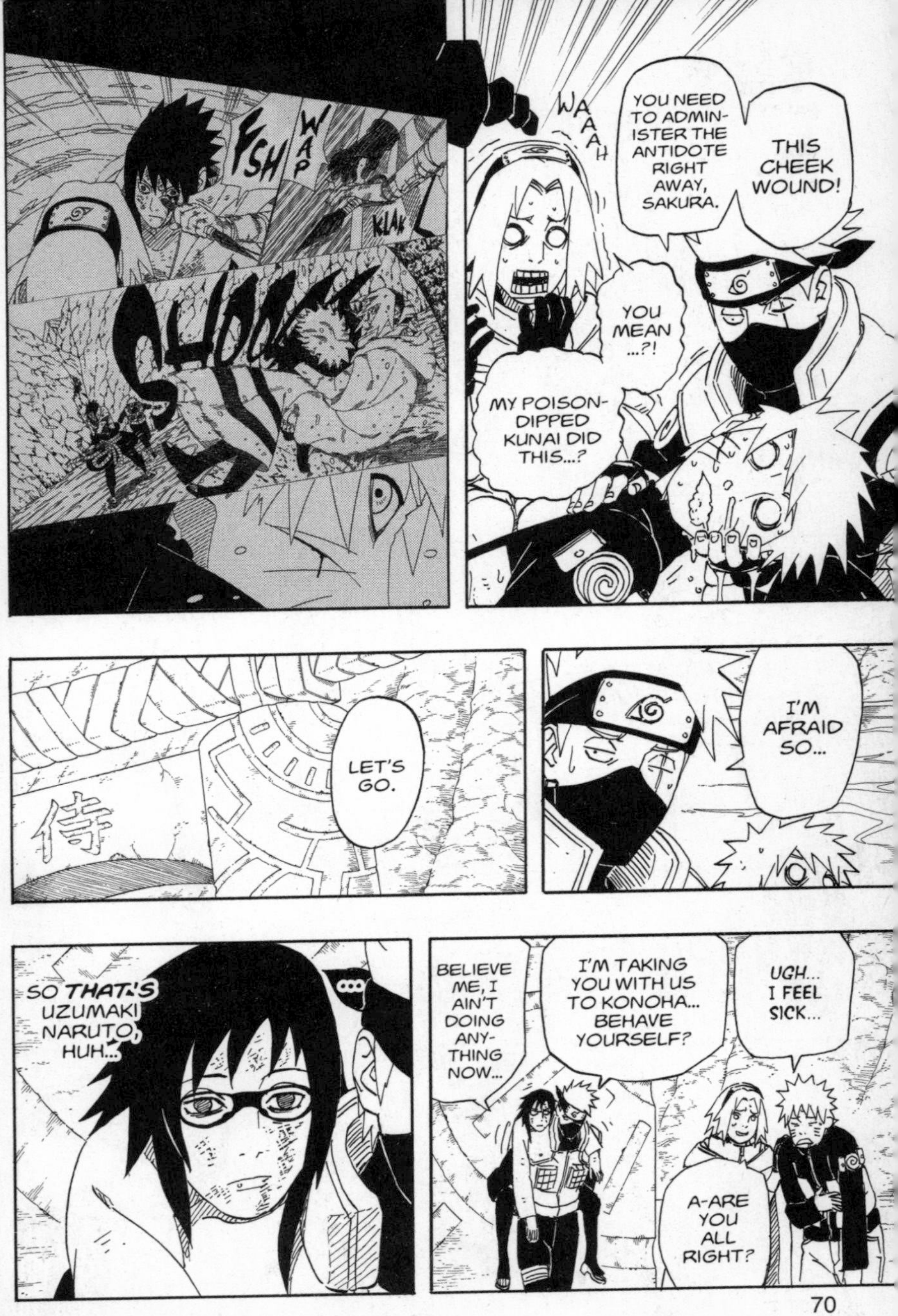
THIS CHEEK WOUND!
YOU NEED TO ADMIN-ISTER THE ANTIDOTE RIGHT AWAY, SAKURA.
WAAAAH
YOU MEAN ...?!
MY POISON-DIPPED KUNAI DID THIS...?
FSH
WAP
KLAK
I'M AFRAID SO...
LET'S GO.
UGH... I FEEL SICK...
I'M TAKING YOU WITH US TO KONOHA... BEHAVE YOURSELF?
BELIEVE ME, I AIN'T DOING ANY-THING NOW...
A-ARE YOU ALL RIGHT?
...
SO THAT'S UZUMAKI NARUTO, HUH...

READ THIS WAY

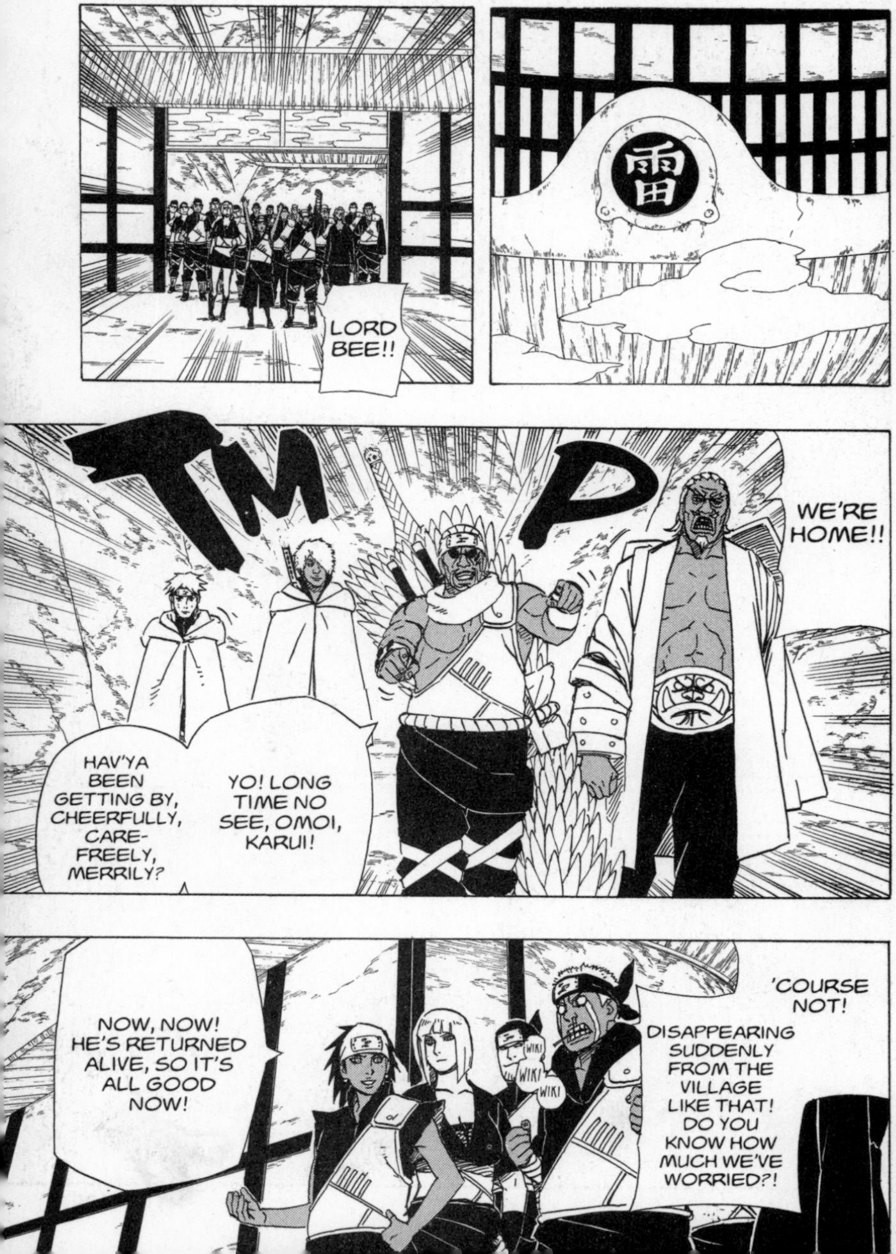
LORD BEE!!
TMP
WE'RE HOME!!
YO! LONG TIME NO SEE, OMOI, KARUI!
HAV'YA BEEN GETTING BY, CHEERFULLY, CAREFREELY, MERRILY?
'COURSE NOT!
DISAPPEARING SUDDENLY FROM THE VILLAGE LIKE THAT! DO YOU KNOW HOW MUCH WE'VE WORRIED?!
WIKI WIKI WIKI
NOW, NOW! HE'S RETURNED ALIVE, SO IT'S ALL GOOD NOW!

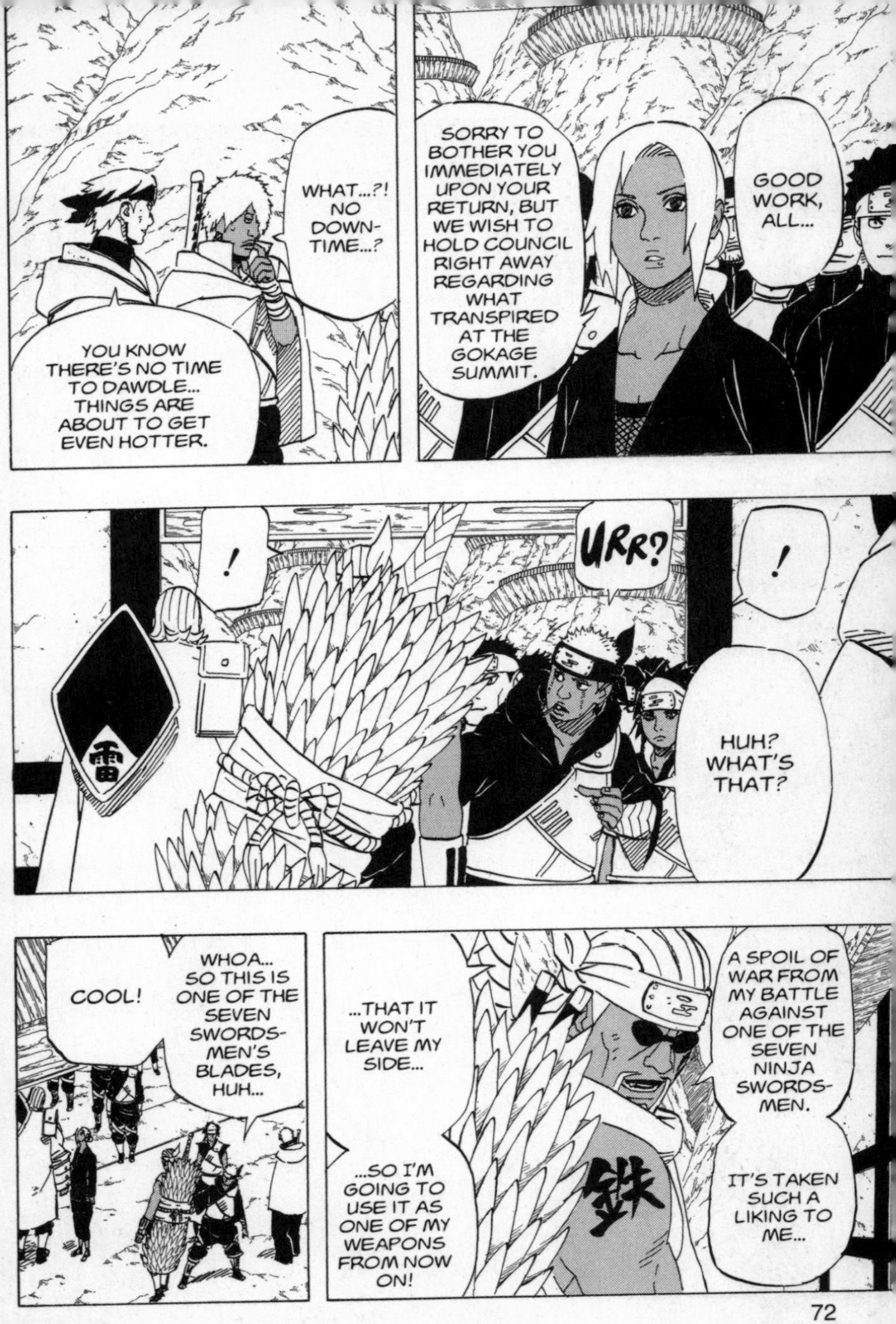
GOOD WORK, ALL...
SORRY TO BOTHER YOU IMMEDIATELY UPON YOUR RETURN, BUT WE WISH TO HOLD COUNCIL RIGHT AWAY REGARDING WHAT TRANSPIRED AT THE GOKAGE SUMMIT.
WHAT...?! NO DOWN-TIME...?
YOU KNOW THERE'S NO TIME TO DAWDLE... THINGS ARE ABOUT TO GET EVEN HOTTER.
!
HUH? WHAT'S THAT?
URR?
!
A SPOIL OF WAR FROM MY BATTLE AGAINST ONE OF THE SEVEN NINJA SWORDS-MEN.
IT'S TAKEN SUCH A LIKING TO ME...
...THAT IT WON'T LEAVE MY SIDE...
...SO I'M GOING TO USE IT AS ONE OF MY WEAPONS FROM NOW ON!
WHOA... SO THIS IS ONE OF THE SEVEN SWORDS-MEN'S BLADES, HUH...
COOL!

READ THIS WAY

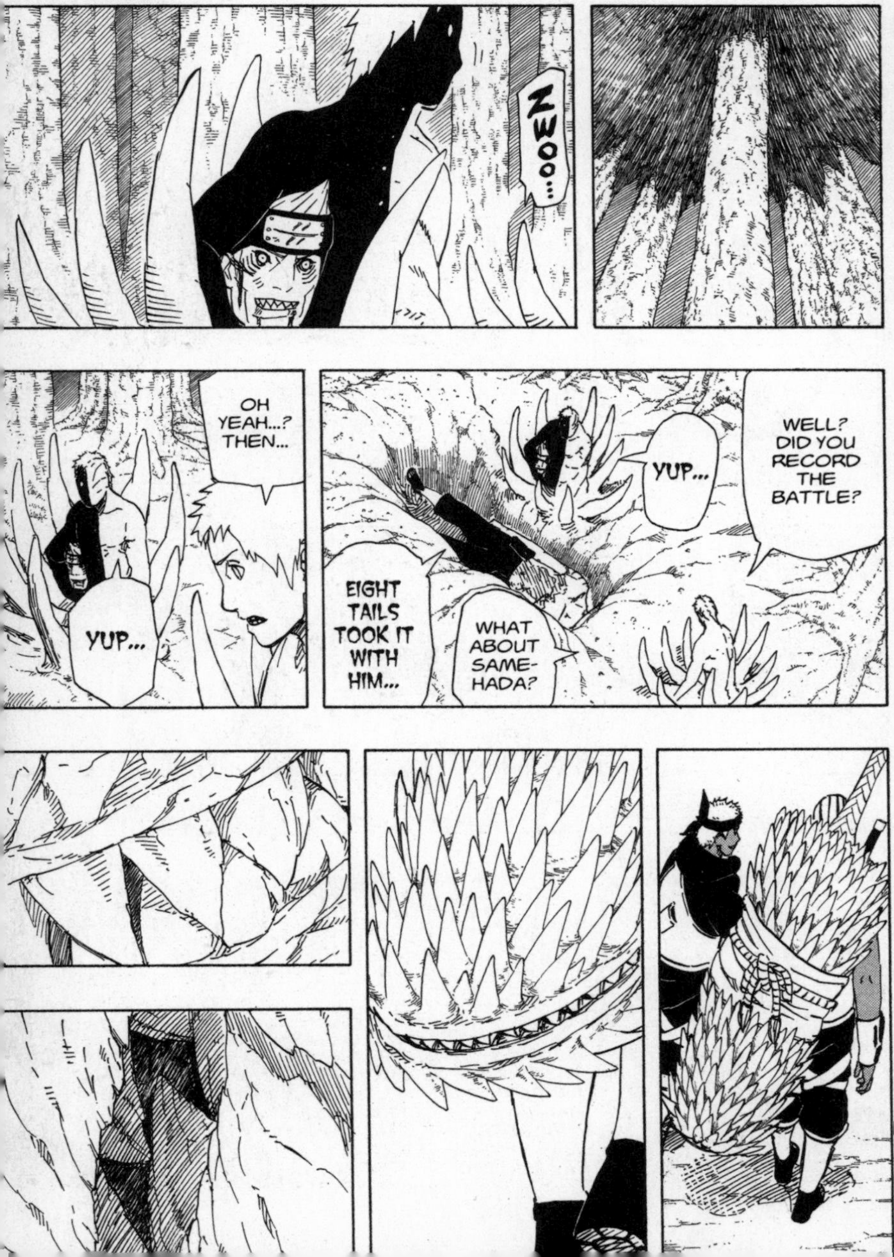
ZWOO...
WELL? DID YOU RECORD THE BATTLE?
YUP...
WHAT ABOUT SAME-HADA?
EIGHT TAILS TOOK IT WITH HIM...
OH YEAH...? THEN...
YUP...

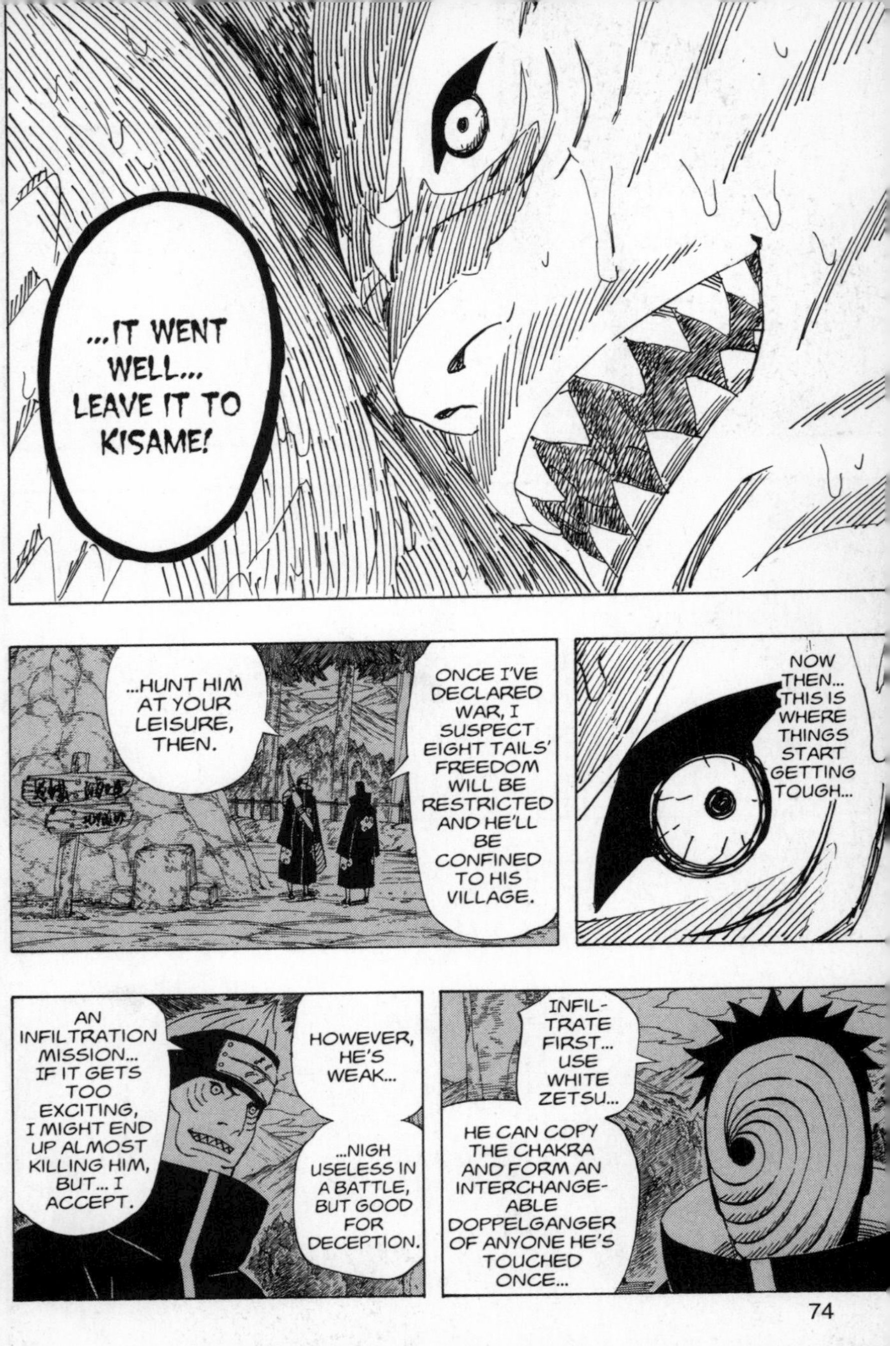
...IT WENT WELL... LEAVE IT TO KISAME!
NOW THEN... THIS IS WHERE THINGS START GETTING TOUGH...
ONCE I'VE DECLARED WAR, I SUSPECT EIGHT TAILS' FREEDOM WILL BE RESTRICTED AND HE'LL BE CONFINED TO HIS VILLAGE.
...HUNT HIM AT YOUR LEISURE, THEN.
INFILTRATE FIRST... USE WHITE ZETSU...
HE CAN COPY THE CHAKRA AND FORM AN INTERCHANGEABLE DOPPELGANGER OF ANYONE HE'S TOUCHED ONCE...
HOWEVER, HE'S WEAK...
...NIGH USELESS IN A BATTLE, BUT GOOD FOR DECEPTION.
AN INFILTRATION MISSION... IF IT GETS TOO EXCITING, I MIGHT END UP ALMOST KILLING HIM, BUT... I ACCEPT.

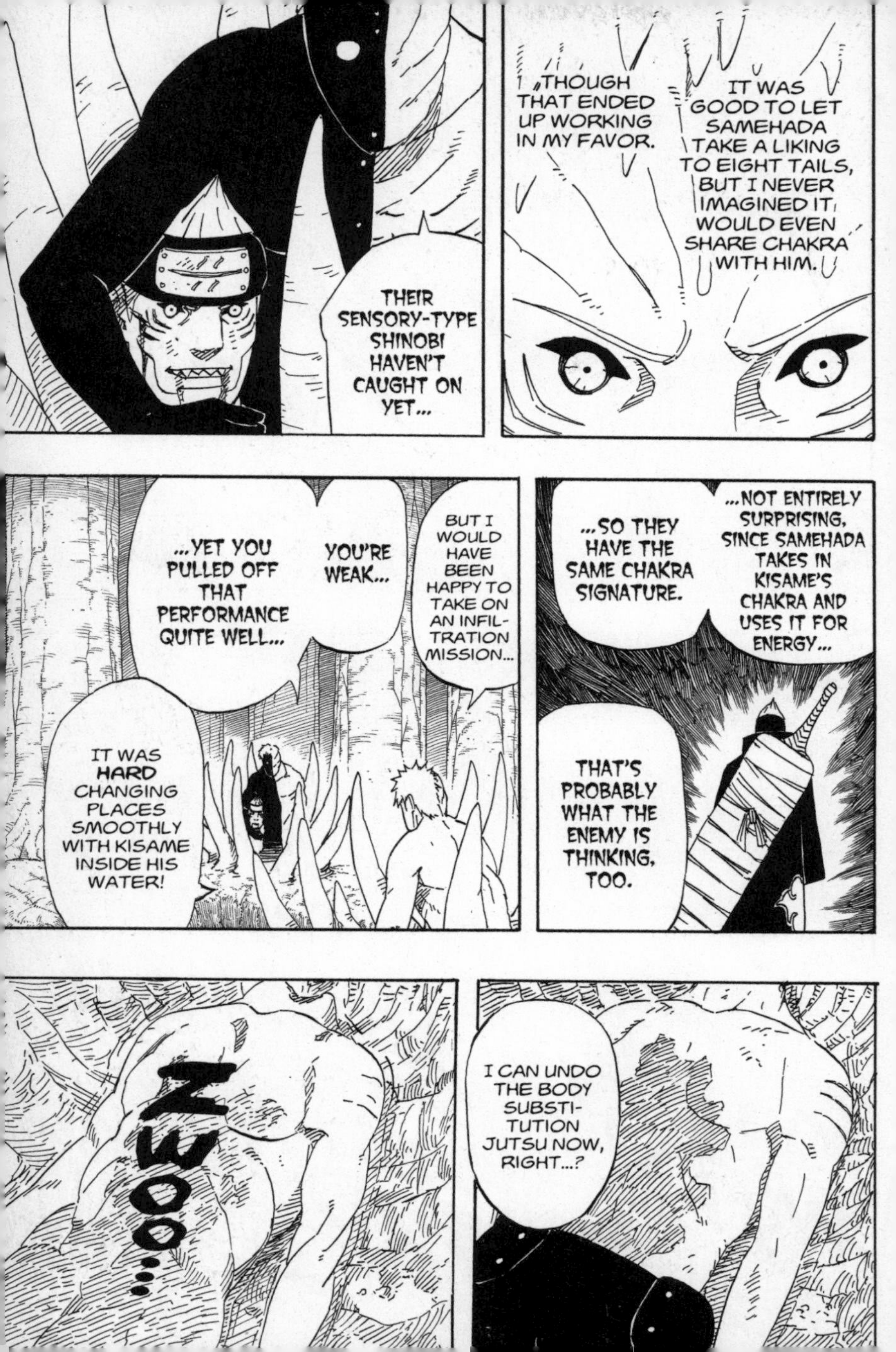
IT WAS GOOD TO LET SAMEHADA TAKE A LIKING TO EIGHT TAILS, BUT I NEVER IMAGINED IT WOULD EVEN SHARE CHAKRA WITH HIM.
...THOUGH THAT ENDED UP WORKING IN MY FAVOR.
THEIR SENSORY-TYPE SHINOBI HAVEN'T CAUGHT ON YET...
...NOT ENTIRELY SURPRISING, SINCE SAMEHADA TAKES IN KISAME'S CHAKRA AND USES IT FOR ENERGY...
...SO THEY HAVE THE SAME CHAKRA SIGNATURE.
THAT'S PROBABLY WHAT THE ENEMY IS THINKING, TOO.
BUT I WOULD HAVE BEEN HAPPY TO TAKE ON AN INFIL-TRATION MISSION...
YOU'RE WEAK...
...YET YOU PULLED OFF THAT PERFORMANCE QUITE WELL...
IT WAS **HARD** CHANGING PLACES SMOOTHLY WITH KISAME INSIDE HIS WATER!
I CAN UNDO THE BODY SUBSTI-TUTION JUTSU NOW, RIGHT...?
NWOO...

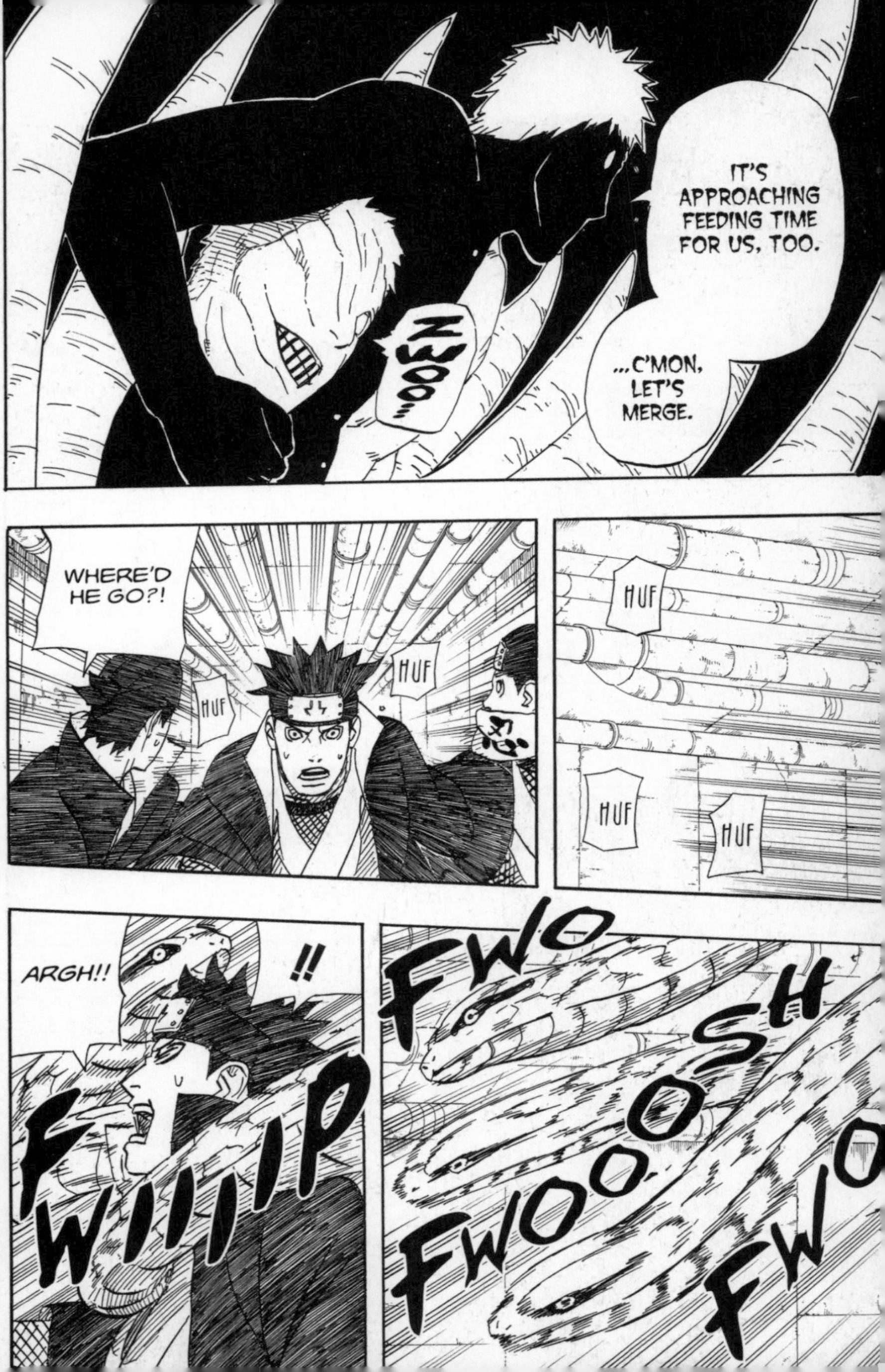
IT'S APPROACHING FEEDING TIME FOR US, TOO.
...C'MON, LET'S MERGE.
FWOO...
HUF
HUF
HUF
WHERE'D HE GO?!
HUF
HUF
FWO
FWOOOOSH
FWO
ARGH!!
!!
FWIIIIP

READ THIS WAY

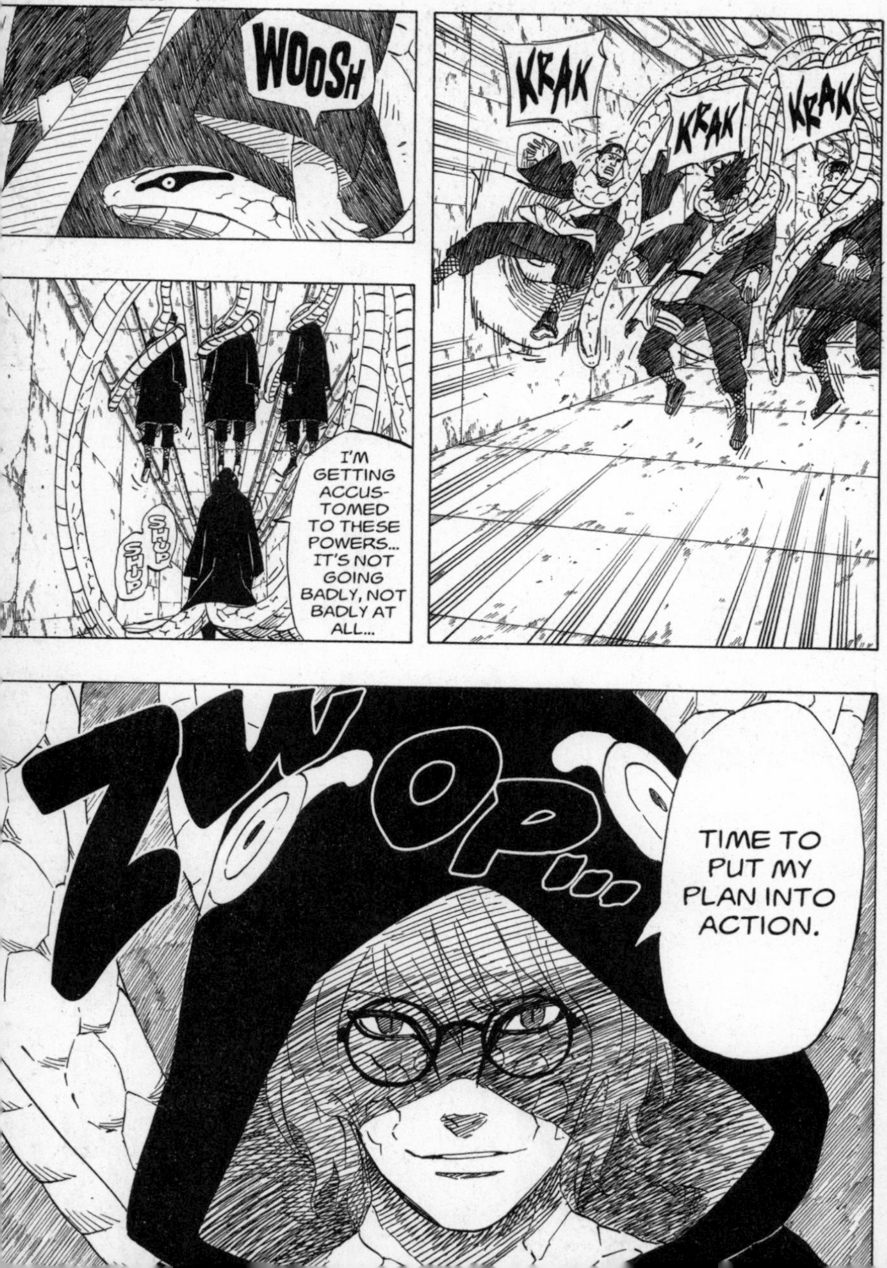
KRAK
KRAK
KRAK
WOOSH
I'M GETTING ACCUS-TOMED TO THESE POWERS... IT'S NOT GOING BADLY, NOT BADLY AT ALL...
SHUP
SHUP
TIME TO PUT MY PLAN INTO ACTION.
ZWOOP...

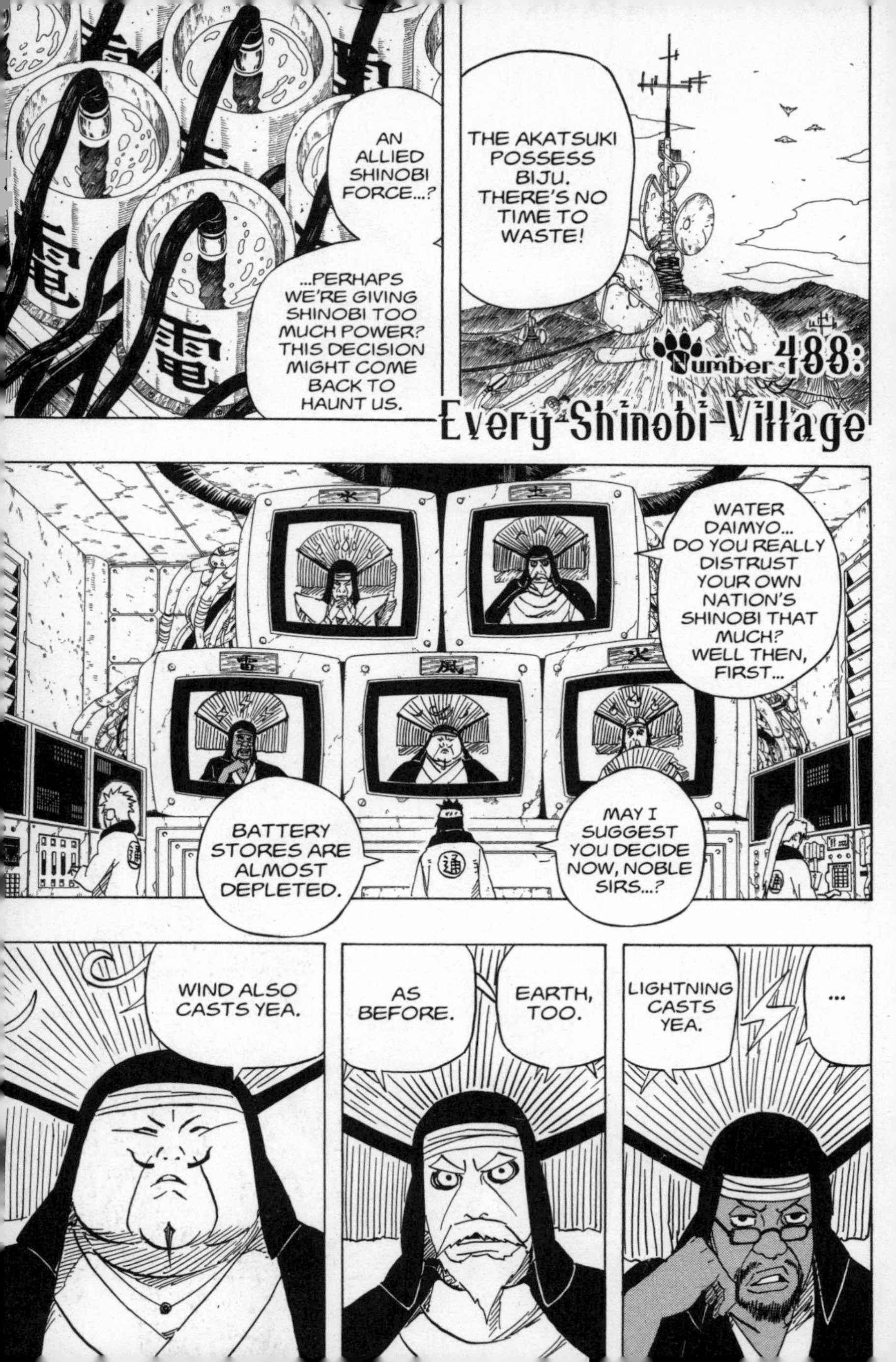
THE AKATSUKI POSSESS BIJU. THERE'S NO TIME TO WASTE!
Number 488: Every Shinobi Village
AN ALLIED SHINOBI FORCE...?
...PERHAPS WE'RE GIVING SHINOBI TOO MUCH POWER? THIS DECISION MIGHT COME BACK TO HAUNT US.
WATER DAIMYO... DO YOU REALLY DISTRUST YOUR OWN NATION'S SHINOBI THAT MUCH? WELL THEN, FIRST...
MAY I SUGGEST YOU DECIDE NOW, NOBLE SIRS...?
BATTERY STORES ARE ALMOST DEPLETED.
...
LIGHTNING CASTS YEA.
EARTH, TOO.
AS BEFORE.
WIND ALSO CASTS YEA.

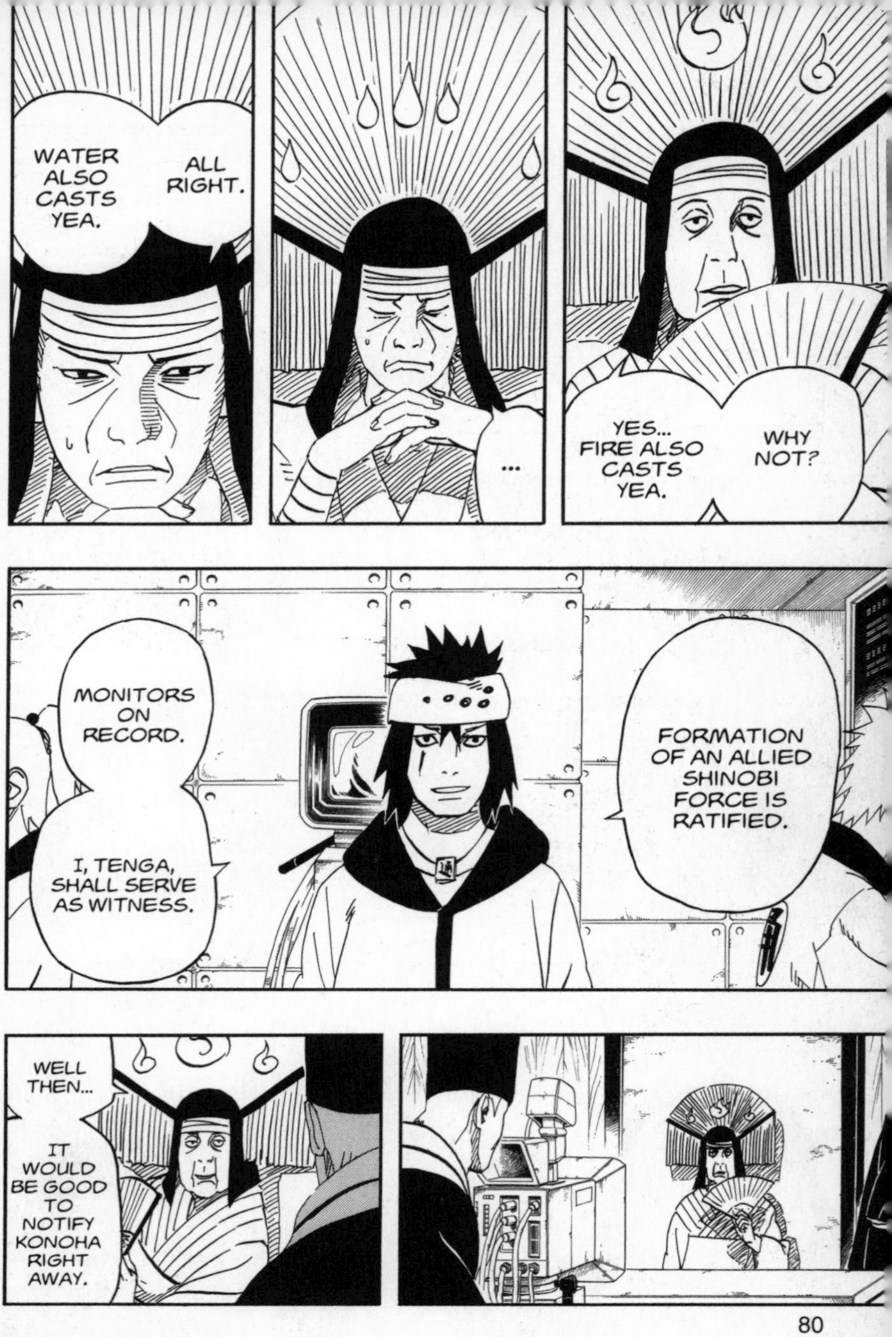
WHY NOT?
YES... FIRE ALSO CASTS YEA.
...
ALL RIGHT.
WATER ALSO CASTS YEA.
FORMATION OF AN ALLIED SHINOBI FORCE IS RATIFIED.
MONITORS ON RECORD.
I, TENGA, SHALL SERVE AS WITNESS.
WELL THEN...
IT WOULD BE GOOD TO NOTIFY KONOHA RIGHT AWAY.

READ THIS WAY

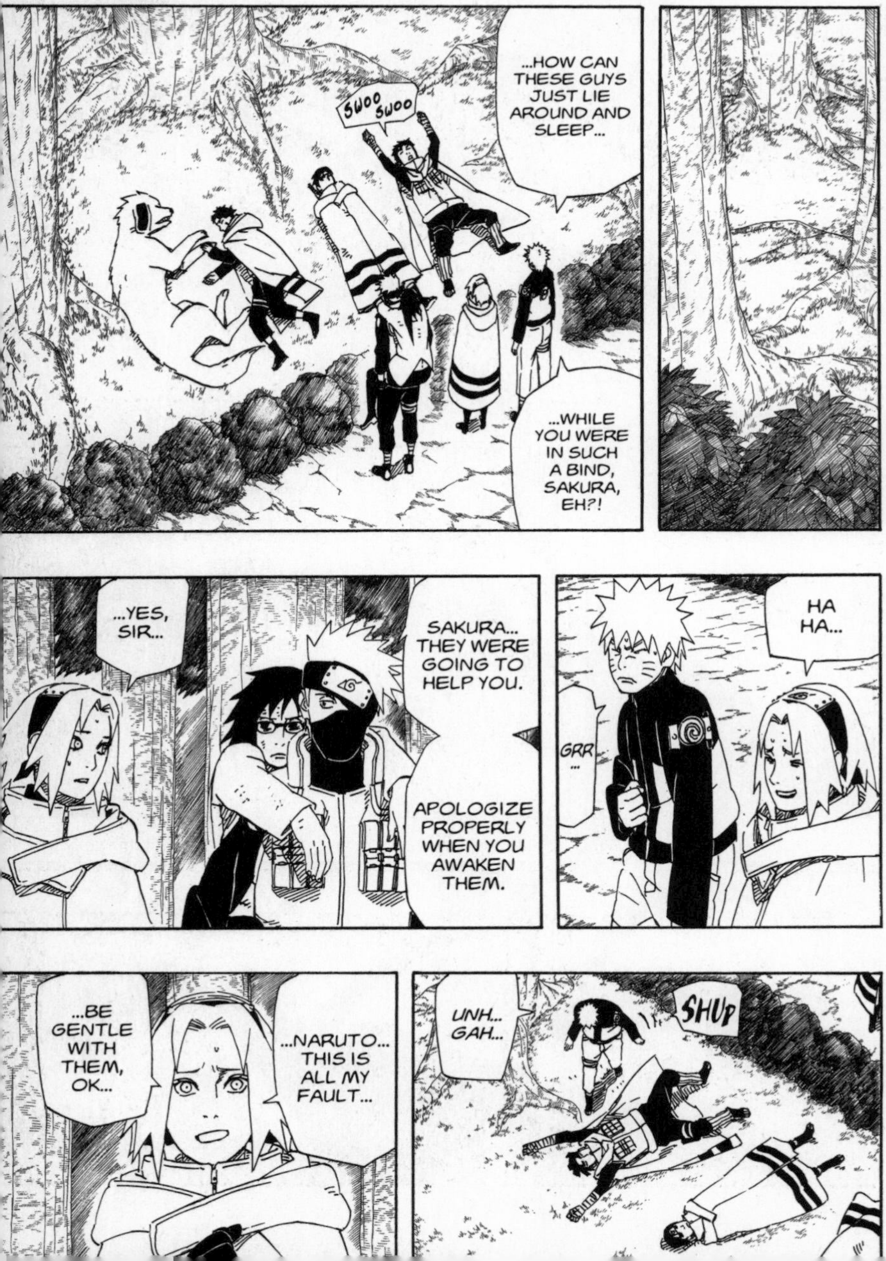
...HOW CAN THESE GUYS JUST LIE AROUND AND SLEEP...
SWOO SWOO
...WHILE YOU WERE IN SUCH A BIND, SAKURA, EH?!
HA HA...
GRR...
SAKURA... THEY WERE GOING TO HELP YOU.
APOLOGIZE PROPERLY WHEN YOU AWAKEN THEM.
...YES, SIR...
SHUP
UNH... GAH...
...NARUTO... THIS IS ALL MY FAULT...
...BE GENTLE WITH THEM, OK...

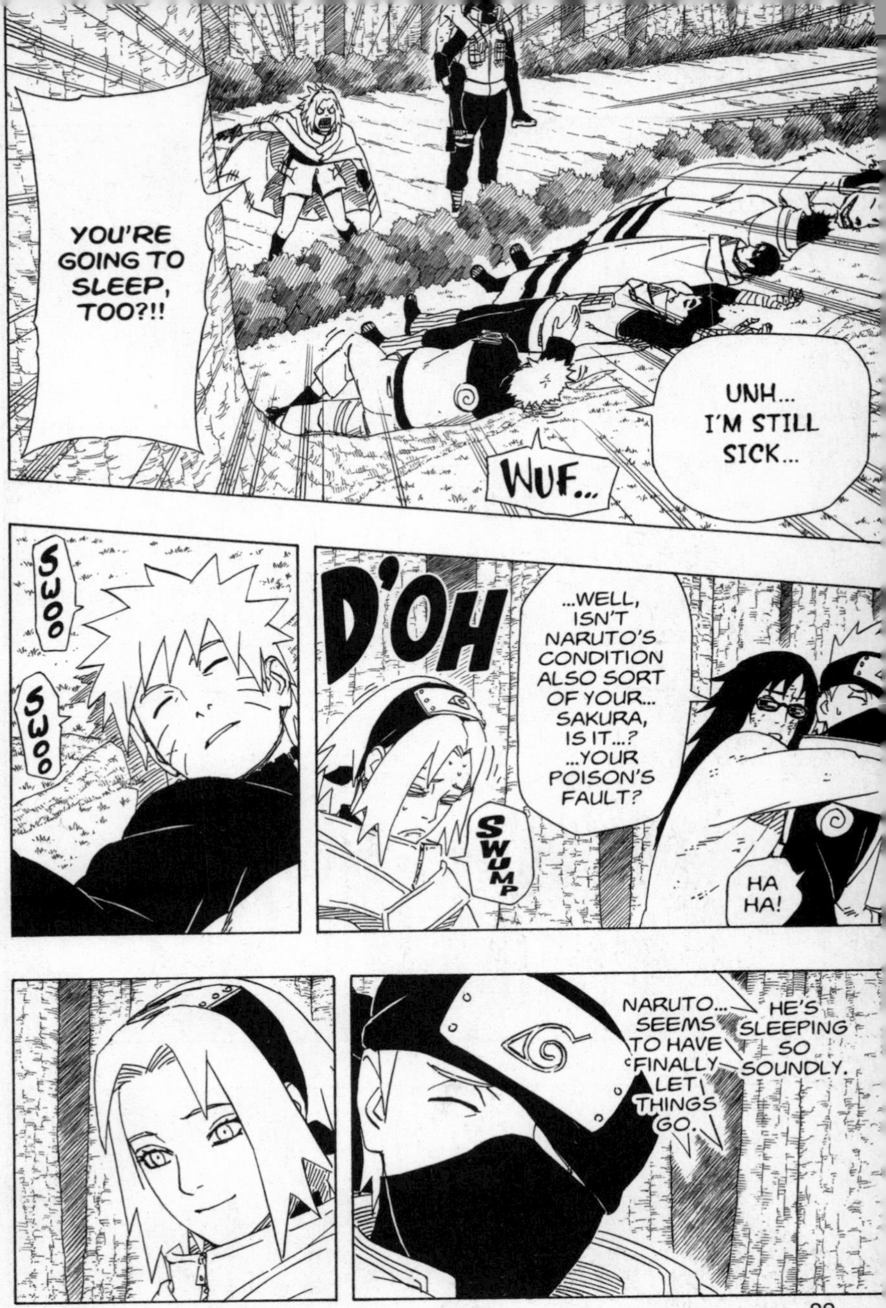
UNH... I'M STILL SICK...
WUF...
YOU'RE GOING TO SLEEP, TOO?!!
HA HA!
...WELL, ISN'T NARUTO'S CONDITION ALSO SORT OF YOUR... SAKURA, IS IT...? ...YOUR POISON'S FAULT?
D'OH
SWUMP
SWOO
SWOO
HE'S SLEEPING SO SOUNDLY.
NARUTO... SEEMS TO HAVE FINALLY LET THINGS GO.

READ THIS WAY

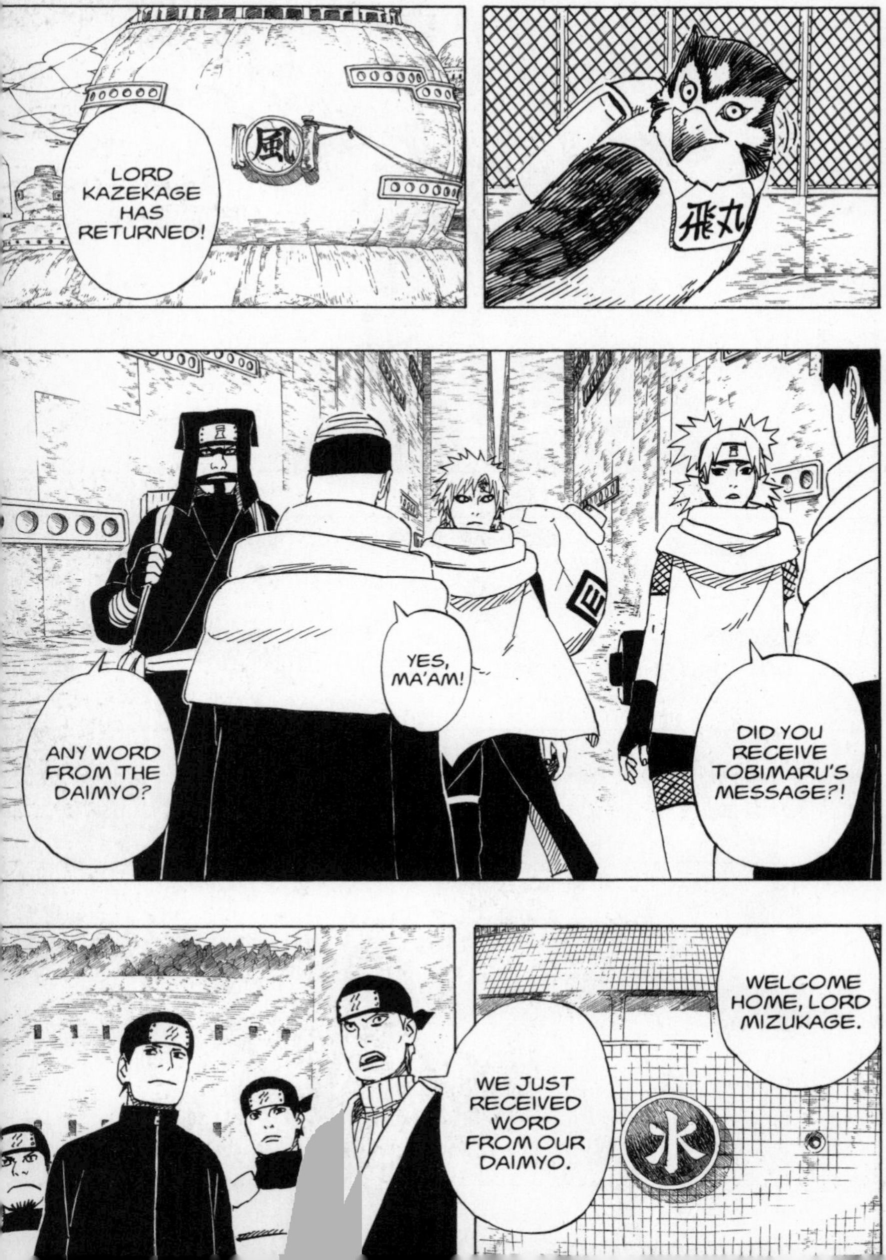
飛丸
風
LORD KAZEKAGE HAS RETURNED!
DID YOU RECEIVE TOBIMARU'S MESSAGE?!
YES, MA'AM!
ANY WORD FROM THE DAIMYO?
WELCOME HOME, LORD MIZUKAGE.
水
WE JUST RECEIVED WORD FROM OUR DAIMYO.

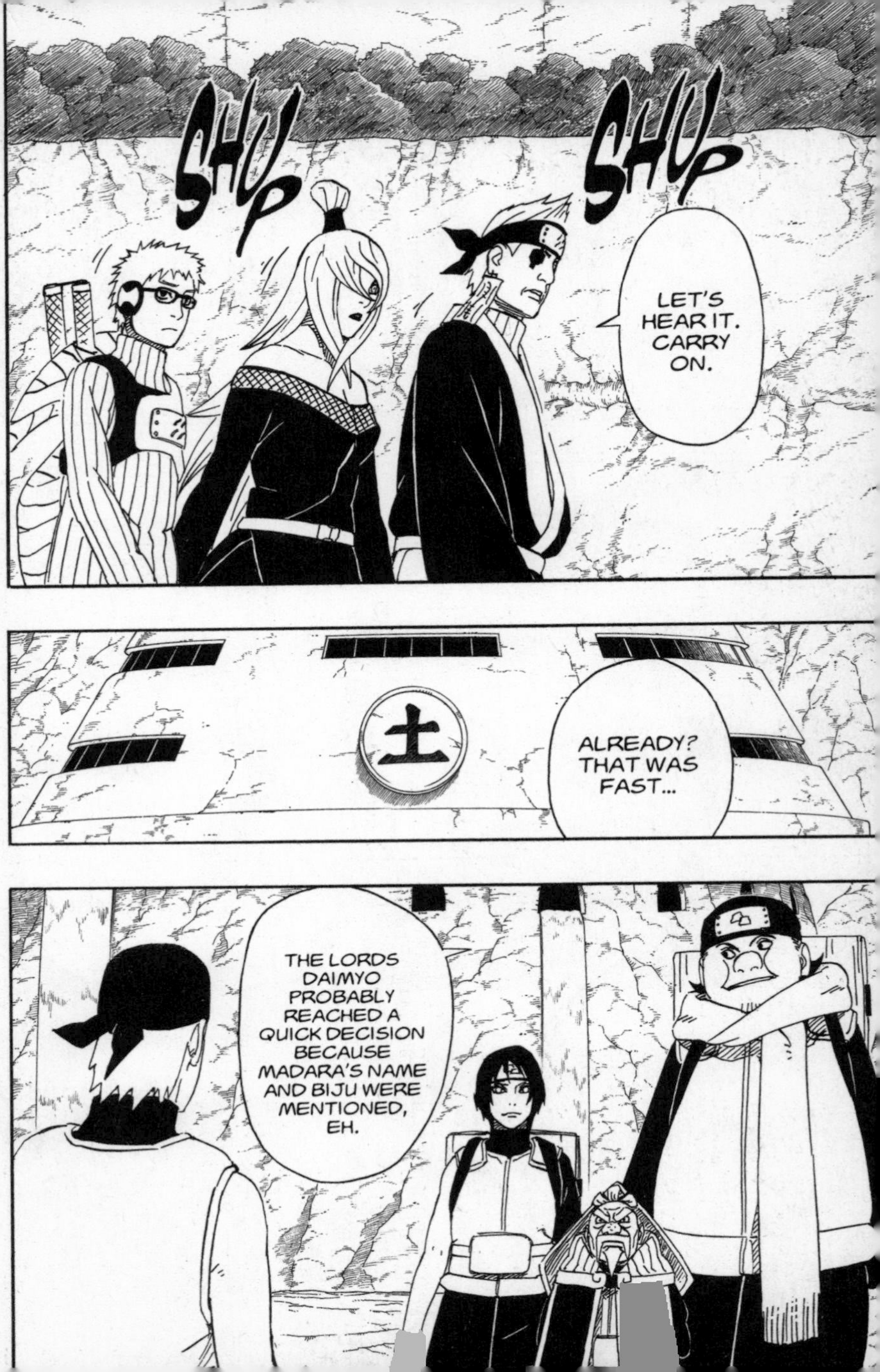
SHUP
SHUP
LET'S HEAR IT. CARRY ON.
ALREADY? THAT WAS FAST...
THE LORDS DAIMYO PROBABLY REACHED A QUICK DECISION BECAUSE MADARA'S NAME AND BIJU WERE MENTIONED, EH.

READ THIS WAY

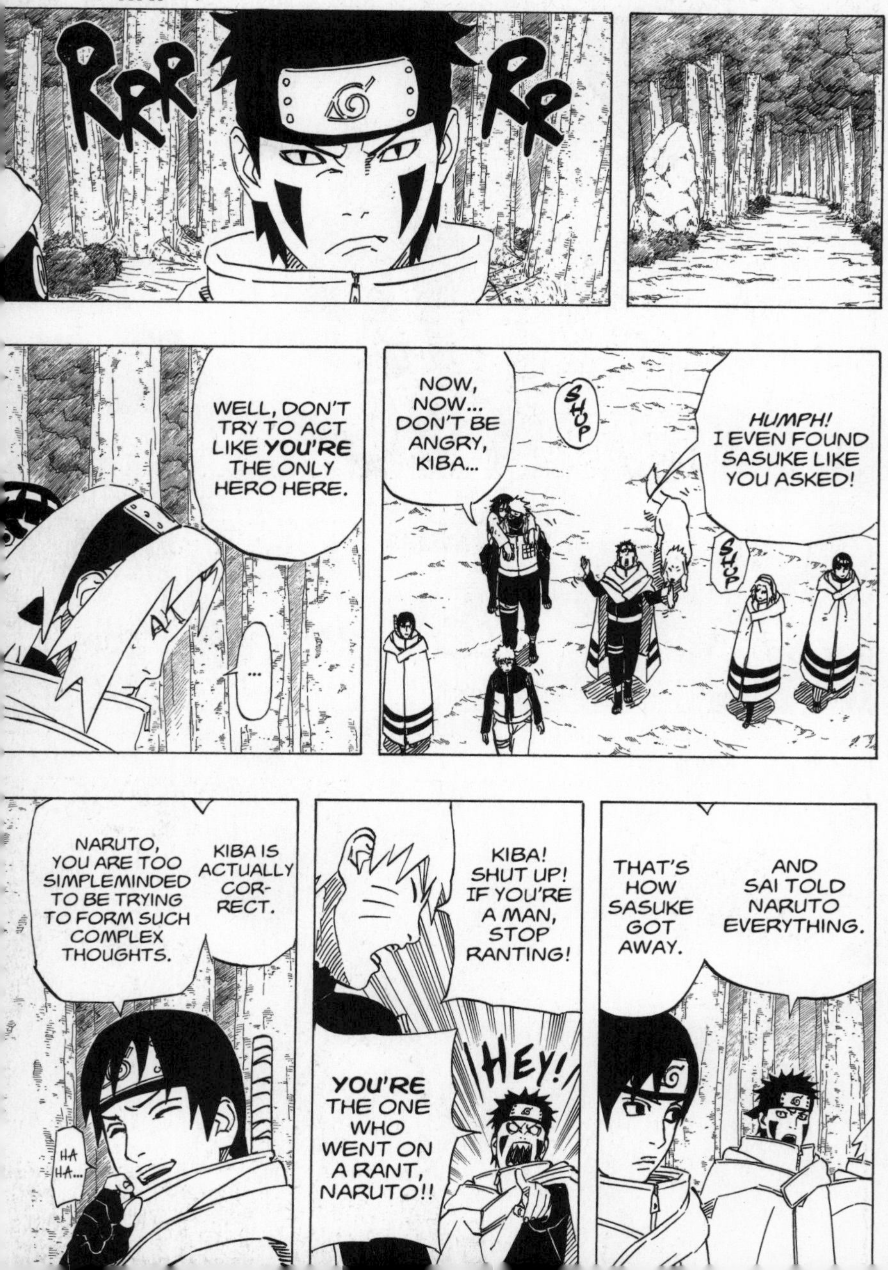
RRR
RR
HUMPH! I EVEN FOUND SASUKE LIKE YOU ASKED!
SHUP
NOW, NOW... DON'T BE ANGRY, KIBA...
SHUP
WELL, DON'T TRY TO ACT LIKE **YOU'RE** THE ONLY HERO HERE.
...
AND SAI TOLD NARUTO EVERYTHING.
THAT'S HOW SASUKE GOT AWAY.
KIBA! SHUT UP! IF YOU'RE A MAN, STOP RANTING!
HEY!
YOU'RE THE ONE WHO WENT ON A RANT, NARUTO!!
KIBA IS ACTUALLY COR-RECT.
NARUTO, YOU ARE TOO SIMPLEMINDED TO BE TRYING TO FORM SUCH COMPLEX THOUGHTS.
HA HA...

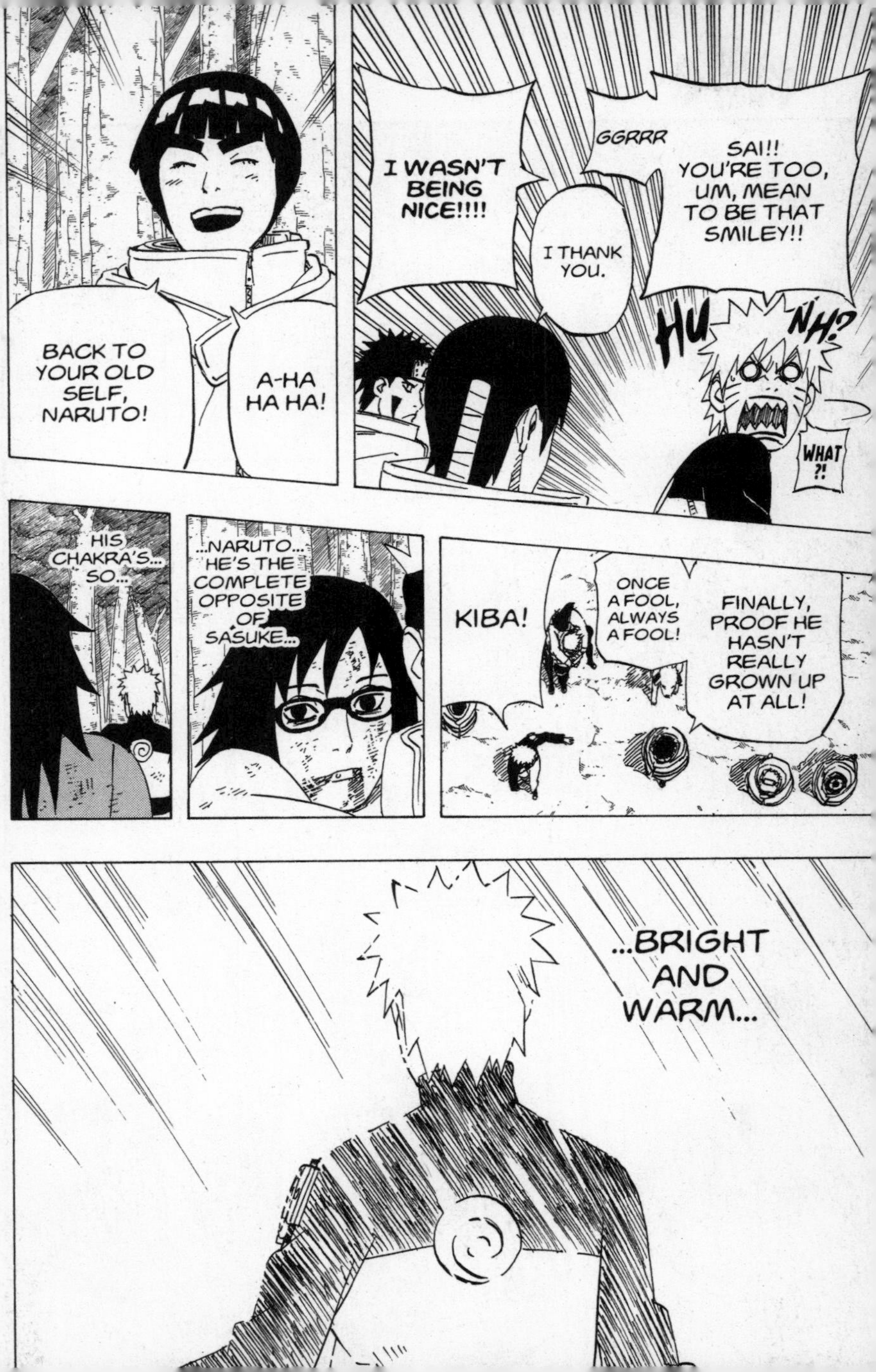
SAI!! YOU'RE TOO, UM, MEAN TO BE THAT SMILEY!!
GGRRR
I THANK YOU.
I WASN'T BEING NICE!!!!
HU-NH?
WHAT ?!
A-HA HA HA!
BACK TO YOUR OLD SELF, NARUTO!
FINALLY, PROOF HE HASN'T REALLY GROWN UP AT ALL!
ONCE A FOOL, ALWAYS A FOOL!
KIBA!
...NARUTO... HE'S THE COMPLETE OPPOSITE OF SASUKE...
HIS CHAKRA'S... SO...
...BRIGHT AND WARM...

READ THIS WAY

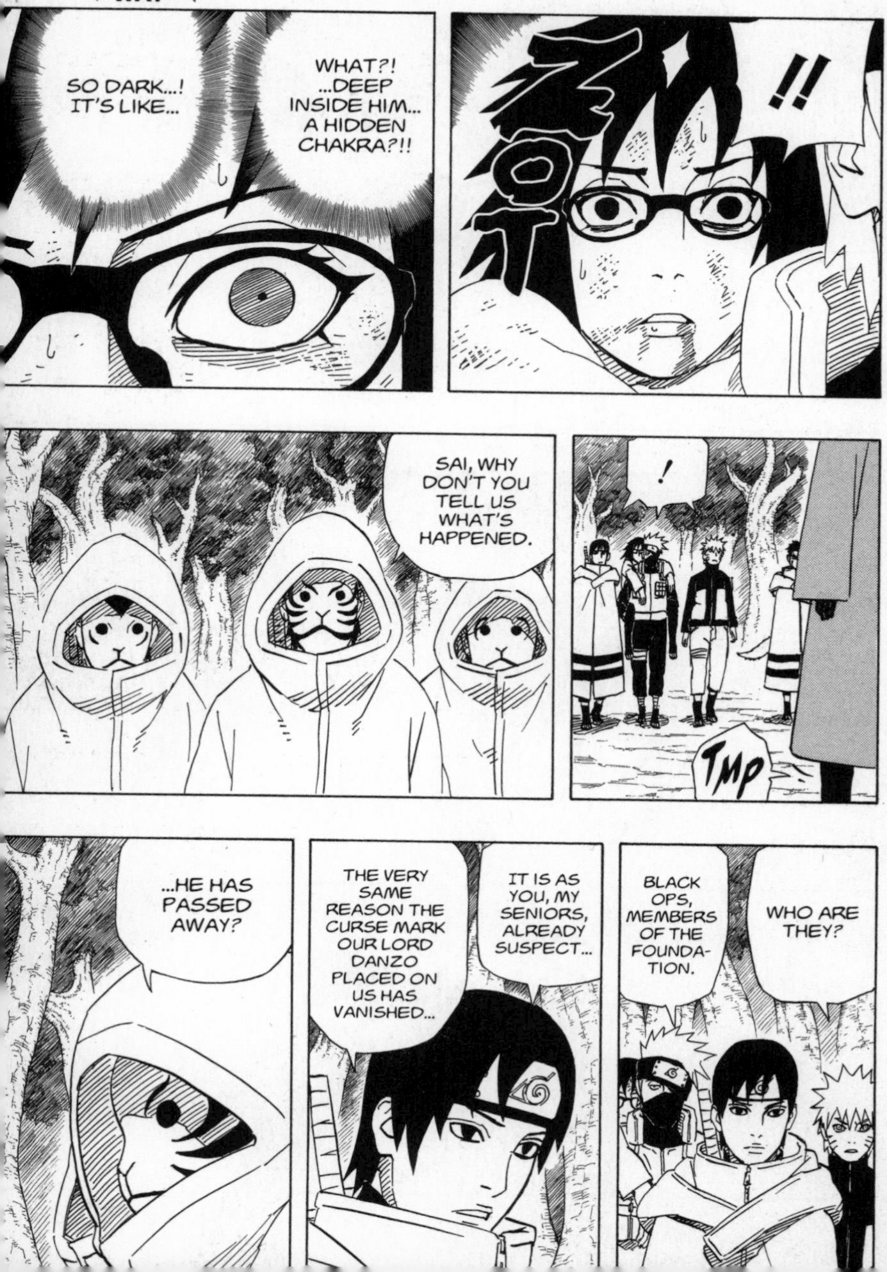
!!
WHAT?! ...DEEP INSIDE HIM... A HIDDEN CHAKRA?!!
SO DARK...! IT'S LIKE...
!
TMP
SAI, WHY DON'T YOU TELL US WHAT'S HAPPENED.
WHO ARE THEY?
BLACK OPS, MEMBERS OF THE FOUNDATION.
IT IS AS YOU, MY SENIORS, ALREADY SUSPECT...
THE VERY SAME REASON THE CURSE MARK OUR LORD DANZO PLACED ON US HAS VANISHED...
...HE HAS PASSED AWAY?

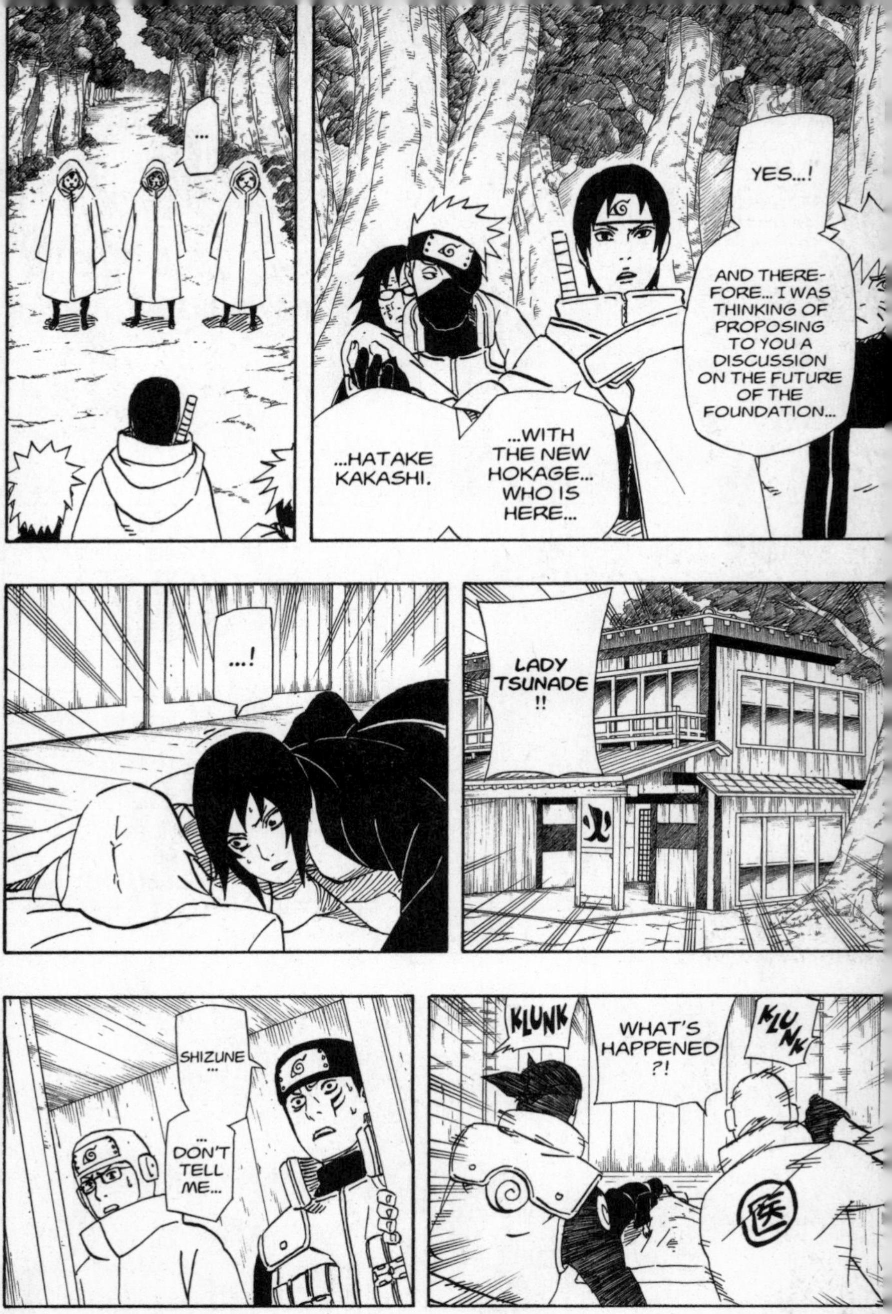
YES...!
AND THEREFORE... I WAS THINKING OF PROPOSING TO YOU A DISCUSSION ON THE FUTURE OF THE FOUNDATION...
...WITH THE NEW HOKAGE... WHO IS HERE...
...HATAKE KAKASHI.
...
LADY TSUNADE !!
...!
KLUNK
WHAT'S HAPPENED ?!
KLUNK
SHIZUNE ...
... DON'T TELL ME...

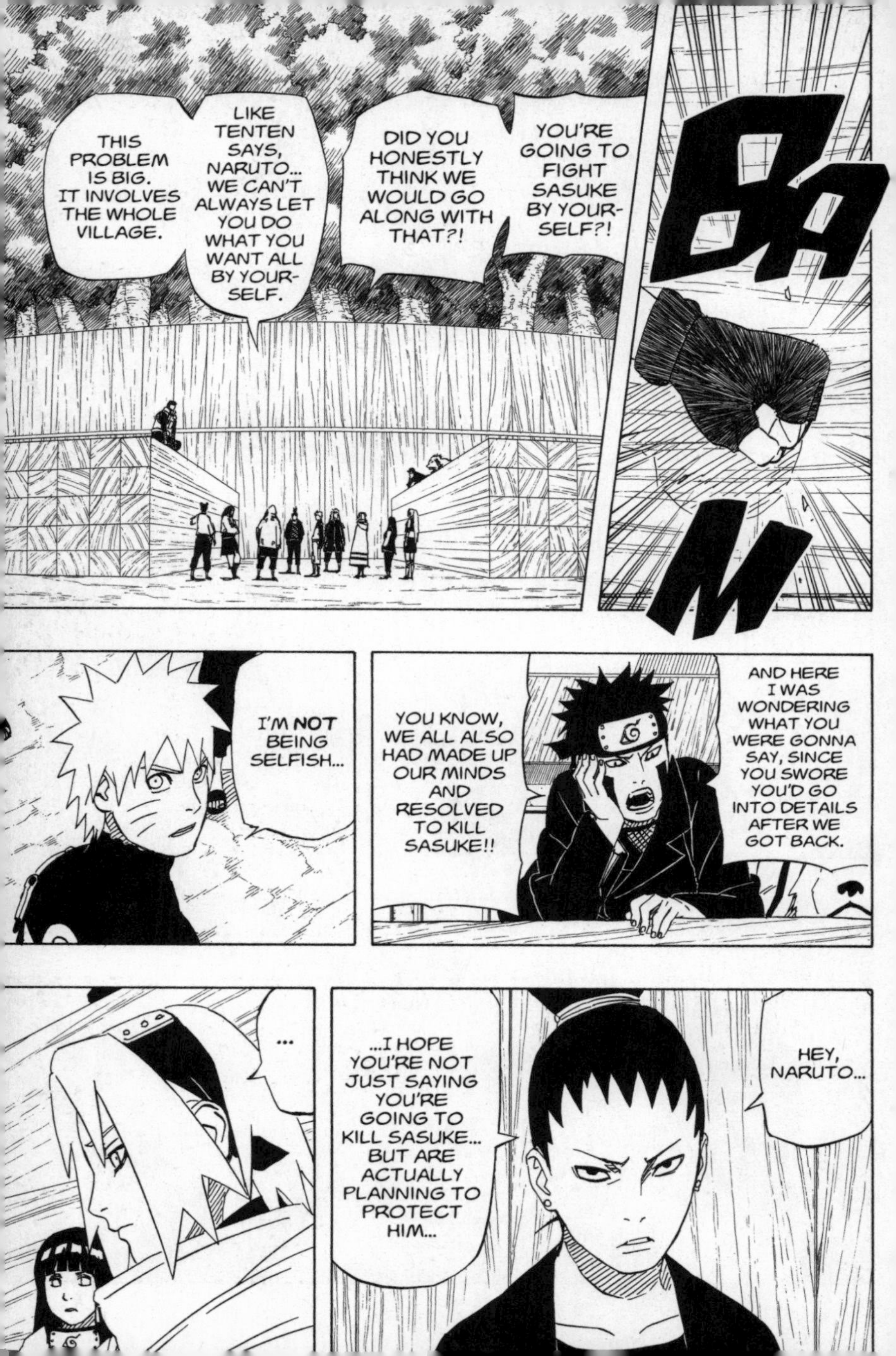
BAM
YOU'RE GOING TO FIGHT SASUKE BY YOURSELF?!
DID YOU HONESTLY THINK WE WOULD GO ALONG WITH THAT?!
LIKE TENTEN SAYS, NARUTO... WE CAN'T ALWAYS LET YOU DO WHAT YOU WANT ALL BY YOURSELF.
THIS PROBLEM IS BIG. IT INVOLVES THE WHOLE VILLAGE.
AND HERE I WAS WONDERING WHAT YOU WERE GONNA SAY, SINCE YOU SWORE YOU'D GO INTO DETAILS AFTER WE GOT BACK.
YOU KNOW, WE ALL ALSO HAD MADE UP OUR MINDS AND RESOLVED TO KILL SASUKE!!
I'M **NOT** BEING SELFISH...
HEY, NARUTO...
...I HOPE YOU'RE NOT JUST SAYING YOU'RE GOING TO KILL SASUKE... BUT ARE ACTUALLY PLANNING TO PROTECT HIM...
...

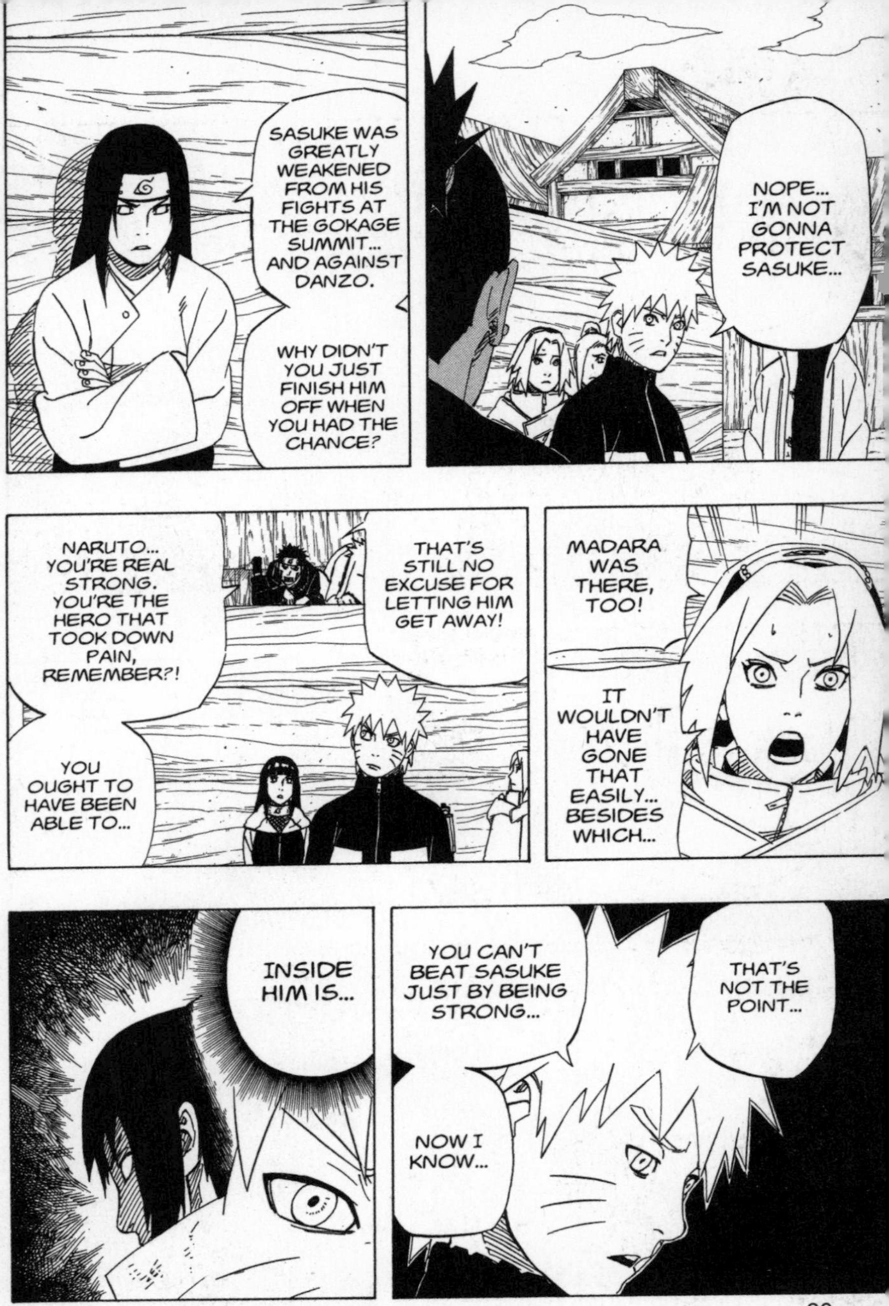

NOPE... I'M NOT GONNA PROTECT SASUKE...
SASUKE WAS GREATLY WEAKENED FROM HIS FIGHTS AT THE GOKAGE SUMMIT... AND AGAINST DANZO.
WHY DIDN'T YOU JUST FINISH HIM OFF WHEN YOU HAD THE CHANCE?
MADARA WAS THERE, TOO!
IT WOULDN'T HAVE GONE THAT EASILY... BESIDES WHICH...
THAT'S STILL NO EXCUSE FOR LETTING HIM GET AWAY!
NARUTO... YOU'RE REAL STRONG. YOU'RE THE HERO THAT TOOK DOWN PAIN, REMEMBER?!
YOU OUGHT TO HAVE BEEN ABLE TO...
THAT'S NOT THE POINT...
YOU CAN'T BEAT SASUKE JUST BY BEING STRONG...
NOW I KNOW...
INSIDE HIM IS...

READ THIS WAY

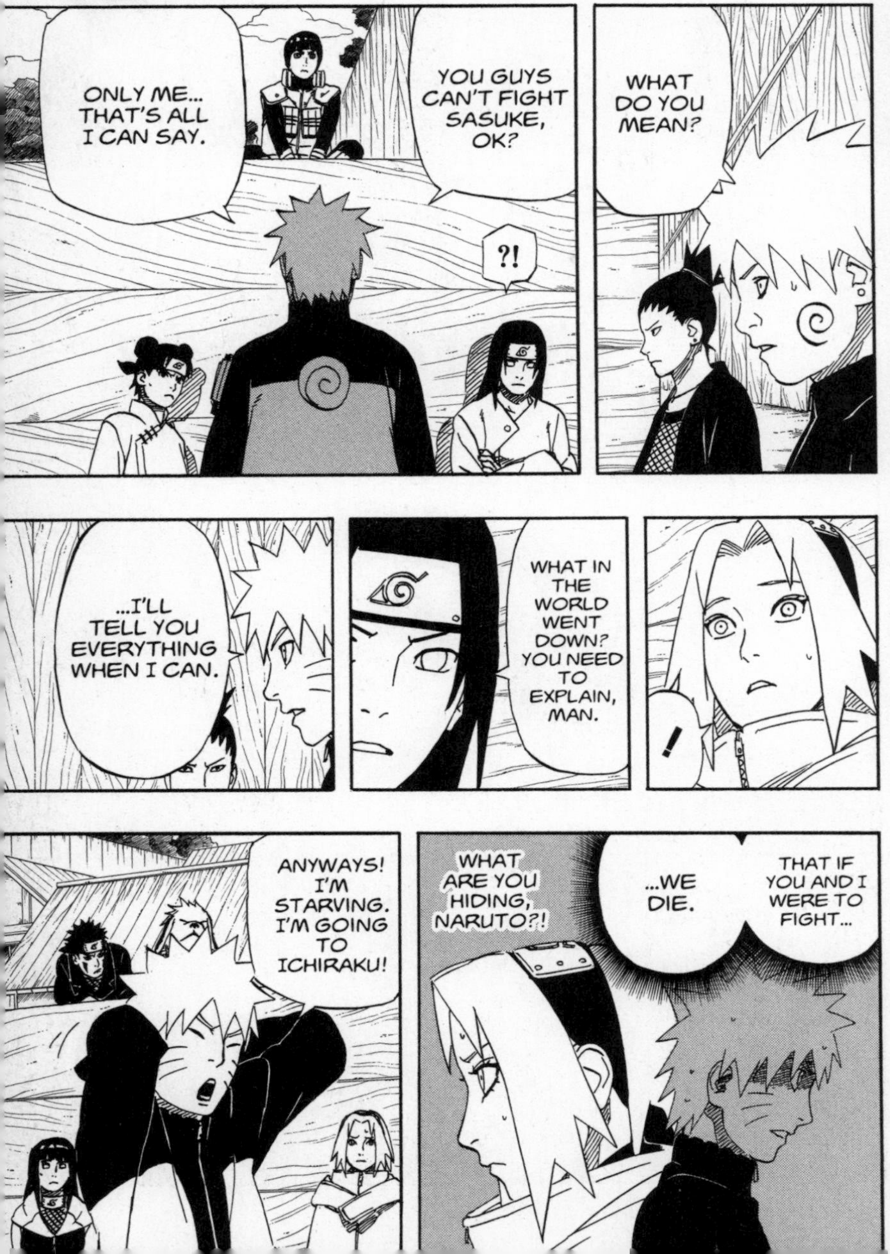
WHAT DO YOU MEAN?
YOU GUYS CAN'T FIGHT SASUKE, OK?
ONLY ME... THAT'S ALL I CAN SAY.
?!
!
WHAT IN THE WORLD WENT DOWN? YOU NEED TO EXPLAIN, MAN.
...I'LL TELL YOU EVERYTHING WHEN I CAN.
THAT IF YOU AND I WERE TO FIGHT...
...WE DIE.
WHAT ARE YOU HIDING, NARUTO?!
ANYWAYS! I'M STARVING. I'M GOING TO ICHIRAKU!

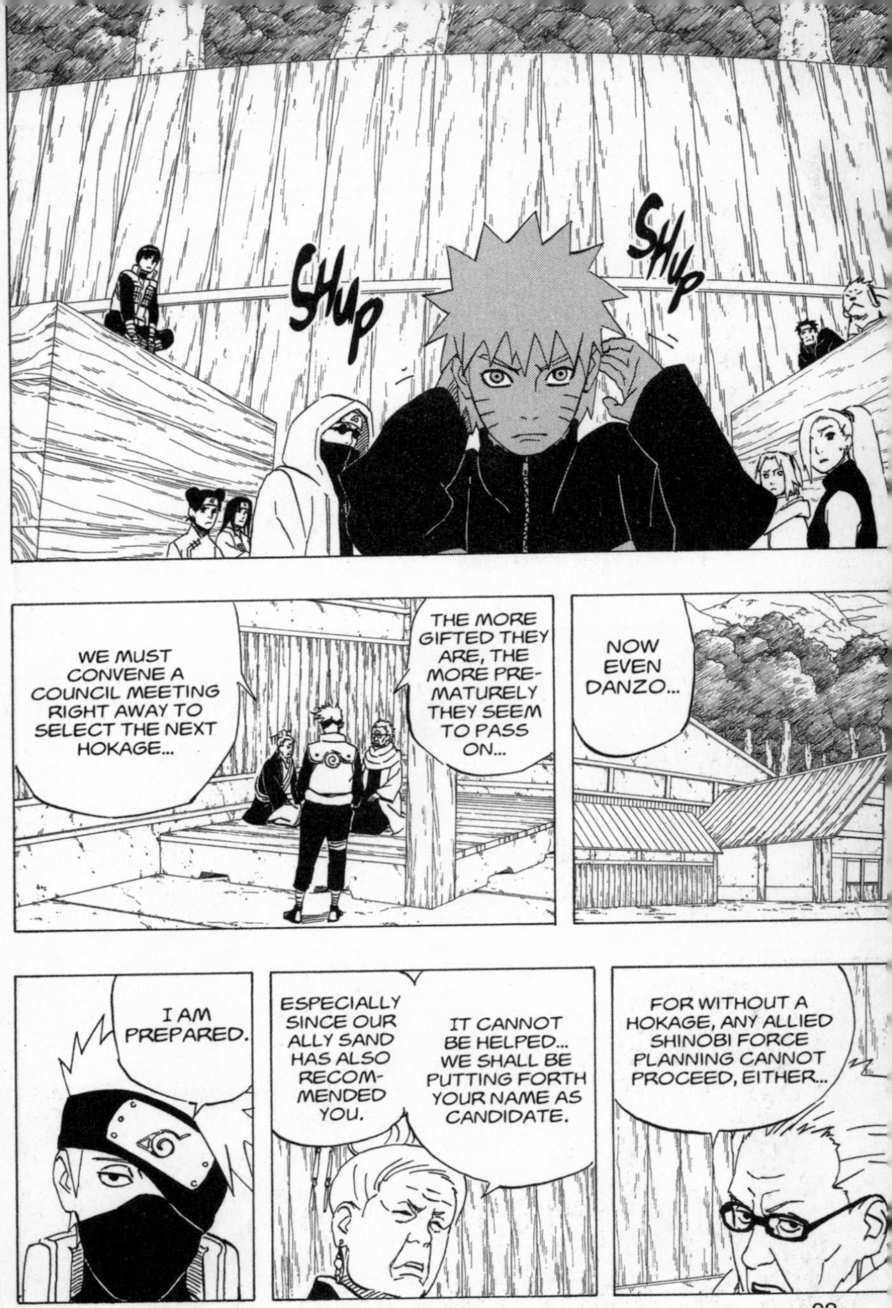
SHUP
SHUP
NOW EVEN DANZO...
THE MORE GIFTED THEY ARE, THE MORE PRE-MATURELY THEY SEEM TO PASS ON...
WE MUST CONVENE A COUNCIL MEETING RIGHT AWAY TO SELECT THE NEXT HOKAGE...
FOR WITHOUT A HOKAGE, ANY ALLIED SHINOBI FORCE PLANNING CANNOT PROCEED, EITHER...
IT CANNOT BE HELPED... WE SHALL BE PUTTING FORTH YOUR NAME AS CANDIDATE.
ESPECIALLY SINCE OUR ALLY SAND HAS ALSO RECOM-MENDED YOU.
I AM PREPARED.

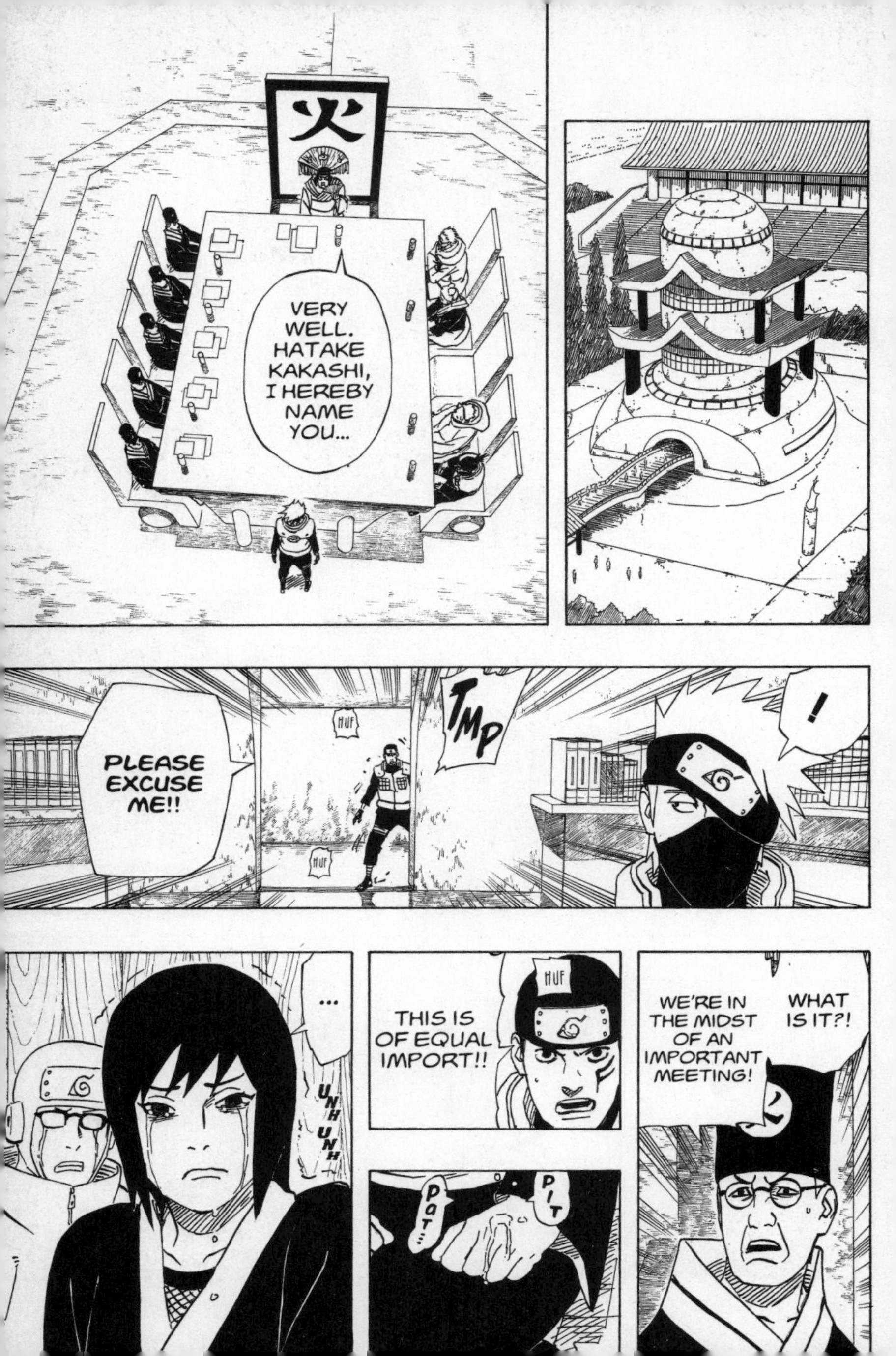
火
VERY WELL. HATAKE KAKASHI, I HEREBY NAME YOU...
!
TMP
HUF
HUF
PLEASE EXCUSE ME!!
WHAT IS IT?!
WE'RE IN THE MIDST OF AN IMPORTANT MEETING!
HUF
THIS IS OF EQUAL IMPORT!!
PIT
PAT...
...
UNH UNH

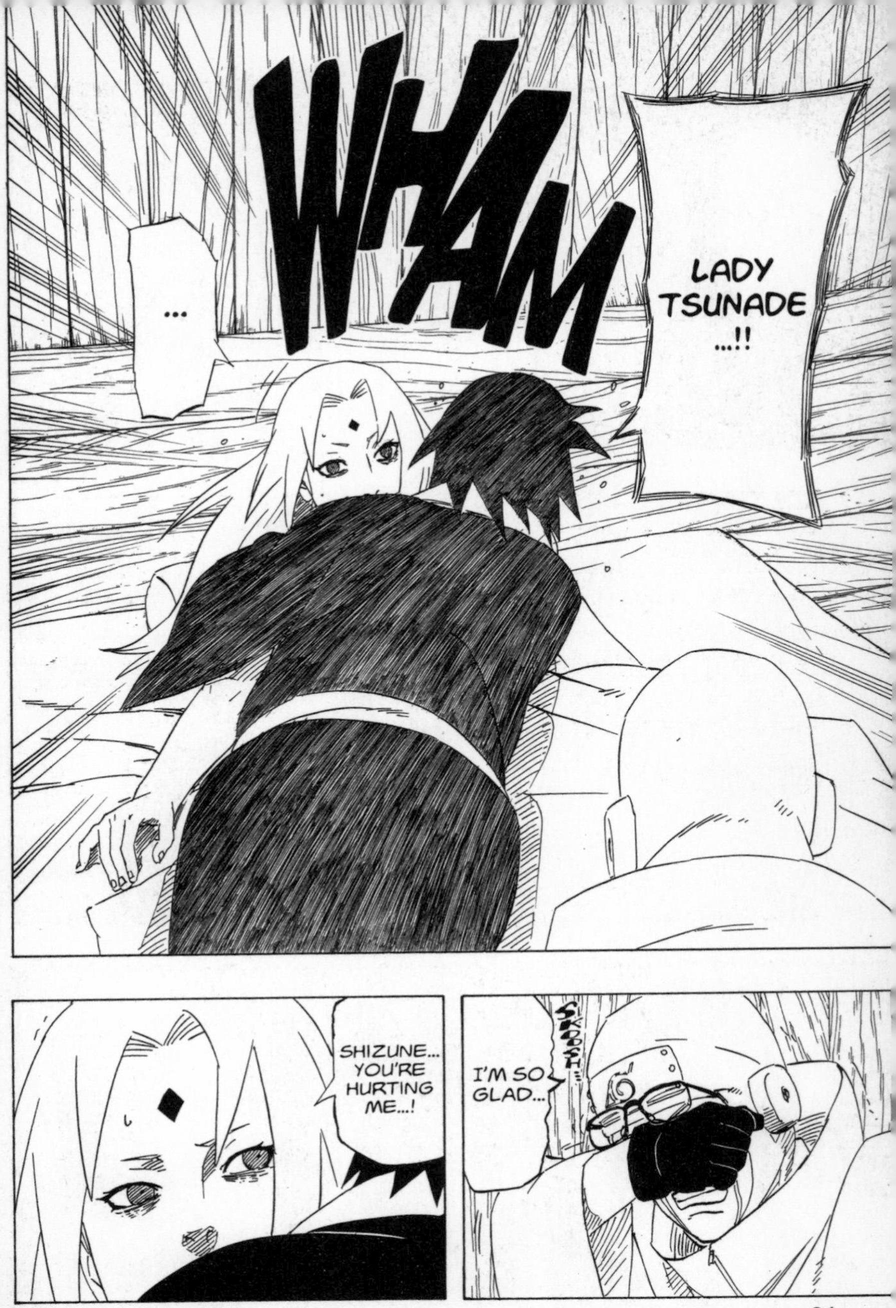
LADY TSUNADE ...!!
WHAM
...
SKOOSH...
I'M SO GLAD...
SHIZUNE... YOU'RE HURTING ME...!

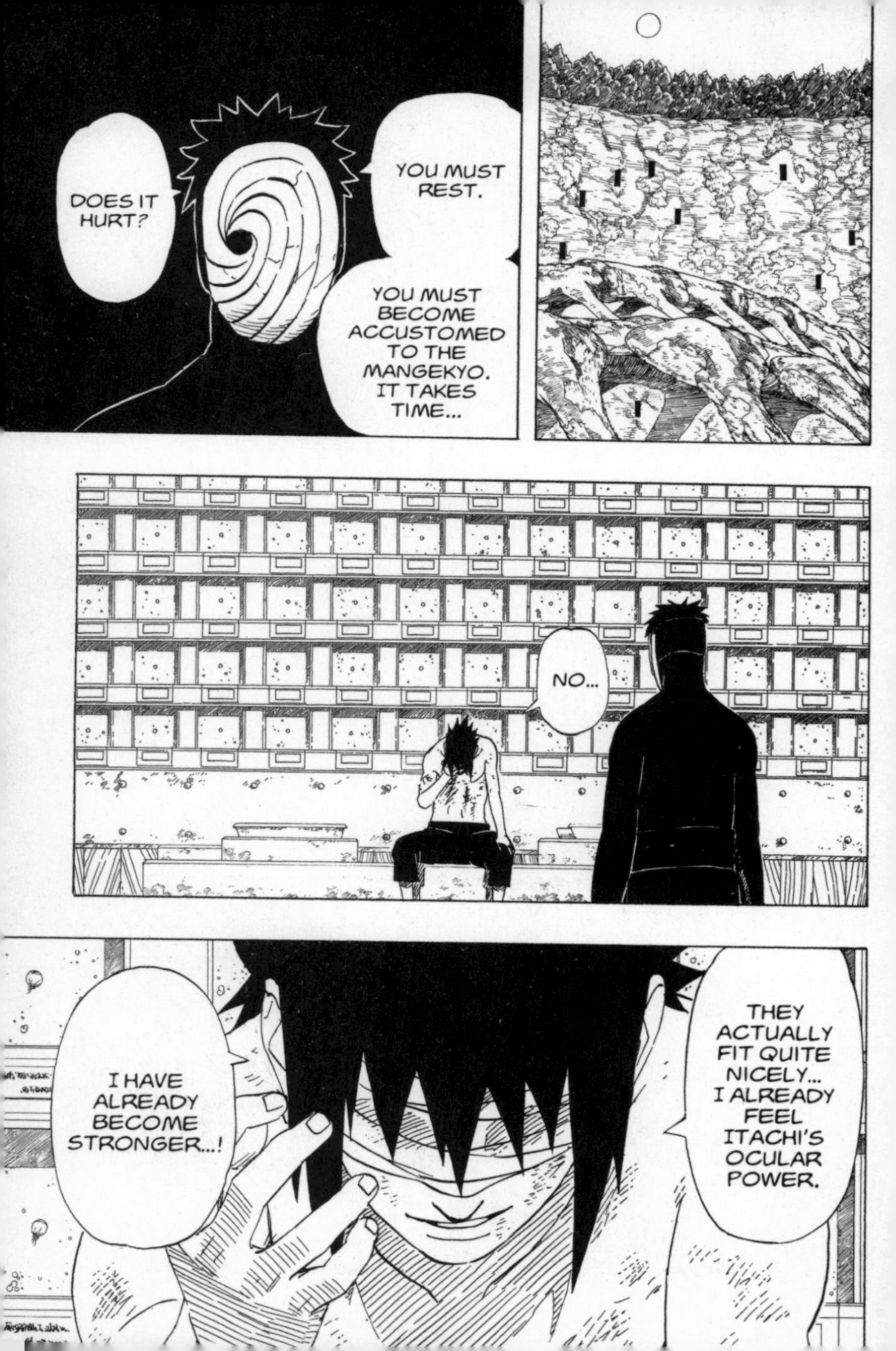
YOU MUST REST.
YOU MUST BECOME ACCUSTOMED TO THE MANGEKYO. IT TAKES TIME...
DOES IT HURT?
NO...
THEY ACTUALLY FIT QUITE NICELY... I ALREADY FEEL ITACHI'S OCULAR POWER.
I HAVE ALREADY BECOME STRONGER...!

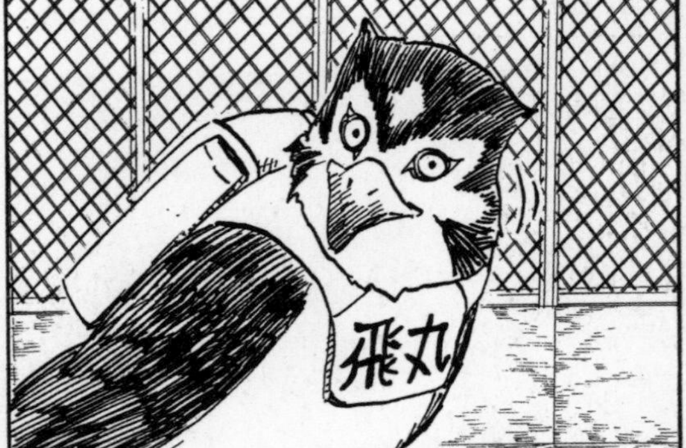
飛丸

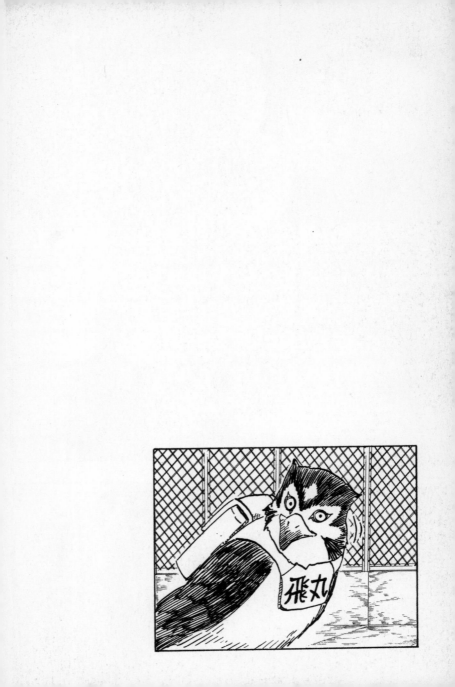

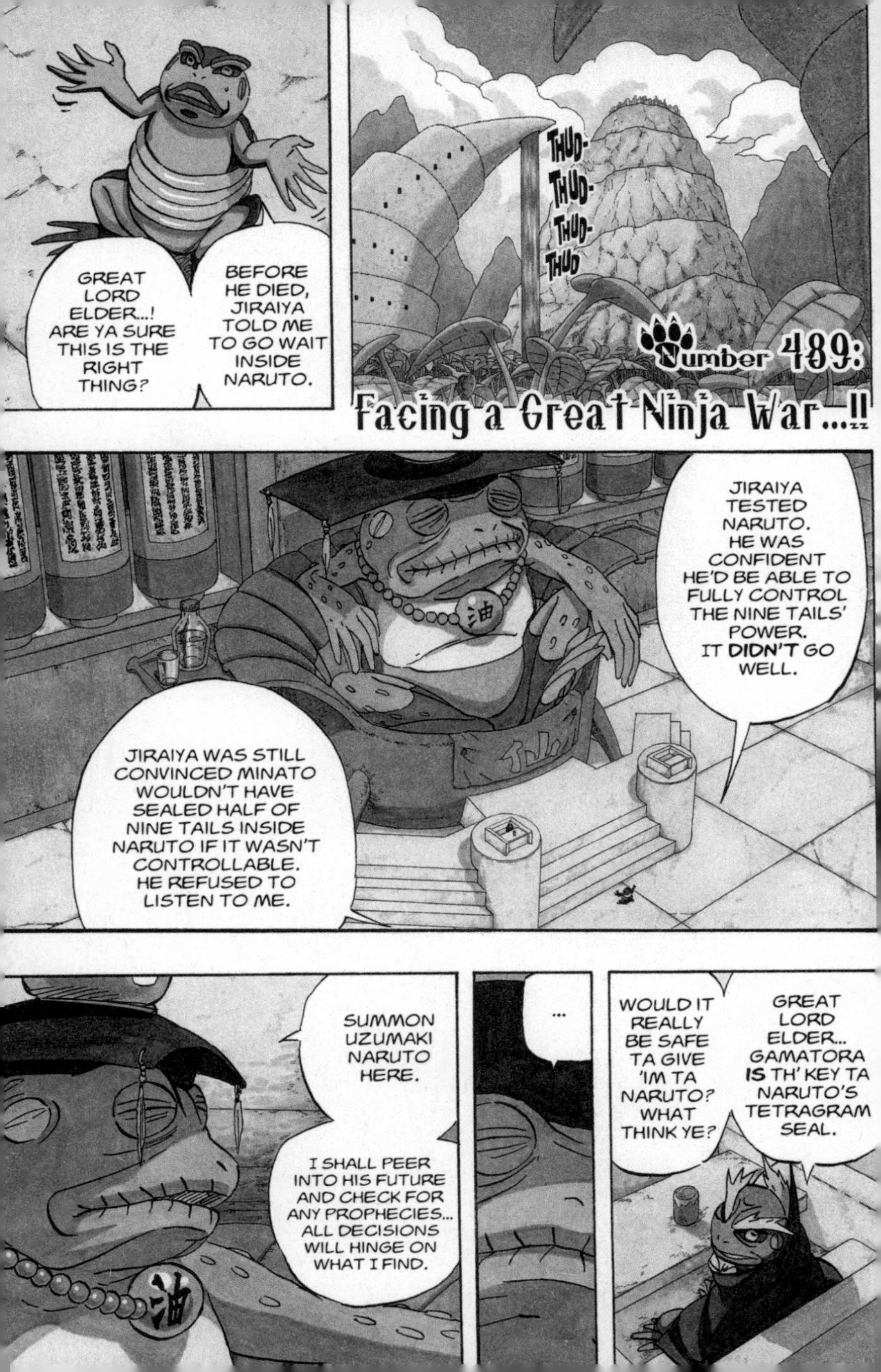
THUD-THUD-THUD-THUD
Number 489:
Facing a Great Ninja War...!!
BEFORE HE DIED, JIRAIYA TOLD ME TO GO WAIT INSIDE NARUTO.
GREAT LORD ELDER...! ARE YA SURE THIS IS THE RIGHT THING?
JIRAIYA TESTED NARUTO. HE WAS CONFIDENT HE'D BE ABLE TO FULLY CONTROL THE NINE TAILS' POWER. IT **DIDN'T** GO WELL.
JIRAIYA WAS STILL CONVINCED MINATO WOULDN'T HAVE SEALED HALF OF NINE TAILS INSIDE NARUTO IF IT WASN'T CONTROLLABLE. HE REFUSED TO LISTEN TO ME.
GREAT LORD ELDER... GAMATORA **IS** TH' KEY TA NARUTO'S TETRAGRAM SEAL.
WOULD IT REALLY BE SAFE TA GIVE 'IM TA NARUTO? WHAT THINK YE?
...
SUMMON UZUMAKI NARUTO HERE.
I SHALL PEER INTO HIS FUTURE AND CHECK FOR ANY PROPHECIES... ALL DECISIONS WILL HINGE ON WHAT I FIND.

Facing a Great Ninja War...!!

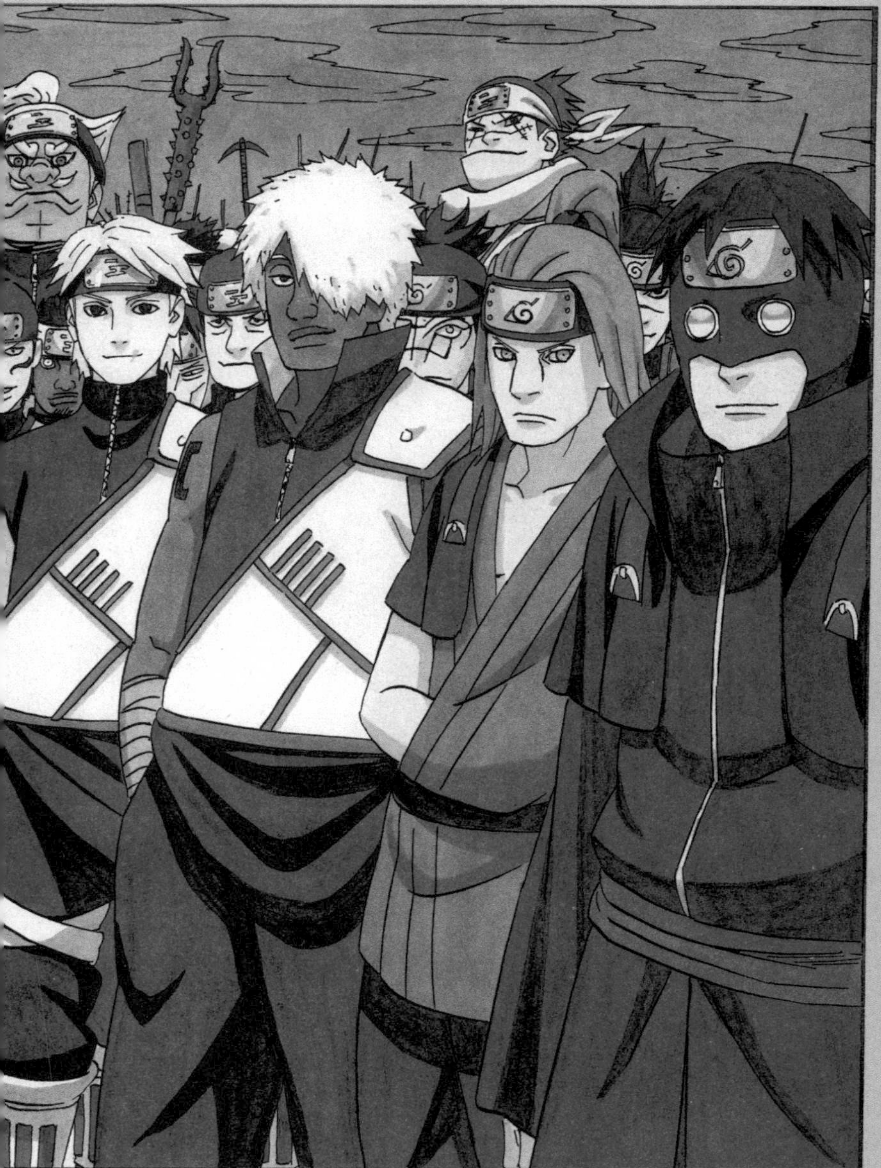

Number 489:

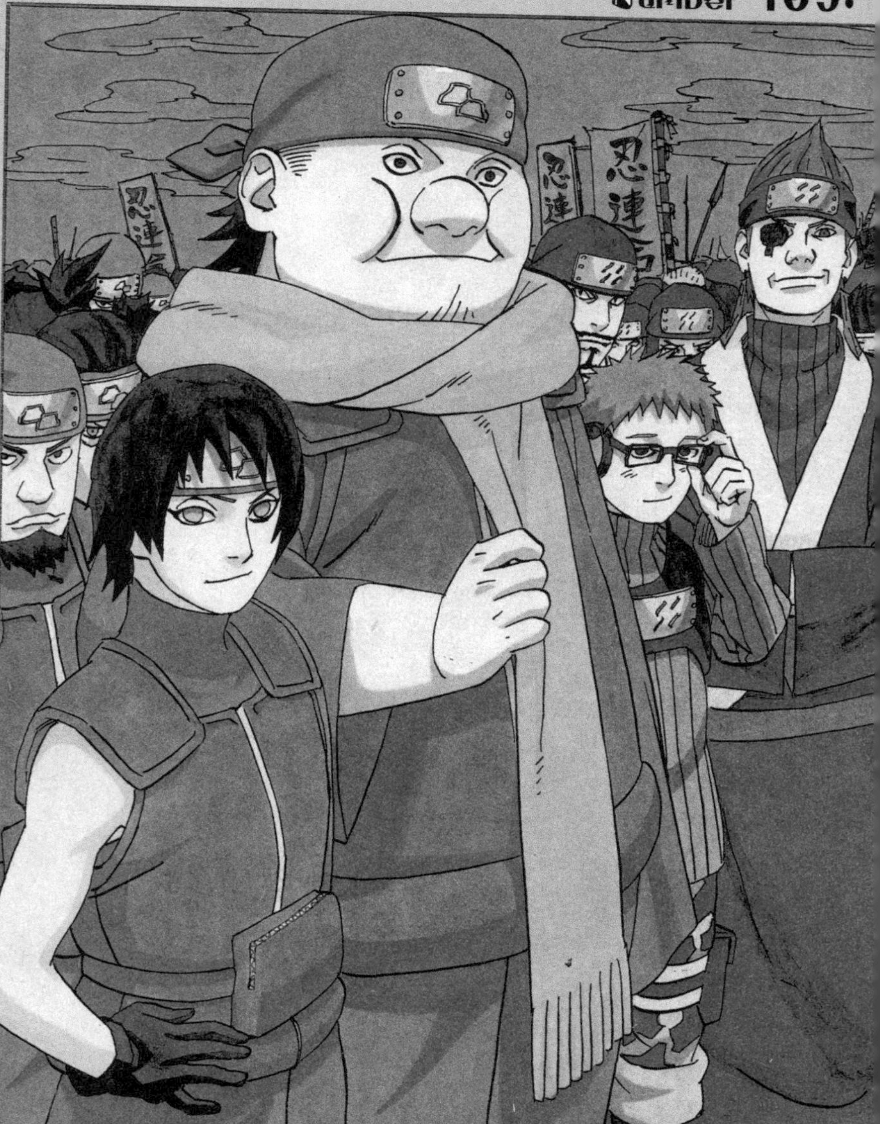
忍連合

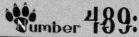

NARUTO

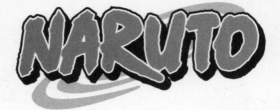

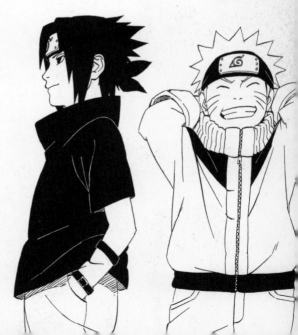

READ THIS WAY

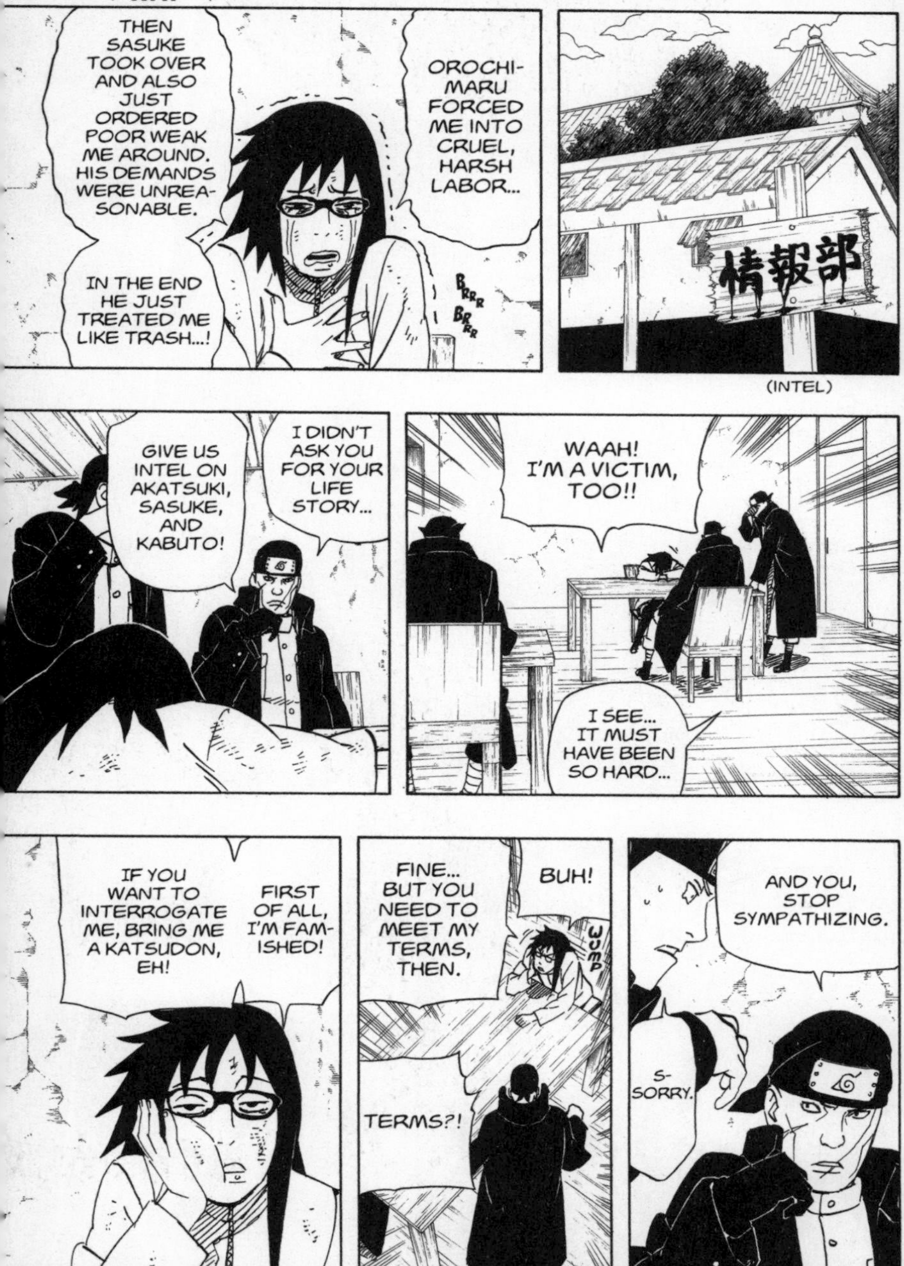
情報部
(INTEL)
OROCHIMARU FORCED ME INTO CRUEL, HARSH LABOR...
THEN SASUKE TOOK OVER AND ALSO JUST ORDERED POOR WEAK ME AROUND. HIS DEMANDS WERE UNREASONABLE.
IN THE END HE JUST TREATED ME LIKE TRASH...!
BRRR BRRR
WAAH! I'M A VICTIM, TOO!!
I SEE... IT MUST HAVE BEEN SO HARD...
I DIDN'T ASK YOU FOR YOUR LIFE STORY...
GIVE US INTEL ON AKATSUKI, SASUKE, AND KABUTO!
AND YOU, STOP SYMPATHIZING.
S-SORRY.
BUH!
WUMP
FINE... BUT YOU NEED TO MEET MY TERMS, THEN.
TERMS?!
FIRST OF ALL, I'M FAMISHED!
IF YOU WANT TO INTERROGATE ME, BRING ME A KATSUDON, EH!

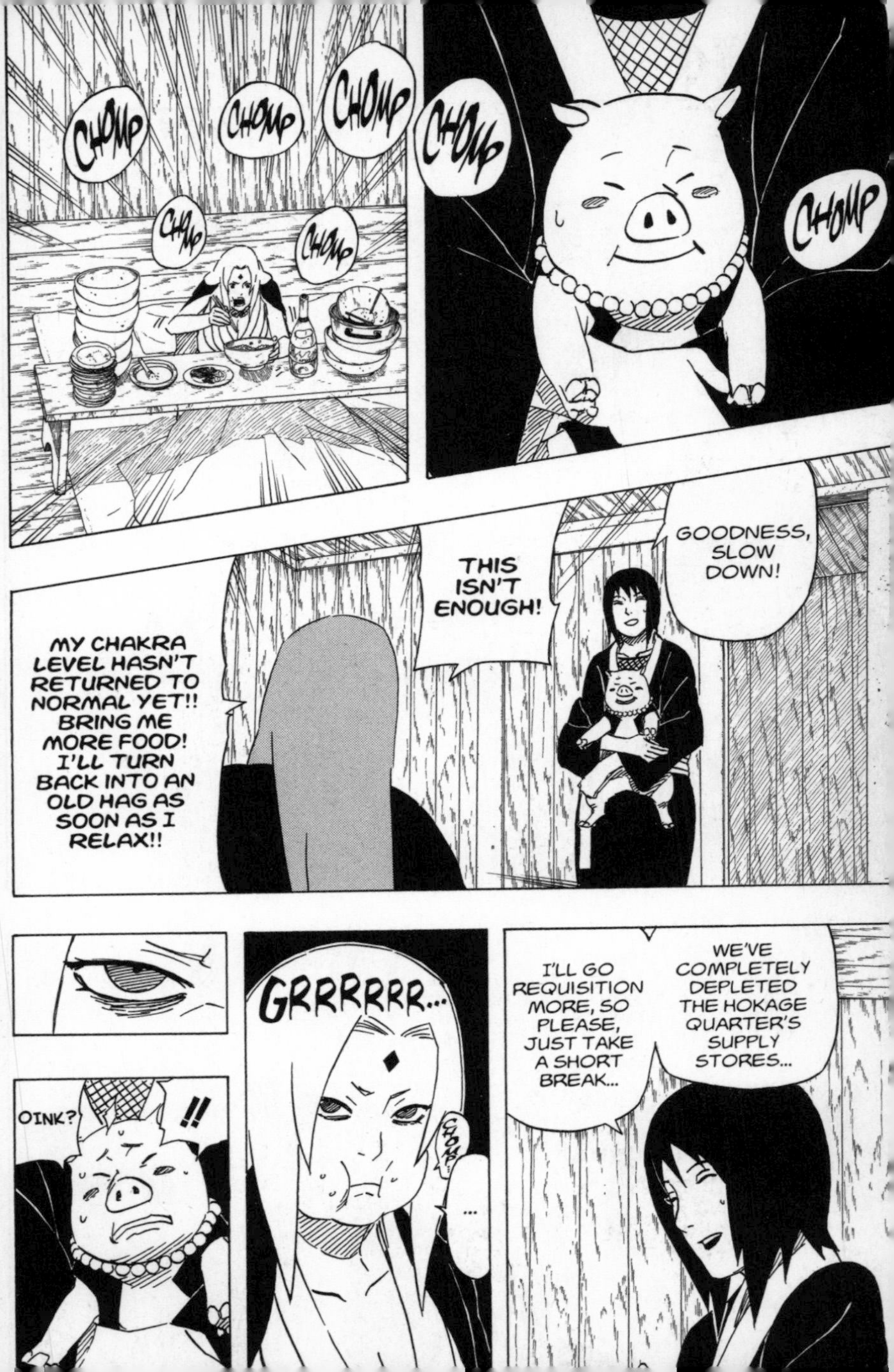
CHOMP
CHOMP
CHOMP
CHOMP
CHOMP
CHOMP
CHOMP
GOODNESS, SLOW DOWN!
THIS ISN'T ENOUGH!
MY CHAKRA LEVEL HASN'T RETURNED TO NORMAL YET!! BRING ME MORE FOOD! I'LL TURN BACK INTO AN OLD HAG AS SOON AS I RELAX!!
WE'VE COMPLETELY DEPLETED THE HOKAGE QUARTER'S SUPPLY STORES...
I'LL GO REQUISITION MORE, SO PLEASE, JUST TAKE A SHORT BREAK...
GRRRRRR...
CHOMP...
...
OINK?
!!

READ THIS WAY

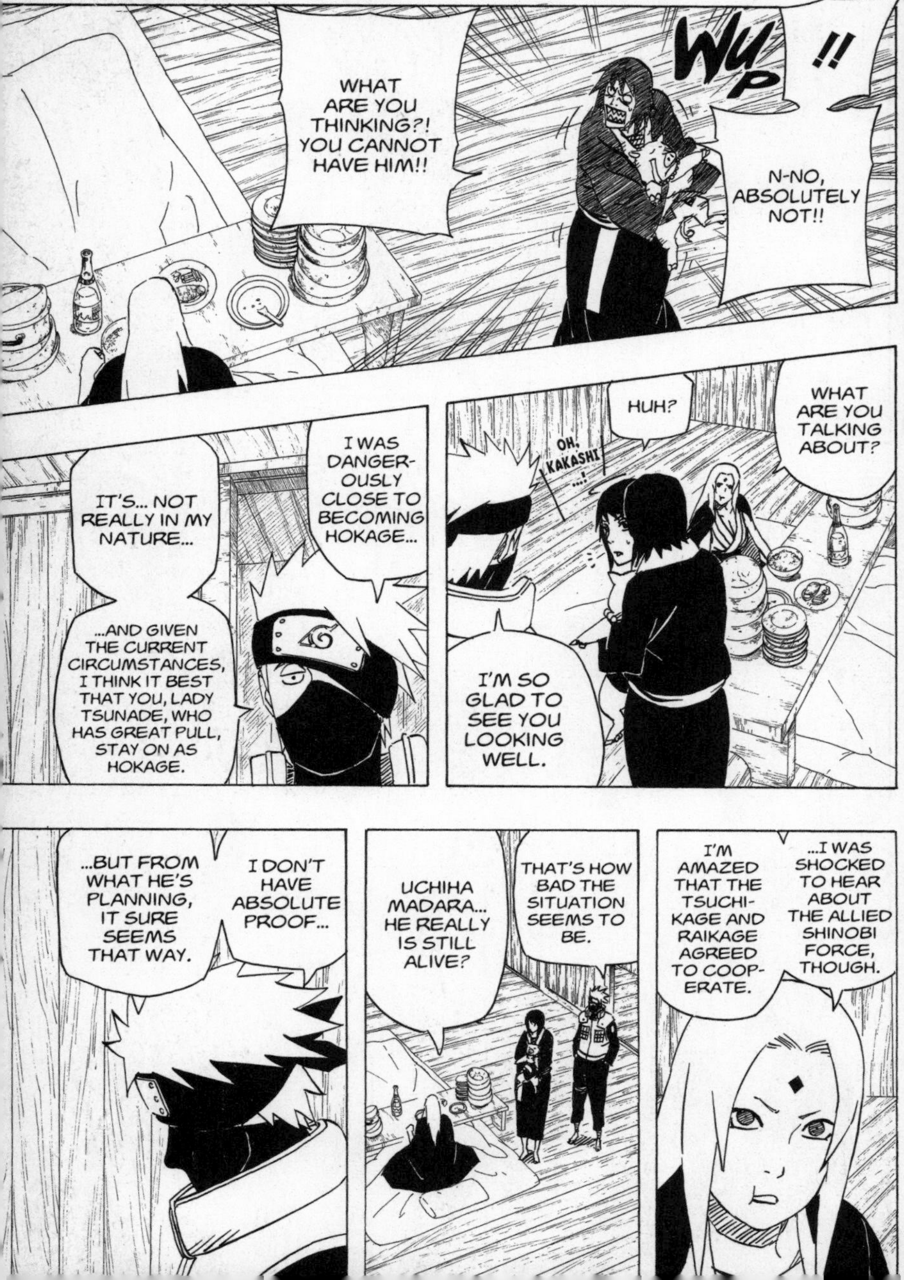
WUP!!
N-NO, ABSOLUTELY NOT!!
WHAT ARE YOU THINKING?! YOU CANNOT HAVE HIM!!
WHAT ARE YOU TALKING ABOUT?
HUH?
OH, KAKASHI...!
I'M SO GLAD TO SEE YOU LOOKING WELL.
I WAS DANGER-OUSLY CLOSE TO BECOMING HOKAGE...
IT'S... NOT REALLY IN MY NATURE...
...AND GIVEN THE CURRENT CIRCUMSTANCES, I THINK IT BEST THAT YOU, LADY TSUNADE, WHO HAS GREAT PULL, STAY ON AS HOKAGE.
...I WAS SHOCKED TO HEAR ABOUT THE ALLIED SHINOBI FORCE, THOUGH.
I'M AMAZED THAT THE TSUCHI-KAGE AND RAIKAGE AGREED TO COOP-ERATE.
THAT'S HOW BAD THE SITUATION SEEMS TO BE.
UCHIHA MADARA... HE REALLY IS STILL ALIVE?
I DON'T HAVE ABSOLUTE PROOF...
...BUT FROM WHAT HE'S PLANNING, IT SURE SEEMS THAT WAY.

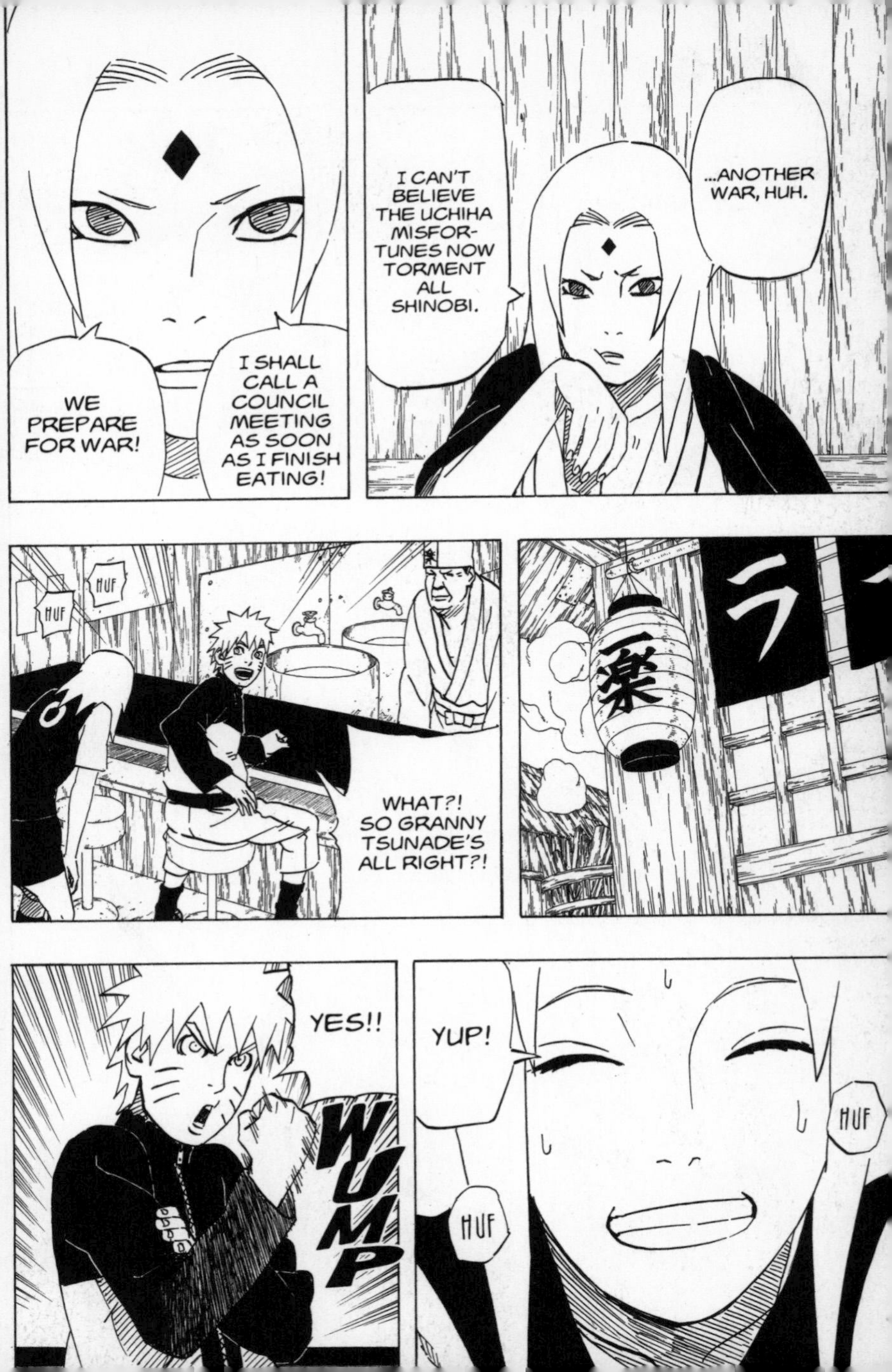
...ANOTHER WAR, HUH.
I CAN'T BELIEVE THE UCHIHA MISFORTUNES NOW TORMENT ALL SHINOBI.
I SHALL CALL A COUNCIL MEETING AS SOON AS I FINISH EATING!
WE PREPARE FOR WAR!
ラ
一楽
HUF
HUF
WHAT?! SO GRANNY TSUNADE'S ALL RIGHT?!
YUP!
HUF
HUF
YES!!
WUMP

READ THIS WAY

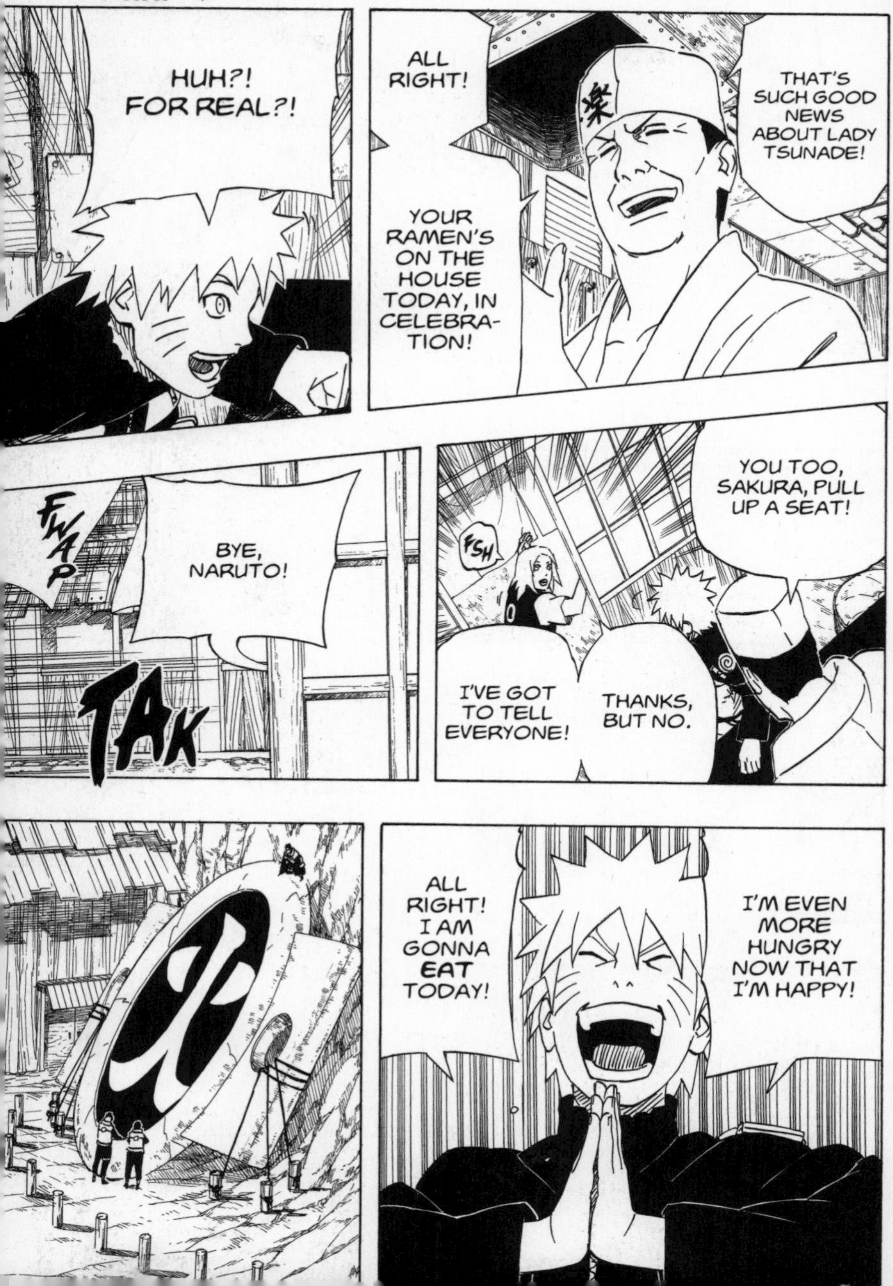
THAT'S SUCH GOOD NEWS ABOUT LADY TSUNADE!
ALL RIGHT!
YOUR RAMEN'S ON THE HOUSE TODAY, IN CELEBRATION!
HUH?! FOR REAL?!
YOU TOO, SAKURA, PULL UP A SEAT!
FSH
THANKS, BUT NO.
I'VE GOT TO TELL EVERYONE!
BYE, NARUTO!
FWAP
TAK
I'M EVEN MORE HUNGRY NOW THAT I'M HAPPY!
ALL RIGHT! I AM GONNA EAT TODAY!

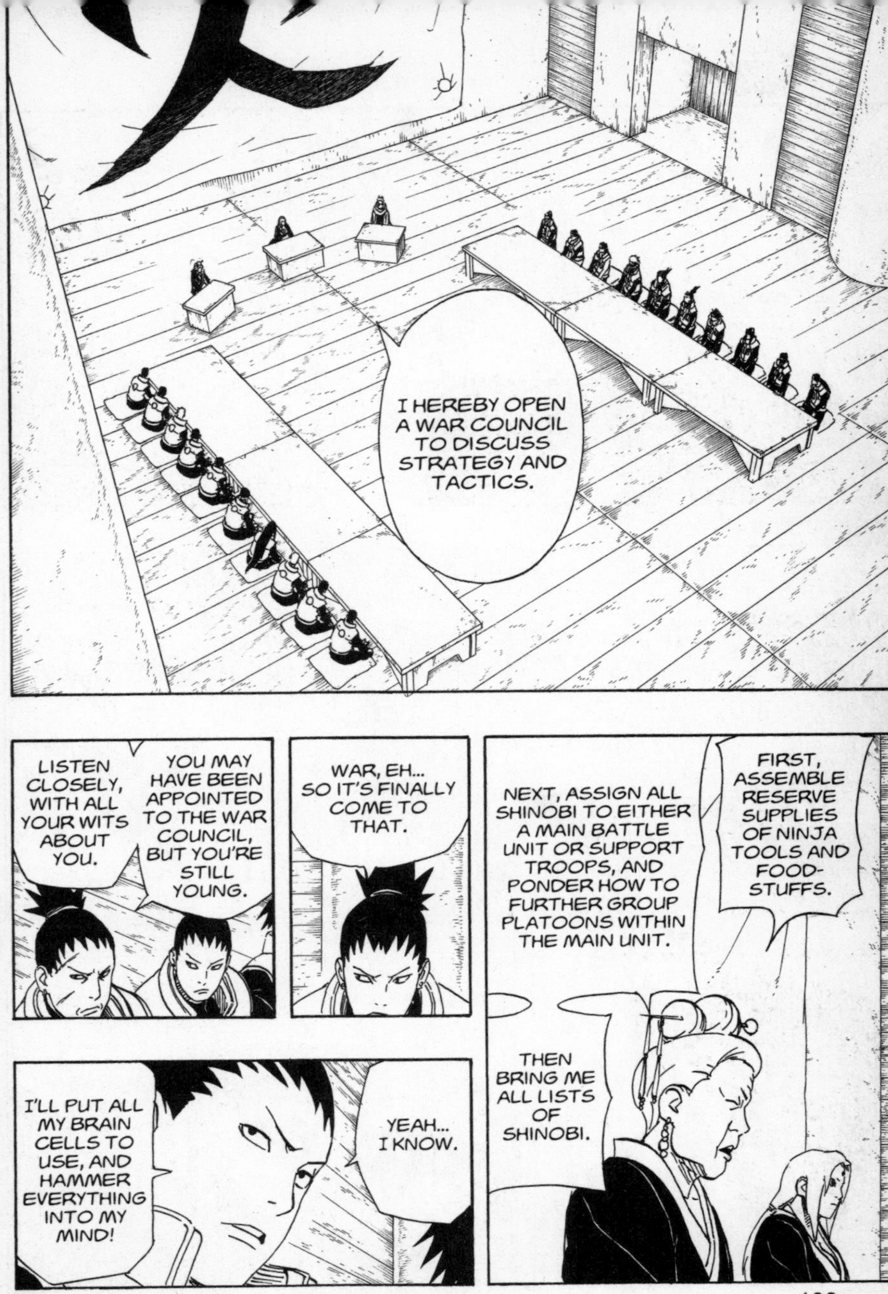
I HEREBY OPEN A WAR COUNCIL TO DISCUSS STRATEGY AND TACTICS.
FIRST, ASSEMBLE RESERVE SUPPLIES OF NINJA TOOLS AND FOOD-STUFFS.
NEXT, ASSIGN ALL SHINOBI TO EITHER A MAIN BATTLE UNIT OR SUPPORT TROOPS, AND PONDER HOW TO FURTHER GROUP PLATOONS WITHIN THE MAIN UNIT.
THEN BRING ME ALL LISTS OF SHINOBI.
WAR, EH... SO IT'S FINALLY COME TO THAT.
YOU MAY HAVE BEEN APPOINTED TO THE WAR COUNCIL, BUT YOU'RE STILL YOUNG.
LISTEN CLOSELY, WITH ALL YOUR WITS ABOUT YOU.
YEAH... I KNOW.
I'LL PUT ALL MY BRAIN CELLS TO USE, AND HAMMER EVERYTHING INTO MY MIND!

READ THIS WAY

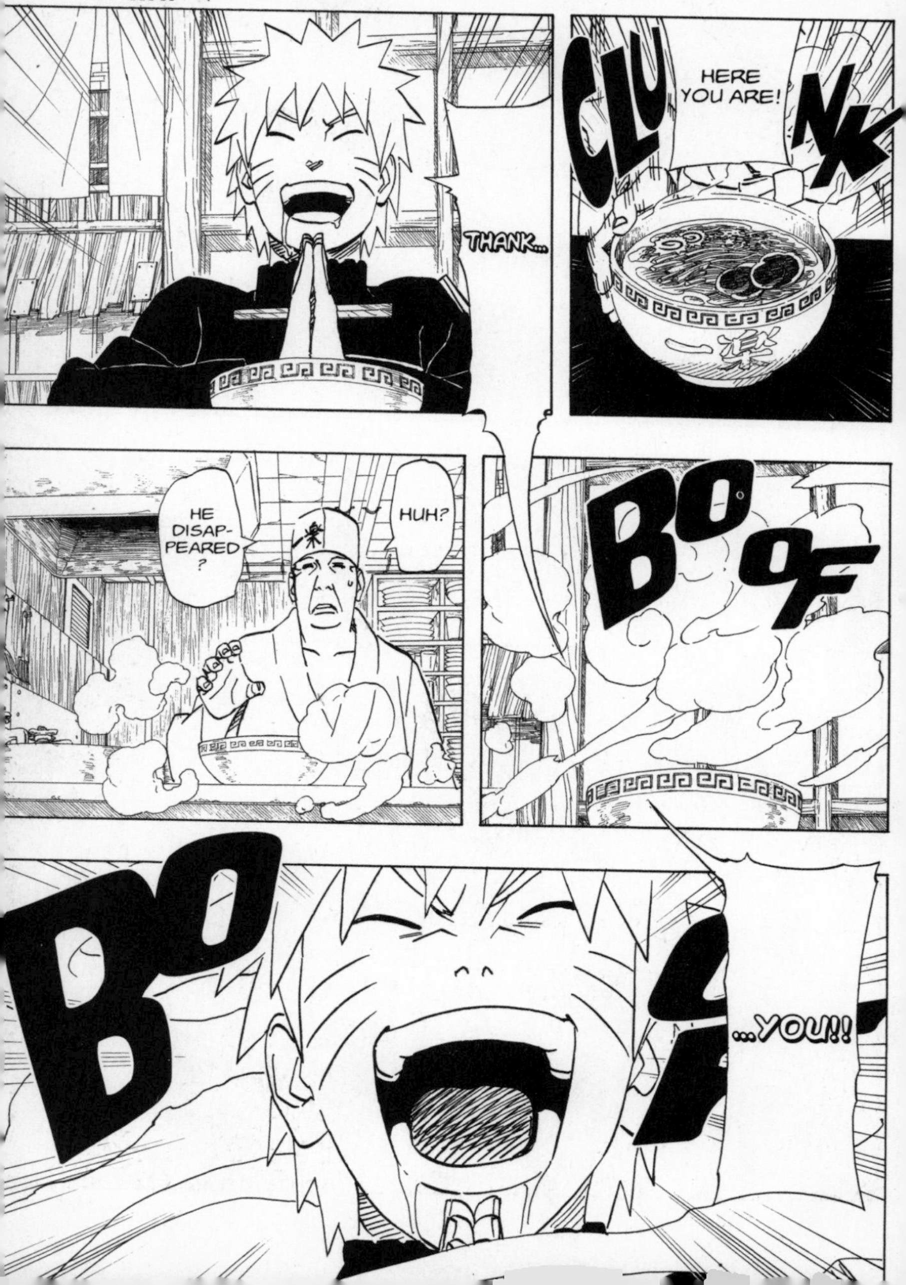
CLUNK
HERE YOU ARE!
THANK...
BOOOF
HUH?
HE DISAP-PEARED?
...YOU!!

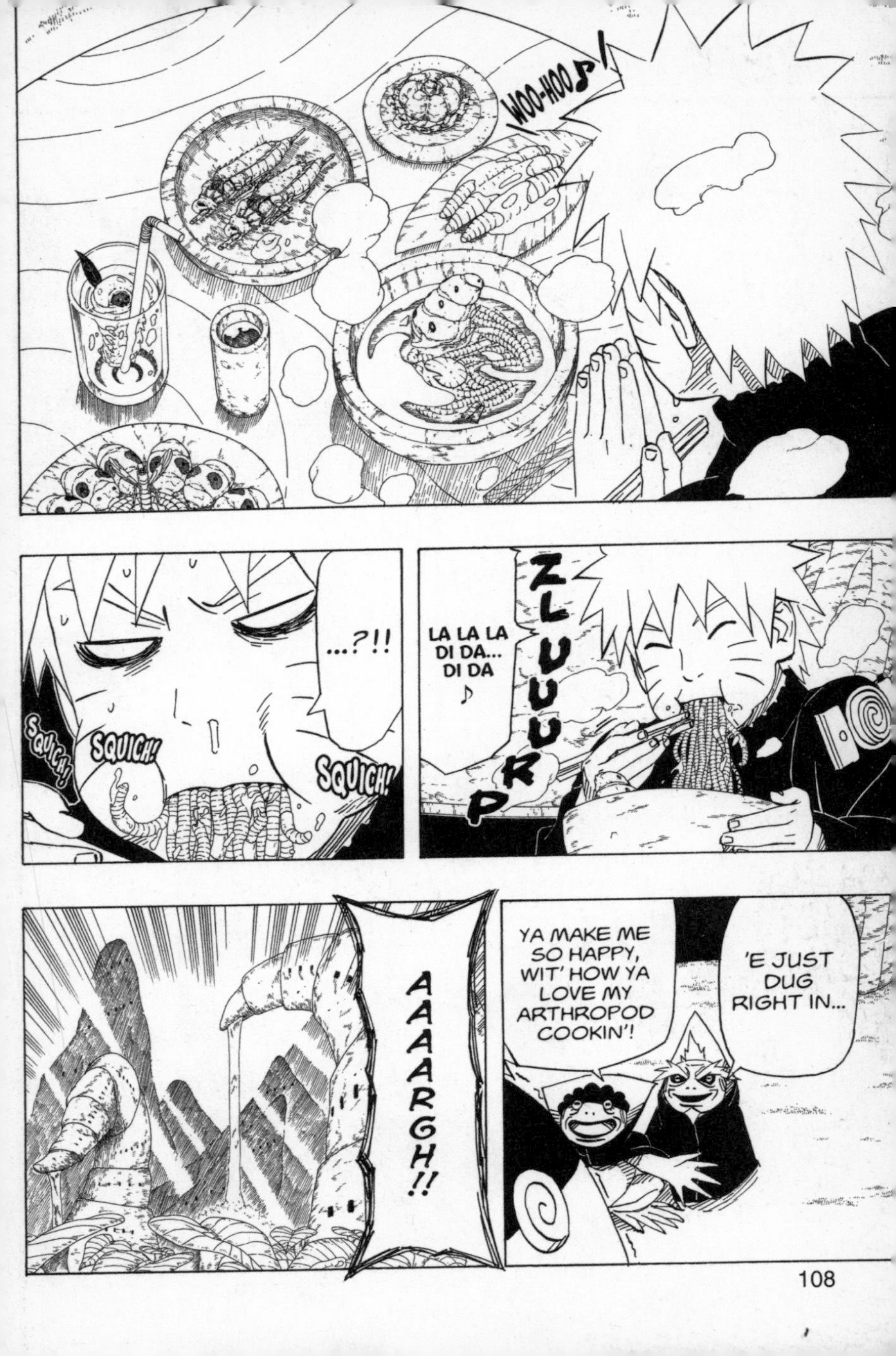
WOO-HOO ♪
ZLUUURP
LA LA LA DI DA... DI DA ♪
...?!!
SQUICH!
SQUICH!
SQUICH!
'E JUST DUG RIGHT IN...
YA MAKE ME SO HAPPY, WIT' HOW YA LOVE MY ARTHROPOD COOKIN'!
AAAARGH!!

READ THIS WAY

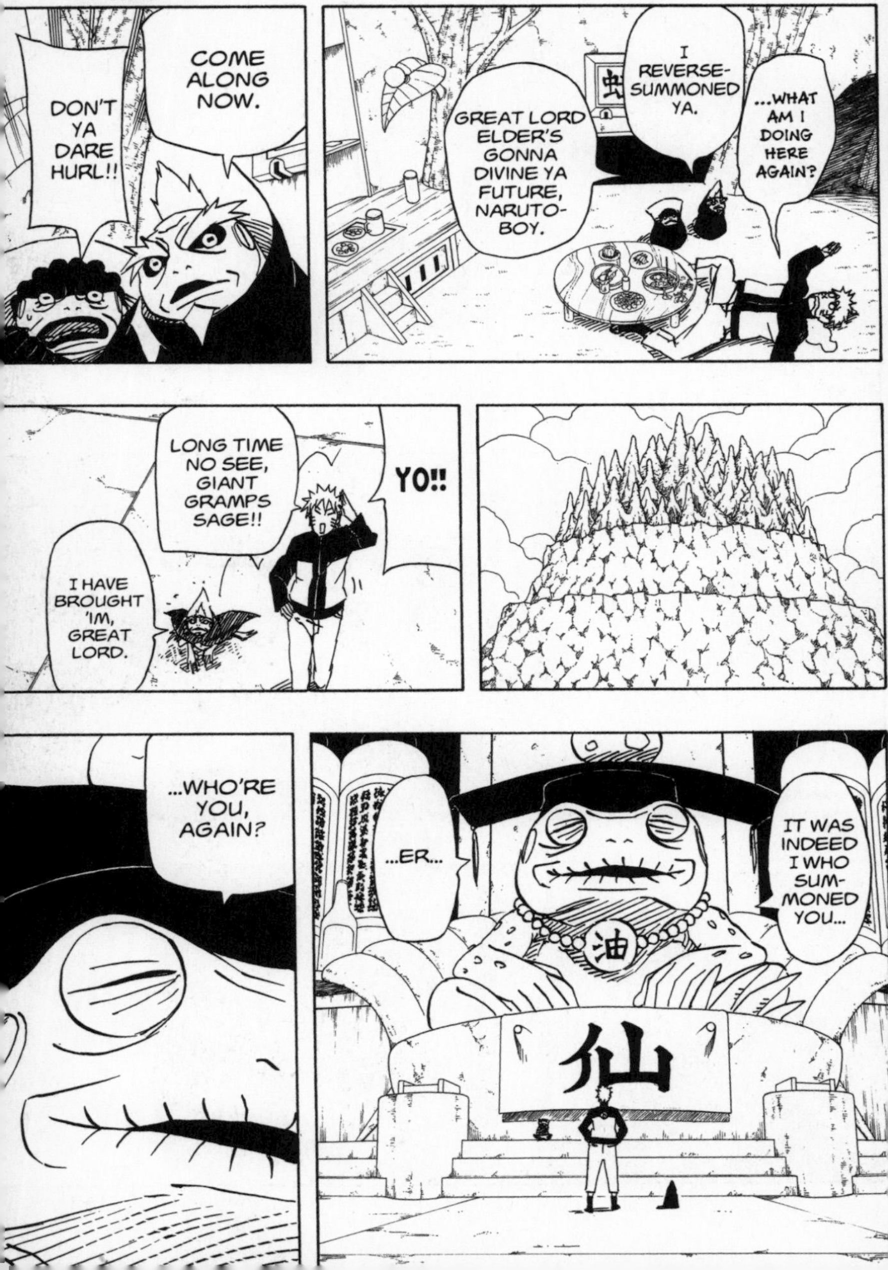
...WHAT AM I DOING HERE AGAIN?
I REVERSE-SUMMONED YA.
GREAT LORD ELDER'S GONNA DIVINE YA FUTURE, NARUTO-BOY.
COME ALONG NOW.
DON'T YA DARE HURL!!
YO!!
LONG TIME NO SEE, GIANT GRAMPS SAGE!!
I HAVE BROUGHT 'IM, GREAT LORD.
IT WAS INDEED I WHO SUMMONED YOU...
...ER...
油
仙
...WHO'RE YOU, AGAIN?

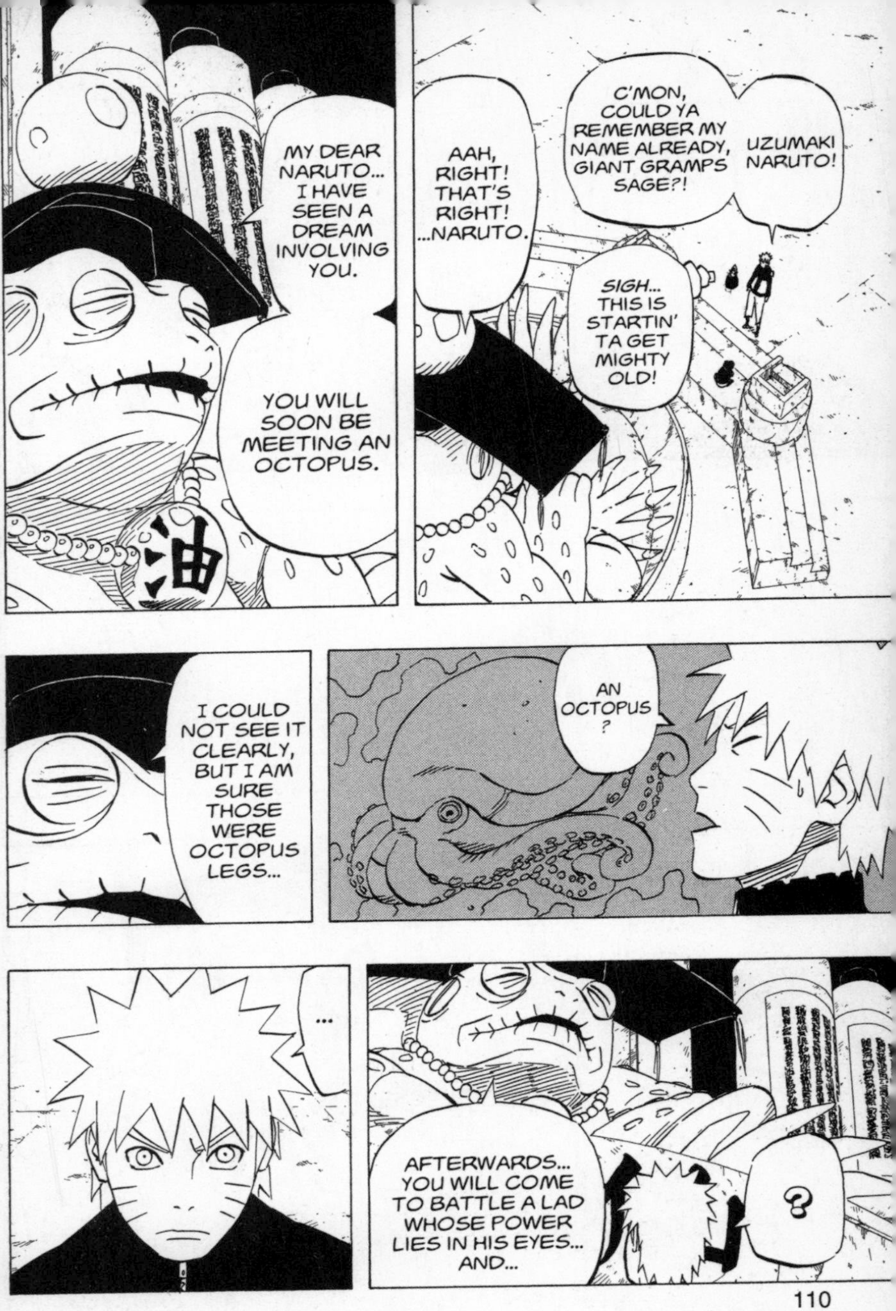
UZUMAKI NARUTO!
C'MON, COULD YA REMEMBER MY NAME ALREADY, GIANT GRAMPS SAGE?!
AAH, RIGHT! THAT'S RIGHT! ...NARUTO.
SIGH... THIS IS STARTIN' TA GET MIGHTY OLD!
MY DEAR NARUTO... I HAVE SEEN A DREAM INVOLVING YOU.
YOU WILL SOON BE MEETING AN OCTOPUS.
AN OCTOPUS?
I COULD NOT SEE IT CLEARLY, BUT I AM SURE THOSE WERE OCTOPUS LEGS...
?
AFTERWARDS... YOU WILL COME TO BATTLE A LAD WHOSE POWER LIES IN HIS EYES... AND...
...

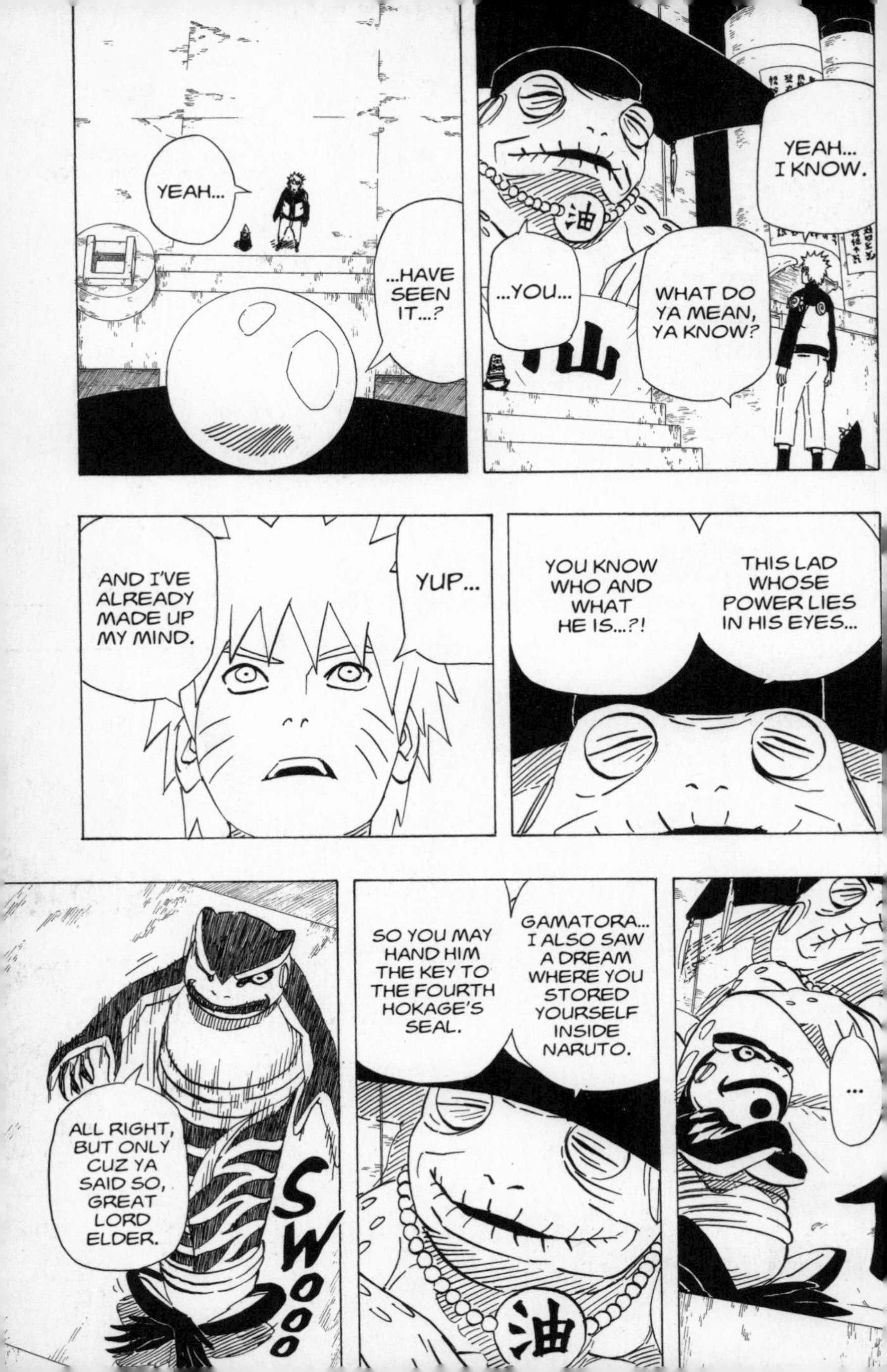
YEAH... I KNOW.
WHAT DO YA MEAN, YA KNOW?
...YOU...
...HAVE SEEN IT...?
YEAH...
THIS LAD WHOSE POWER LIES IN HIS EYES...
YOU KNOW WHO AND WHAT HE IS...?!
YUP...
AND I'VE ALREADY MADE UP MY MIND.
...
GAMATORA... I ALSO SAW A DREAM WHERE YOU STORED YOURSELF INSIDE NARUTO.
SO YOU MAY HAND HIM THE KEY TO THE FOURTH HOKAGE'S SEAL.
ALL RIGHT, BUT ONLY CUZ YA SAID SO, GREAT LORD ELDER.
SWOOOO

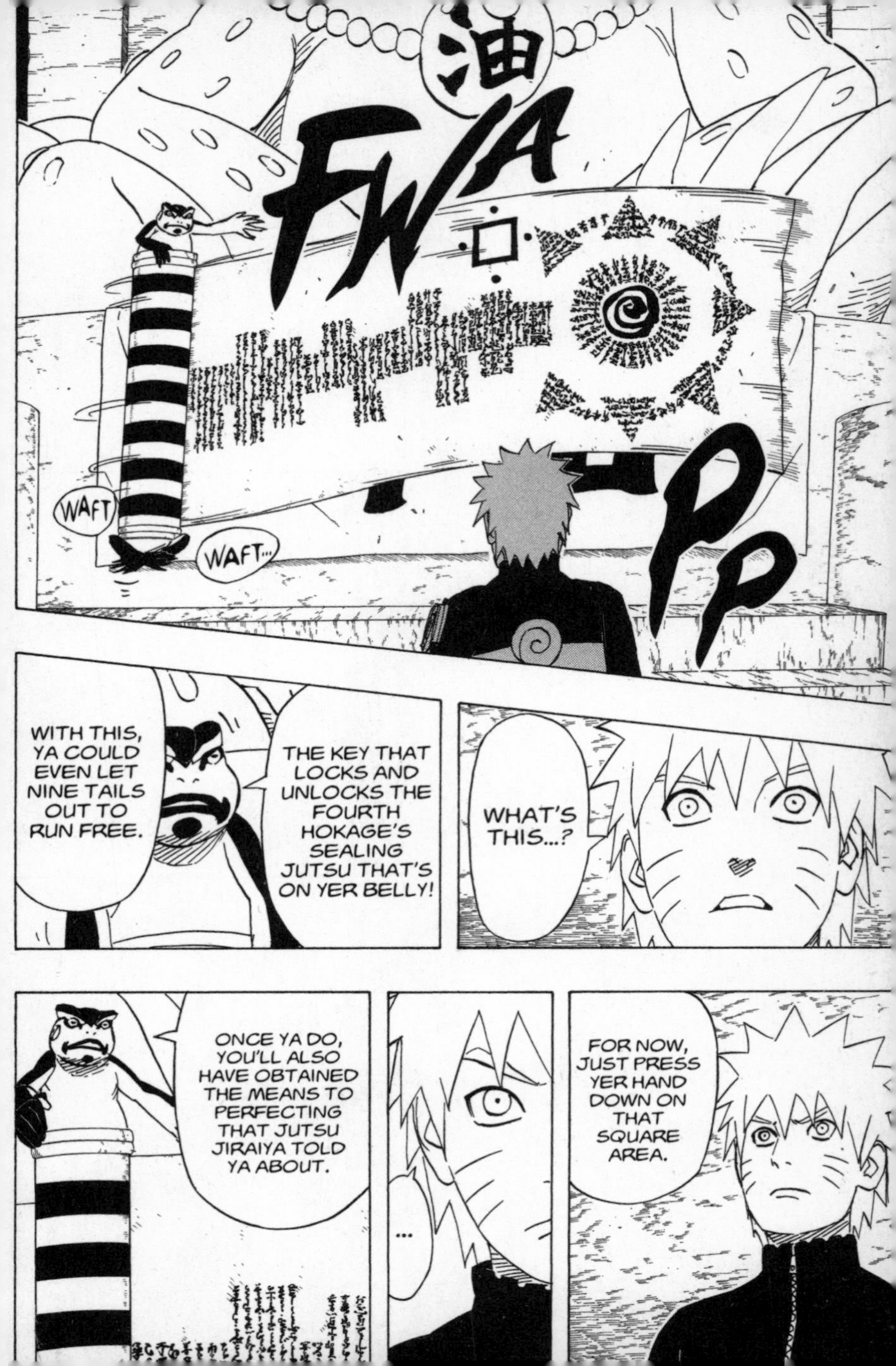
油
FWAPP
WAFT
WAFT...
WHAT'S THIS...?
THE KEY THAT LOCKS AND UNLOCKS THE FOURTH HOKAGE'S SEALING JUTSU THAT'S ON YER BELLY!
WITH THIS, YA COULD EVEN LET NINE TAILS OUT TO RUN FREE.
FOR NOW, JUST PRESS YER HAND DOWN ON THAT SQUARE AREA.
...
ONCE YA DO, YOU'LL ALSO HAVE OBTAINED THE MEANS TO PERFECTING THAT JUTSU JIRAIYA TOLD YA ABOUT.

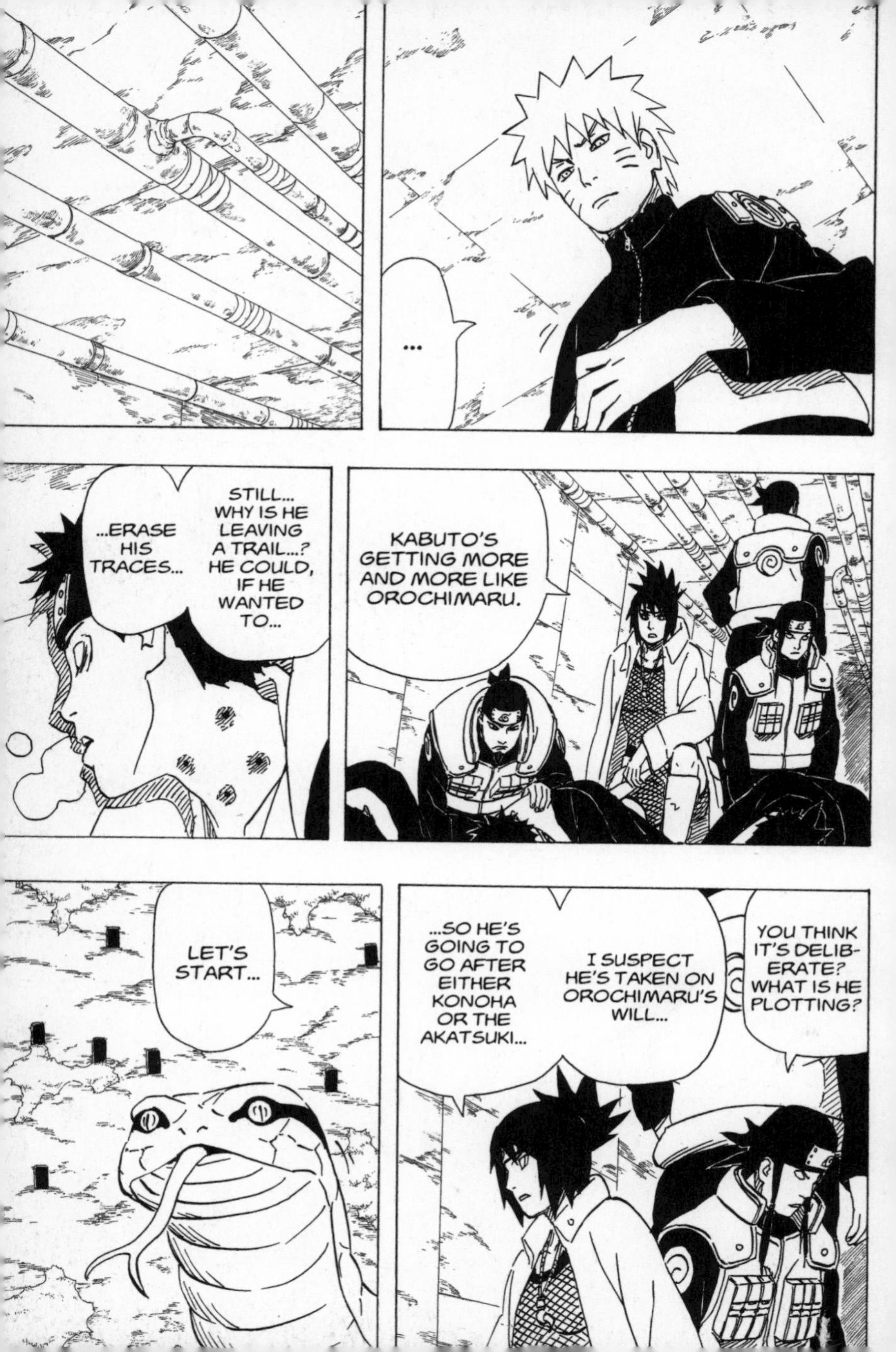
...
KABUTO'S GETTING MORE AND MORE LIKE OROCHIMARU.
STILL... WHY IS HE LEAVING A TRAIL...? HE COULD, IF HE WANTED TO...
...ERASE HIS TRACES...
YOU THINK IT'S DELIB-ERATE? WHAT IS HE PLOTTING?
I SUSPECT HE'S TAKEN ON OROCHIMARU'S WILL...
...SO HE'S GOING TO GO AFTER EITHER KONOHA OR THE AKATSUKI...
LET'S START...

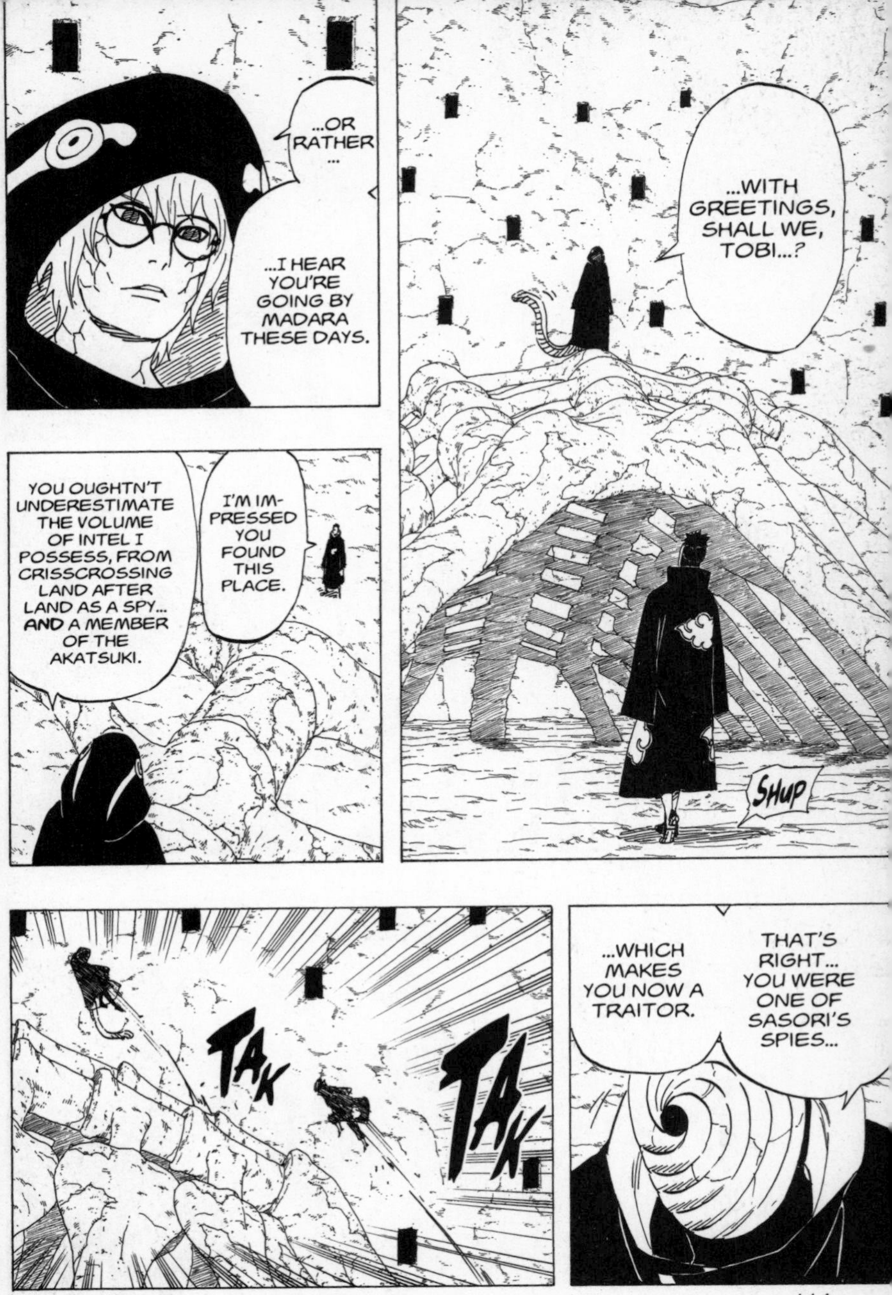

...WITH GREETINGS, SHALL WE, TOBI...?
SHUP
...OR RATHER ...
...I HEAR YOU'RE GOING BY MADARA THESE DAYS.
I'M IM-PRESSED YOU FOUND THIS PLACE.
YOU OUGHTN'T UNDERESTIMATE THE VOLUME OF INTEL I POSSESS, FROM CRISSCROSSING LAND AFTER LAND AS A SPY... **AND** A MEMBER OF THE AKATSUKI.
THAT'S RIGHT... YOU WERE ONE OF SASORI'S SPIES...
...WHICH MAKES YOU NOW A TRAITOR.
TAK
TAK

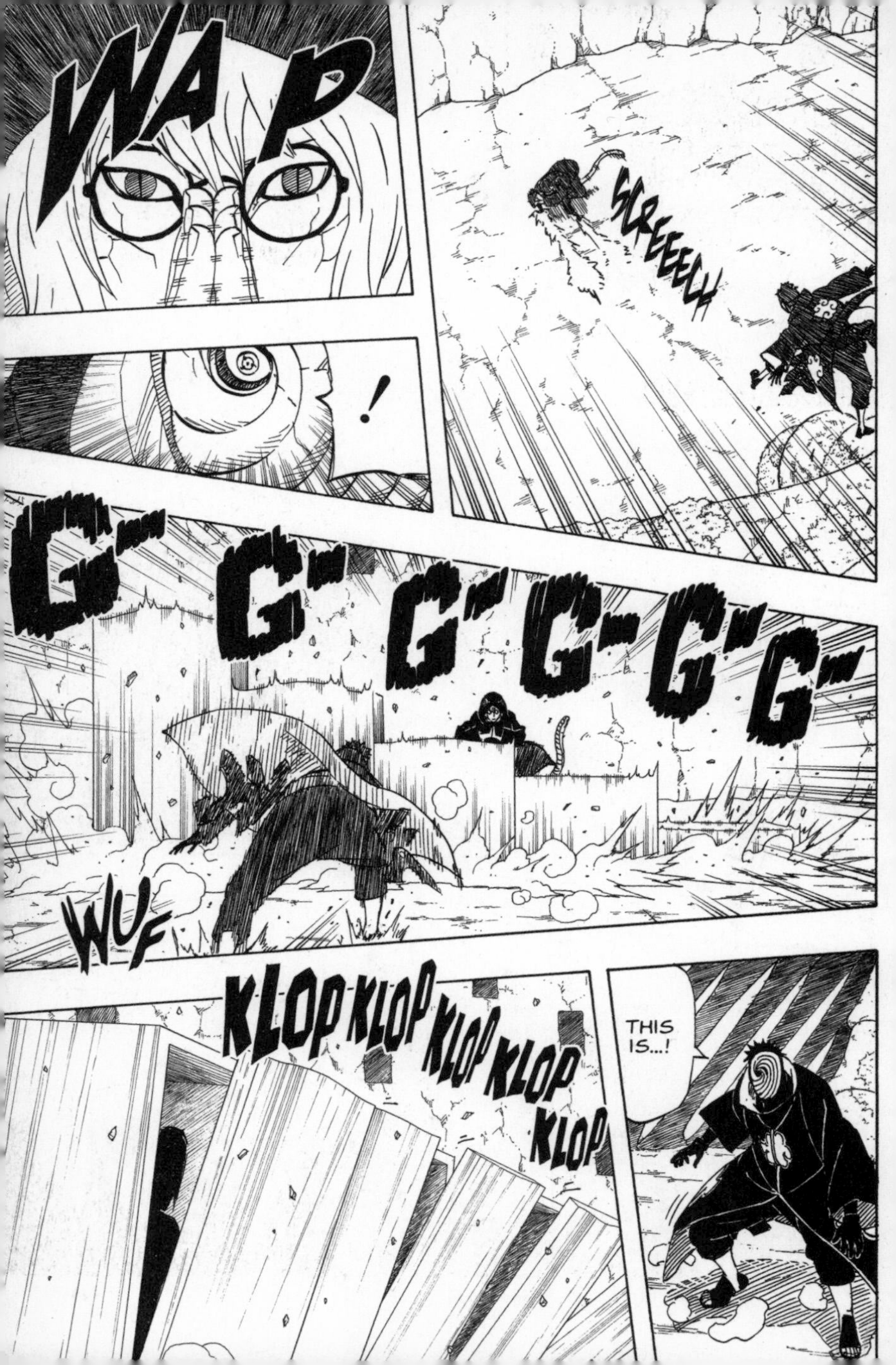
SCREEECH
WAP
!
G G G G-G G
WUF
THIS IS...!
KLOP KLOP KLOP KLOP KLOP

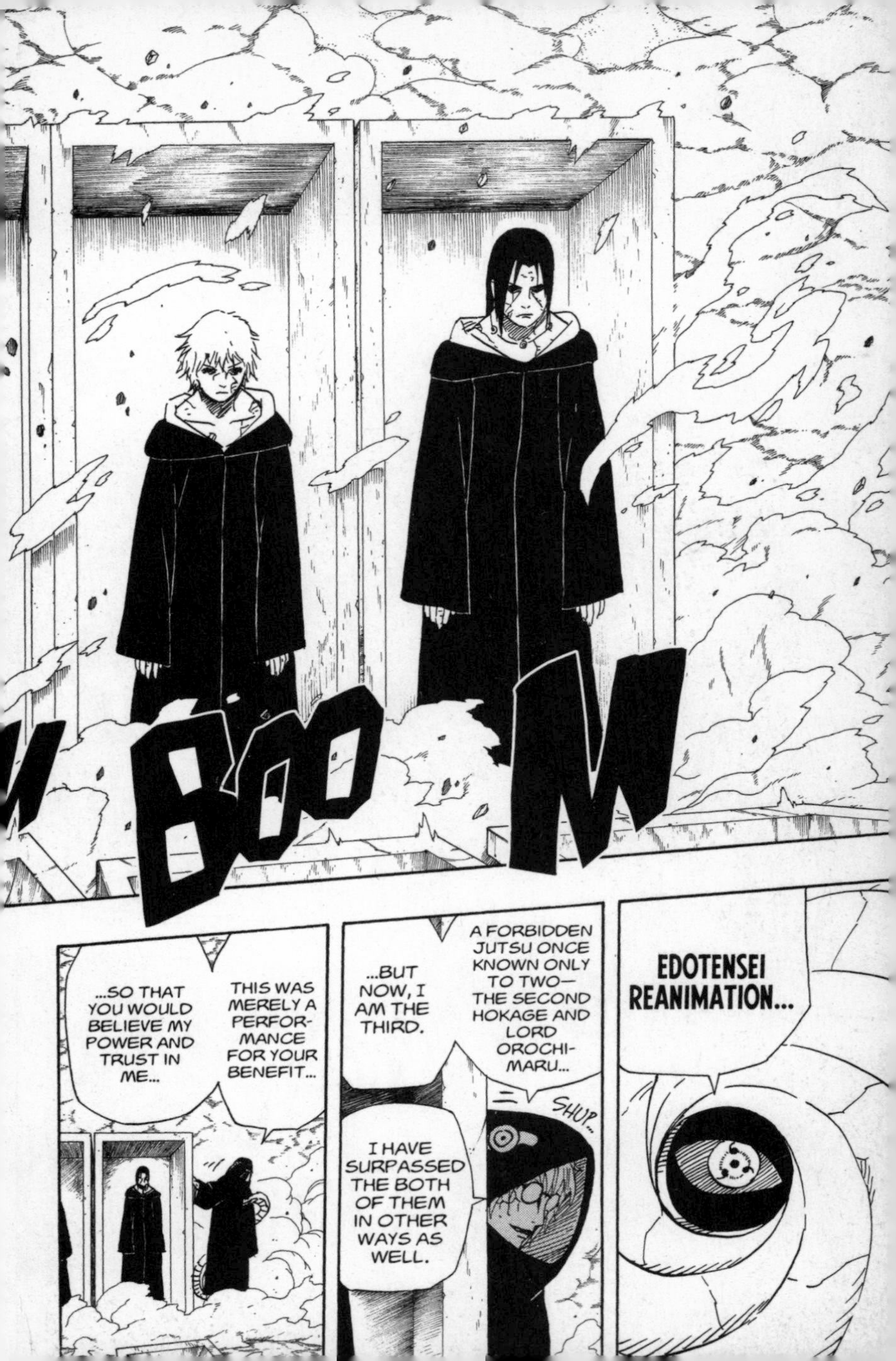
BOOM
EDOTENSEI REANIMATION...
A FORBIDDEN JUTSU ONCE KNOWN ONLY TO TWO—THE SECOND HOKAGE AND LORD OROCHIMARU...
...BUT NOW, I AM THE THIRD.
SHUP...
I HAVE SURPASSED THE BOTH OF THEM IN OTHER WAYS AS WELL.
THIS WAS MERELY A PERFORMANCE FOR YOUR BENEFIT...
...SO THAT YOU WOULD BELIEVE MY POWER AND TRUST IN ME...

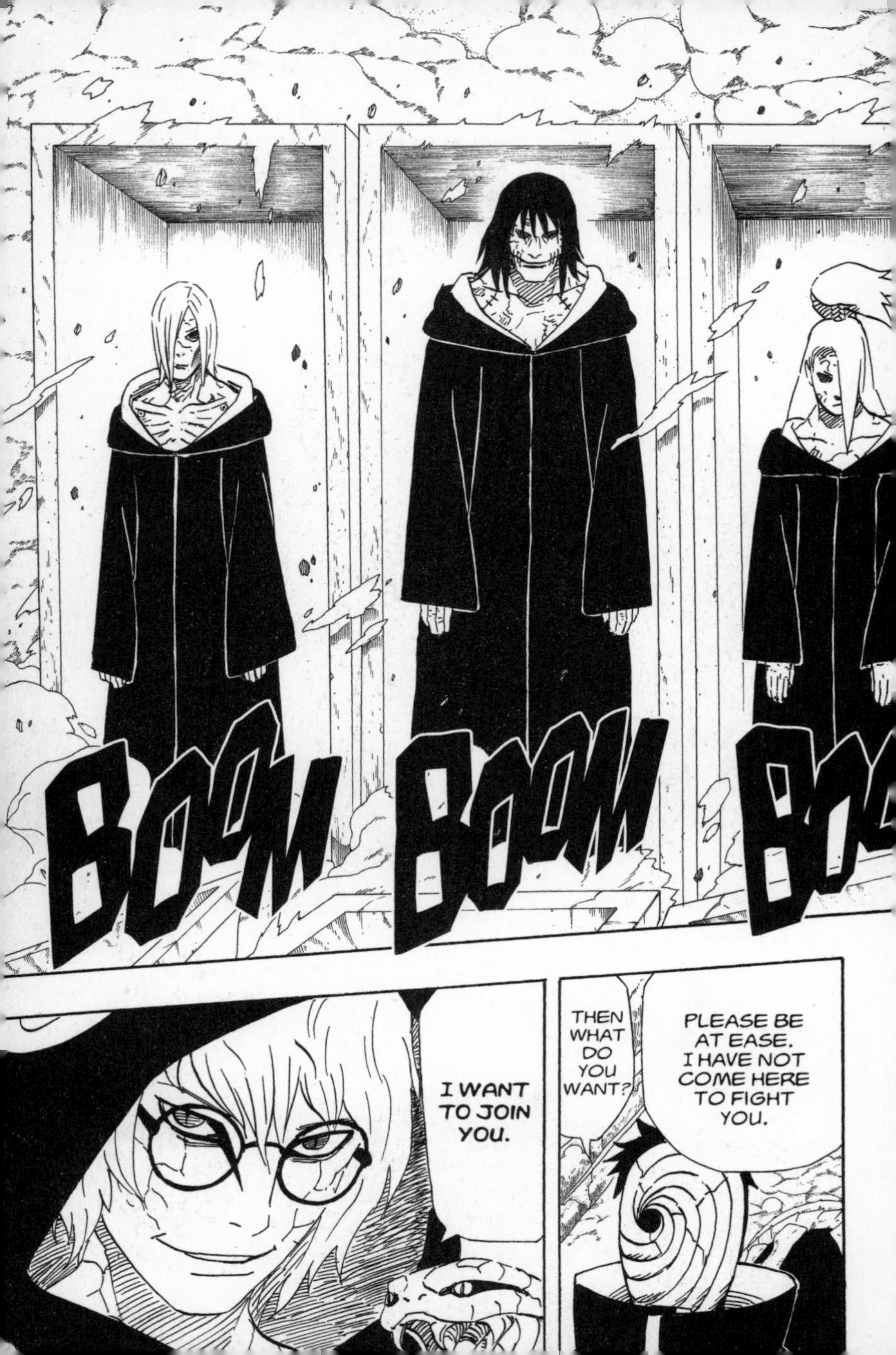
BOO
BOOM
BOOM
PLEASE BE AT EASE. I HAVE NOT COME HERE TO FIGHT YOU.
THEN WHAT DO YOU WANT?
I WANT TO JOIN YOU.

NARUTO

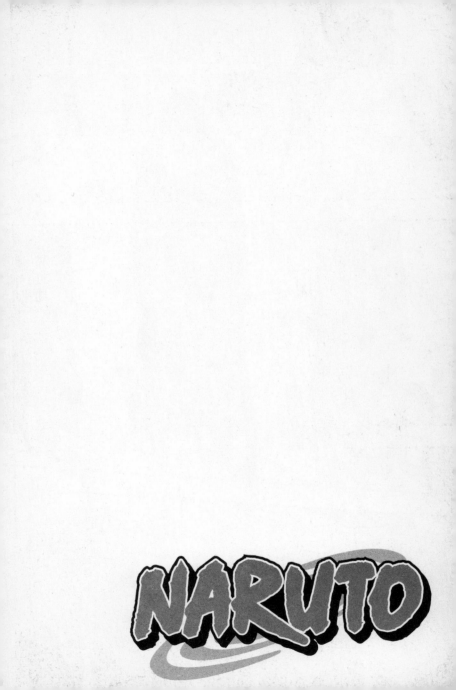

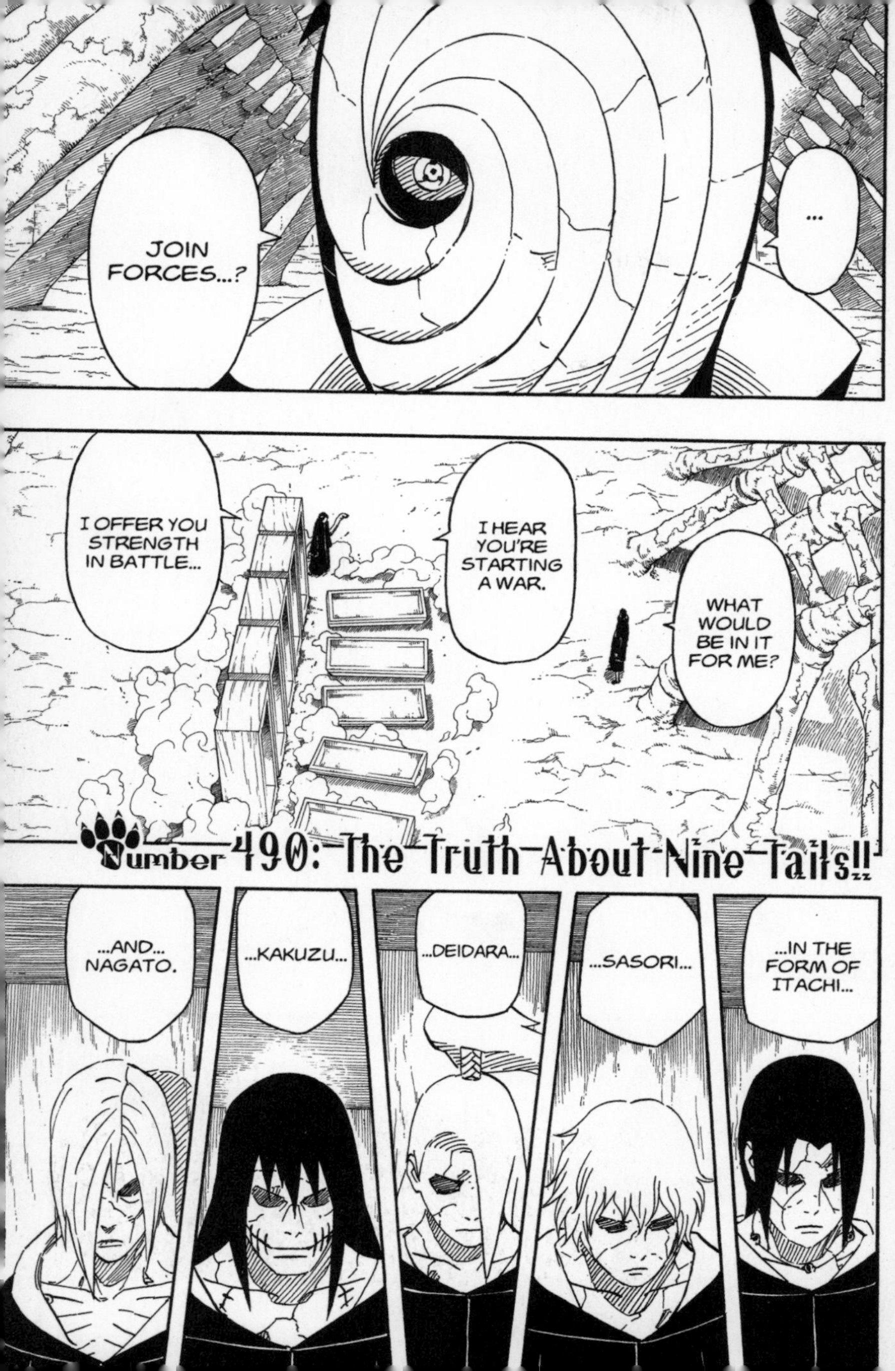
...
JOIN FORCES...?
WHAT WOULD BE IN IT FOR ME?
I HEAR YOU'RE STARTING A WAR.
I OFFER YOU STRENGTH IN BATTLE...
Number 490: The Truth About Nine Tails!!
...IN THE FORM OF ITACHI...
...SASORI...
...DEIDARA...
...KAKUZU...
...AND... NAGATO.

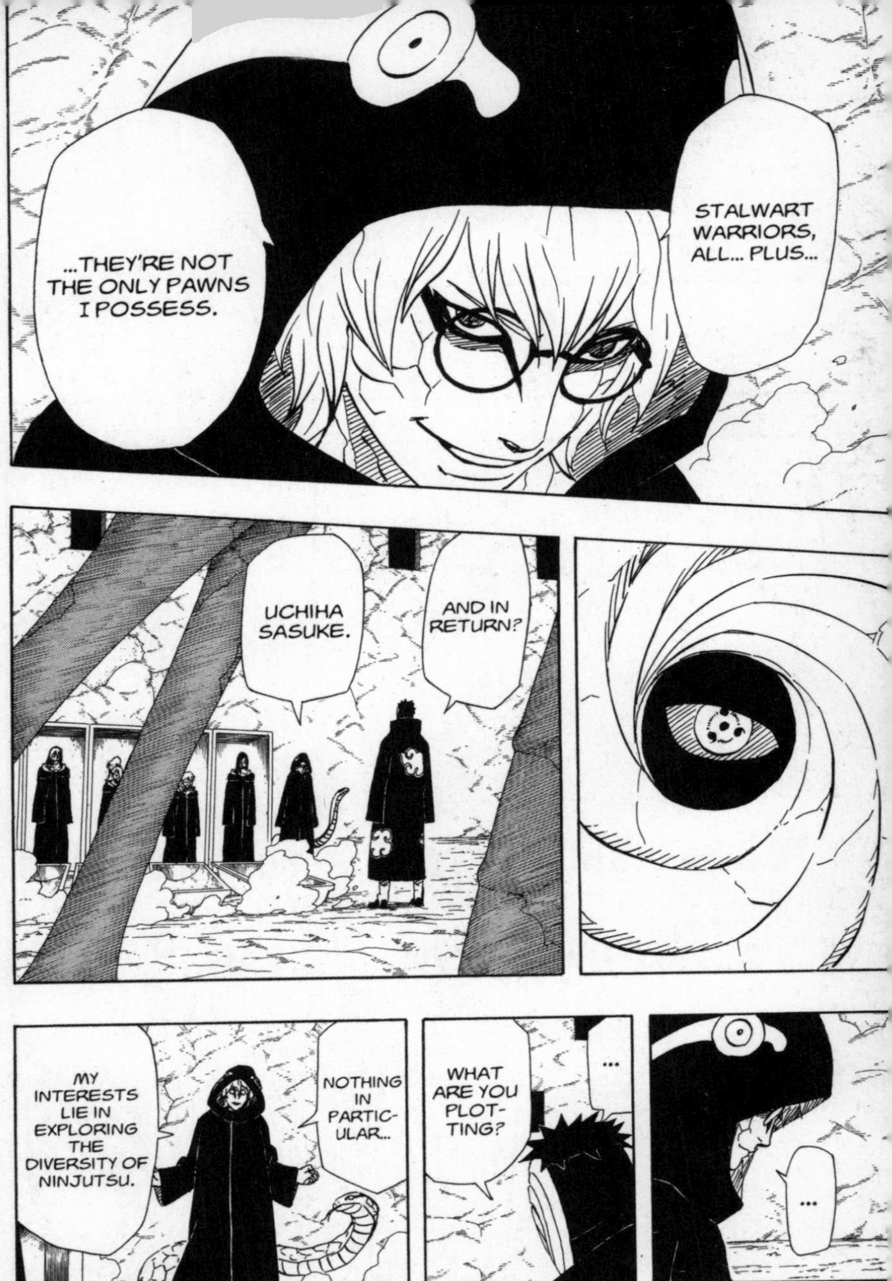
STALWART WARRIORS, ALL... PLUS...
...THEY'RE NOT THE ONLY PAWNS I POSSESS.
AND IN RETURN?
UCHIHA SASUKE.
...
...
WHAT ARE YOU PLOT-TING?
NOTHING IN PARTIC-ULAR...
MY INTERESTS LIE IN EXPLORING THE DIVERSITY OF NINJUTSU.

READ THIS WAY

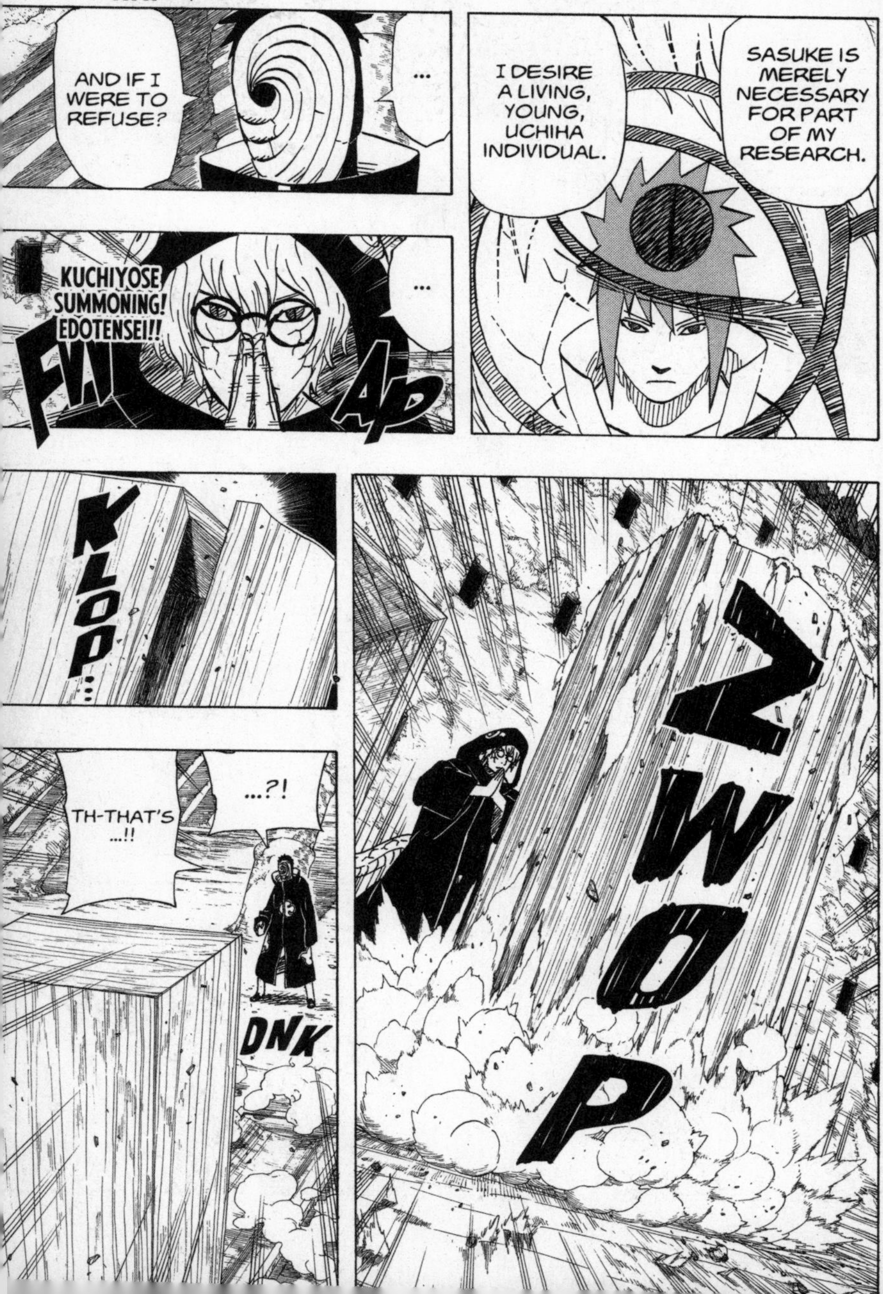
SASUKE IS MERELY NECESSARY FOR PART OF MY RESEARCH.
I DESIRE A LIVING, YOUNG, UCHIHA INDIVIDUAL.
...
AND IF I WERE TO REFUSE?
...
KUCHIYOSE SUMMONING! EDOTENSEI!!
FWAP
ZWOOP
KLOP...
...?!
TH-THAT'S ...!!
DNK

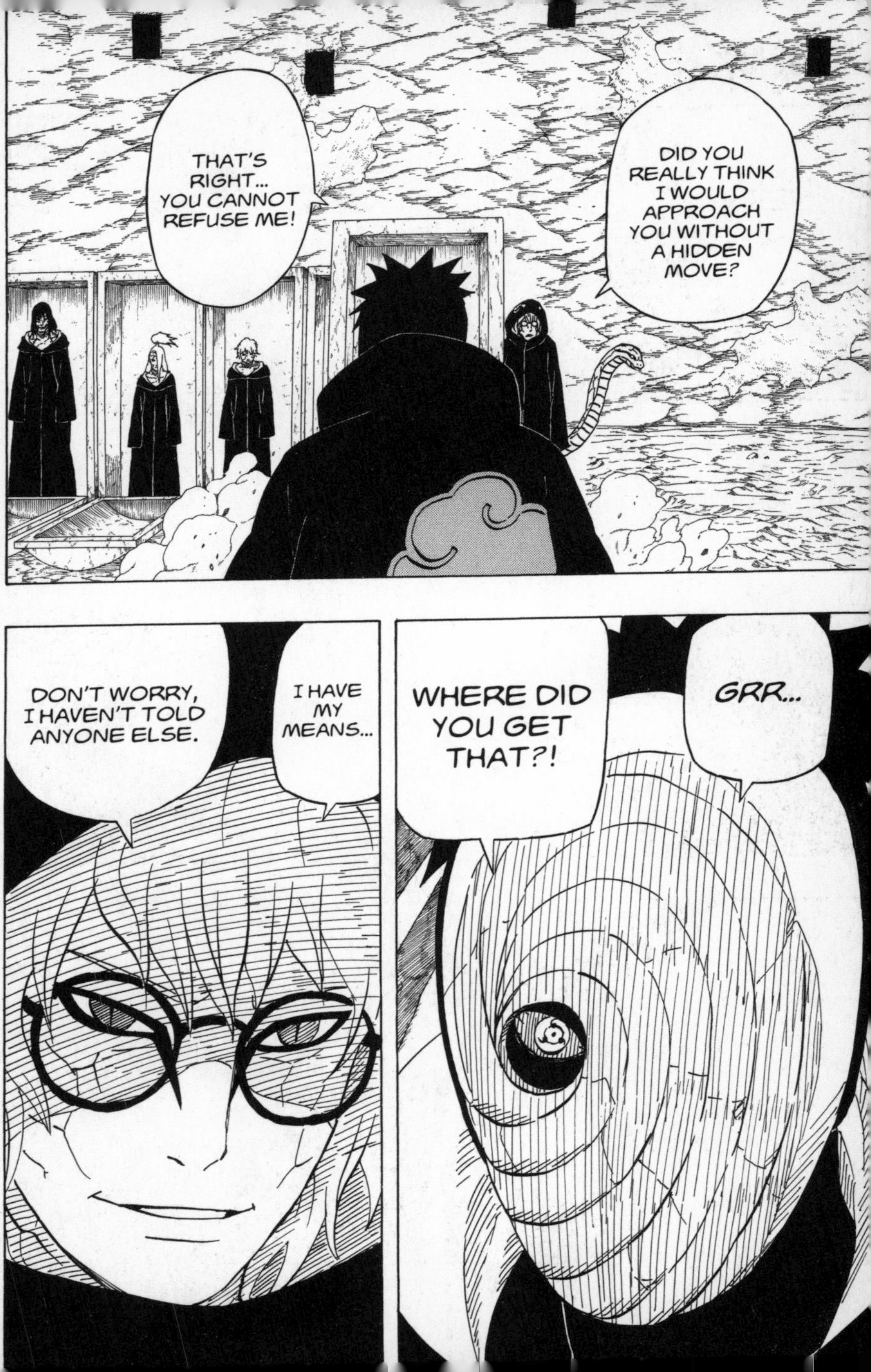
DID YOU REALLY THINK I WOULD APPROACH YOU WITHOUT A HIDDEN MOVE?
THAT'S RIGHT... YOU CANNOT REFUSE ME!
GRR...
WHERE DID YOU GET THAT?!
I HAVE MY MEANS...
DON'T WORRY, I HAVEN'T TOLD ANYONE ELSE.

READ THIS WAY

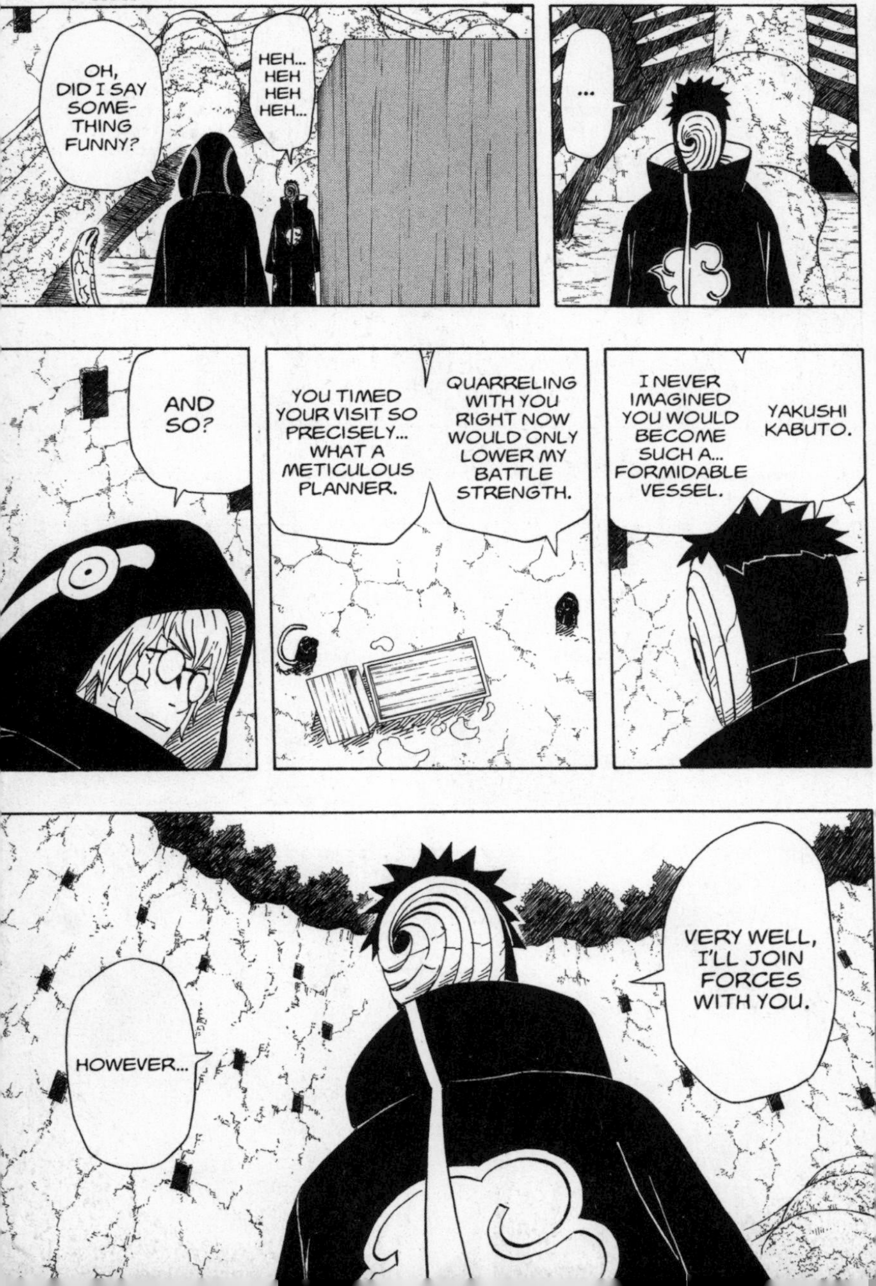
...
HEH... HEH HEH HEH...
OH, DID I SAY SOMETHING FUNNY?
YAKUSHI KABUTO.
I NEVER IMAGINED YOU WOULD BECOME SUCH A... FORMIDABLE VESSEL.
QUARRELING WITH YOU RIGHT NOW WOULD ONLY LOWER MY BATTLE STRENGTH.
YOU TIMED YOUR VISIT SO PRECISELY... WHAT A METICULOUS PLANNER.
AND SO?
VERY WELL, I'LL JOIN FORCES WITH YOU.
HOWEVER...

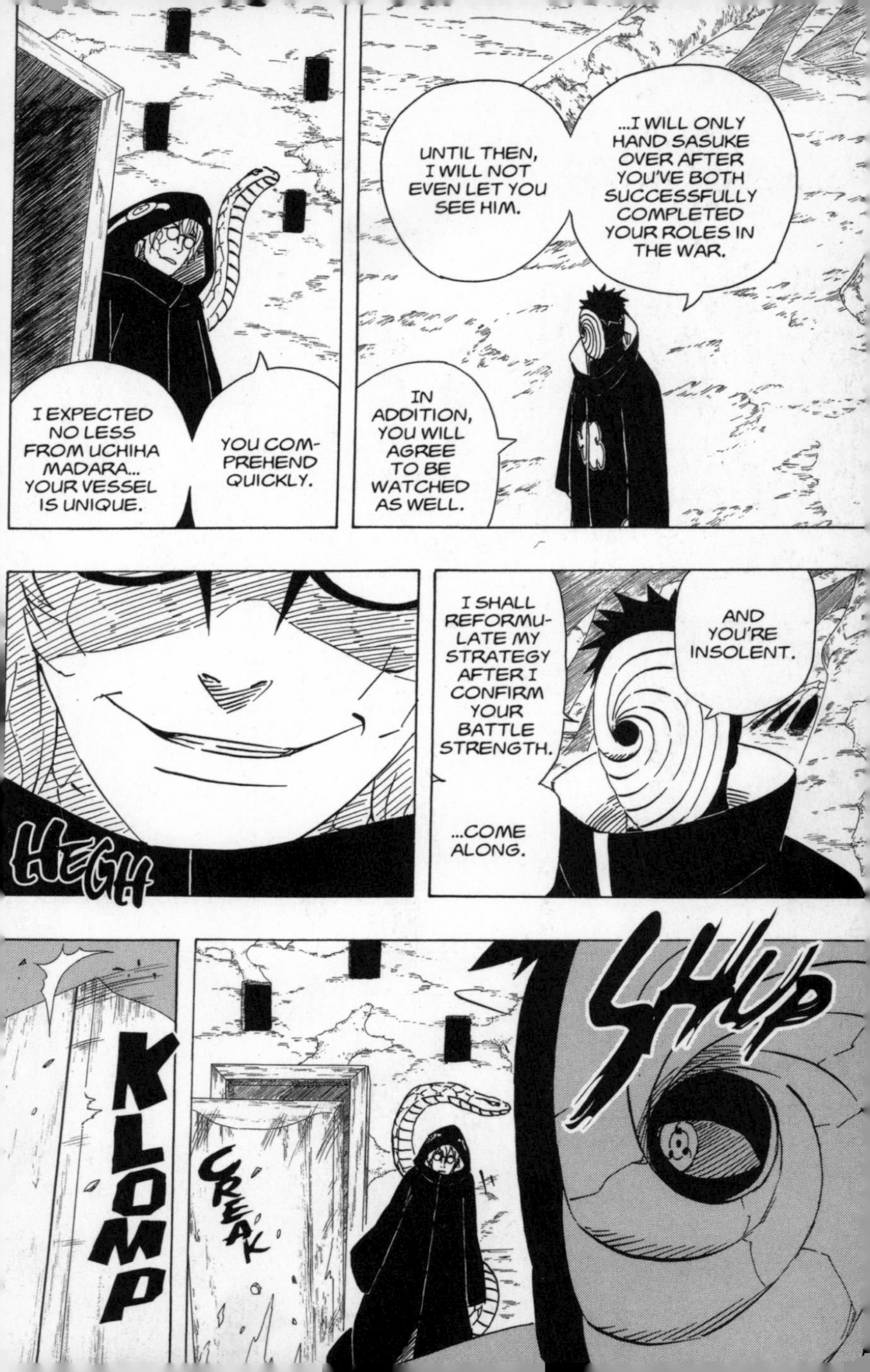
...I WILL ONLY HAND SASUKE OVER AFTER YOU'VE BOTH SUCCESSFULLY COMPLETED YOUR ROLES IN THE WAR.
UNTIL THEN, I WILL NOT EVEN LET YOU SEE HIM.
IN ADDITION, YOU WILL AGREE TO BE WATCHED AS WELL.
YOU COM-PREHEND QUICKLY.
I EXPECTED NO LESS FROM UCHIHA MADARA... YOUR VESSEL IS UNIQUE.
AND YOU'RE INSOLENT.
I SHALL REFORMU-LATE MY STRATEGY AFTER I CONFIRM YOUR BATTLE STRENGTH.
...COME ALONG.
HEGH
SHUP
CREAK
KLOMP

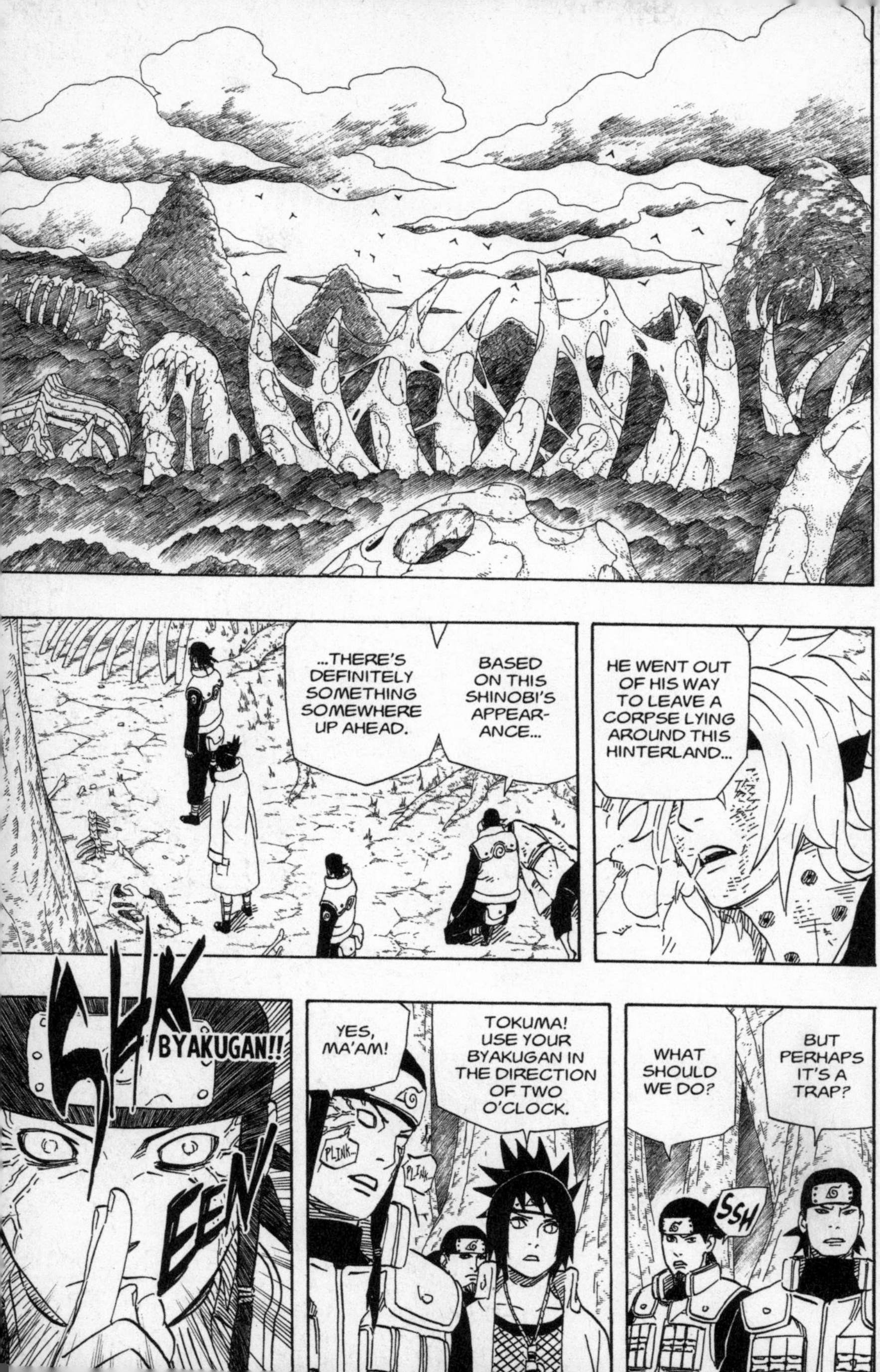
HE WENT OUT OF HIS WAY TO LEAVE A CORPSE LYING AROUND THIS HINTERLAND...
BASED ON THIS SHINOBI'S APPEAR-ANCE...
...THERE'S DEFINITELY SOMETHING SOMEWHERE UP AHEAD.
BUT PERHAPS IT'S A TRAP?
SSH
WHAT SHOULD WE DO?
TOKUMA! USE YOUR BYAKUGAN IN THE DIRECTION OF TWO O'CLOCK.
YES, MA'AM!
PLINK
PLINK
BYAKUGAN!!
EEN

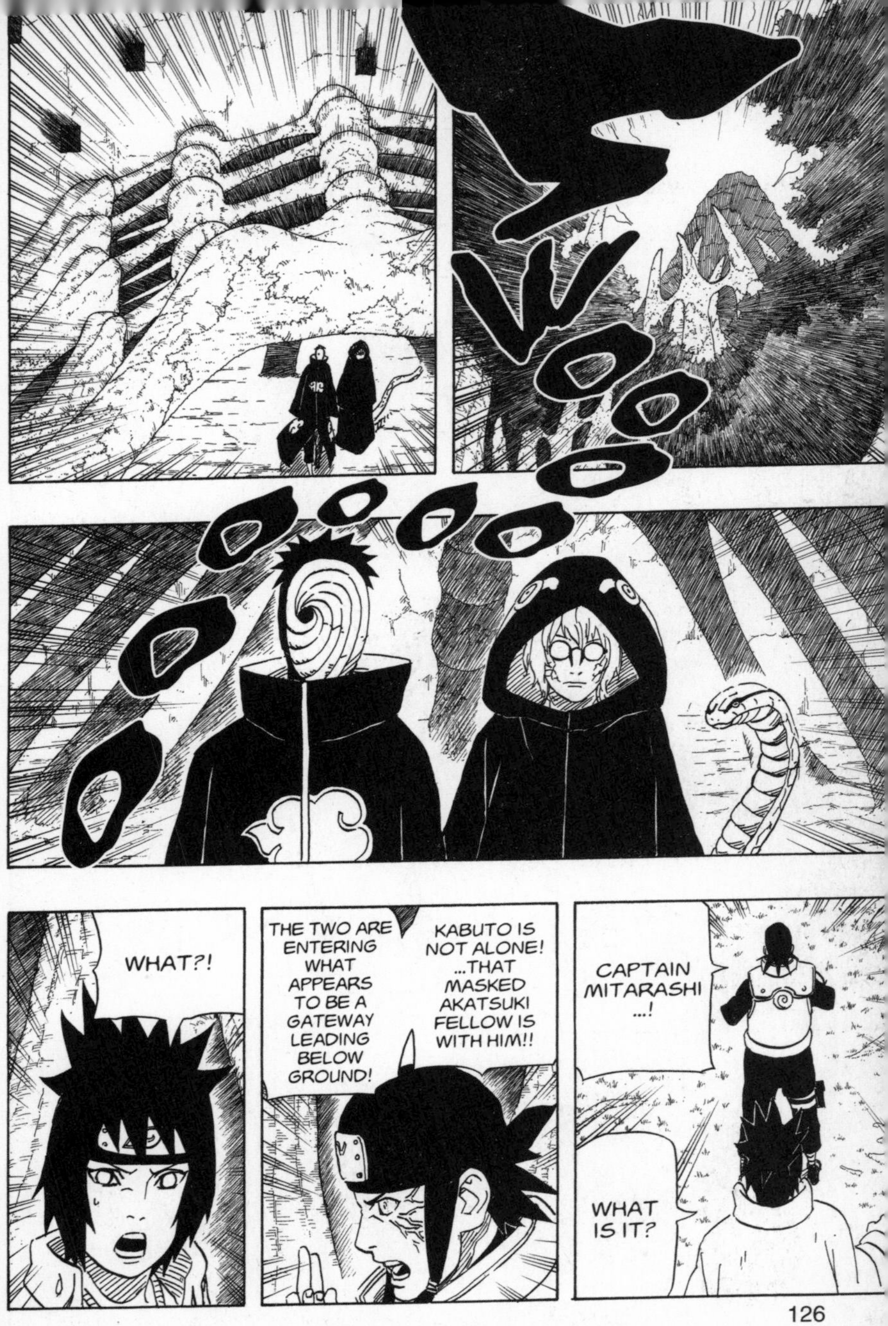

VWOOOOOOOOO
CAPTAIN MITARASHI ...!
WHAT IS IT?
KABUTO IS NOT ALONE! ...THAT MASKED AKATSUKI FELLOW IS WITH HIM!!
THE TWO ARE ENTERING WHAT APPEARS TO BE A GATEWAY LEADING BELOW GROUND!
WHAT?!

READ THIS WAY

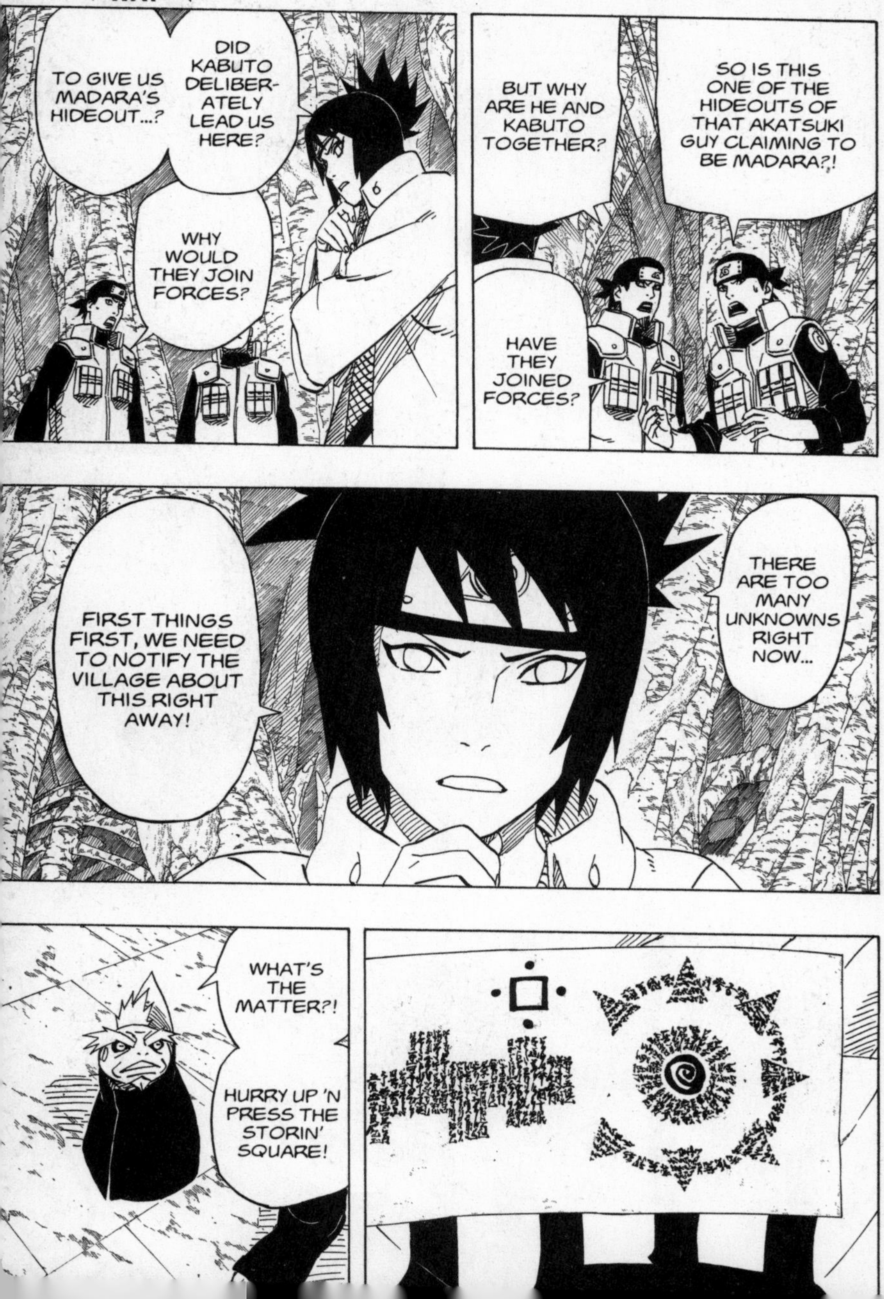
SO IS THIS ONE OF THE HIDEOUTS OF THAT AKATSUKI GUY CLAIMING TO BE MADARA?!
BUT WHY ARE HE AND KABUTO TOGETHER?
HAVE THEY JOINED FORCES?
DID KABUTO DELIBERATELY LEAD US HERE?
TO GIVE US MADARA'S HIDEOUT...?
WHY WOULD THEY JOIN FORCES?
THERE ARE TOO MANY UNKNOWNS RIGHT NOW...
FIRST THINGS FIRST, WE NEED TO NOTIFY THE VILLAGE ABOUT THIS RIGHT AWAY!
WHAT'S THE MATTER?!
HURRY UP 'N PRESS THE STORIN' SQUARE!

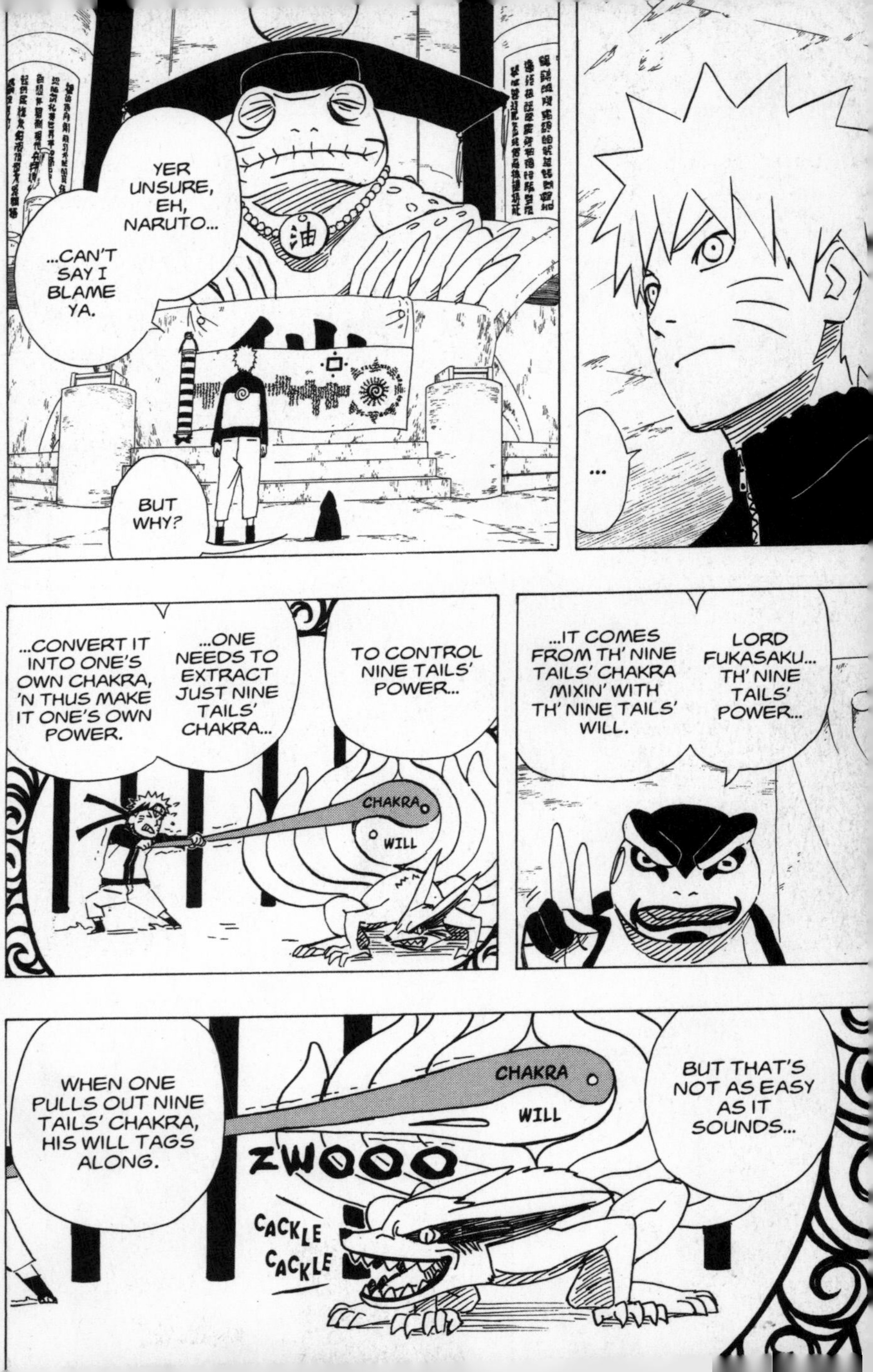
...
YER UNSURE, EH, NARUTO...
...CAN'T SAY I BLAME YA.
BUT WHY?
LORD FUKASAKU... TH' NINE TAILS' POWER...
...IT COMES FROM TH' NINE TAILS' CHAKRA MIXIN' WITH TH' NINE TAILS' WILL.
TO CONTROL NINE TAILS' POWER...
...ONE NEEDS TO EXTRACT JUST NINE TAILS' CHAKRA...
...CONVERT IT INTO ONE'S OWN CHAKRA, 'N THUS MAKE IT ONE'S OWN POWER.
CHAKRA
WILL
BUT THAT'S NOT AS EASY AS IT SOUNDS...
WHEN ONE PULLS OUT NINE TAILS' CHAKRA, HIS WILL TAGS ALONG.
CHAKRA
WILL
ZWOOO
CACKLE
CACKLE

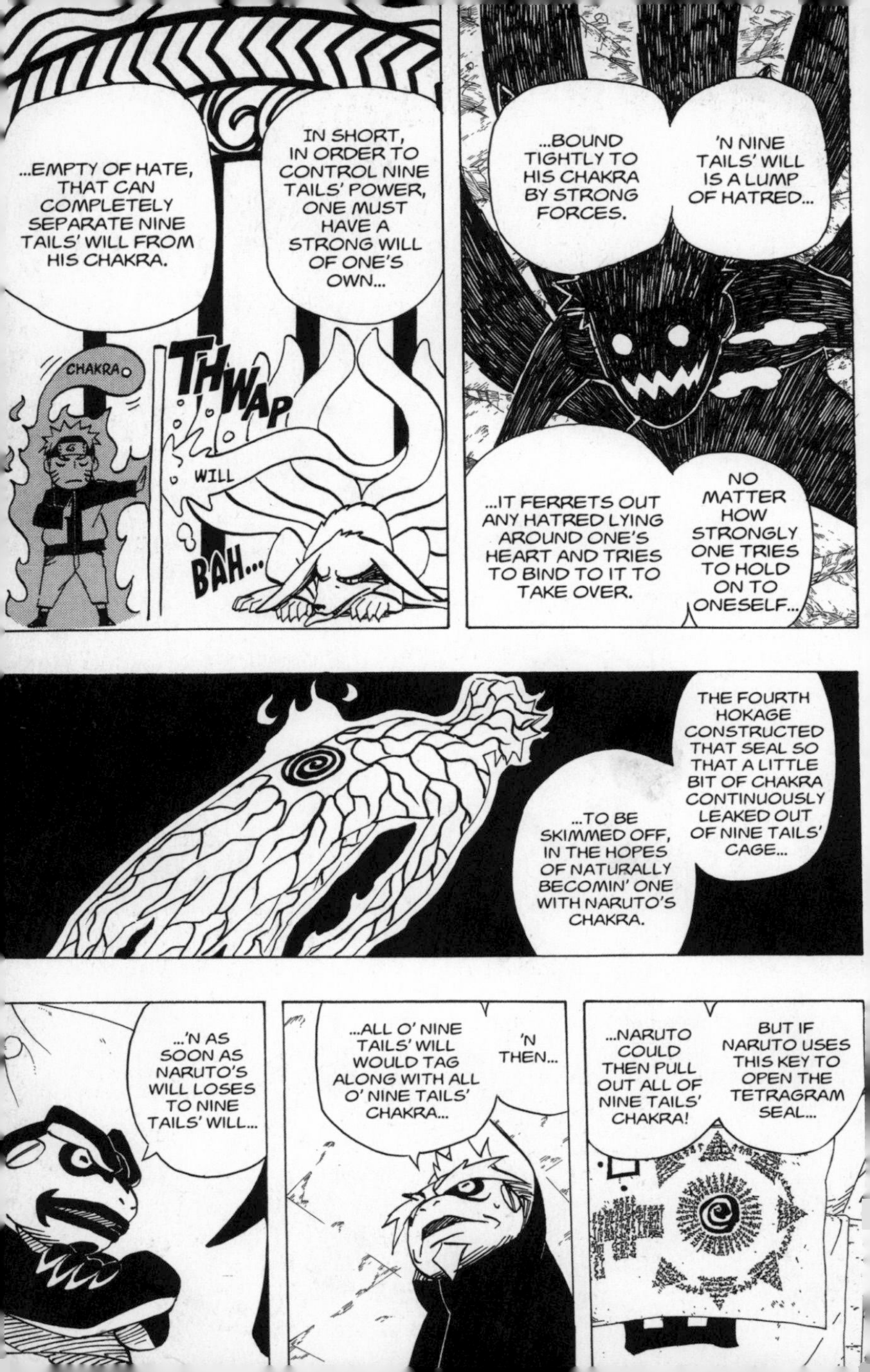
'N NINE TAILS' WILL IS A LUMP OF HATRED...
...BOUND TIGHTLY TO HIS CHAKRA BY STRONG FORCES.
NO MATTER HOW STRONGLY ONE TRIES TO HOLD ON TO ONESELF...
...IT FERRETS OUT ANY HATRED LYING AROUND ONE'S HEART AND TRIES TO BIND TO IT TO TAKE OVER.
IN SHORT, IN ORDER TO CONTROL NINE TAILS' POWER, ONE MUST HAVE A STRONG WILL OF ONE'S OWN...
...EMPTY OF HATE, THAT CAN COMPLETELY SEPARATE NINE TAILS' WILL FROM HIS CHAKRA.
THWAP
CHAKRA
WILL
BAH...
THE FOURTH HOKAGE CONSTRUCTED THAT SEAL SO THAT A LITTLE BIT OF CHAKRA CONTINUOUSLY LEAKED OUT OF NINE TAILS' CAGE...
...TO BE SKIMMED OFF, IN THE HOPES OF NATURALLY BECOMIN' ONE WITH NARUTO'S CHAKRA.
BUT IF NARUTO USES THIS KEY TO OPEN THE TETRAGRAM SEAL...
...NARUTO COULD THEN PULL OUT ALL OF NINE TAILS' CHAKRA!
'N THEN...
...ALL O' NINE TAILS' WILL WOULD TAG ALONG WITH ALL O' NINE TAILS' CHAKRA...
...'N AS SOON AS NARUTO'S WILL LOSES TO NINE TAILS' WILL...

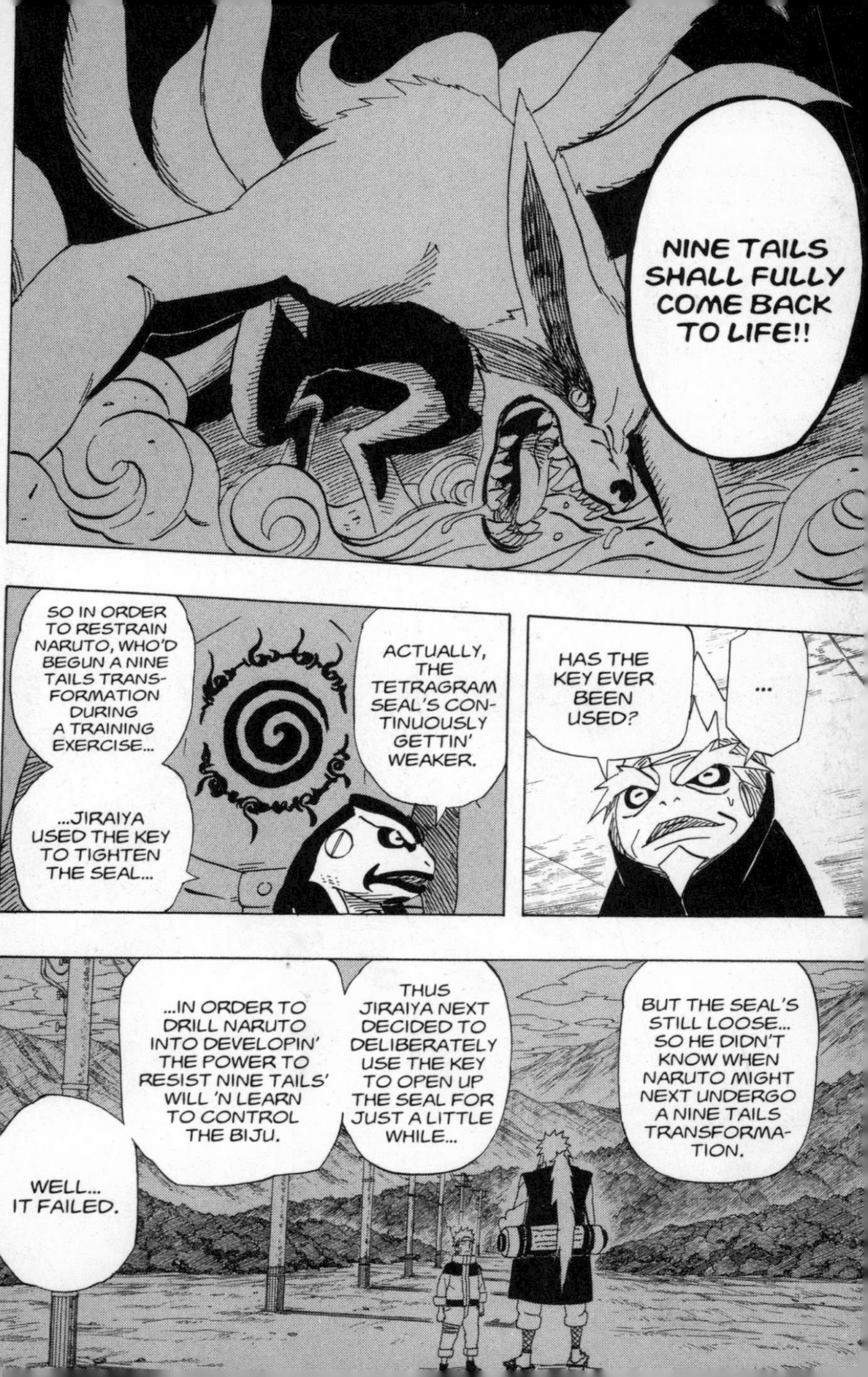
NINE TAILS SHALL FULLY COME BACK TO LIFE!!
...
HAS THE KEY EVER BEEN USED?
ACTUALLY, THE TETRAGRAM SEAL'S CON-TINUOUSLY GETTIN' WEAKER.
SO IN ORDER TO RESTRAIN NARUTO, WHO'D BEGUN A NINE TAILS TRANS-FORMATION DURING A TRAINING EXERCISE...
...JIRAIYA USED THE KEY TO TIGHTEN THE SEAL...
BUT THE SEAL'S STILL LOOSE... SO HE DIDN'T KNOW WHEN NARUTO MIGHT NEXT UNDERGO A NINE TAILS TRANSFORMA-TION.
THUS JIRAIYA NEXT DECIDED TO DELIBERATELY USE THE KEY TO OPEN UP THE SEAL FOR JUST A LITTLE WHILE...
...IN ORDER TO DRILL NARUTO INTO DEVELOPIN' THE POWER TO RESIST NINE TAILS' WILL 'N LEARN TO CONTROL THE BIJU.
WELL... IT FAILED.

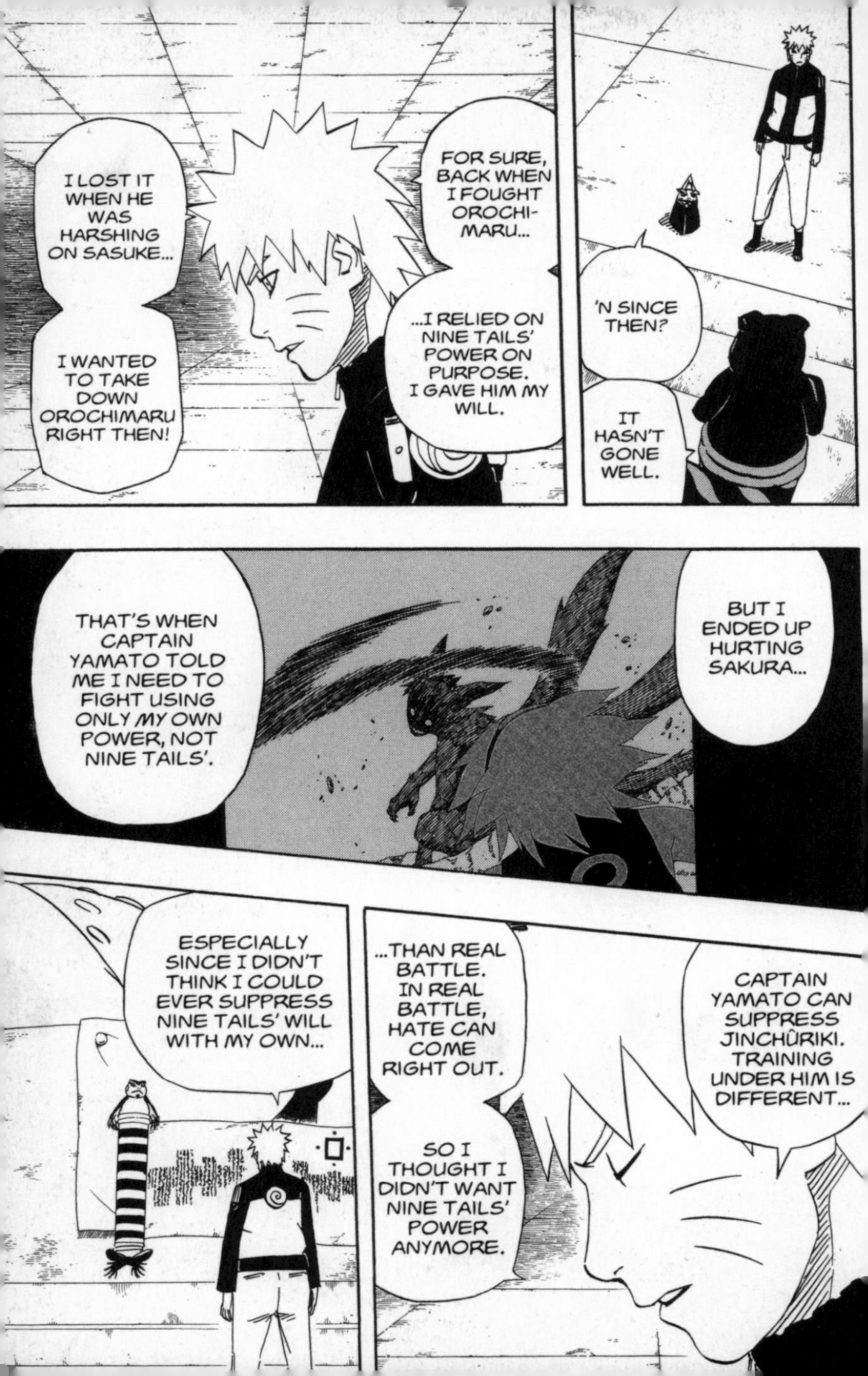
'N SINCE THEN?
IT HASN'T GONE WELL.
FOR SURE, BACK WHEN I FOUGHT OROCHI-MARU...
...I RELIED ON NINE TAILS' POWER ON PURPOSE. I GAVE HIM MY WILL.
I LOST IT WHEN HE WAS HARSHING ON SASUKE...
I WANTED TO TAKE DOWN OROCHIMARU RIGHT THEN!
BUT I ENDED UP HURTING SAKURA...
THAT'S WHEN CAPTAIN YAMATO TOLD ME I NEED TO FIGHT USING ONLY *MY OWN* POWER, NOT NINE TAILS'.
CAPTAIN YAMATO CAN SUPPRESS JINCHÛRIKI. TRAINING UNDER HIM IS DIFFERENT...
...THAN REAL BATTLE. IN REAL BATTLE, HATE CAN COME RIGHT OUT.
SO I THOUGHT I DIDN'T WANT NINE TAILS' POWER ANYMORE.
ESPECIALLY SINCE I DIDN'T THINK I COULD EVER SUPPRESS NINE TAILS' WILL WITH *MY* OWN...

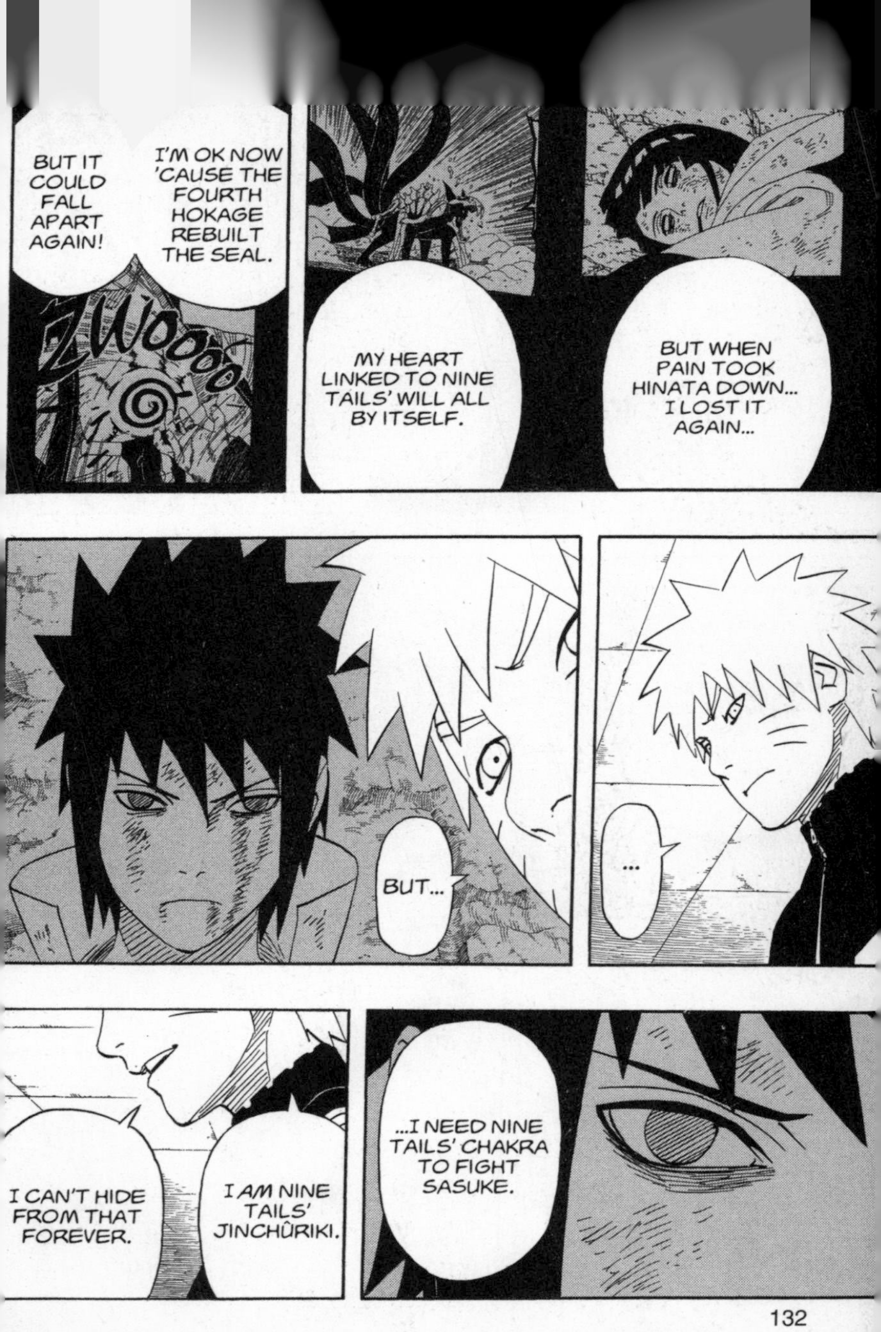
BUT WHEN PAIN TOOK HINATA DOWN... I LOST IT AGAIN...
MY HEART LINKED TO NINE TAILS' WILL ALL BY ITSELF.
I'M OK NOW 'CAUSE THE FOURTH HOKAGE REBUILT THE SEAL.
BUT IT COULD FALL APART AGAIN!
ZWOOOO
...
BUT...
...I NEED NINE TAILS' CHAKRA TO FIGHT SASUKE.
I *AM* NINE TAILS' JINCHÛRIKI.
I CAN'T HIDE FROM THAT FOREVER.

READ THIS WAY

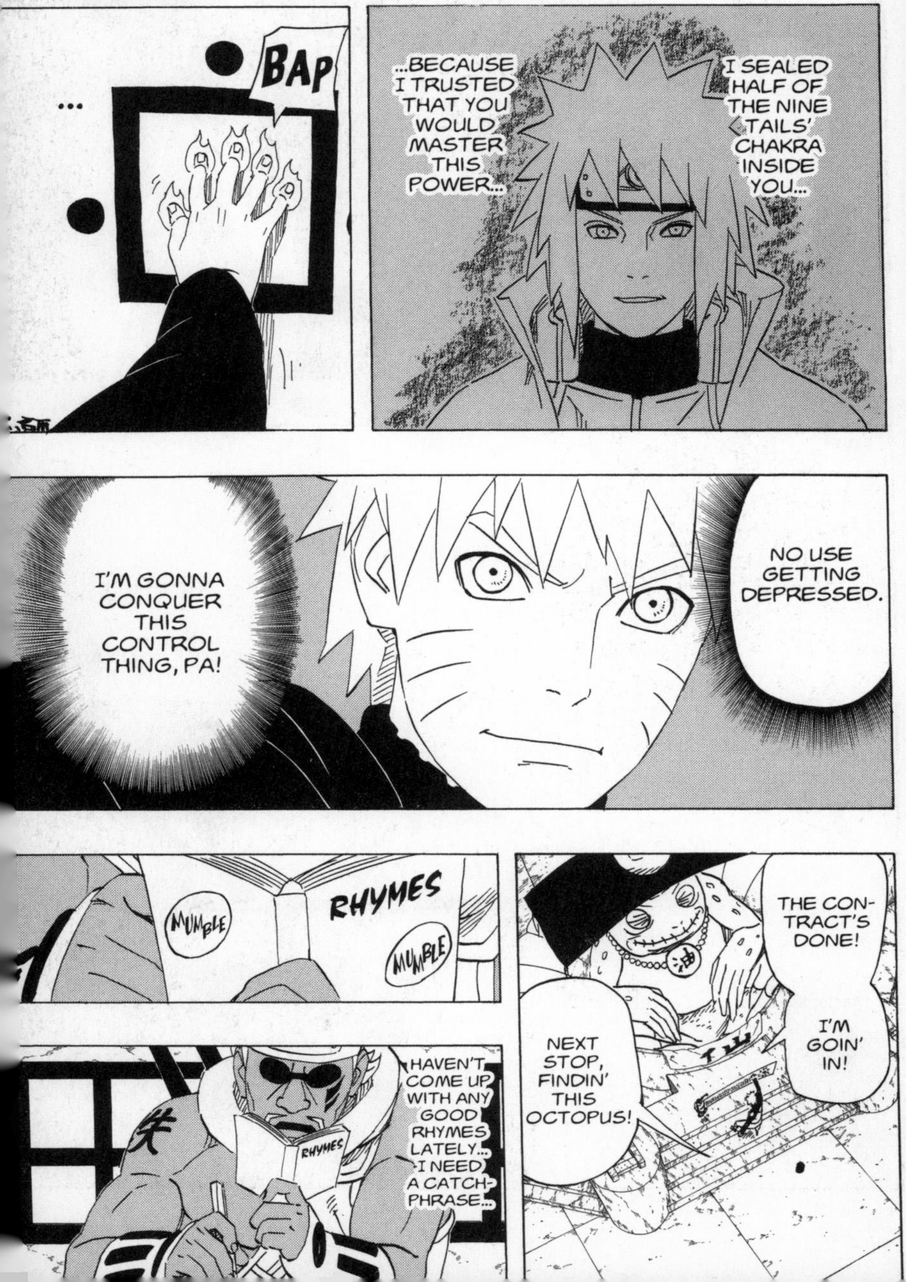
I SEALED HALF OF THE NINE TAILS' CHAKRA INSIDE YOU...
...BECAUSE I TRUSTED THAT YOU WOULD MASTER THIS POWER...
BAP
...
NO USE GETTING DEPRESSED.
I'M GONNA CONQUER THIS CONTROL THING, PA!
THE CON-TRACT'S DONE!
I'M GOIN' IN!
NEXT STOP, FINDIN' THIS OCTOPUS!
RHYMES
MUMBLE
MUMBLE
HAVEN'T COME UP WITH ANY GOOD RHYMES LATELY... I NEED A CATCH-PHRASE...
RHYMES

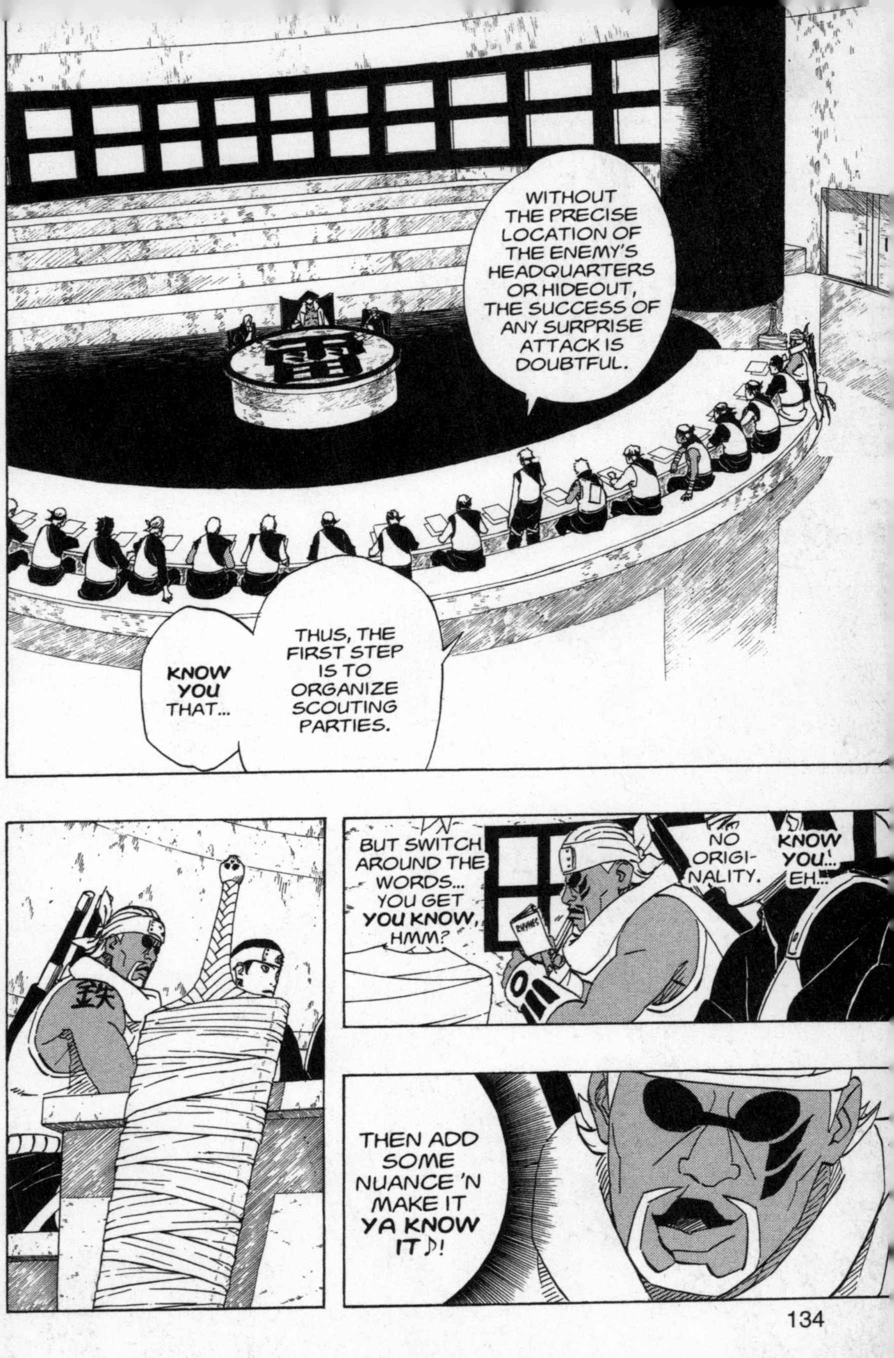
WITHOUT THE PRECISE LOCATION OF THE ENEMY'S HEADQUARTERS OR HIDEOUT, THE SUCCESS OF ANY SURPRISE ATTACK IS DOUBTFUL.
THUS, THE FIRST STEP IS TO ORGANIZE SCOUTING PARTIES.
KNOW YOU THAT...
KNOW YOU... EH...
NO ORIGINALITY.
BUT SWITCH AROUND THE WORDS... YOU GET YOU KNOW, HMM?
RHYMES
THEN ADD SOME NUANCE 'N MAKE IT YA KNOW IT♪!
鉄

READ THIS WAY

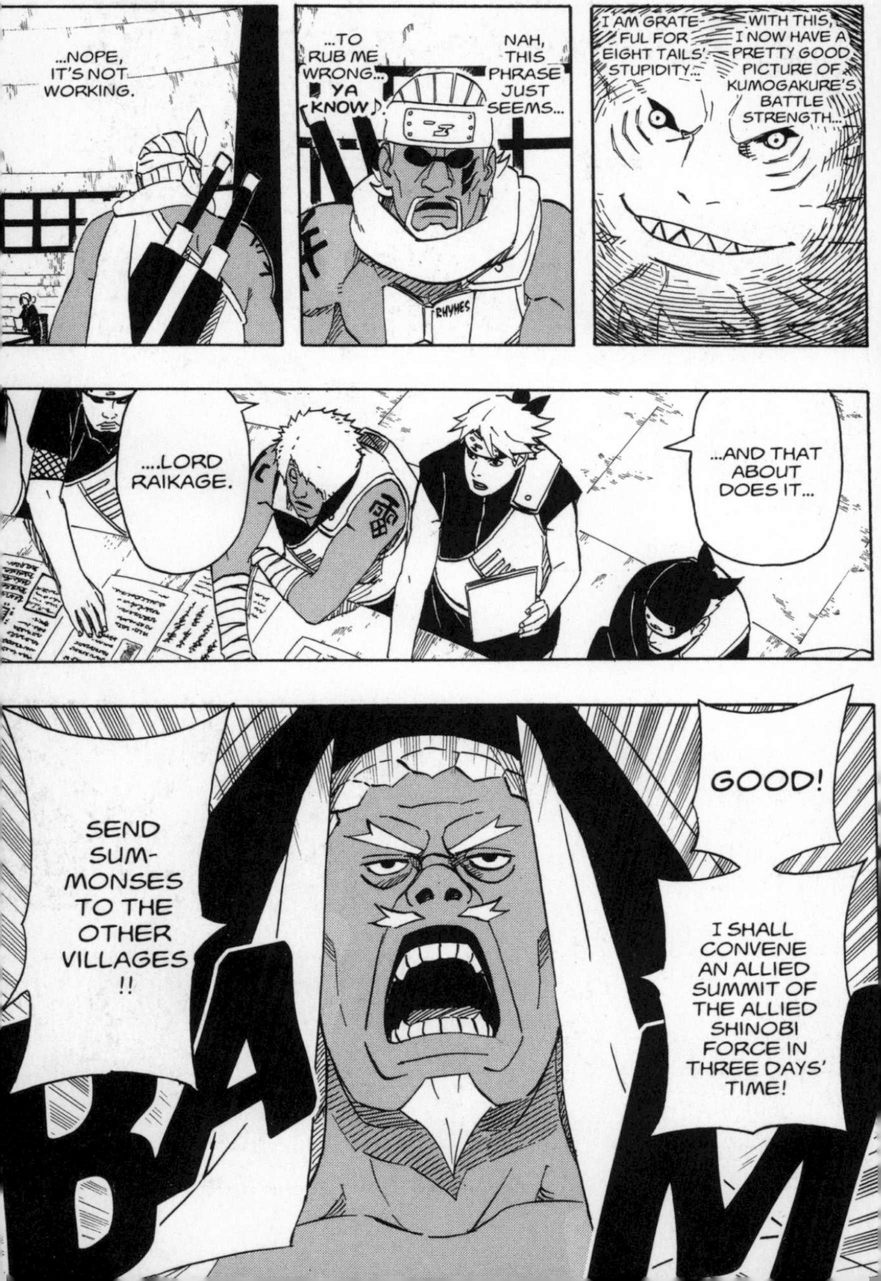
WITH THIS, I NOW HAVE A PRETTY GOOD PICTURE OF KUMOGAKURE'S BATTLE STRENGTH...
I AM GRATEFUL FOR EIGHT TAILS' STUPIDITY...
NAH, THIS PHRASE JUST SEEMS...
...TO RUB ME WRONG... YA KNOW♪
RHYMES
...NOPE, IT'S NOT WORKING.
...AND THAT ABOUT DOES IT...
....LORD RAIKAGE.
GOOD!
I SHALL CONVENE AN ALLIED SUMMIT OF THE ALLIED SHINOBI FORCE IN THREE DAYS' TIME!
SEND SUMMONSES TO THE OTHER VILLAGES!!

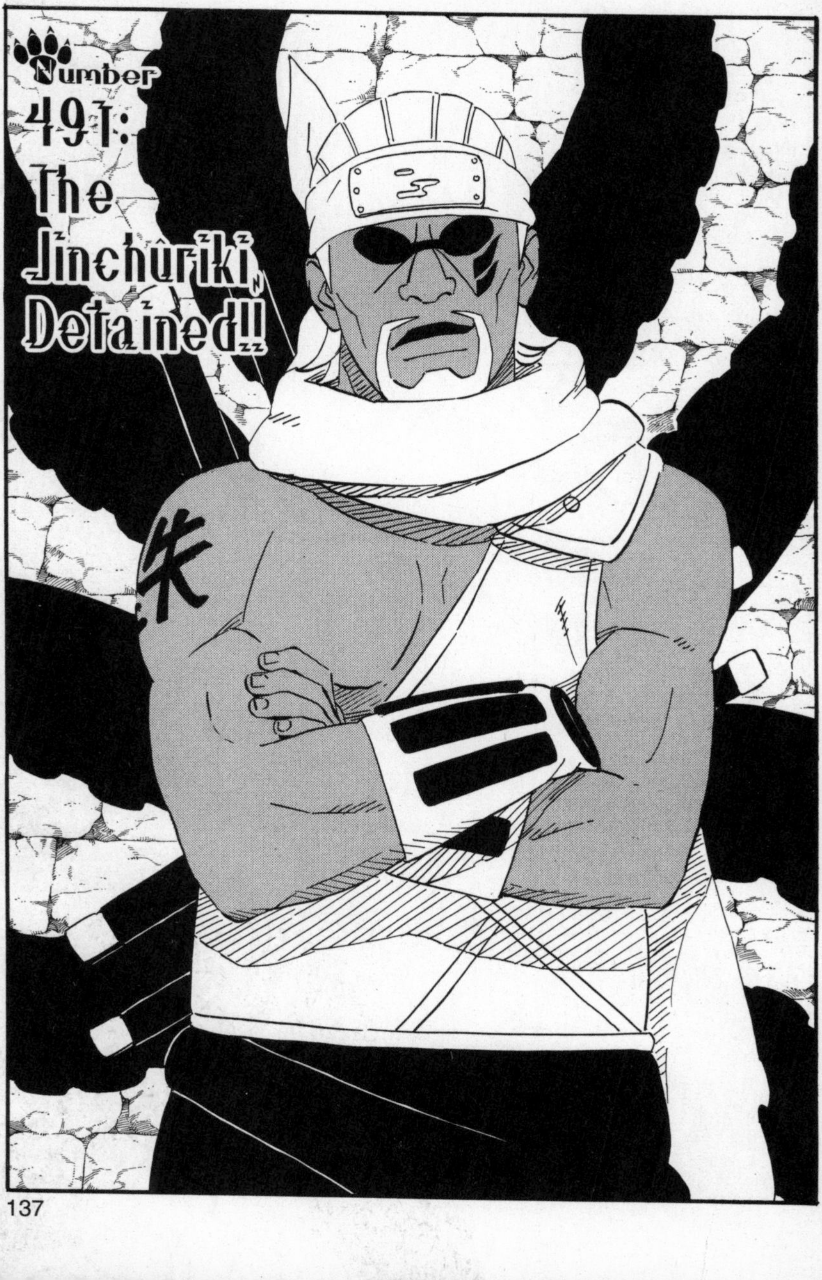
Number 491: The Jinchûriki Detained!!

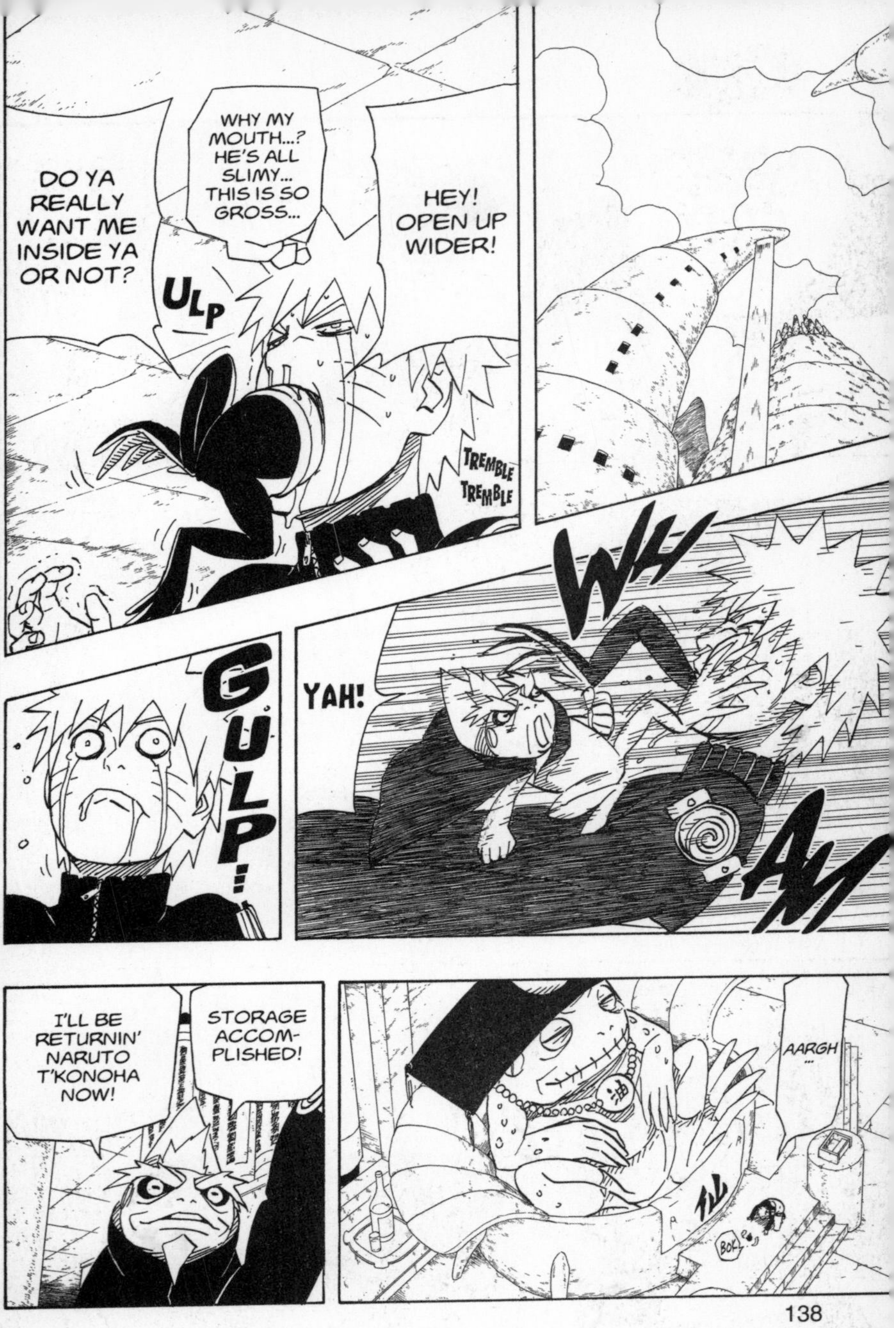
HEY! OPEN UP WIDER!
WHY MY MOUTH...? HE'S ALL SLIMY... THIS IS SO GROSS...
DO YA REALLY WANT ME INSIDE YA OR NOT?
TREMBLE TREMBLE
ULP
WHAM
YAH!
GULP!!
AARGH ...
BOK
STORAGE ACCOMPLISHED!
I'LL BE RETURNIN' NARUTO T'KONOHA NOW!

READ THIS WAY

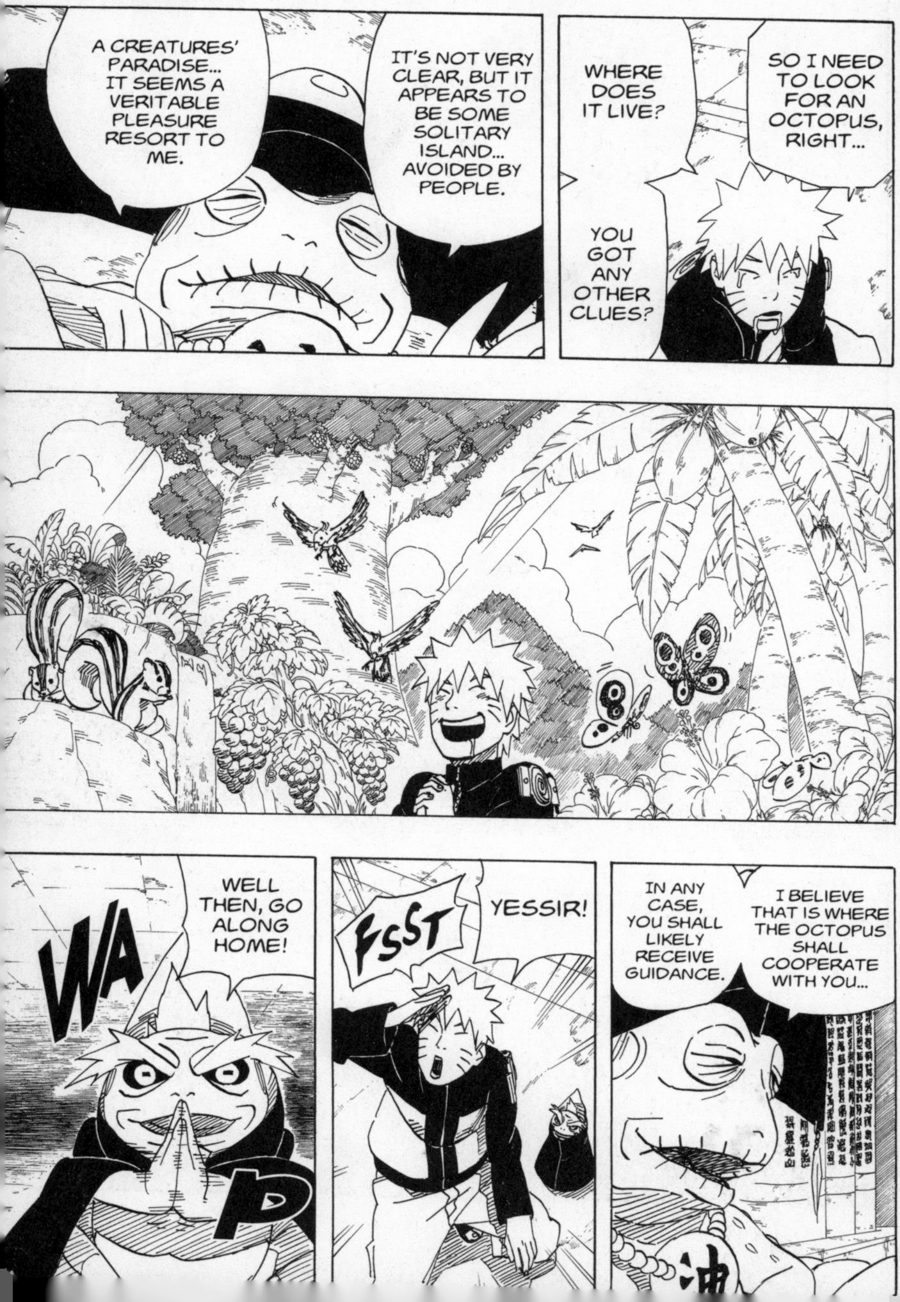

SO I NEED TO LOOK FOR AN OCTOPUS, RIGHT...
WHERE DOES IT LIVE?
YOU GOT ANY OTHER CLUES?
IT'S NOT VERY CLEAR, BUT IT APPEARS TO BE SOME SOLITARY ISLAND... AVOIDED BY PEOPLE.
A CREATURES' PARADISE... IT SEEMS A VERITABLE PLEASURE RESORT TO ME.
I BELIEVE THAT IS WHERE THE OCTOPUS SHALL COOPERATE WITH YOU...
IN ANY CASE, YOU SHALL LIKELY RECEIVE GUIDANCE.
YESSIR!
FSST
WELL THEN, GO ALONG HOME!
WAP

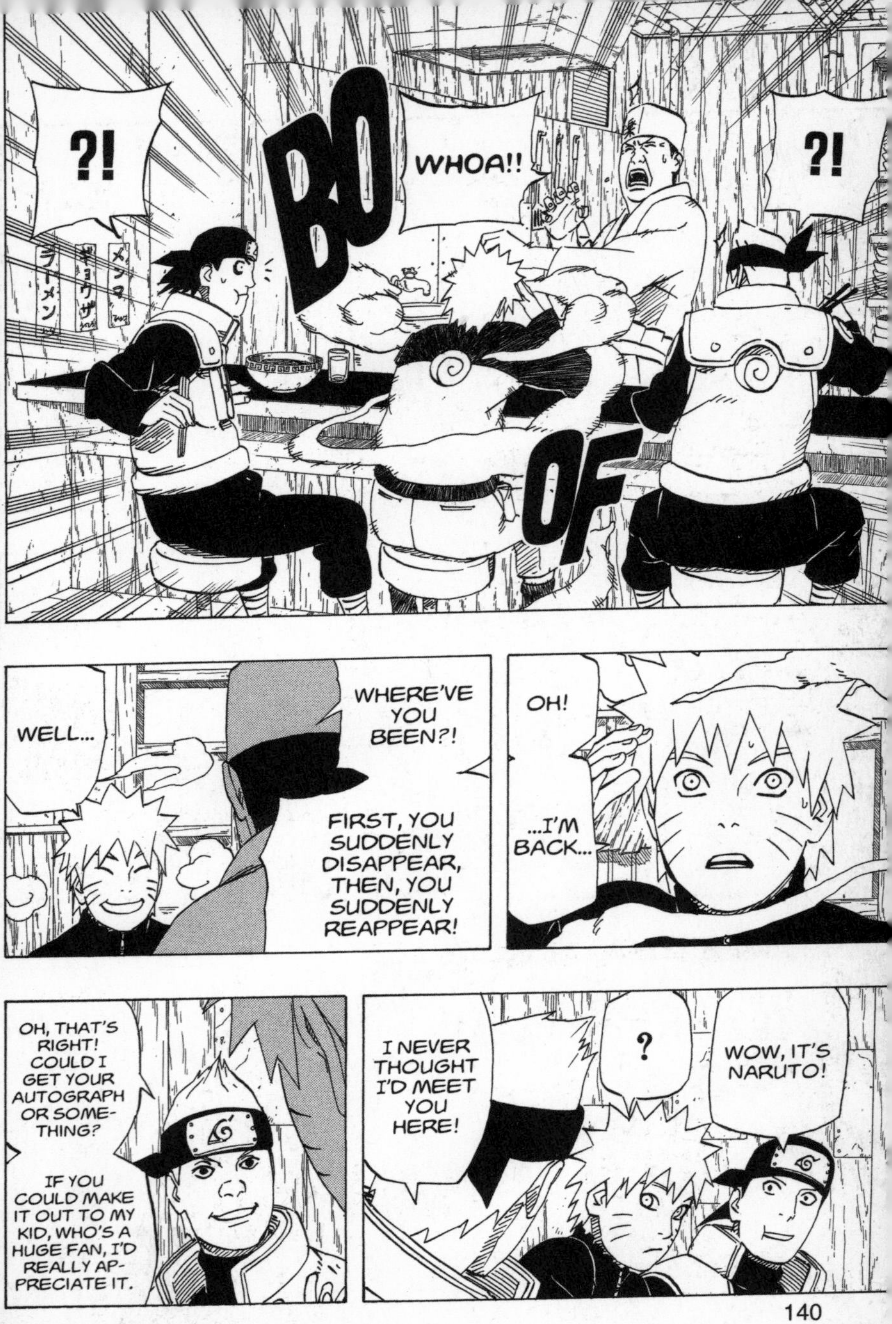
?!
WHOA!!
BO
OF
?!
メンマ
ギョウザ
ラーメン
OH!
...I'M BACK...
WHERE'VE YOU BEEN?!
FIRST, YOU SUDDENLY DISAPPEAR, THEN, YOU SUDDENLY REAPPEAR!
WELL...
WOW, IT'S NARUTO!
?
I NEVER THOUGHT I'D MEET YOU HERE!
OH, THAT'S RIGHT! COULD I GET YOUR AUTOGRAPH OR SOME-THING?
IF YOU COULD MAKE IT OUT TO MY KID, WHO'S A HUGE FAN, I'D REALLY AP-PRECIATE IT.

READ THIS WAY

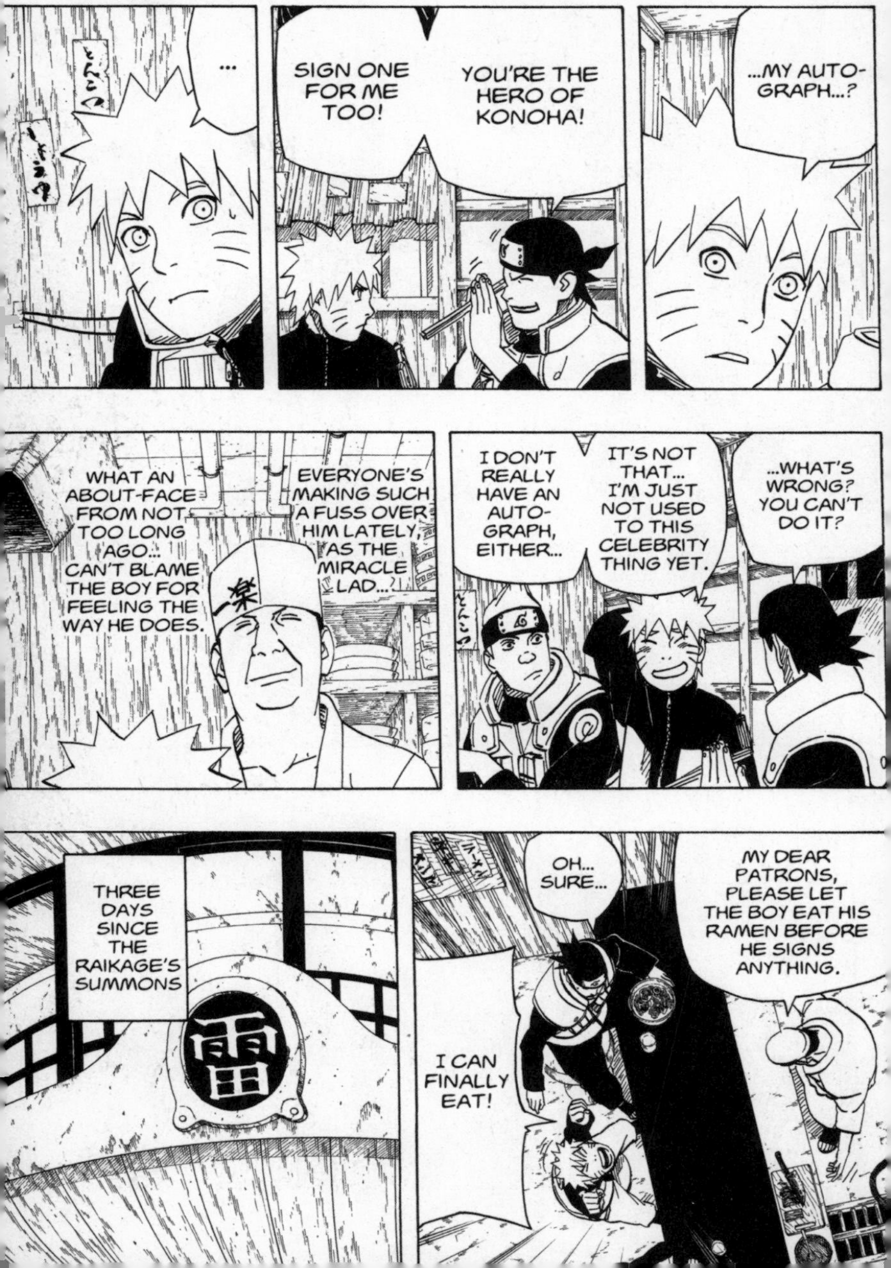

...MY AUTO-GRAPH...?
YOU'RE THE HERO OF KONOHA!
SIGN ONE FOR ME TOO!
...
...WHAT'S WRONG? YOU CAN'T DO IT?
IT'S NOT THAT... I'M JUST NOT USED TO THIS CELEBRITY THING YET.
I DON'T REALLY HAVE AN AUTO-GRAPH, EITHER...
EVERYONE'S MAKING SUCH A FUSS OVER HIM LATELY, AS THE MIRACLE LAD...?
WHAT AN ABOUT-FACE FROM NOT TOO LONG AGO... CAN'T BLAME THE BOY FOR FEELING THE WAY HE DOES.
MY DEAR PATRONS, PLEASE LET THE BOY EAT HIS RAMEN BEFORE HE SIGNS ANYTHING.
OH... SURE...
I CAN FINALLY EAT!
THREE DAYS SINCE THE RAIKAGE'S SUMMONS

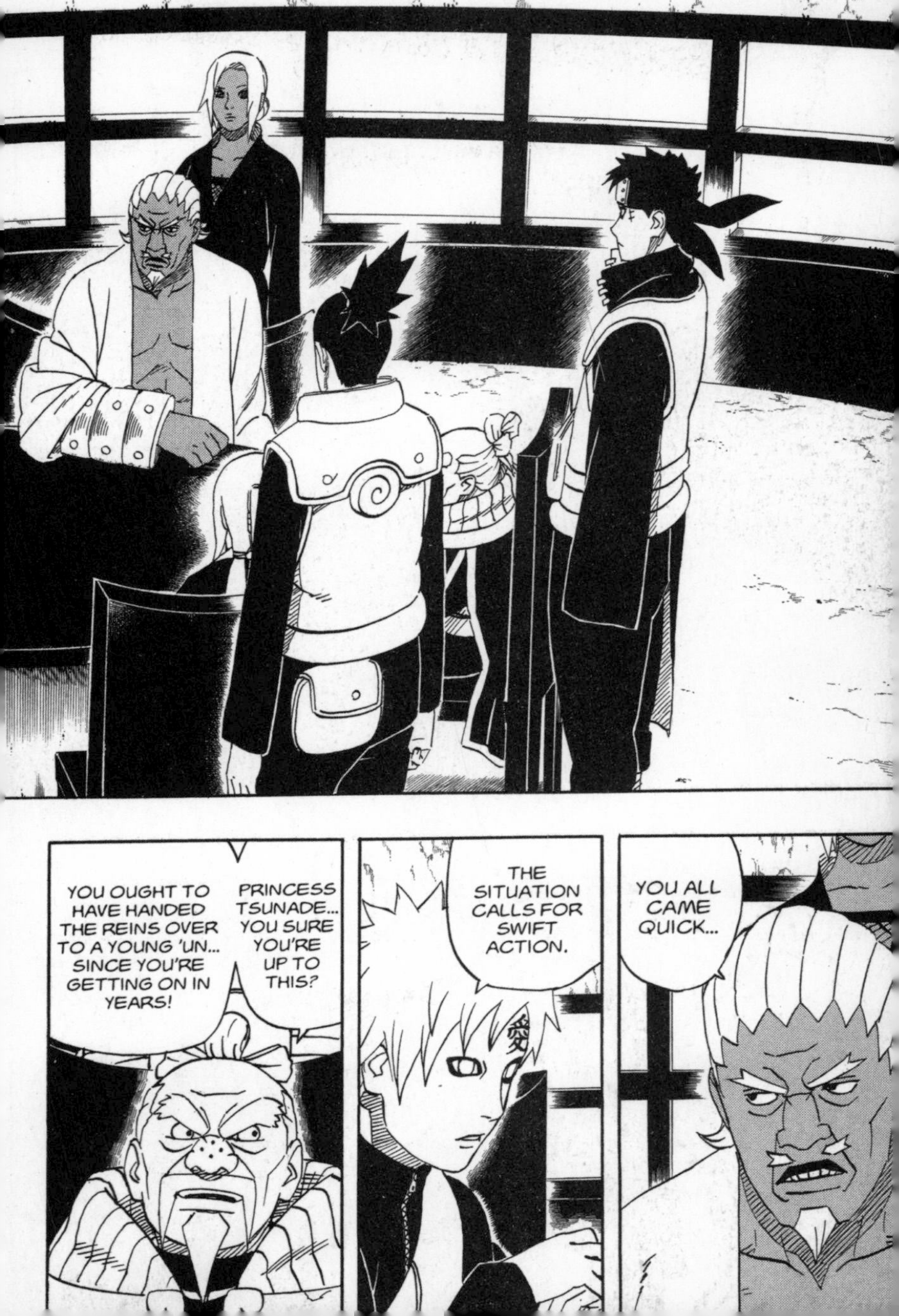
YOU ALL CAME QUICK...
THE SITUATION CALLS FOR SWIFT ACTION.
PRINCESS TSUNADE... YOU SURE YOU'RE UP TO THIS?
YOU OUGHT TO HAVE HANDED THE REINS OVER TO A YOUNG 'UN... SINCE YOU'RE GETTING ON IN YEARS!

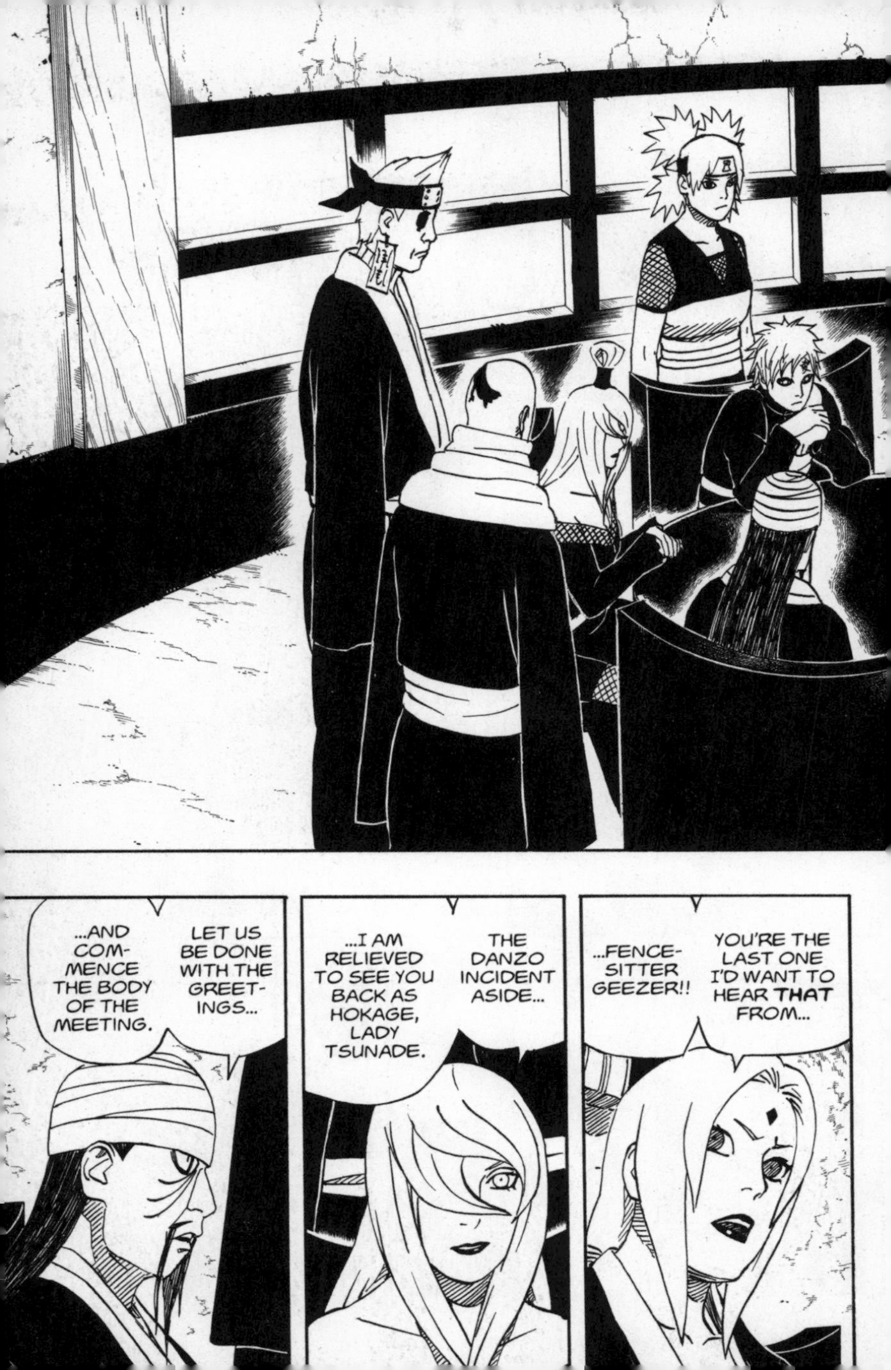
YOU'RE THE LAST ONE I'D WANT TO HEAR **THAT** FROM...
...FENCE-SITTER GEEZER!!
THE DANZO INCIDENT ASIDE...
...I AM RELIEVED TO SEE YOU BACK AS HOKAGE, LADY TSUNADE.
LET US BE DONE WITH THE GREETINGS...
...AND COMMENCE THE BODY OF THE MEETING.

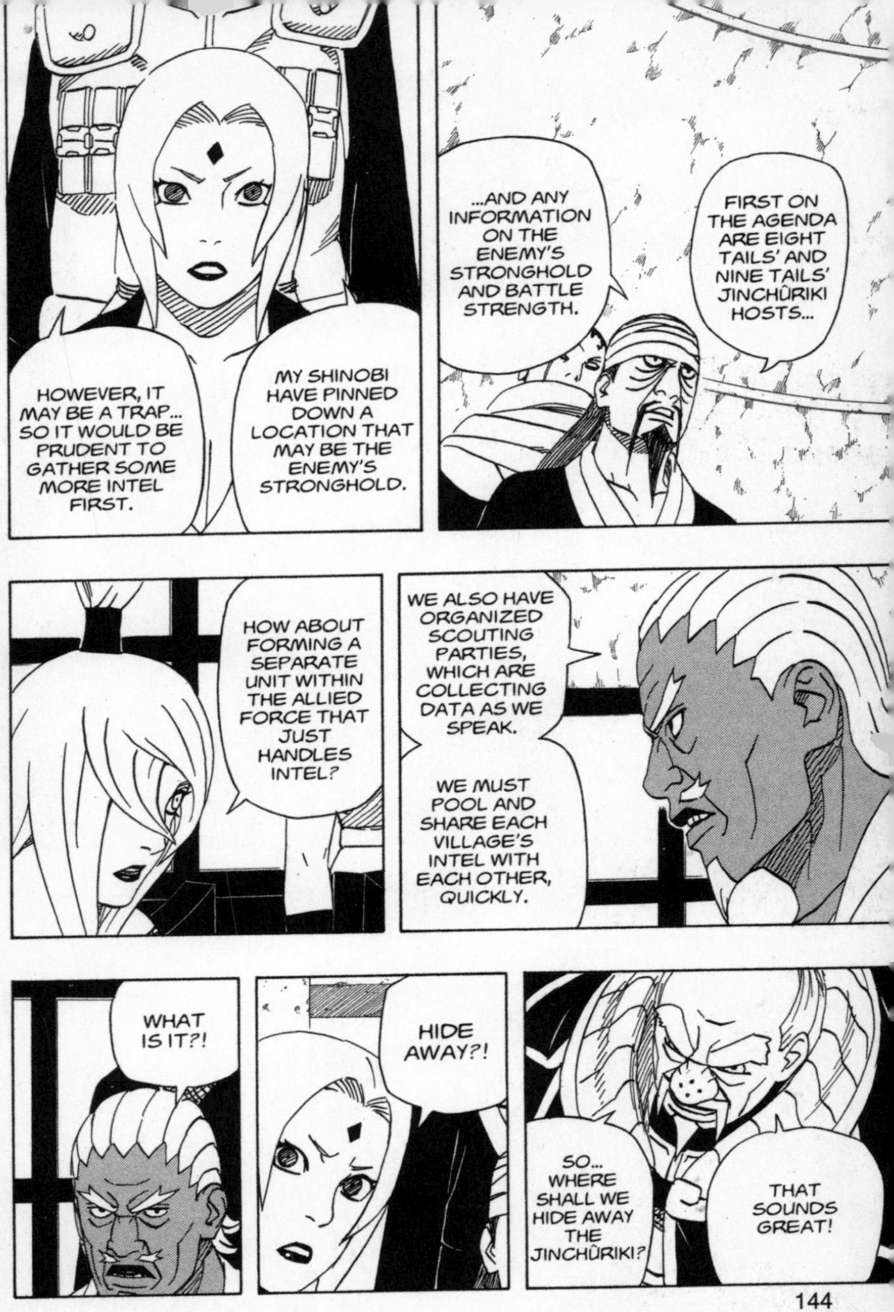
FIRST ON THE AGENDA ARE EIGHT TAILS' AND NINE TAILS' JINCHÛRIKI HOSTS...
...AND ANY INFORMATION ON THE ENEMY'S STRONGHOLD AND BATTLE STRENGTH.
MY SHINOBI HAVE PINNED DOWN A LOCATION THAT MAY BE THE ENEMY'S STRONGHOLD.
HOWEVER, IT MAY BE A TRAP... SO IT WOULD BE PRUDENT TO GATHER SOME MORE INTEL FIRST.
WE ALSO HAVE ORGANIZED SCOUTING PARTIES, WHICH ARE COLLECTING DATA AS WE SPEAK.
WE MUST POOL AND SHARE EACH VILLAGE'S INTEL WITH EACH OTHER, QUICKLY.
HOW ABOUT FORMING A SEPARATE UNIT WITHIN THE ALLIED FORCE THAT JUST HANDLES INTEL?
THAT SOUNDS GREAT!
SO... WHERE SHALL WE HIDE AWAY THE JINCHÛRIKI?
HIDE AWAY?!
WHAT IS IT?!

READ THIS WAY

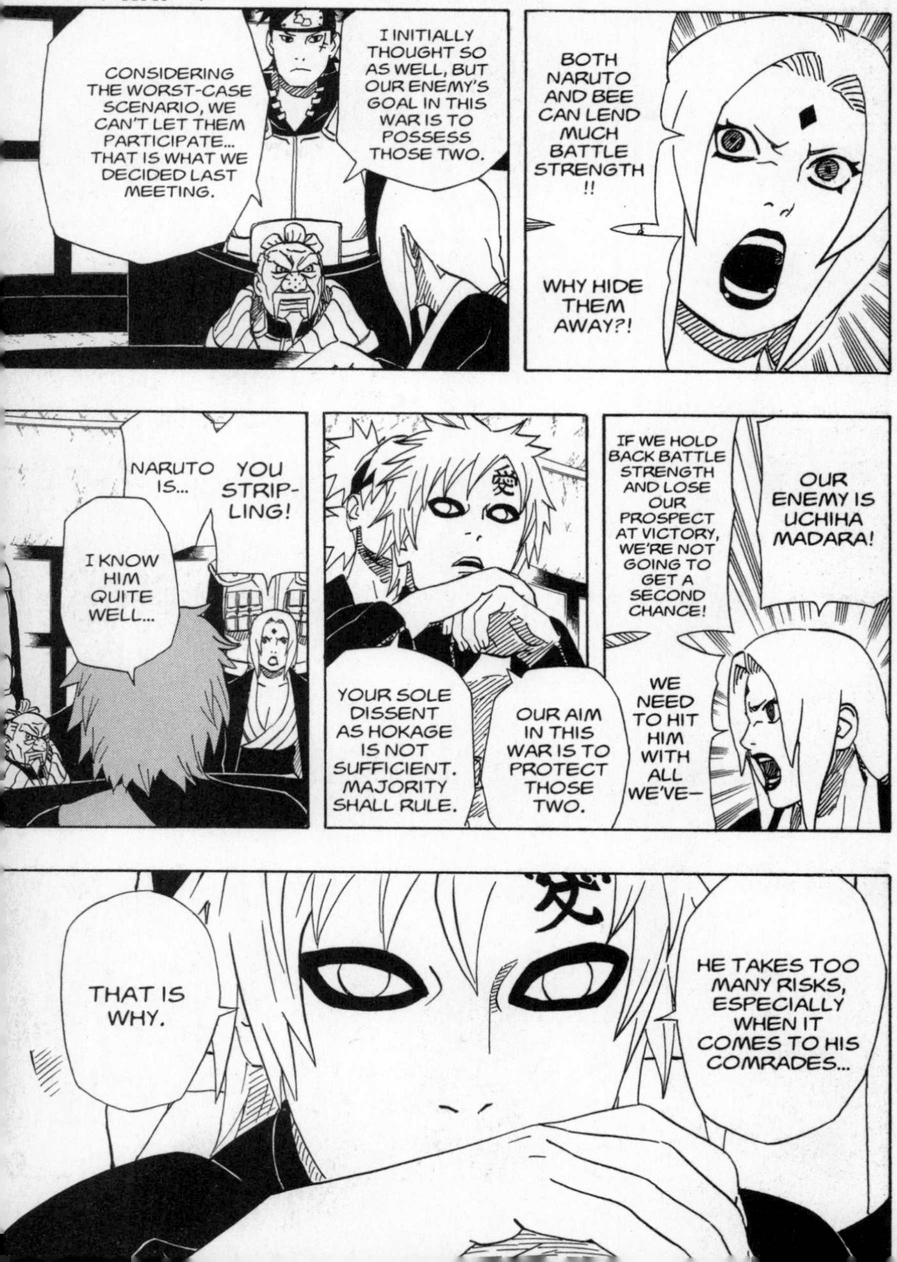
BOTH NARUTO AND BEE CAN LEND MUCH BATTLE STRENGTH !!
WHY HIDE THEM AWAY?!
I INITIALLY THOUGHT SO AS WELL, BUT OUR ENEMY'S GOAL IN THIS WAR IS TO POSSESS THOSE TWO.
CONSIDERING THE WORST-CASE SCENARIO, WE CAN'T LET THEM PARTICIPATE... THAT IS WHAT WE DECIDED LAST MEETING.
OUR ENEMY IS UCHIHA MADARA!
IF WE HOLD BACK BATTLE STRENGTH AND LOSE OUR PROSPECT AT VICTORY, WE'RE NOT GOING TO GET A SECOND CHANCE!
WE NEED TO HIT HIM WITH ALL WE'VE—
OUR AIM IN THIS WAR IS TO PROTECT THOSE TWO.
YOUR SOLE DISSENT AS HOKAGE IS NOT SUFFICIENT. MAJORITY SHALL RULE.
YOU STRIP-LING!
NARUTO IS...
I KNOW HIM QUITE WELL...
HE TAKES TOO MANY RISKS, ESPECIALLY WHEN IT COMES TO HIS COMRADES...
THAT IS WHY.

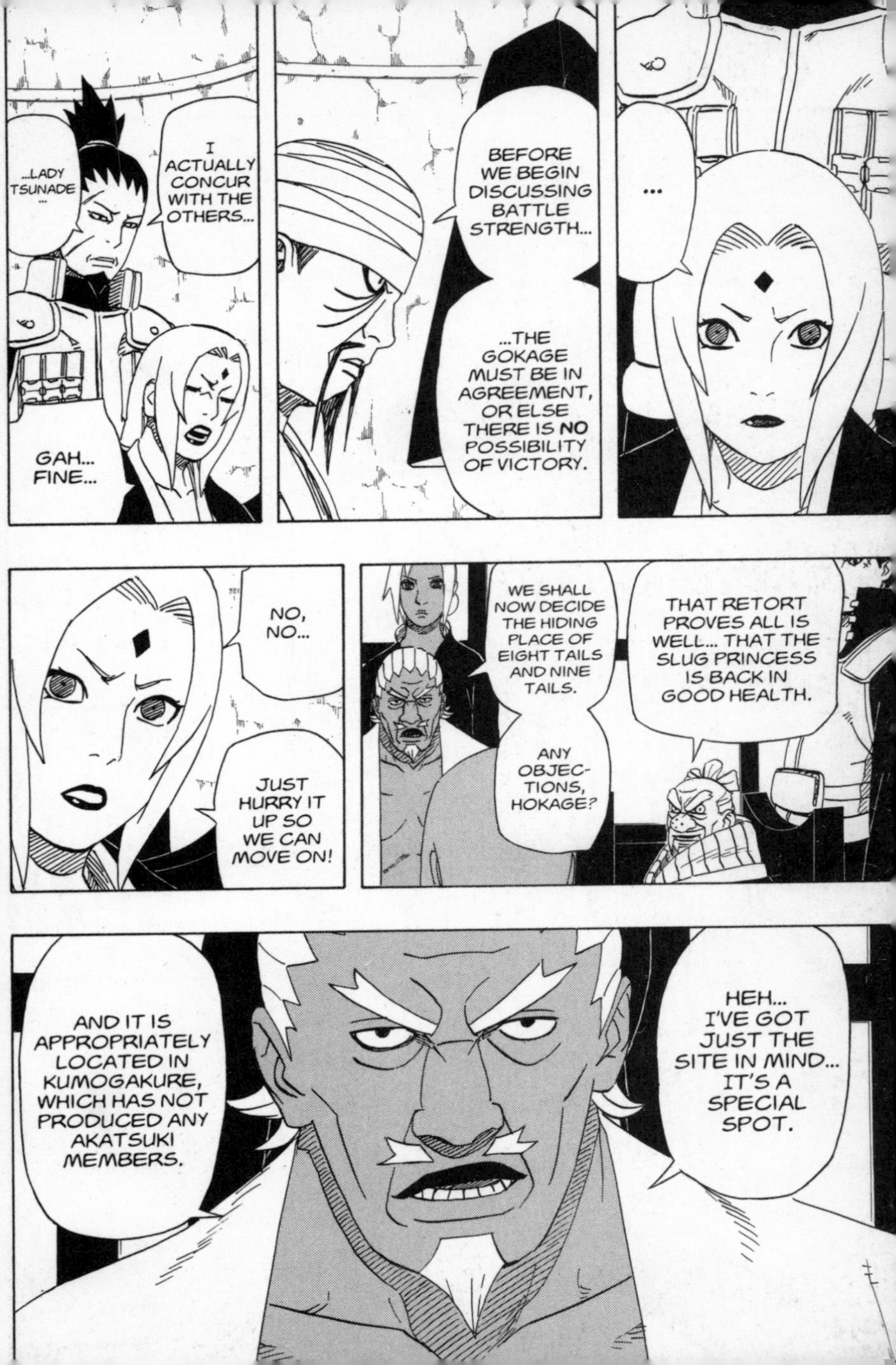
...
BEFORE WE BEGIN DISCUSSING BATTLE STRENGTH...
...THE GOKAGE MUST BE IN AGREEMENT, OR ELSE THERE IS **NO** POSSIBILITY OF VICTORY.
I ACTUALLY CONCUR WITH THE OTHERS...
...LADY TSUNADE ...
GAH... FINE...
THAT RETORT PROVES ALL IS WELL... THAT THE SLUG PRINCESS IS BACK IN GOOD HEALTH.
WE SHALL NOW DECIDE THE HIDING PLACE OF EIGHT TAILS AND NINE TAILS.
ANY OBJEC-TIONS, HOKAGE?
NO, NO...
JUST HURRY IT UP SO WE CAN MOVE ON!
HEH... I'VE GOT JUST THE SITE IN MIND... IT'S A SPECIAL SPOT.
AND IT IS APPROPRIATELY LOCATED IN KUMOGAKURE, WHICH HAS NOT PRODUCED ANY AKATSUKI MEMBERS.

READ THIS WAY

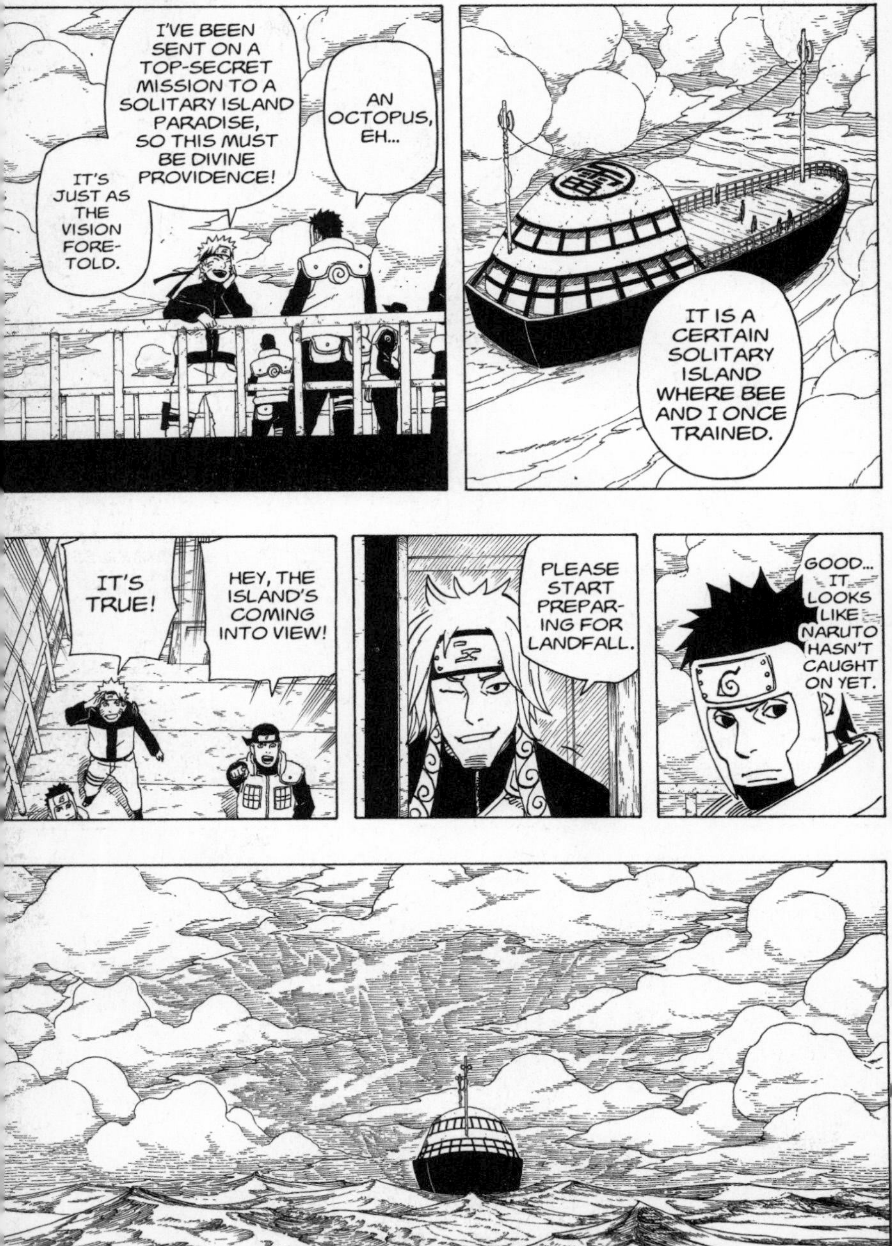
IT IS A CERTAIN SOLITARY ISLAND WHERE BEE AND I ONCE TRAINED.
AN OCTOPUS, EH...
I'VE BEEN SENT ON A TOP-SECRET MISSION TO A SOLITARY ISLAND PARADISE, SO THIS MUST BE DIVINE PROVIDENCE!
IT'S JUST AS THE VISION FORE-TOLD.
GOOD... IT LOOKS LIKE NARUTO HASN'T CAUGHT ON YET.
PLEASE START PREPAR-ING FOR LANDFALL.
HEY, THE ISLAND'S COMING INTO VIEW!
IT'S TRUE!

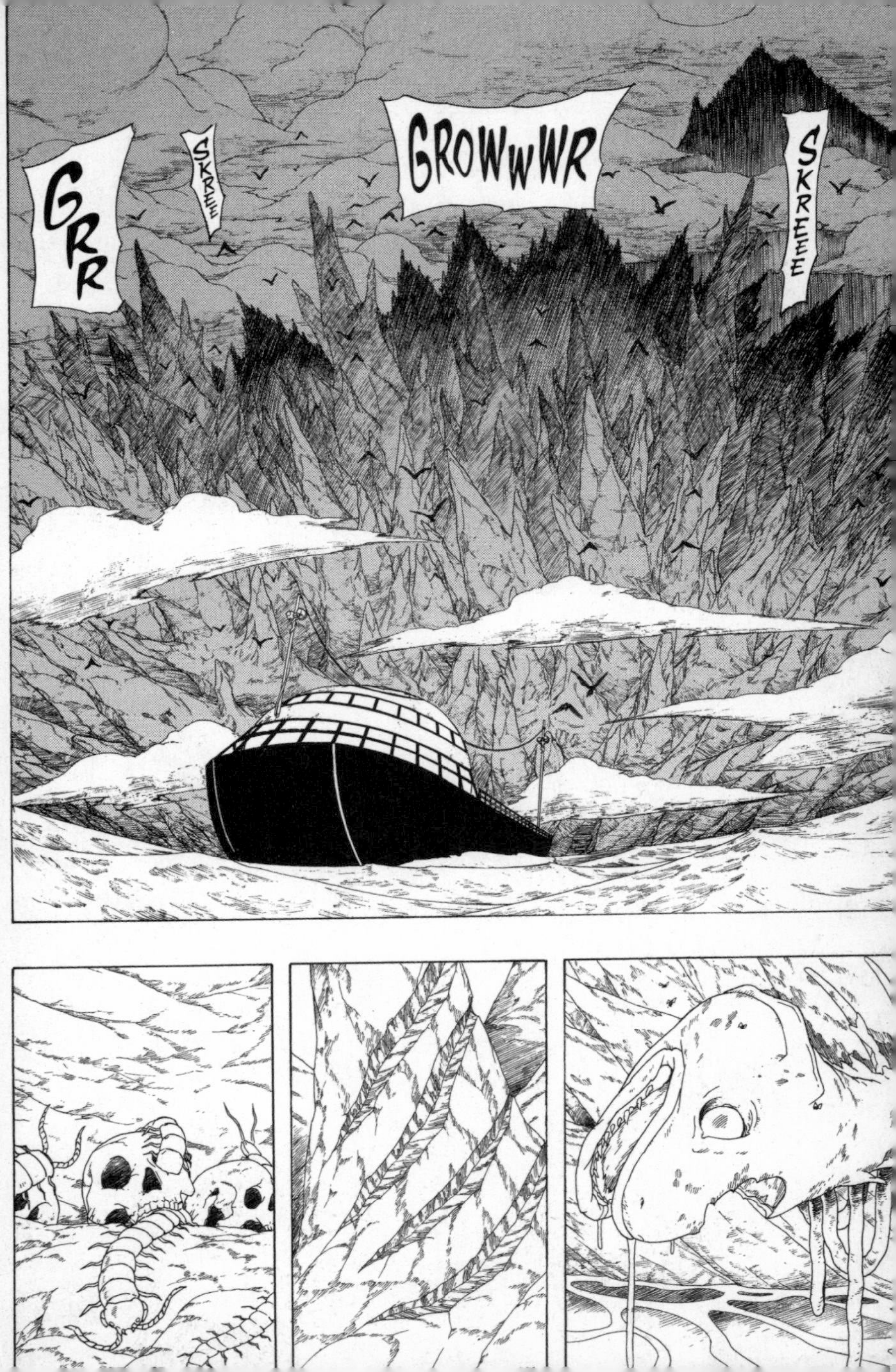
SKREEE
GROWWWR
SKREE
GRR

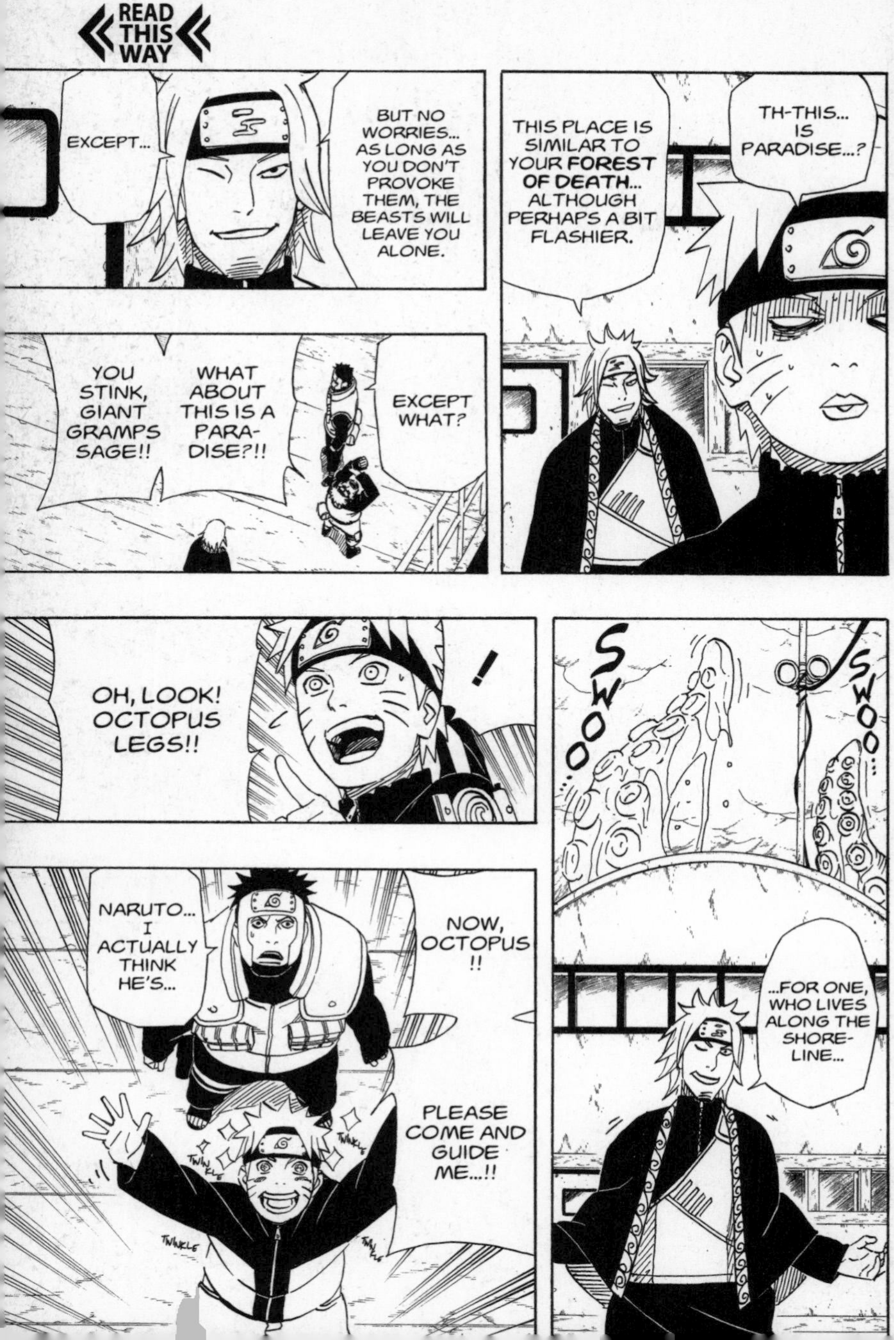
READ THIS WAY
TH-THIS... IS PARADISE...?
THIS PLACE IS SIMILAR TO YOUR FOREST OF DEATH... ALTHOUGH PERHAPS A BIT FLASHIER.
BUT NO WORRIES... AS LONG AS YOU DON'T PROVOKE THEM, THE BEASTS WILL LEAVE YOU ALONE.
EXCEPT...
EXCEPT WHAT?
WHAT ABOUT THIS IS A PARA-DISE?!!
YOU STINK, GIANT GRAMPS SAGE!!
SWOOO...
SWOOO...
...FOR ONE, WHO LIVES ALONG THE SHORE-LINE...
!
OH, LOOK! OCTOPUS LEGS!!
NOW, OCTOPUS!!
PLEASE COME AND GUIDE ME...!!
NARUTO... I ACTUALLY THINK HE'S...
TWINKLE
TWINKLE
TWINKLE
TWINKLE

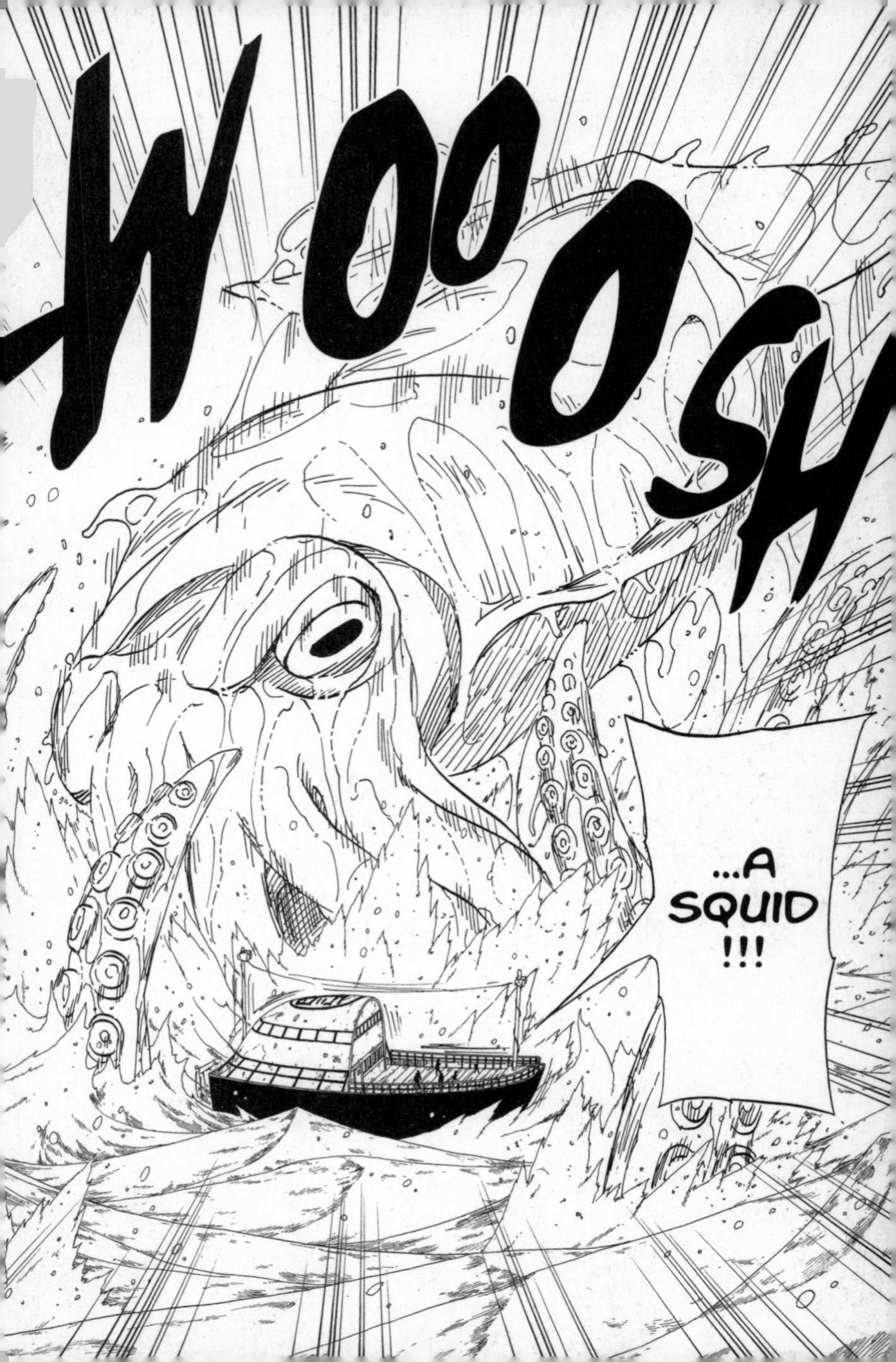
WHOOOOSH
...A SQUID !!!

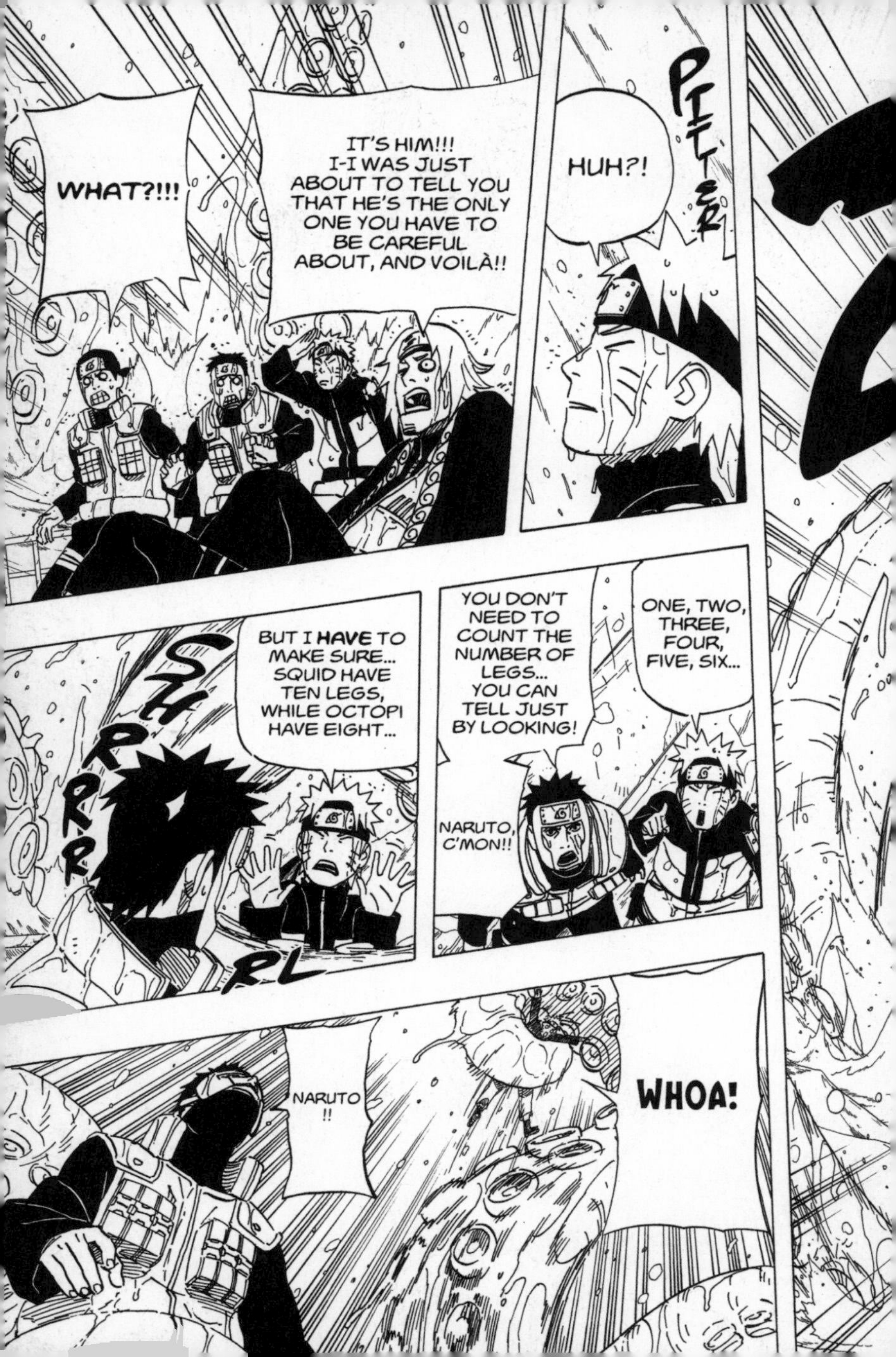
PITTER
HUH?!
IT'S HIM!!! I-I WAS JUST ABOUT TO TELL YOU THAT HE'S THE ONLY ONE YOU HAVE TO BE CAREFUL ABOUT, AND VOILÀ!!
WHAT?!!!
ONE, TWO, THREE, FOUR, FIVE, SIX...
YOU DON'T NEED TO COUNT THE NUMBER OF LEGS... YOU CAN TELL JUST BY LOOKING!
NARUTO, C'MON!!
BUT I **HAVE** TO MAKE SURE... SQUID HAVE TEN LEGS, WHILE OCTOPI HAVE EIGHT...
SHRRRR
RL
WHOA!
NARUTO !!

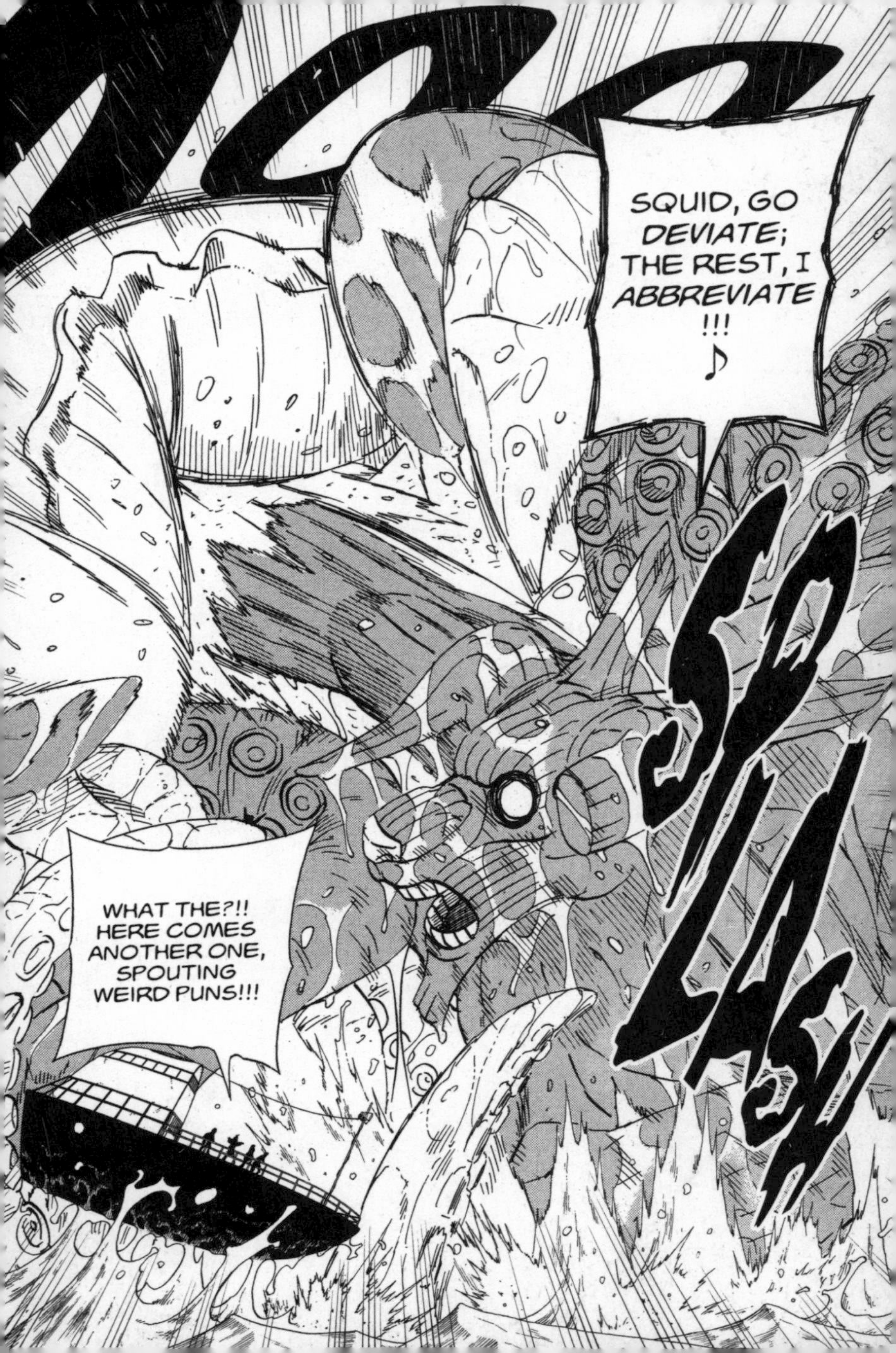
SQUID, GO DEVIATE; THE REST, I ABBREVIATE!!! ♪
SPLASH
WHAT THE?!! HERE COMES ANOTHER ONE, SPOUTING WEIRD PUNS!!!

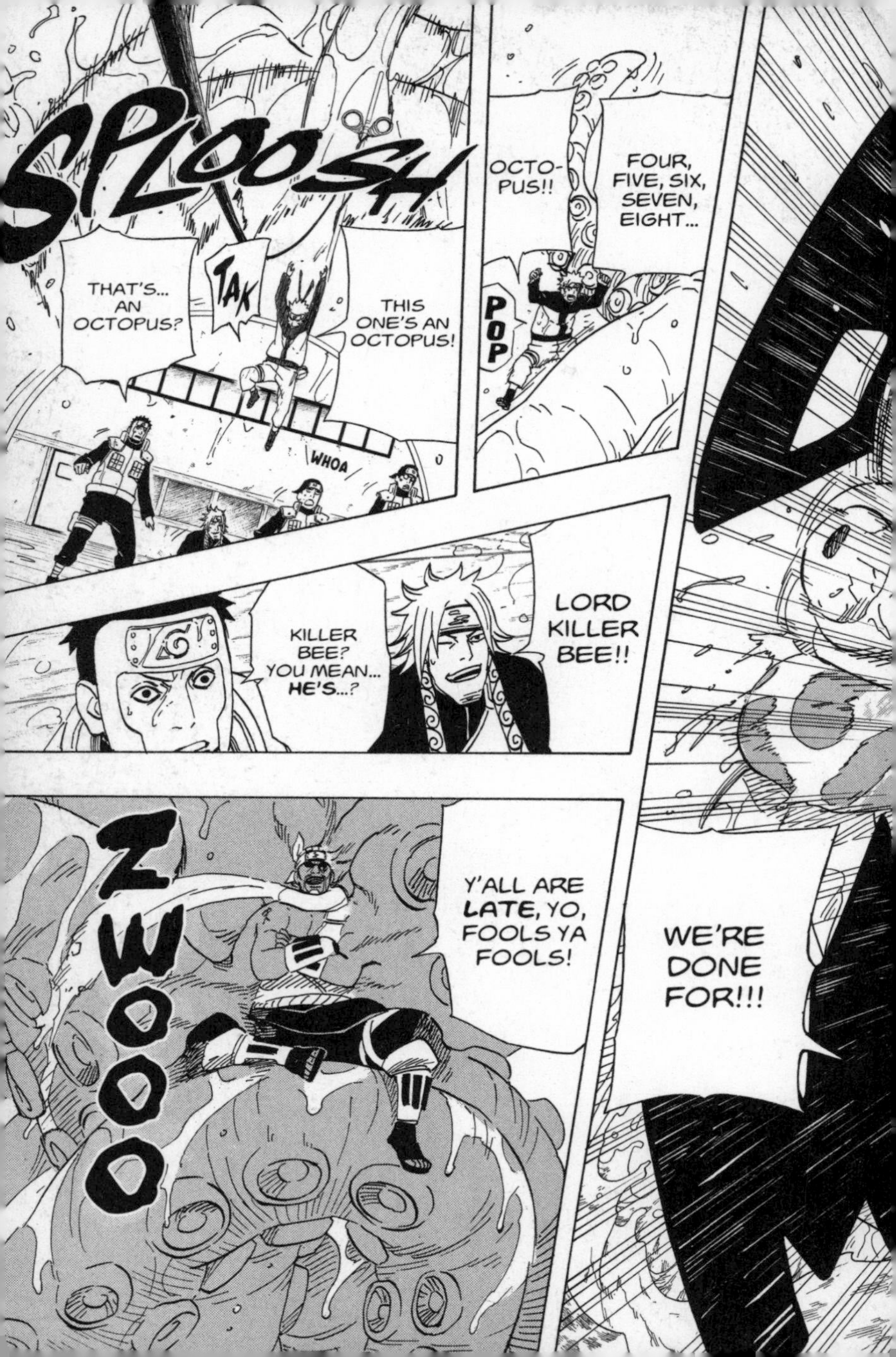
WE'RE DONE FOR!!!
FOUR, FIVE, SIX, SEVEN, EIGHT...
OCTO-PUS!!
POP
SPLOOSH
THIS ONE'S AN OCTOPUS!
TAK
THAT'S... AN OCTOPUS?
WHOA
LORD KILLER BEE!!
KILLER BEE? YOU MEAN... **HE'S**...?
Y'ALL ARE **LATE**, YO, FOOLS YA FOOLS!
ZWOOO

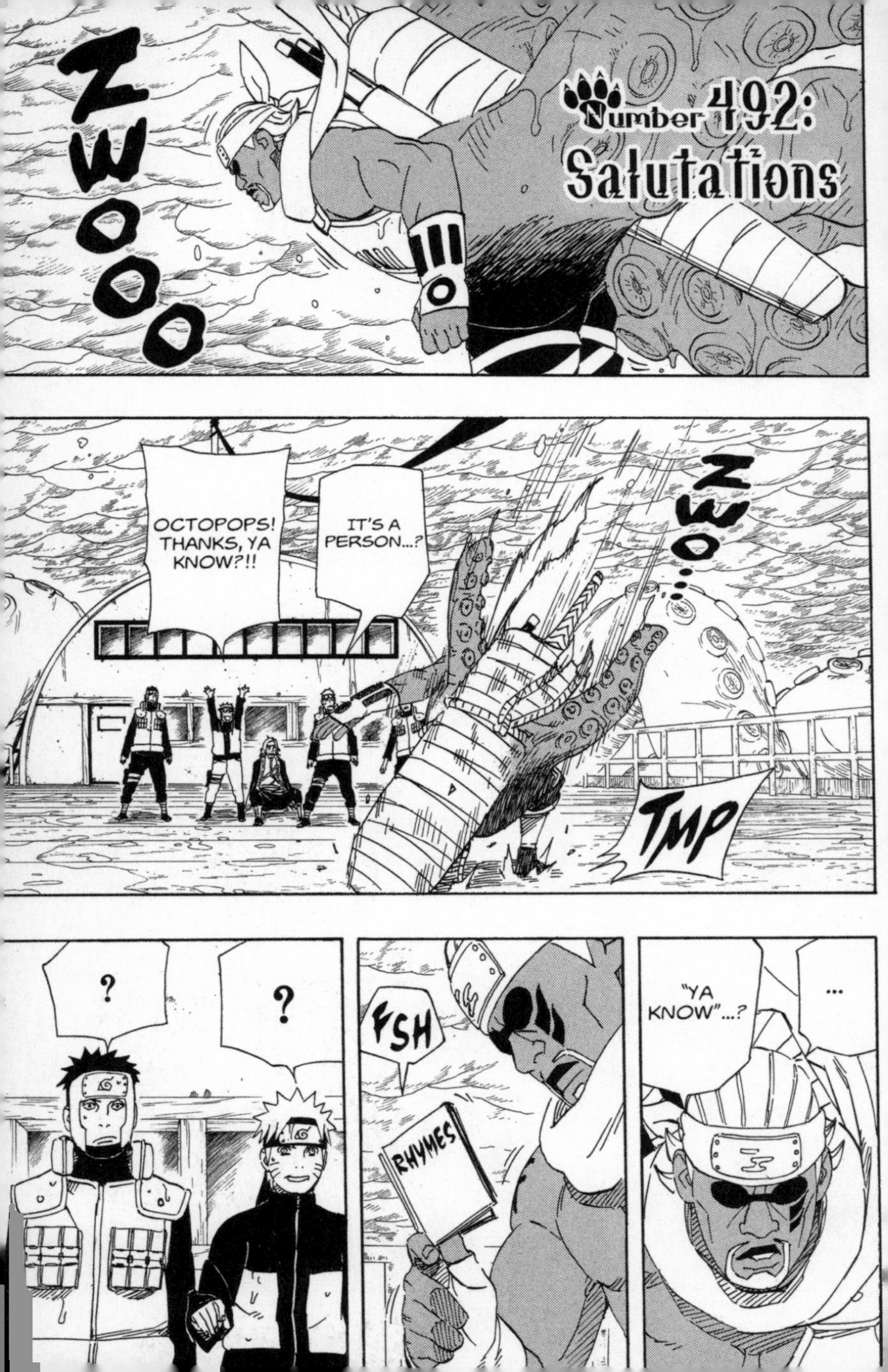
Number 492:
Salutations
ZWOOO
ZWO...
TMP
IT'S A PERSON...?
OCTOPOPS! THANKS, YA KNOW?!!
...
"YA KNOW"...?
FSH
RHYMES
?
?

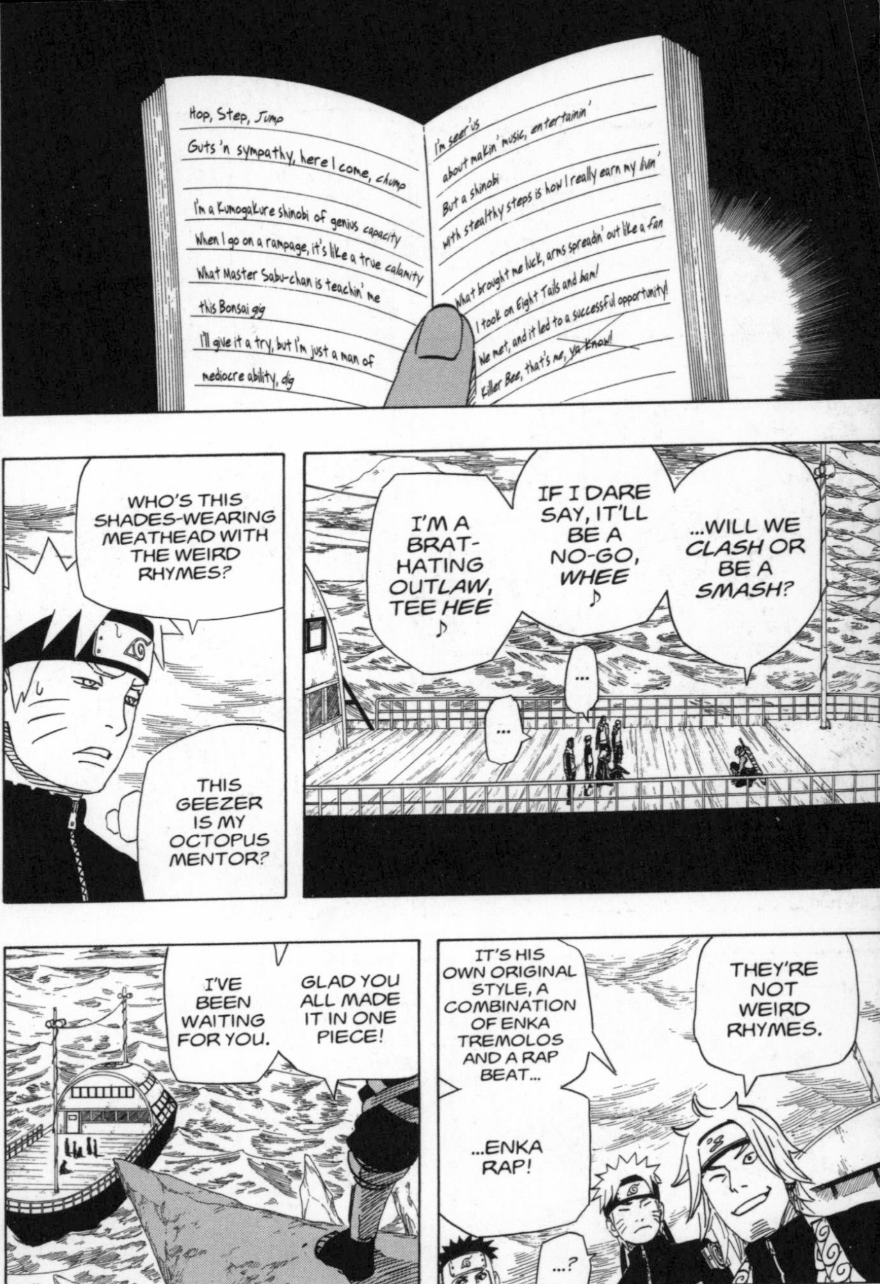
Hop, Step, Jump
Guts 'n sympathy, here I come, chump
I'm a Kumogakure shinobi of genius capacity
When I go on a rampage, it's like a true calamity
What Master Sabu-chan is teachin' me
this Bonsai gig
I'll give it a try, but I'm just a man of
mediocre ability, dig
I'm seer'us
about makin' music, entertainin'
But a shinobi
with stealthy steps is how I really earn my livin'
What brought me luck, arms spreadin' out like a fan
I took on Eight Tails and bam!
We met, and it led to a successful opportunity!
Killer Bee, that's me, ya know!
...WILL WE *CLASH* OR BE A *SMASH*?
IF I DARE SAY, IT'LL BE A NO-GO, *WHEE* ♪
I'M A BRAT-HATING OUTLAW, TEE *HEE* ♪
...
...
WHO'S THIS SHADES-WEARING MEATHEAD WITH THE WEIRD RHYMES?
THIS GEEZER IS MY OCTOPUS MENTOR?
THEY'RE NOT WEIRD RHYMES.
IT'S HIS OWN ORIGINAL STYLE, A COMBINATION OF ENKA TREMOLOS AND A RAP BEAT...
...ENKA RAP!
...?
GLAD YOU ALL MADE IT IN ONE PIECE!
I'VE BEEN WAITING FOR YOU.

READ THIS WAY

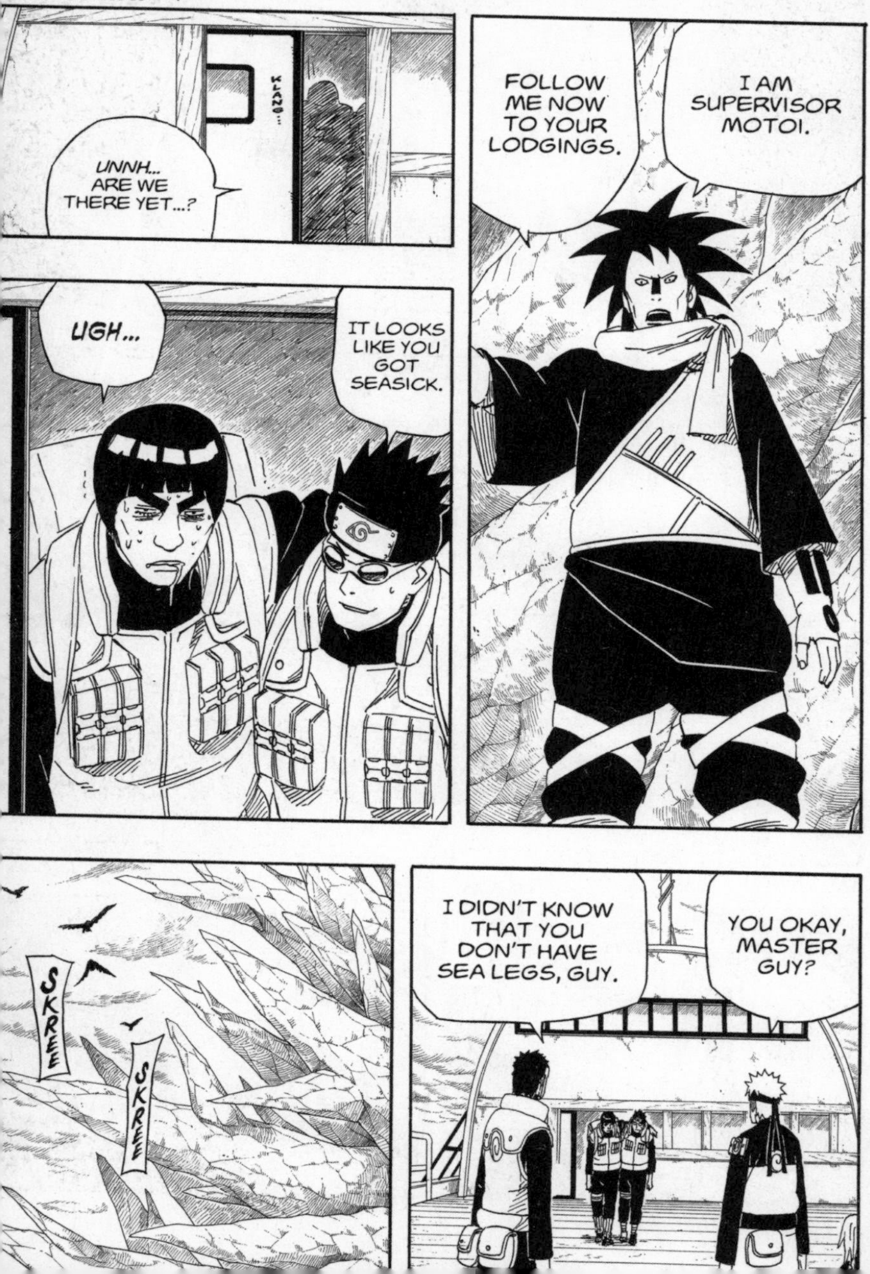
I AM SUPERVISOR MOTOI.
FOLLOW ME NOW TO YOUR LODGINGS.
KLANG...
UNNH... ARE WE THERE YET...?
IT LOOKS LIKE YOU GOT SEASICK.
UGH...
YOU OKAY, MASTER GUY?
I DIDN'T KNOW THAT YOU DON'T HAVE SEA LEGS, GUY.
SKREE
SKREE

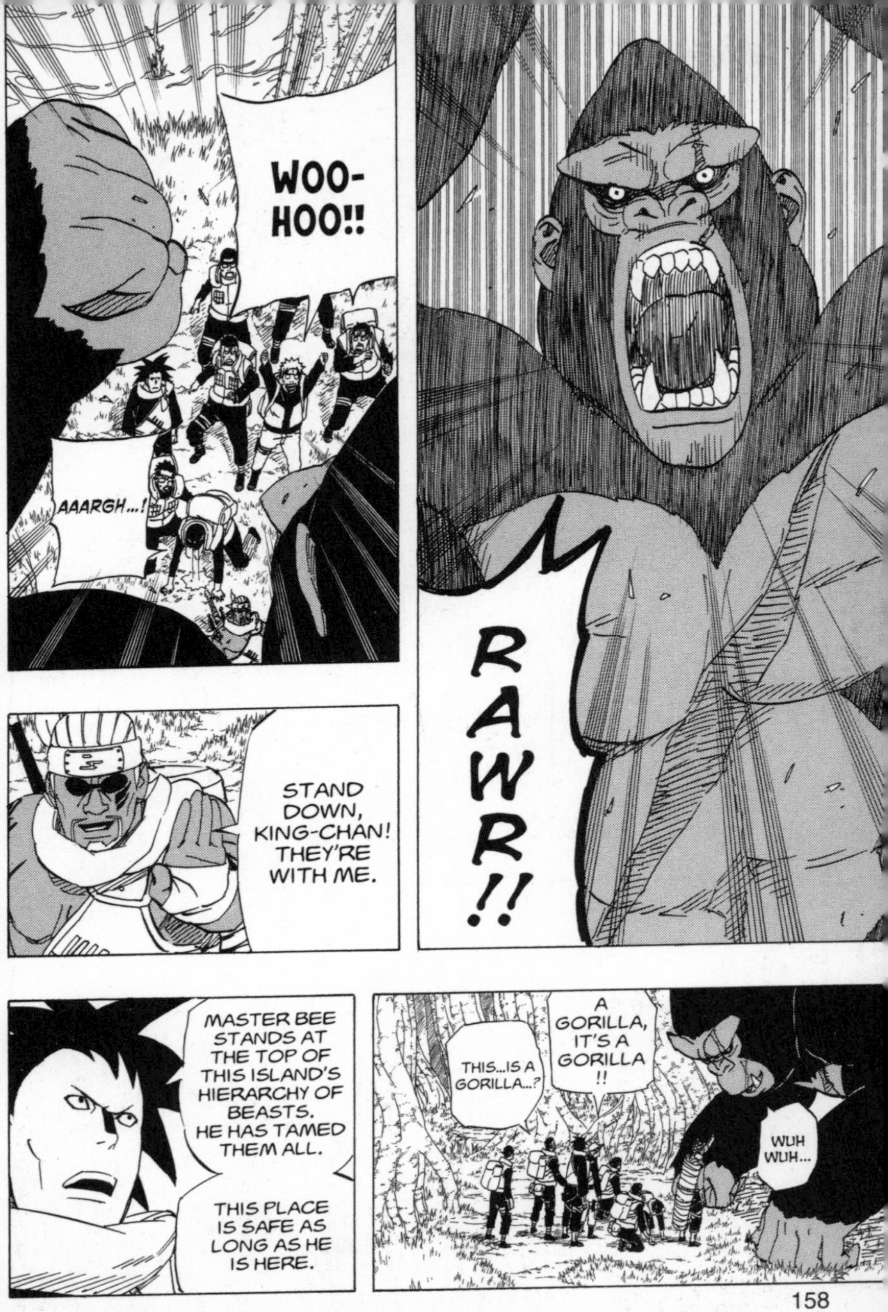
RAWR!!
WOO-HOO!!
AAARGH...!
STAND DOWN, KING-CHAN! THEY'RE WITH ME.
A GORILLA, IT'S A GORILLA!!
THIS...IS A GORILLA...?
WUH WUH...
MASTER BEE STANDS AT THE TOP OF THIS ISLAND'S HIERARCHY OF BEASTS. HE HAS TAMED THEM ALL.
THIS PLACE IS SAFE AS LONG AS HE IS HERE.

READ THIS WAY

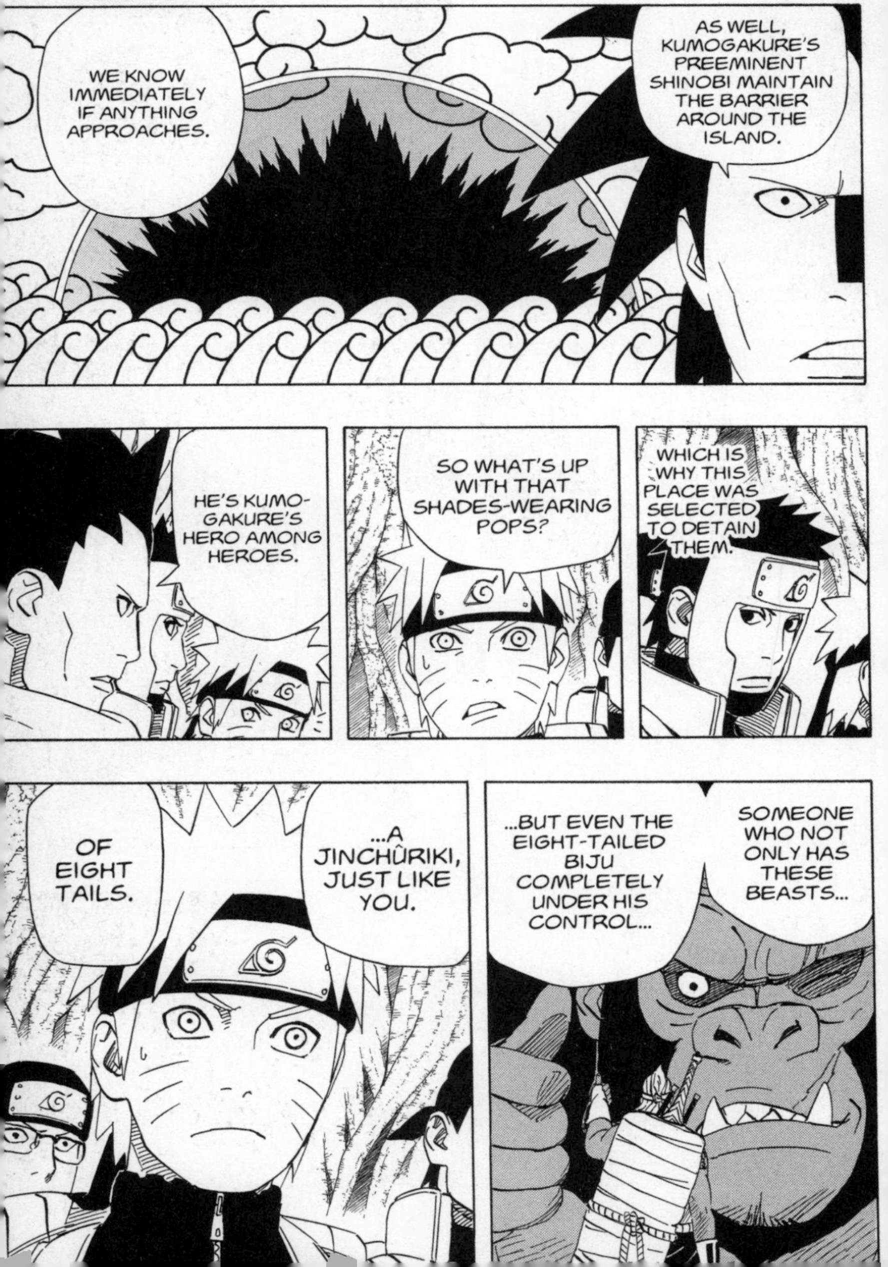
AS WELL, KUMOGAKURE'S PREEMINENT SHINOBI MAINTAIN THE BARRIER AROUND THE ISLAND.
WE KNOW IMMEDIATELY IF ANYTHING APPROACHES.
WHICH IS WHY THIS PLACE WAS SELECTED TO DETAIN THEM.
SO WHAT'S UP WITH THAT SHADES-WEARING POPS?
HE'S KUMO-GAKURE'S HERO AMONG HEROES.
SOMEONE WHO NOT ONLY HAS THESE BEASTS...
...BUT EVEN THE EIGHT-TAILED BIJU COMPLETELY UNDER HIS CONTROL...
...A JINCHÛRIKI, JUST LIKE YOU.
OF EIGHT TAILS.

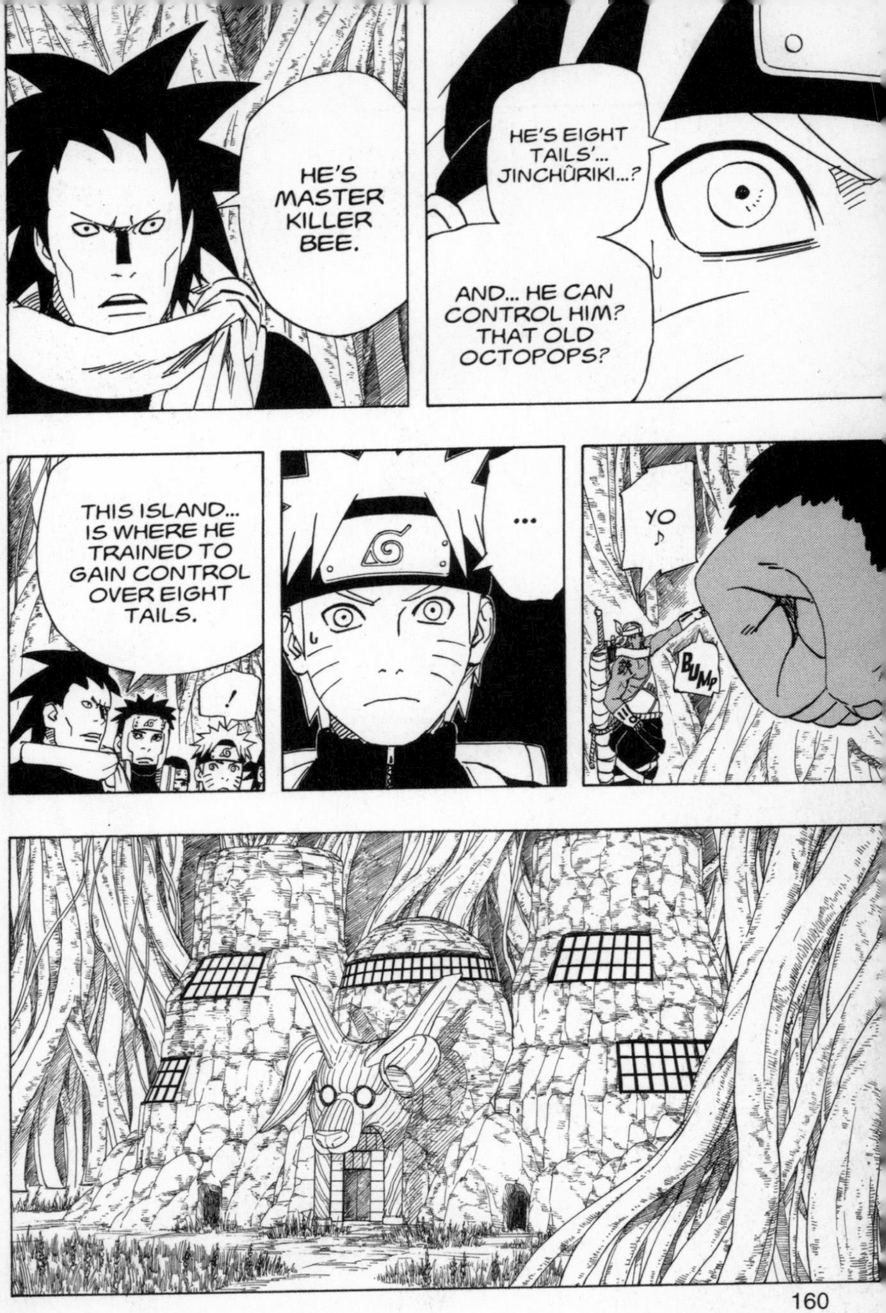
HE'S EIGHT TAILS'... JINCHÛRIKI...?
AND... HE CAN CONTROL HIM? THAT OLD OCTOPOPS?
HE'S MASTER KILLER BEE.
YO ♪
BUMP
...
THIS ISLAND... IS WHERE HE TRAINED TO GAIN CONTROL OVER EIGHT TAILS.
!

READ THIS WAY

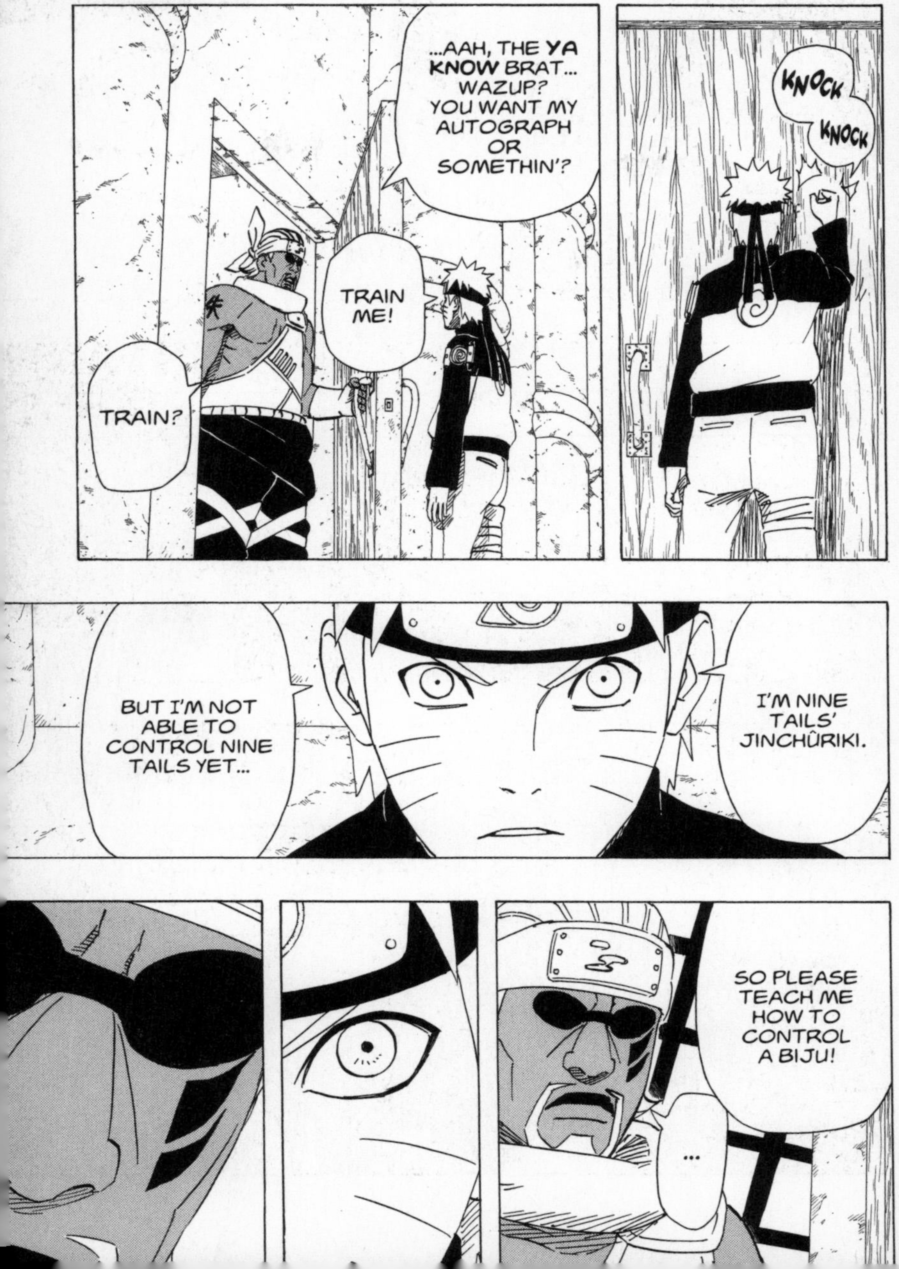
KNOCK
KNOCK
...AAH, THE YA KNOW BRAT... WAZUP? YOU WANT MY AUTOGRAPH OR SOMETHIN'?
TRAIN ME!
TRAIN?
I'M NINE TAILS' JINCHÛRIKI.
BUT I'M NOT ABLE TO CONTROL NINE TAILS YET...
SO PLEASE TEACH ME HOW TO CONTROL A BIJU!
...

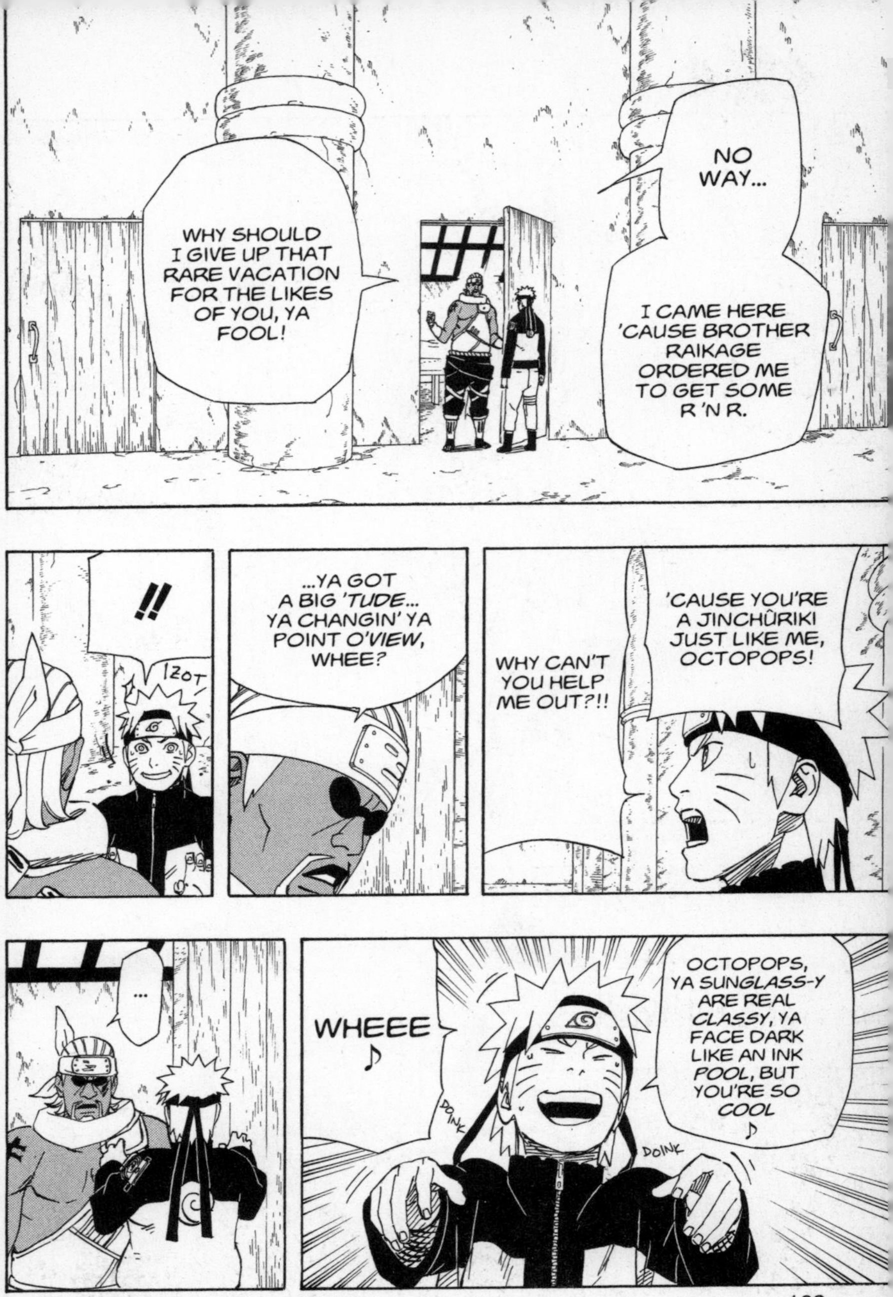
NO WAY...
I CAME HERE 'CAUSE BROTHER RAIKAGE ORDERED ME TO GET SOME R 'N R.
WHY SHOULD I GIVE UP THAT RARE VACATION FOR THE LIKES OF YOU, YA FOOL!
'CAUSE YOU'RE A JINCHÛRIKI JUST LIKE ME, OCTOPOPS!
WHY CAN'T YOU HELP ME OUT?!!
...YA GOT A BIG 'TUDE... YA CHANGIN' YA POINT O'VIEW, WHEE?
!!
ZOT
OCTOPOPS, YA SUNGLASS-Y ARE REAL CLASSY, YA FACE DARK LIKE AN INK POOL, BUT YOU'RE SO COOL ♪
DOINK
WHEEE ♪
DOINK
...

READ THIS WAY

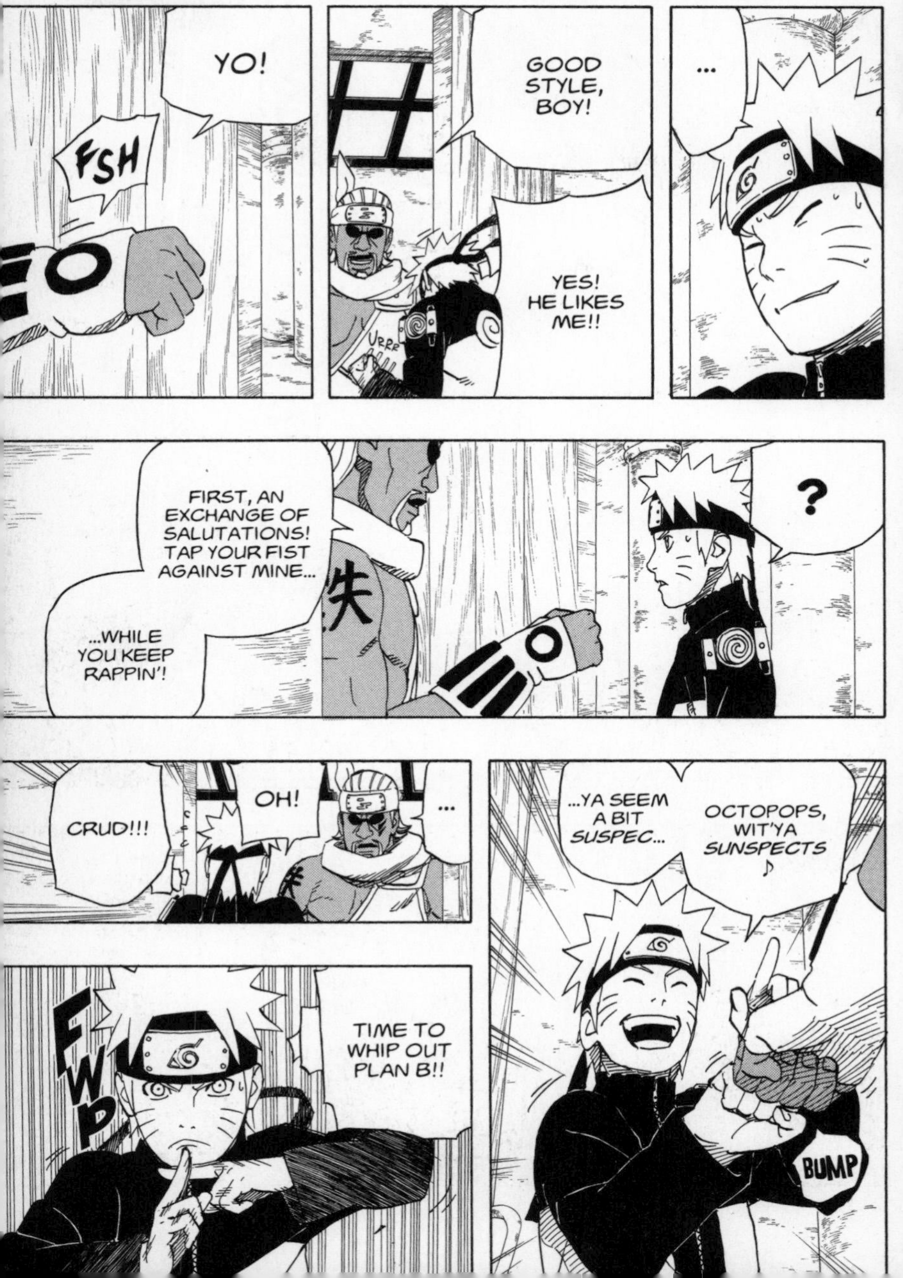
...
GOOD STYLE, BOY!
YES! HE LIKES ME!!
URRR
YO!
FSH
?
FIRST, AN EXCHANGE OF SALUTATIONS! TAP YOUR FIST AGAINST MINE...
...WHILE YOU KEEP RAPPIN'!
OCTOPOPS, WIT'YA SUNSPECTS ♪
...YA SEEM A BIT SUSPEC...
BUMP
...
OH!
CRUD!!!
TIME TO WHIP OUT PLAN B!!
FWP

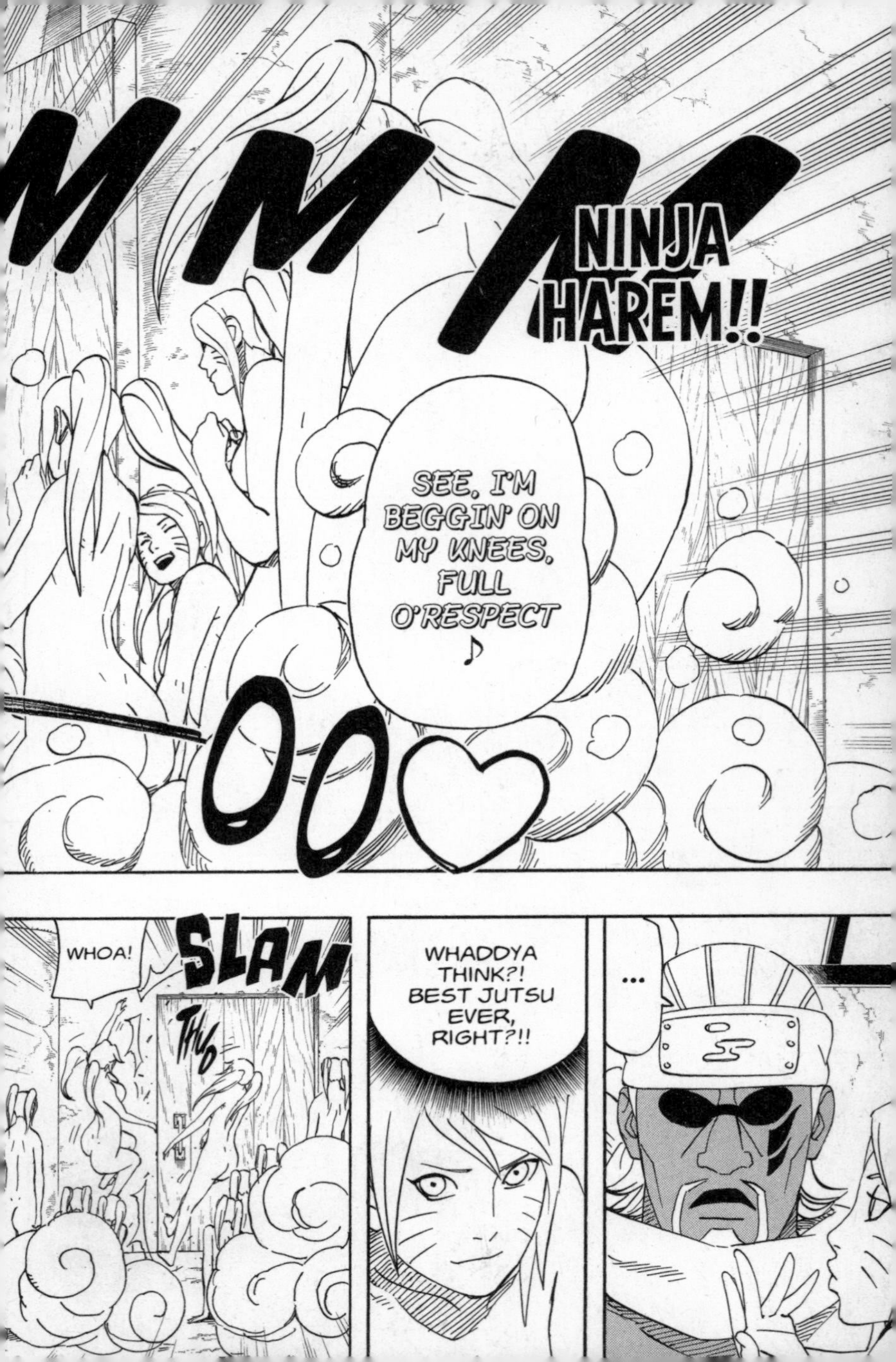
NINJA HAREM!!
SEE, I'M BEGGIN' ON MY KNEES, FULL O'RESPECT ♪
...
WHADDYA THINK?! BEST JUTSU EVER, RIGHT?!!
SLAM
THUD
WHOA!

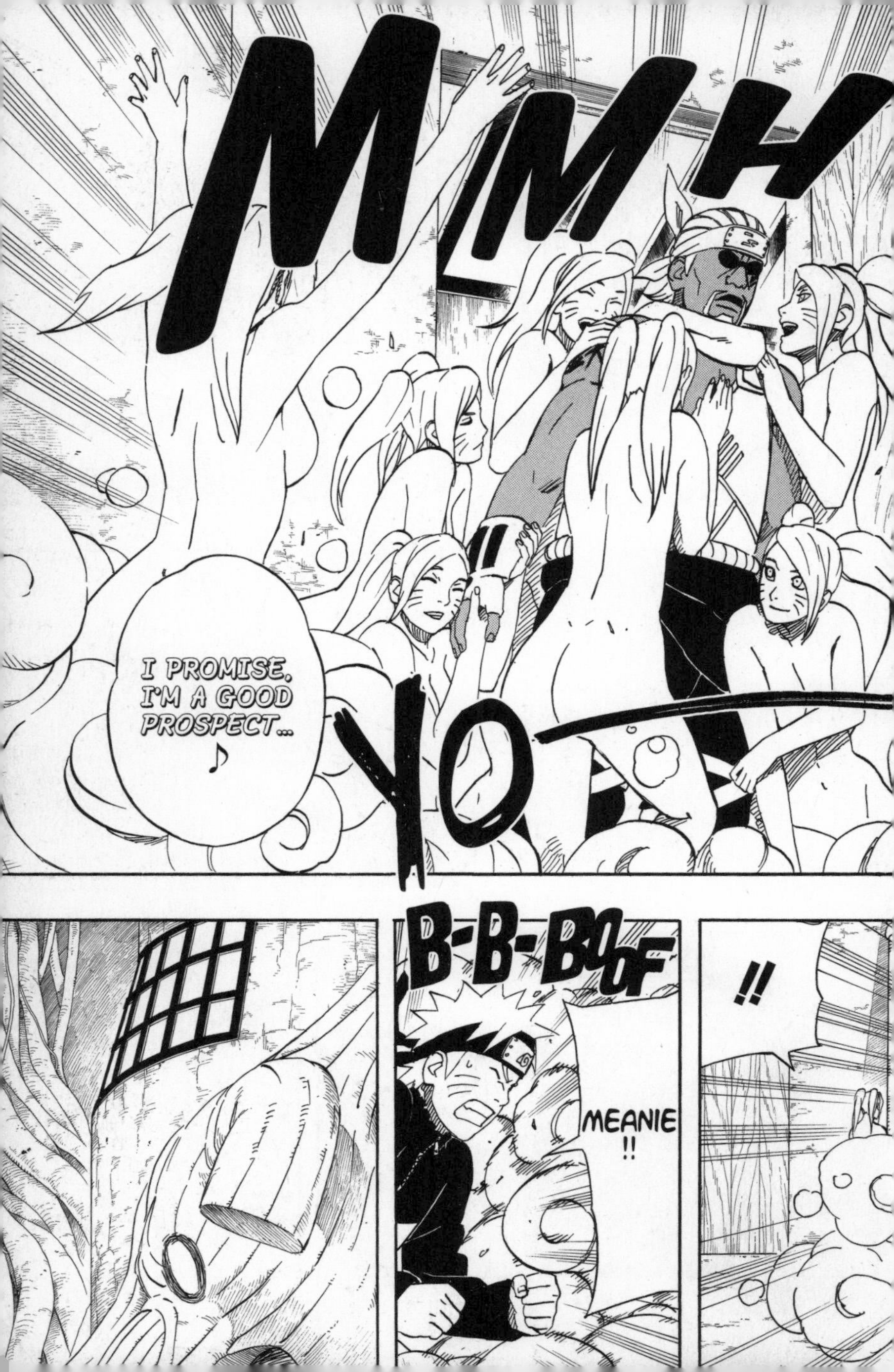
MMH
I PROMISE, I'M A GOOD PROSPECT... ♪
YO
!!
B-B-BOOF
MEANIE !!

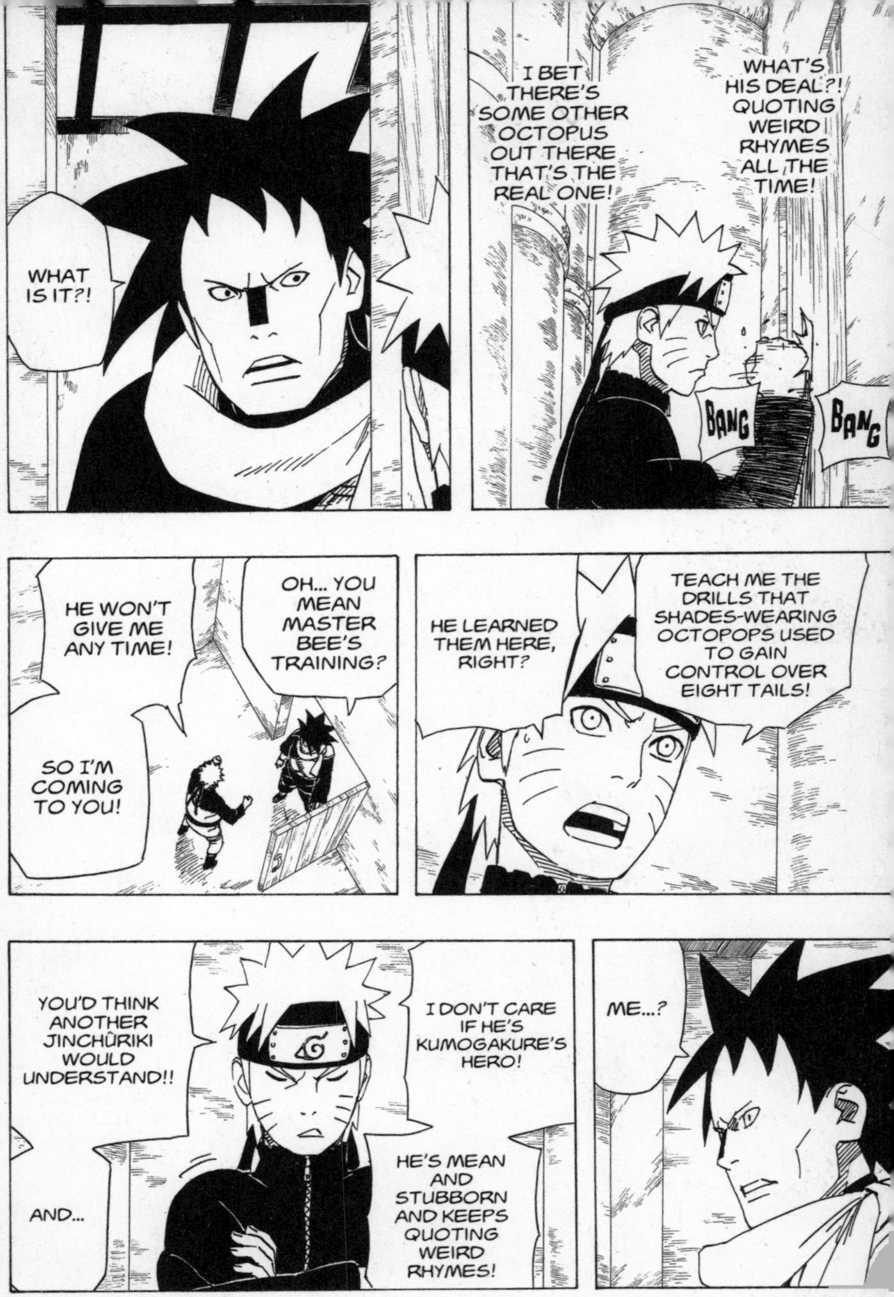
WHAT'S HIS DEAL?! QUOTING WEIRD RHYMES ALL THE TIME!
BANG
BANG
I BET THERE'S SOME OTHER OCTOPUS OUT THERE THAT'S THE REAL ONE!
WHAT IS IT?!
TEACH ME THE DRILLS THAT SHADES-WEARING OCTOPOPS USED TO GAIN CONTROL OVER EIGHT TAILS!
HE LEARNED THEM HERE, RIGHT?
OH... YOU MEAN MASTER BEE'S TRAINING?
HE WON'T GIVE ME ANY TIME!
SO I'M COMING TO YOU!
ME...?
I DON'T CARE IF HE'S KUMOGAKURE'S HERO!
HE'S MEAN AND STUBBORN AND KEEPS QUOTING WEIRD RHYMES!
YOU'D THINK ANOTHER JINCHŪRIKI WOULD UNDERSTAND!!
AND...

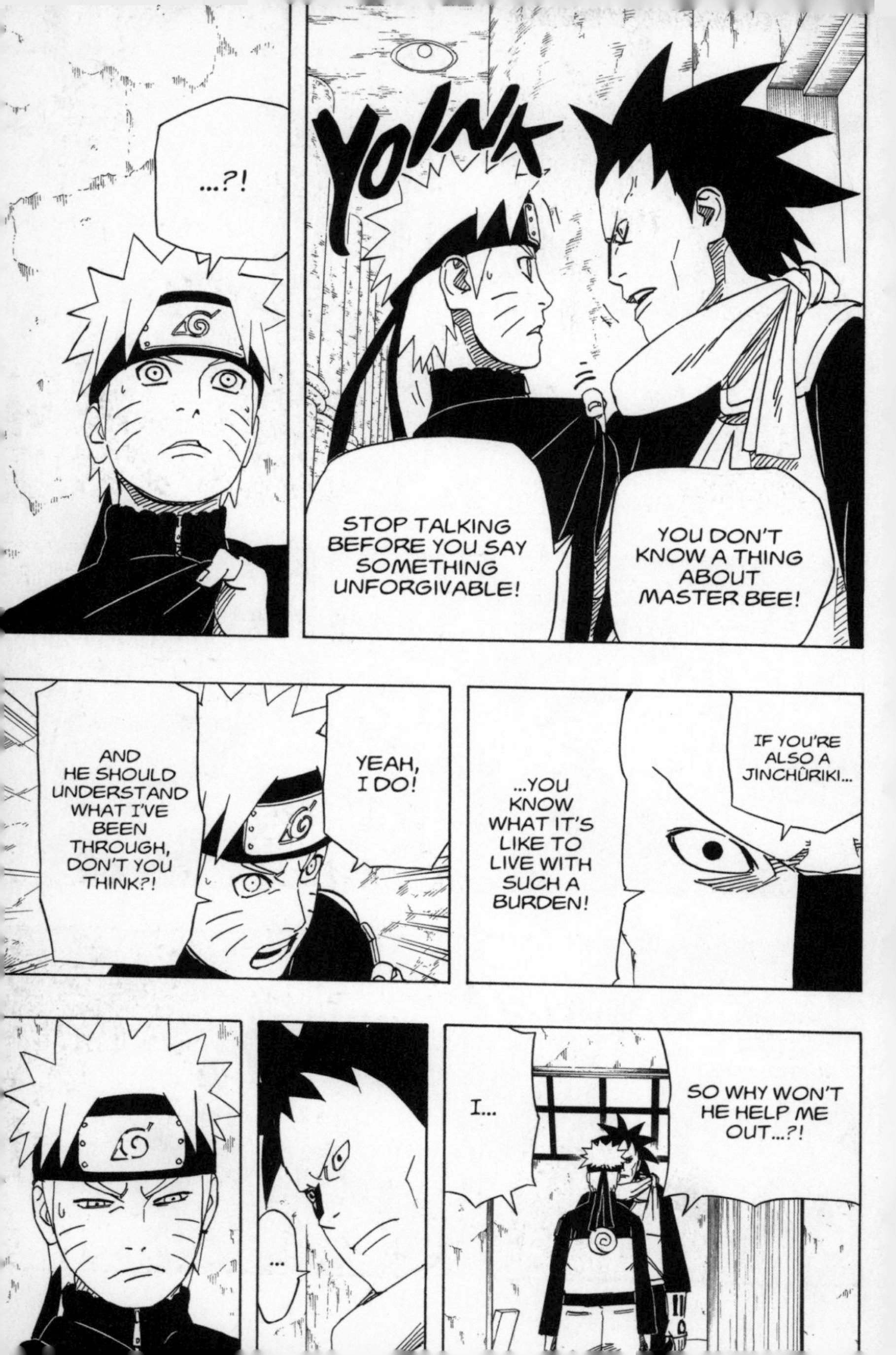
YOINK
YOU DON'T KNOW A THING ABOUT MASTER BEE!
STOP TALKING BEFORE YOU SAY SOMETHING UNFORGIVABLE!
...?!
IF YOU'RE ALSO A JINCHÛRIKI...
...YOU KNOW WHAT IT'S LIKE TO LIVE WITH SUCH A BURDEN!
YEAH, I DO!
AND HE SHOULD UNDERSTAND WHAT I'VE BEEN THROUGH, DON'T YOU THINK?!
SO WHY WON'T HE HELP ME OUT...?!
I...
...

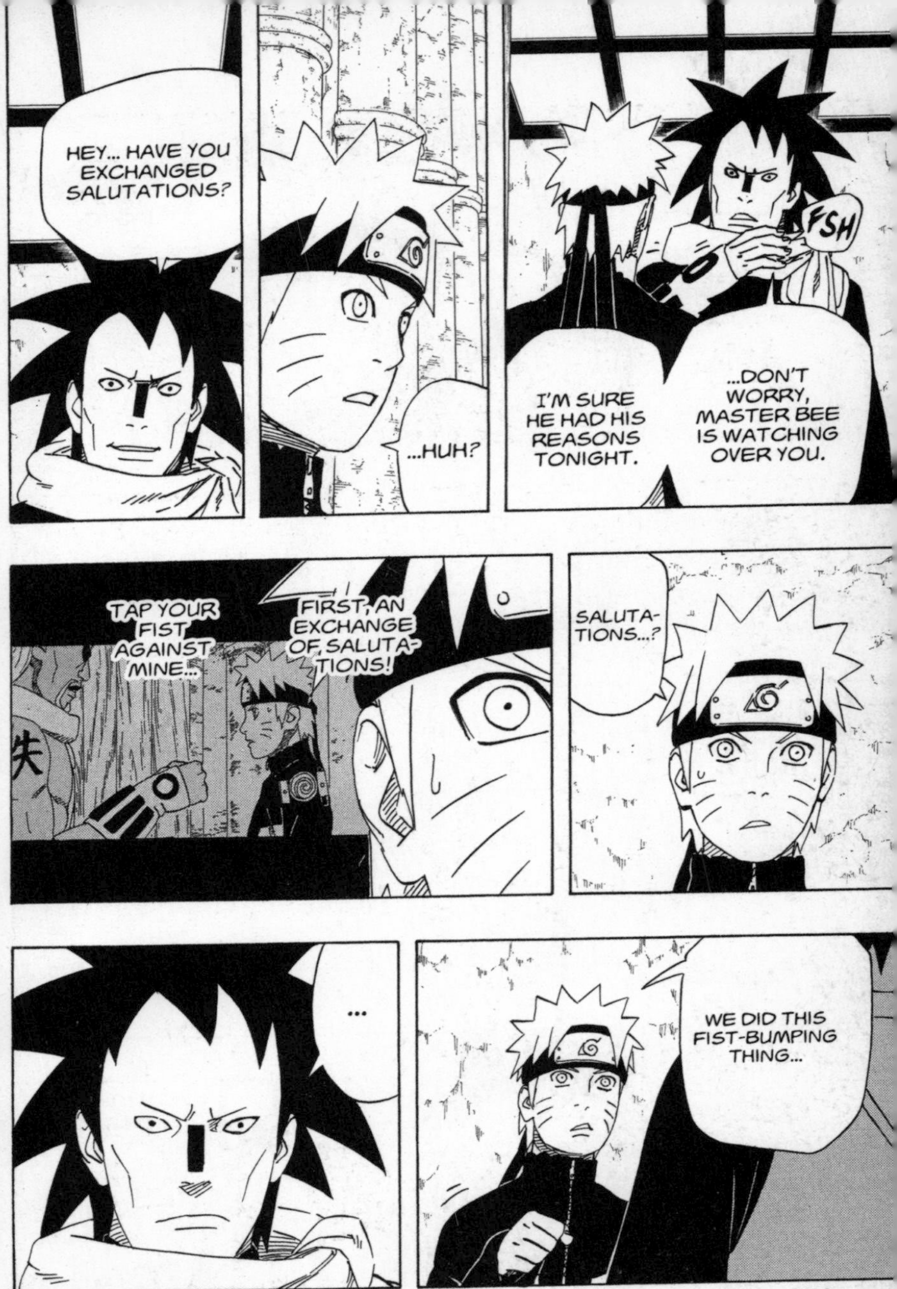
FSH
...DON'T WORRY, MASTER BEE IS WATCHING OVER YOU.
I'M SURE HE HAD HIS REASONS TONIGHT.
...HUH?
HEY... HAVE YOU EXCHANGED SALUTATIONS?
SALUTATIONS...?
FIRST, AN EXCHANGE OF SALUTATIONS!
TAP YOUR FIST AGAINST MINE...
WE DID THIS FIST-BUMPING THING...
...

READ THIS WAY

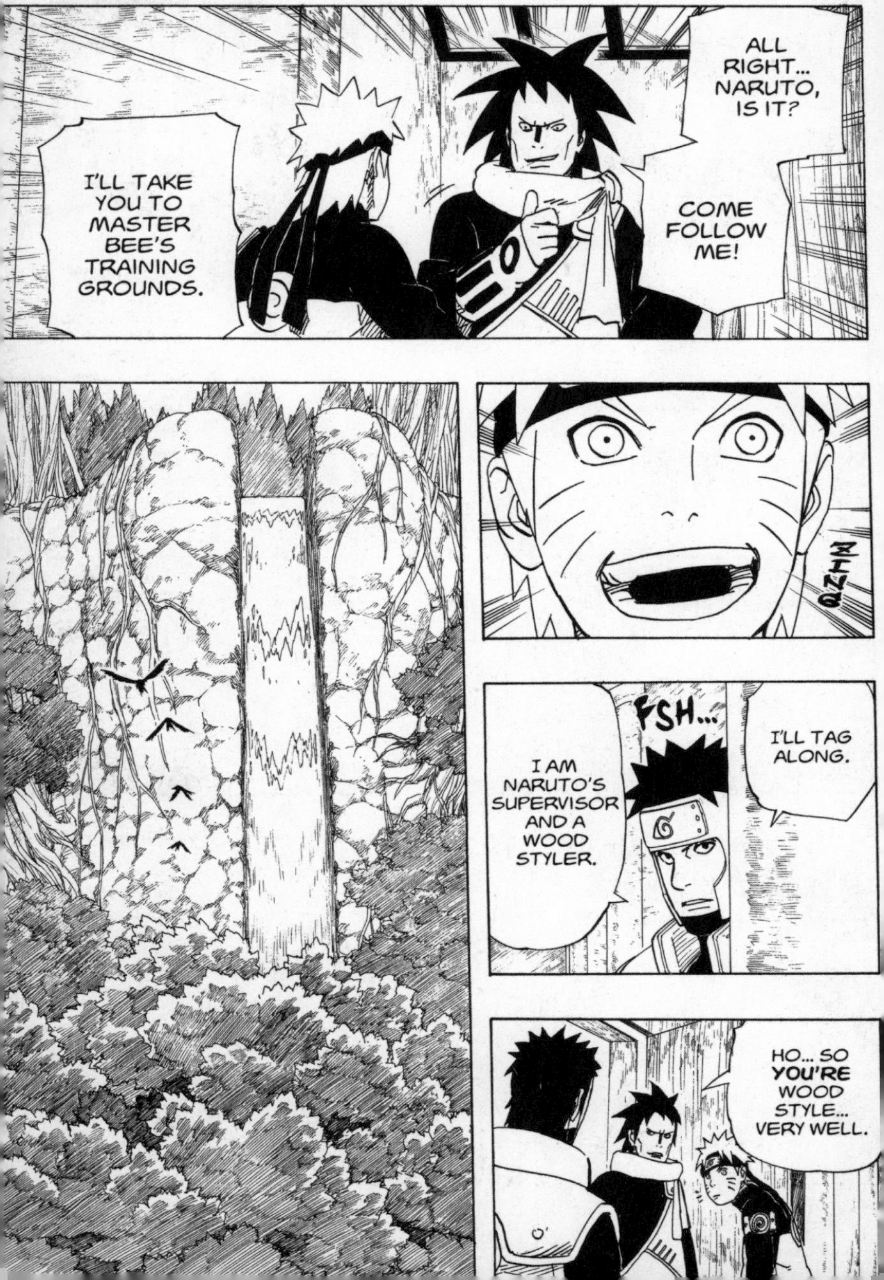
ALL RIGHT... NARUTO, IS IT?
COME FOLLOW ME!
I'LL TAKE YOU TO MASTER BEE'S TRAINING GROUNDS.
ZING
FSH...
I'LL TAG ALONG.
I AM NARUTO'S SUPERVISOR AND A WOOD STYLER.
HO... SO YOU'RE WOOD STYLE... VERY WELL.

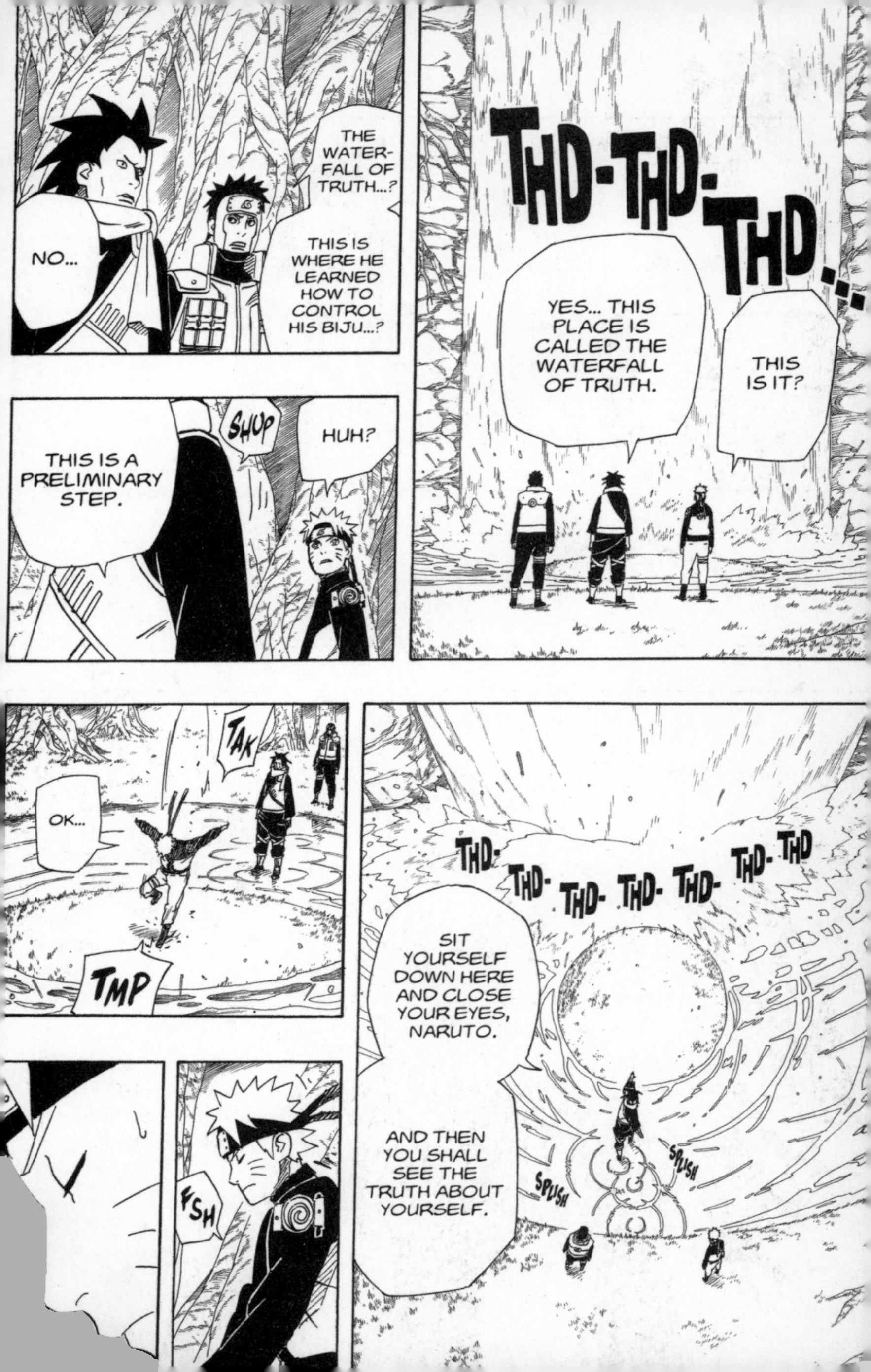
THD-THD-THD...
THIS IS IT?
YES... THIS PLACE IS CALLED THE WATERFALL OF TRUTH.
THE WATERFALL OF TRUTH...?
THIS IS WHERE HE LEARNED HOW TO CONTROL HIS BIJU...?
NO...
HUH?
SHUP
THIS IS A PRELIMINARY STEP.
THD-THD-THD-THD-THD-THD-THD
SIT YOURSELF DOWN HERE AND CLOSE YOUR EYES, NARUTO.
SPLISH
SPLISH
AND THEN YOU SHALL SEE THE TRUTH ABOUT YOURSELF.
TAK
OK...
TMP
FSH

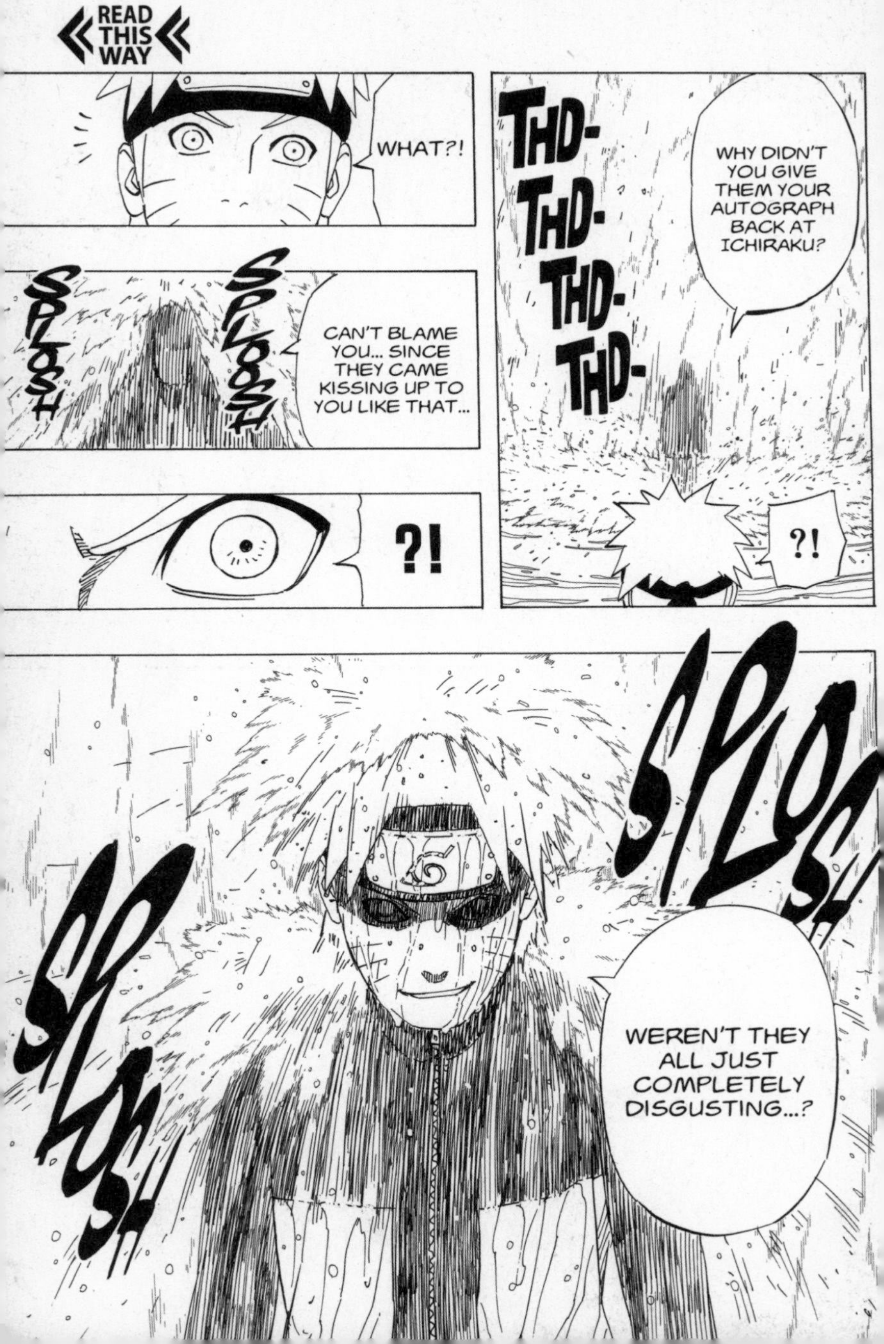
READ THIS WAY
THD- THD- THD- THD-
WHY DIDN'T YOU GIVE THEM YOUR AUTOGRAPH BACK AT ICHIRAKU?
?!
WHAT?!
SPLOOSH
SPLOSH
CAN'T BLAME YOU... SINCE THEY CAME KISSING UP TO YOU LIKE THAT...
?!
SPLOSH
WEREN'T THEY ALL JUST COMPLETELY DISGUSTING...?
SPLOSH

NARUTO

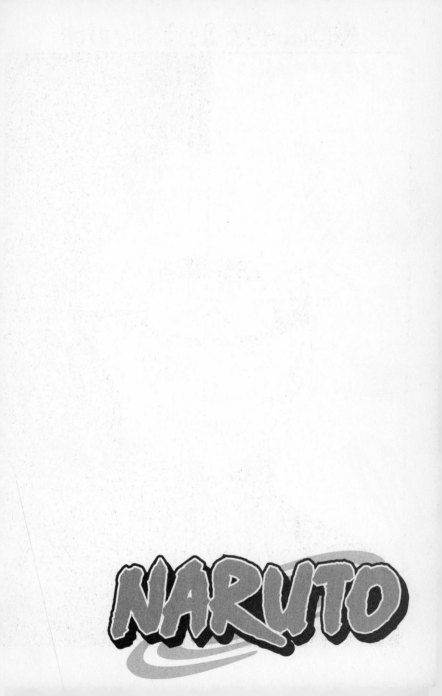

Number 493: Dark Naruto!!

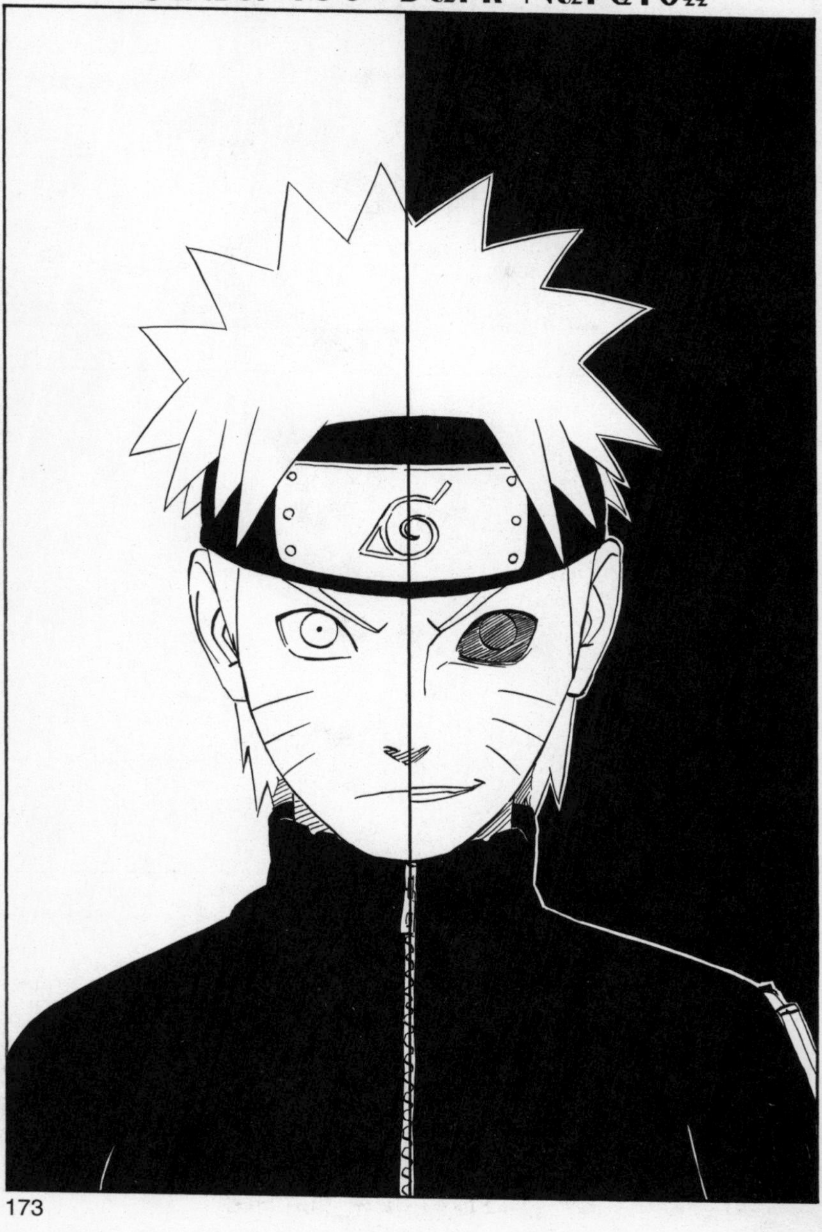

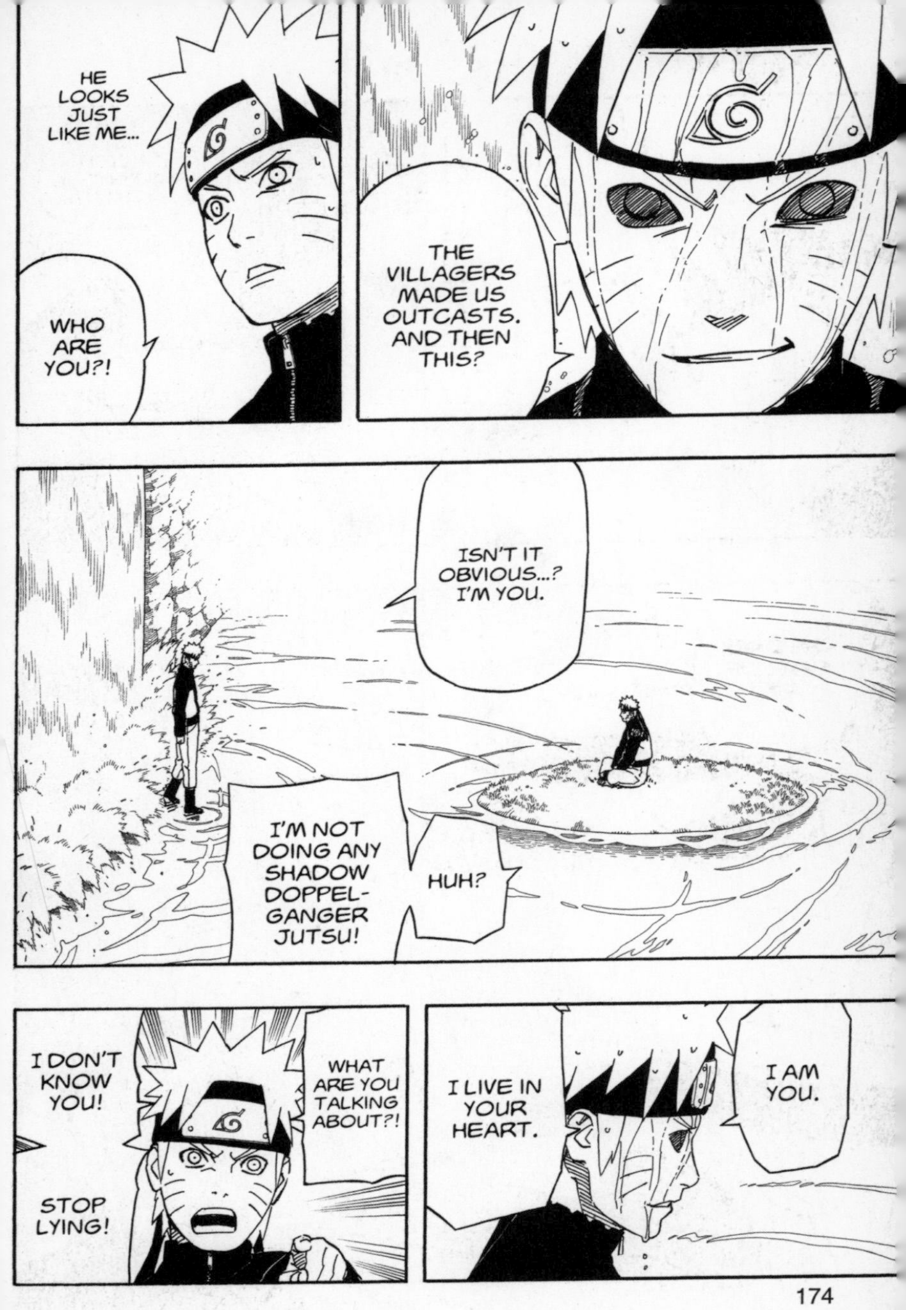
THE VILLAGERS MADE US OUTCASTS. AND THEN THIS?
HE LOOKS JUST LIKE ME...
WHO ARE YOU?!
ISN'T IT OBVIOUS...? I'M YOU.
HUH?
I'M NOT DOING ANY SHADOW DOPPEL-GANGER JUTSU!
I AM YOU.
I LIVE IN YOUR HEART.
WHAT ARE YOU TALKING ABOUT?!
I DON'T KNOW YOU!
STOP LYING!

READ THIS WAY

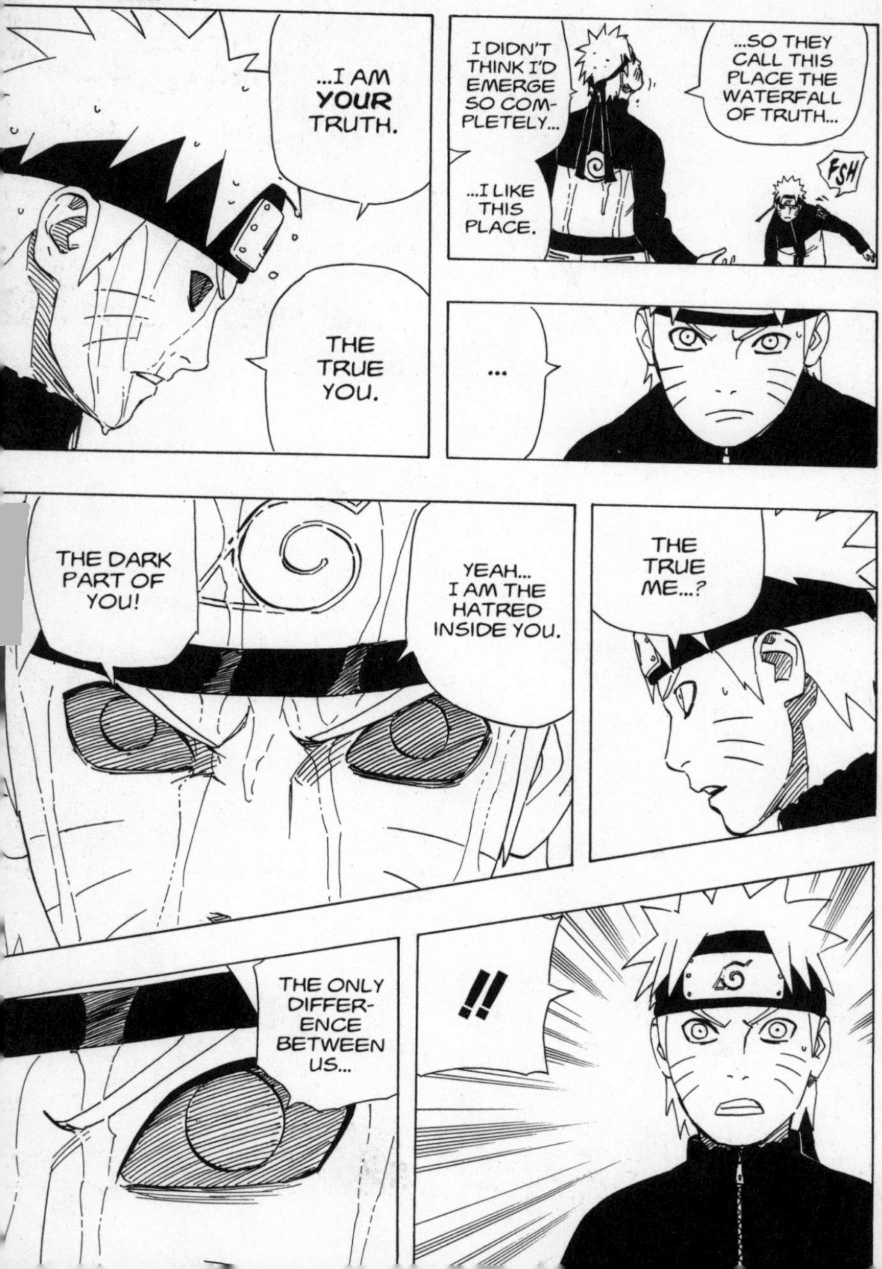

...SO THEY CALL THIS PLACE THE WATERFALL OF TRUTH...
FSH
I DIDN'T THINK I'D EMERGE SO COM-PLETELY...
...I LIKE THIS PLACE.
...
...I AM YOUR TRUTH.
THE TRUE YOU.
THE TRUE ME...?
YEAH... I AM THE HATRED INSIDE YOU.
THE DARK PART OF YOU!
!!
THE ONLY DIFFER-ENCE BETWEEN US...

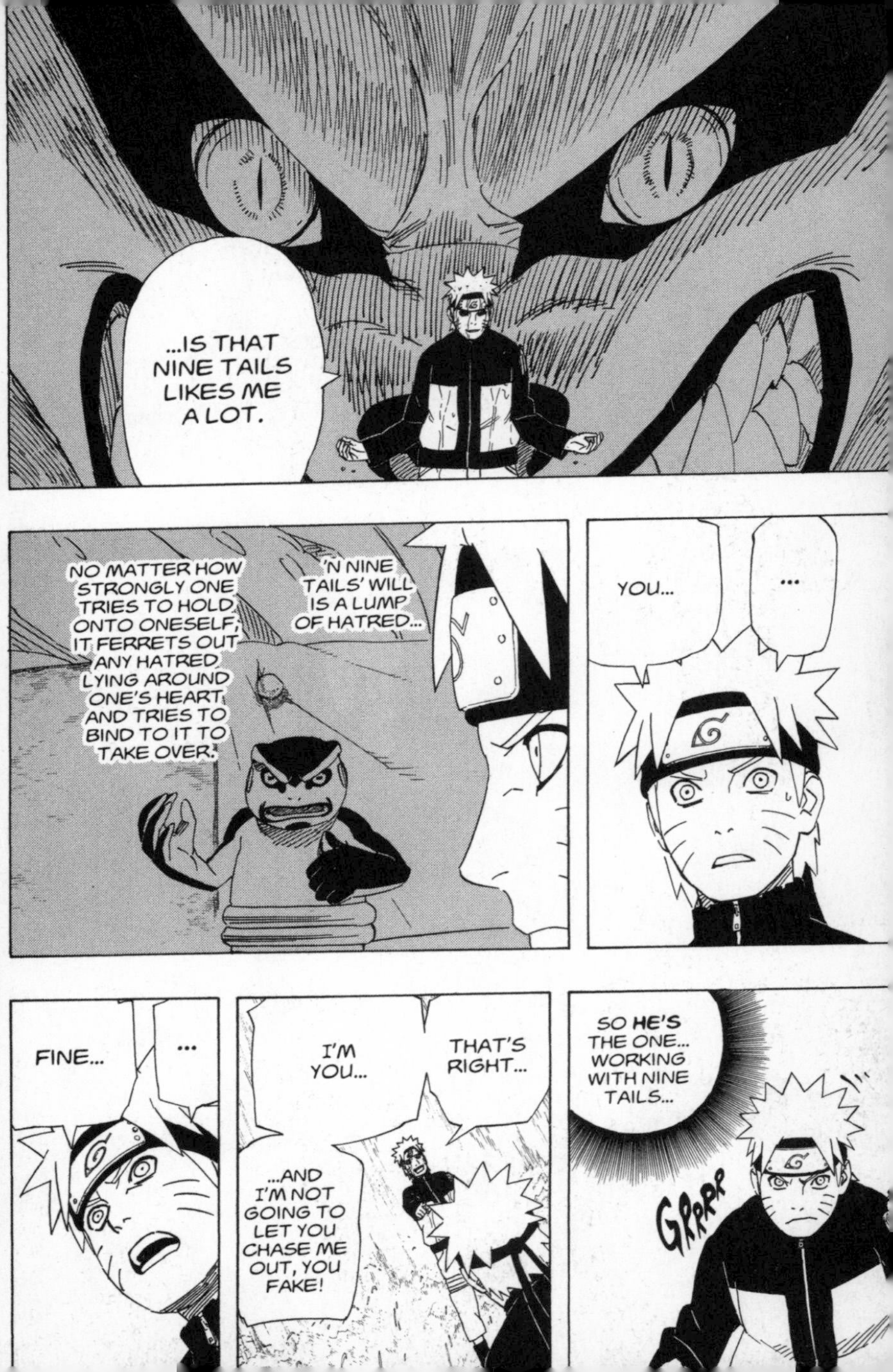
...IS THAT NINE TAILS LIKES ME A LOT.
...
YOU...
'N NINE TAILS' WILL IS A LUMP OF HATRED...
NO MATTER HOW STRONGLY ONE TRIES TO HOLD ONTO ONESELF, IT FERRETS OUT ANY HATRED LYING AROUND ONE'S HEART AND TRIES TO BIND TO IT TO TAKE OVER.
SO HE'S THE ONE... WORKING WITH NINE TAILS...
GRRRR
THAT'S RIGHT...
I'M YOU...
...AND I'M NOT GOING TO LET YOU CHASE ME OUT, YOU FAKE!
...
FINE...

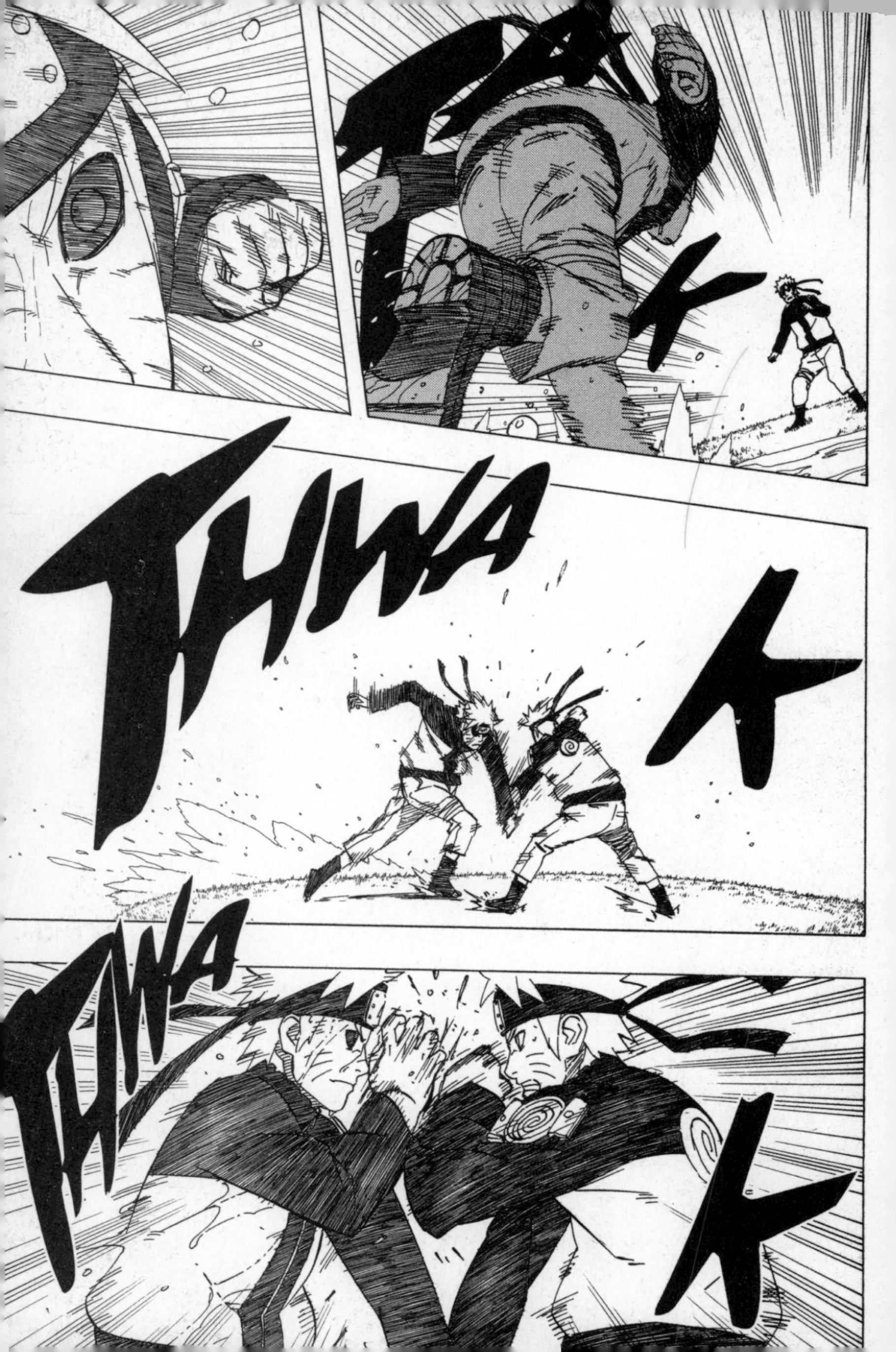
THWAK
THWAK

THOOM

YOU'RE THE FAKE!!

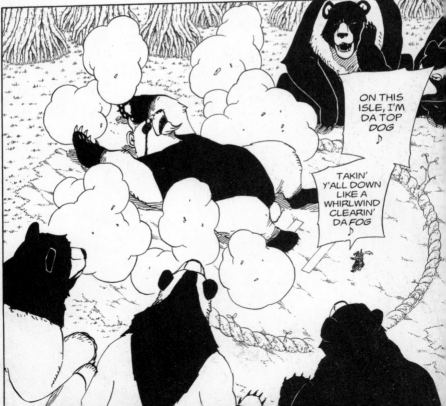

ON THIS ISLE, I'M DA TOP *DOG* ♪

TAKIN' Y'ALL DOWN LIKE A WHIRLWIND CLEARIN' DA FOG ♪

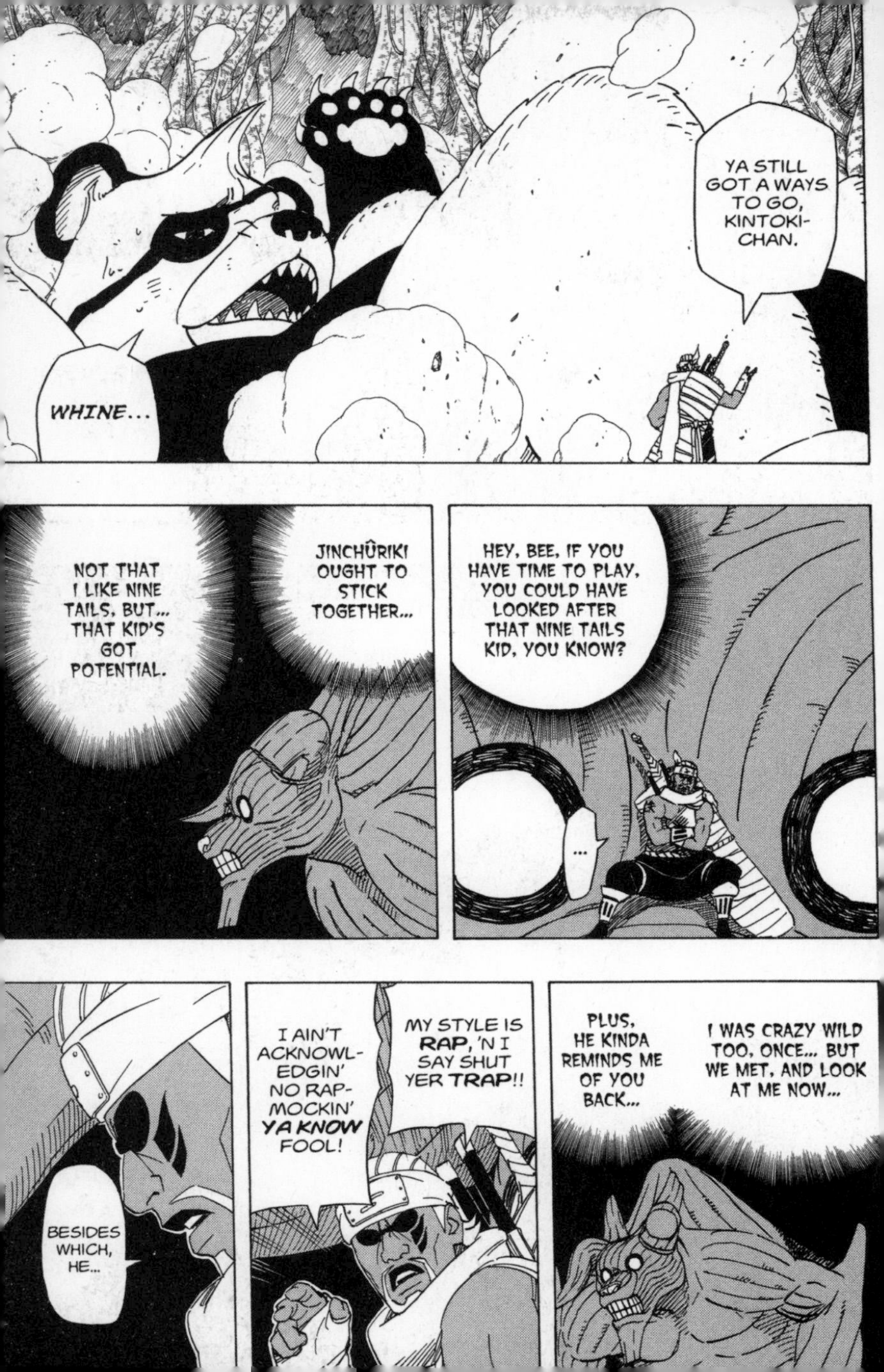
YA STILL GOT A WAYS TO GO, KINTOKI-CHAN.
WHINE...
HEY, BEE, IF YOU HAVE TIME TO PLAY, YOU COULD HAVE LOOKED AFTER THAT NINE TAILS KID, YOU KNOW?
...
JINCHÛRIKI OUGHT TO STICK TOGETHER...
NOT THAT I LIKE NINE TAILS, BUT... THAT KID'S GOT POTENTIAL.
I WAS CRAZY WILD TOO, ONCE... BUT WE MET, AND LOOK AT ME NOW...
PLUS, HE KINDA REMINDS ME OF YOU BACK...
MY STYLE IS **RAP**, 'N I SAY SHUT YER **TRAP**!!
I AIN'T ACKNOWL-EDGIN' NO RAP-MOCKIN' ***YA KNOW*** FOOL!
BESIDES WHICH, HE...

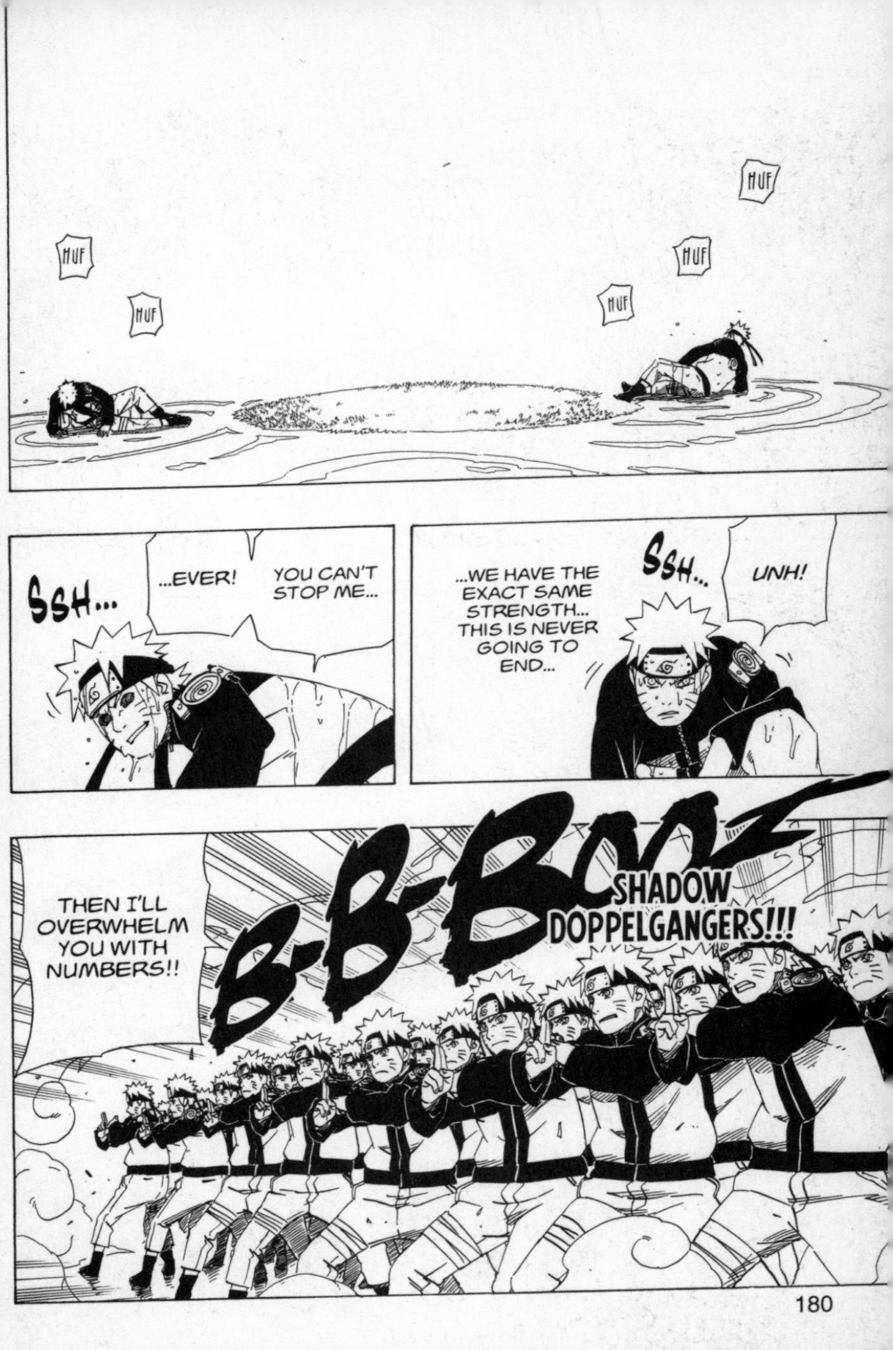
HUF
HUF
HUF
HUF
HUF
UNH!
SSH...
...WE HAVE THE EXACT SAME STRENGTH... THIS IS NEVER GOING TO END...
YOU CAN'T STOP ME...
...EVER!
SSH...
SHADOW DOPPELGANGERS!!!
THEN I'LL OVERWHELM YOU WITH NUMBERS!!

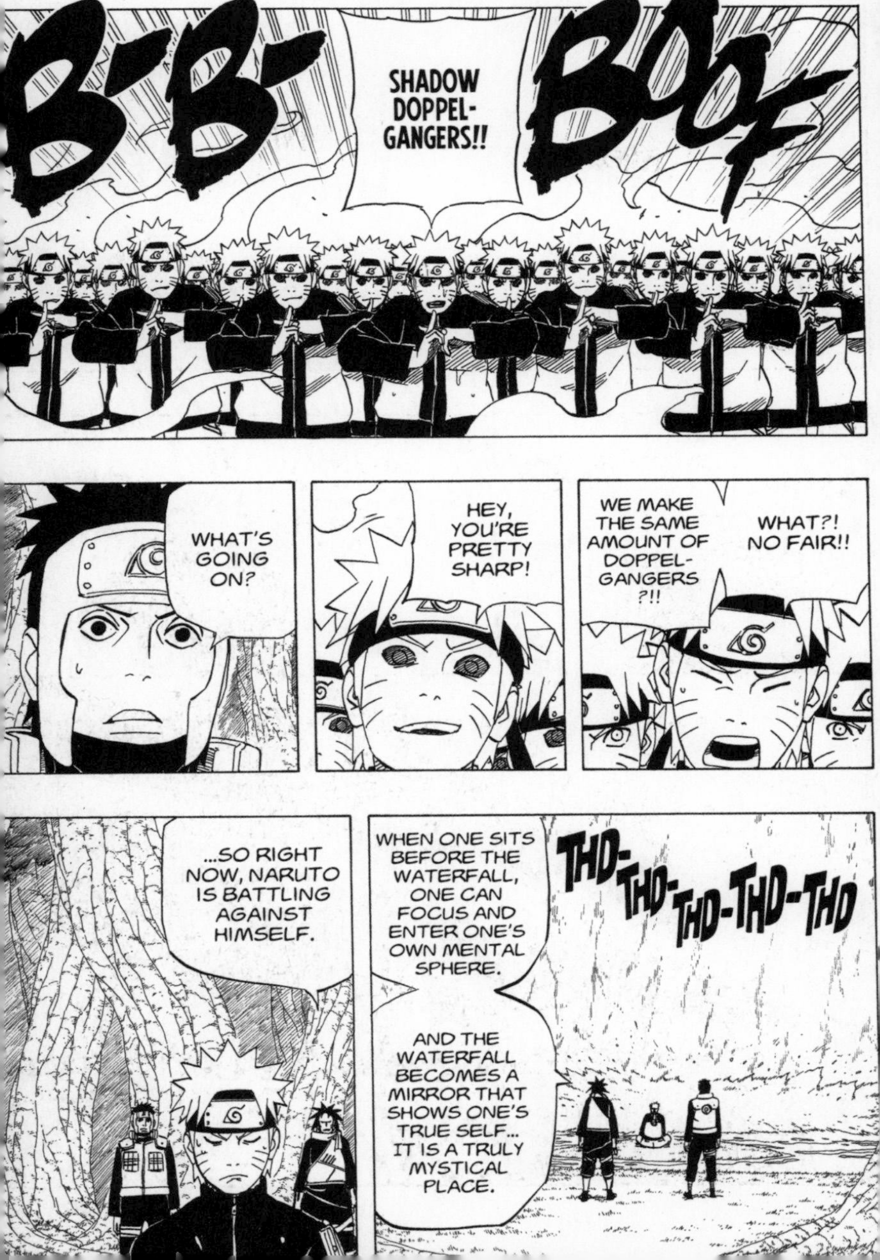
B-B-BOOF
SHADOW DOPPEL-GANGERS!!
WHAT?! NO FAIR!!
WE MAKE THE SAME AMOUNT OF DOPPEL-GANGERS?!!
HEY, YOU'RE PRETTY SHARP!
WHAT'S GOING ON?
THD-THD-THD-THD-THD
WHEN ONE SITS BEFORE THE WATERFALL, ONE CAN FOCUS AND ENTER ONE'S OWN MENTAL SPHERE.
AND THE WATERFALL BECOMES A MIRROR THAT SHOWS ONE'S TRUE SELF... IT IS A TRULY MYSTICAL PLACE.
...SO RIGHT NOW, NARUTO IS BATTLING AGAINST HIMSELF.

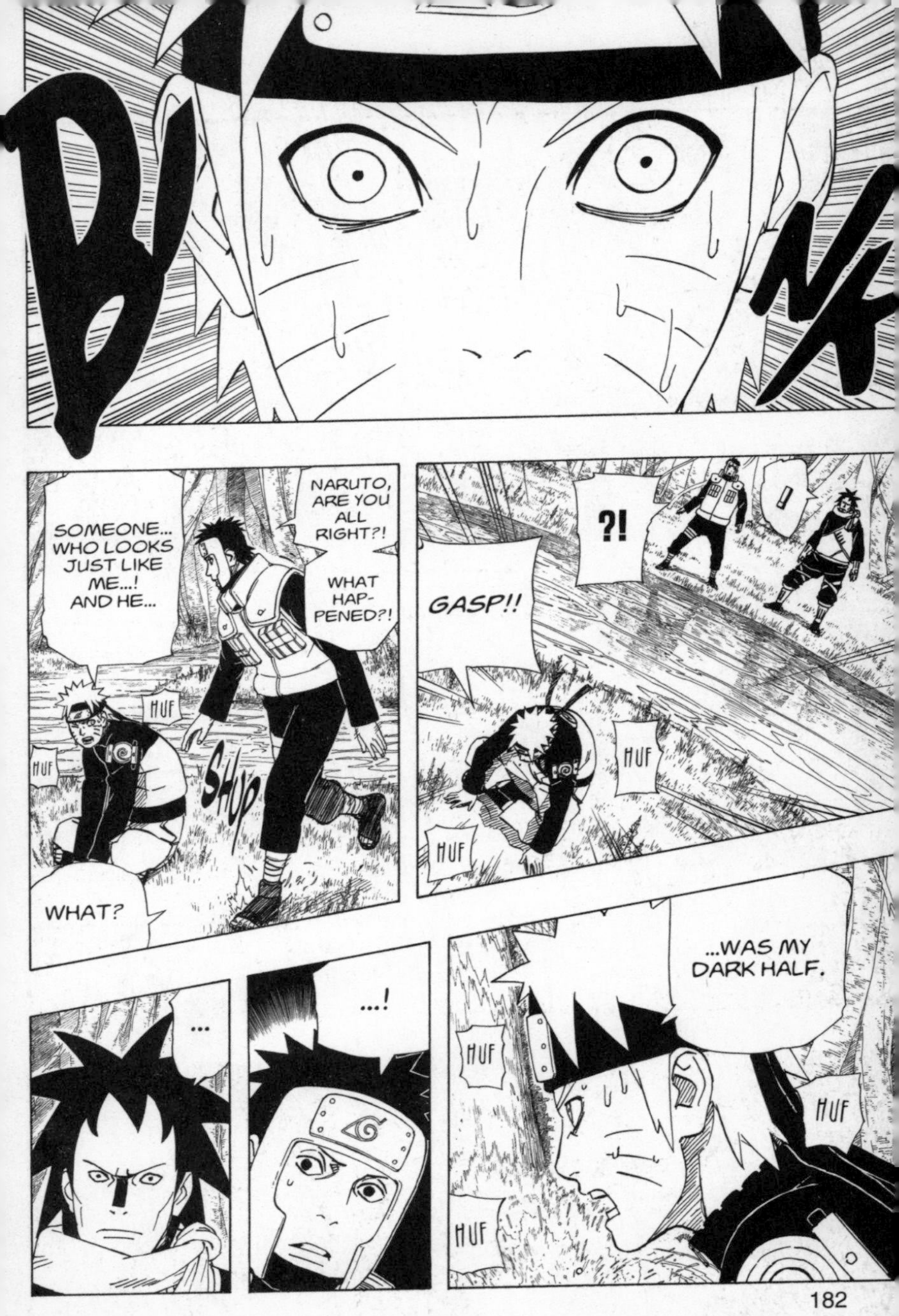
?!
!
GASP!!
HUF
HUF
NARUTO, ARE YOU ALL RIGHT?!
WHAT HAP-PENED?!
SHUP
SOMEONE... WHO LOOKS JUST LIKE ME...! AND HE...
HUF
HUF
WHAT?
...WAS MY DARK HALF.
HUF
HUF
HUF
...!
...

READ THIS WAY

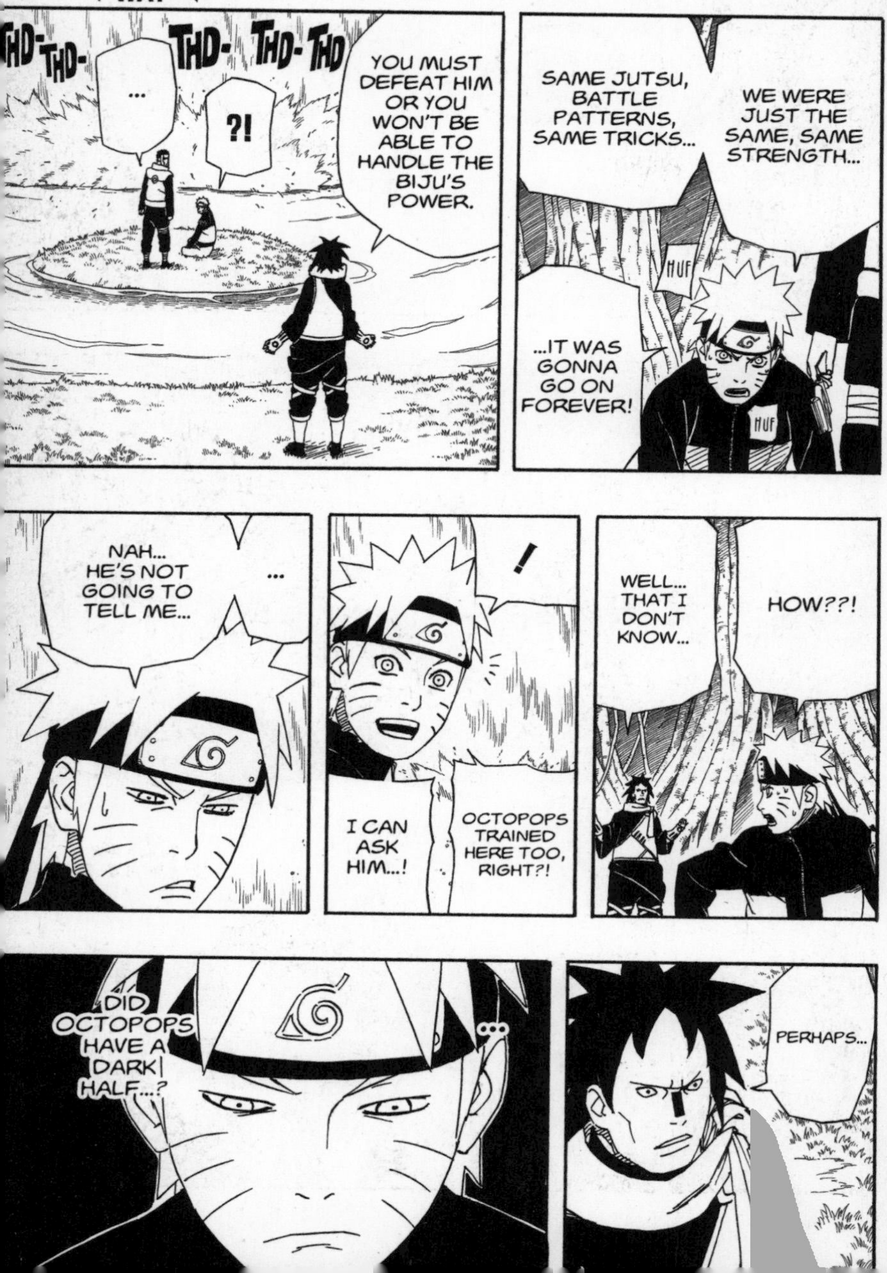
WE WERE JUST THE SAME, SAME STRENGTH...
SAME JUTSU, BATTLE PATTERNS, SAME TRICKS...
HUF
...IT WAS GONNA GO ON FOREVER!
HUF
YOU MUST DEFEAT HIM OR YOU WON'T BE ABLE TO HANDLE THE BIJU'S POWER.
THD- THD- THD- THD- THD
?!
...
HOW??!
WELL... THAT I DON'T KNOW...
!
OCTOPOPS TRAINED HERE TOO, RIGHT?!
I CAN ASK HIM...!
...
NAH... HE'S NOT GOING TO TELL ME...
PERHAPS...
...
DID OCTOPOPS HAVE A DARK HALF...?

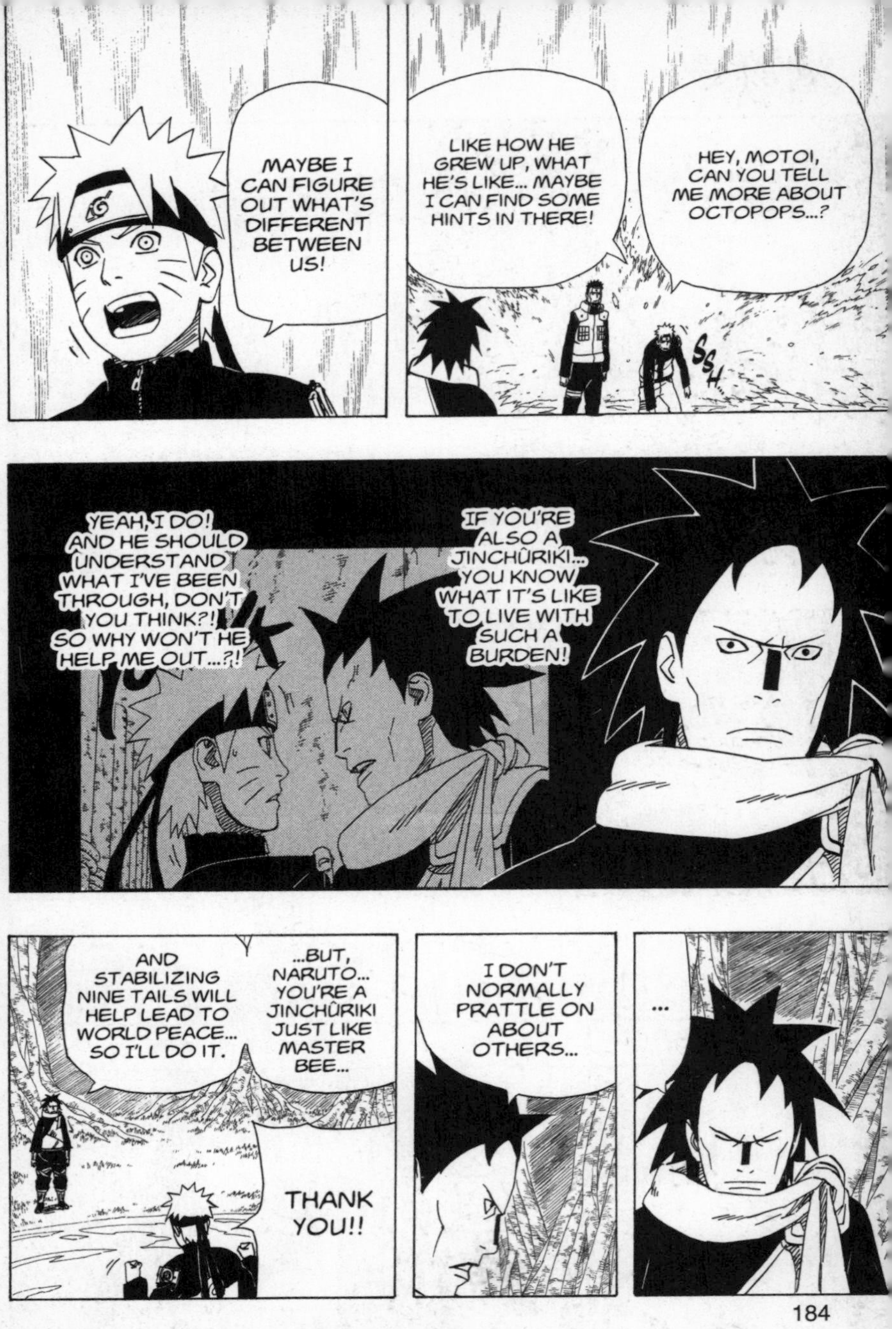
HEY, MOTOI, CAN YOU TELL ME MORE ABOUT OCTOPOPS...?
LIKE HOW HE GREW UP, WHAT HE'S LIKE... MAYBE I CAN FIND SOME HINTS IN THERE!
SSH...
MAYBE I CAN FIGURE OUT WHAT'S DIFFERENT BETWEEN US!
IF YOU'RE ALSO A JINCHÛRIKI... YOU KNOW WHAT IT'S LIKE TO LIVE WITH SUCH A BURDEN!
YEAH, I DO! AND HE SHOULD UNDERSTAND WHAT I'VE BEEN THROUGH, DON'T YOU THINK?! SO WHY WON'T HE HELP ME OUT...?!
...
I DON'T NORMALLY PRATTLE ON ABOUT OTHERS...
...BUT, NARUTO... YOU'RE A JINCHÛRIKI JUST LIKE MASTER BEE...
AND STABILIZING NINE TAILS WILL HELP LEAD TO WORLD PEACE... SO I'LL DO IT.
THANK YOU!!

READ THIS WAY

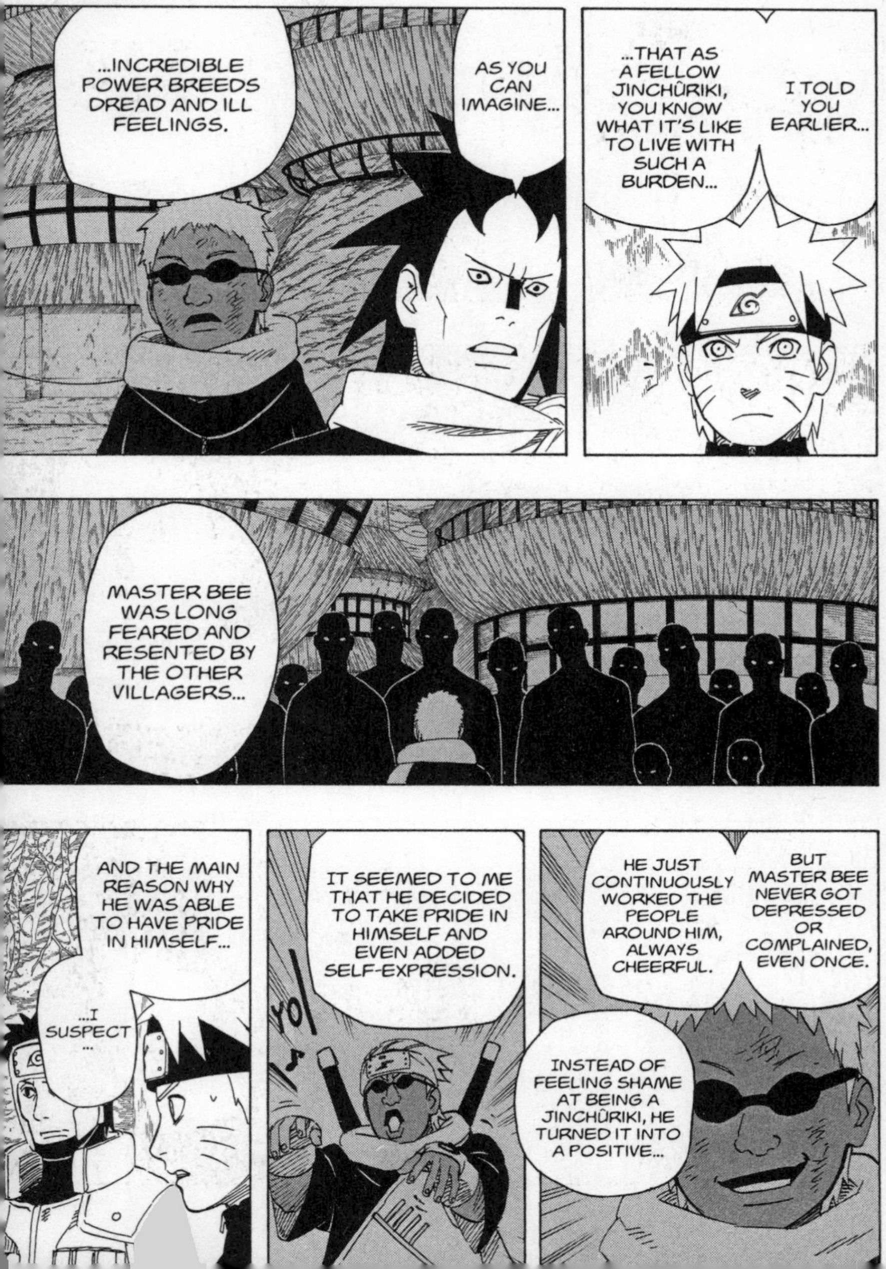
I TOLD YOU EARLIER...
...THAT AS A FELLOW JINCHŪRIKI, YOU KNOW WHAT IT'S LIKE TO LIVE WITH SUCH A BURDEN...
AS YOU CAN IMAGINE...
...INCREDIBLE POWER BREEDS DREAD AND ILL FEELINGS.
MASTER BEE WAS LONG FEARED AND RESENTED BY THE OTHER VILLAGERS...
BUT MASTER BEE NEVER GOT DEPRESSED OR COMPLAINED, EVEN ONCE.
HE JUST CONTINUOUSLY WORKED THE PEOPLE AROUND HIM, ALWAYS CHEERFUL.
INSTEAD OF FEELING SHAME AT BEING A JINCHŪRIKI, HE TURNED IT INTO A POSITIVE...
IT SEEMED TO ME THAT HE DECIDED TO TAKE PRIDE IN HIMSELF AND EVEN ADDED SELF-EXPRESSION.
YO
AND THE MAIN REASON WHY HE WAS ABLE TO HAVE PRIDE IN HIMSELF...
...I SUSPECT...

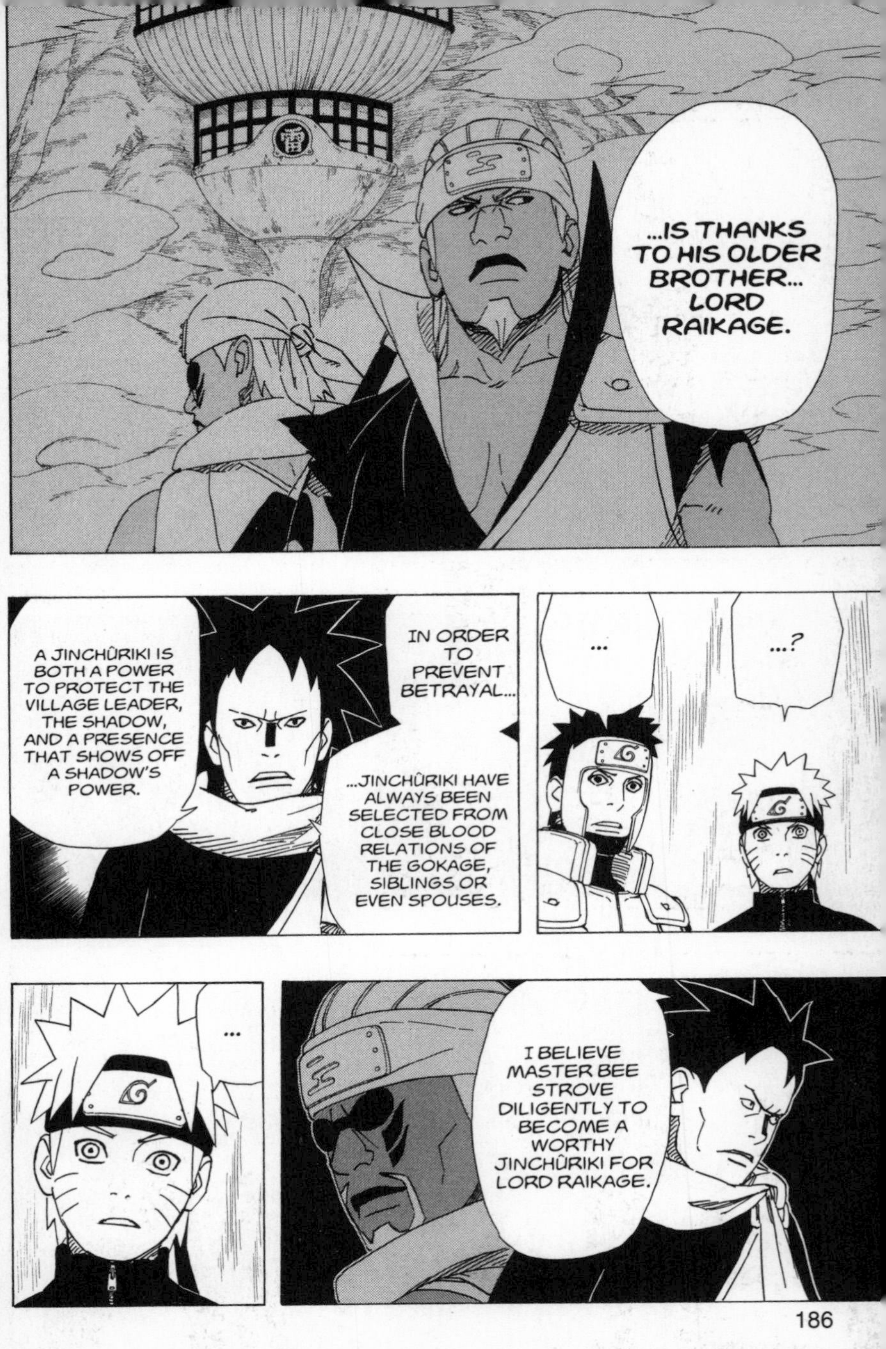
...IS THANKS TO HIS OLDER BROTHER... LORD RAIKAGE.
...?
...
IN ORDER TO PREVENT BETRAYAL...
...JINCHÛRIKI HAVE ALWAYS BEEN SELECTED FROM CLOSE BLOOD RELATIONS OF THE GOKAGE, SIBLINGS OR EVEN SPOUSES.
A JINCHÛRIKI IS BOTH A POWER TO PROTECT THE VILLAGE LEADER, THE SHADOW, AND A PRESENCE THAT SHOWS OFF A SHADOW'S POWER.
I BELIEVE MASTER BEE STROVE DILIGENTLY TO BECOME A WORTHY JINCHÛRIKI FOR LORD RAIKAGE.
...

READ THIS WAY

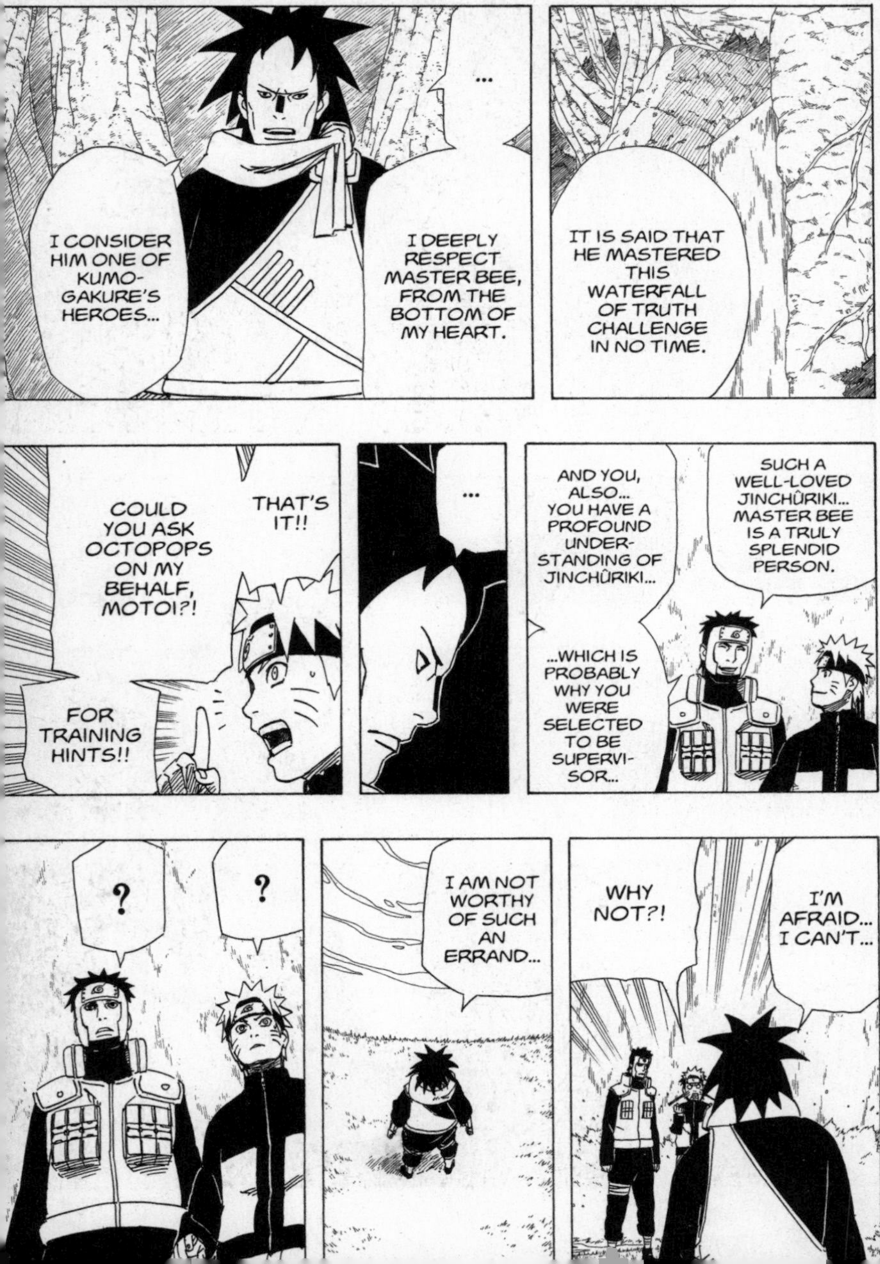
IT IS SAID THAT HE MASTERED THIS WATERFALL OF TRUTH CHALLENGE IN NO TIME.
...
I DEEPLY RESPECT MASTER BEE, FROM THE BOTTOM OF MY HEART.
I CONSIDER HIM ONE OF KUMOGAKURE'S HEROES...
SUCH A WELL-LOVED JINCHŪRIKI... MASTER BEE IS A TRULY SPLENDID PERSON.
AND YOU, ALSO... YOU HAVE A PROFOUND UNDERSTANDING OF JINCHŪRIKI...
...WHICH IS PROBABLY WHY YOU WERE SELECTED TO BE SUPERVISOR...
...
THAT'S IT!!
COULD YOU ASK OCTOPOPS ON MY BEHALF, MOTOI?!
FOR TRAINING HINTS!!
I'M AFRAID... I CAN'T...
WHY NOT?!
I AM NOT WORTHY OF SUCH AN ERRAND...
?
?

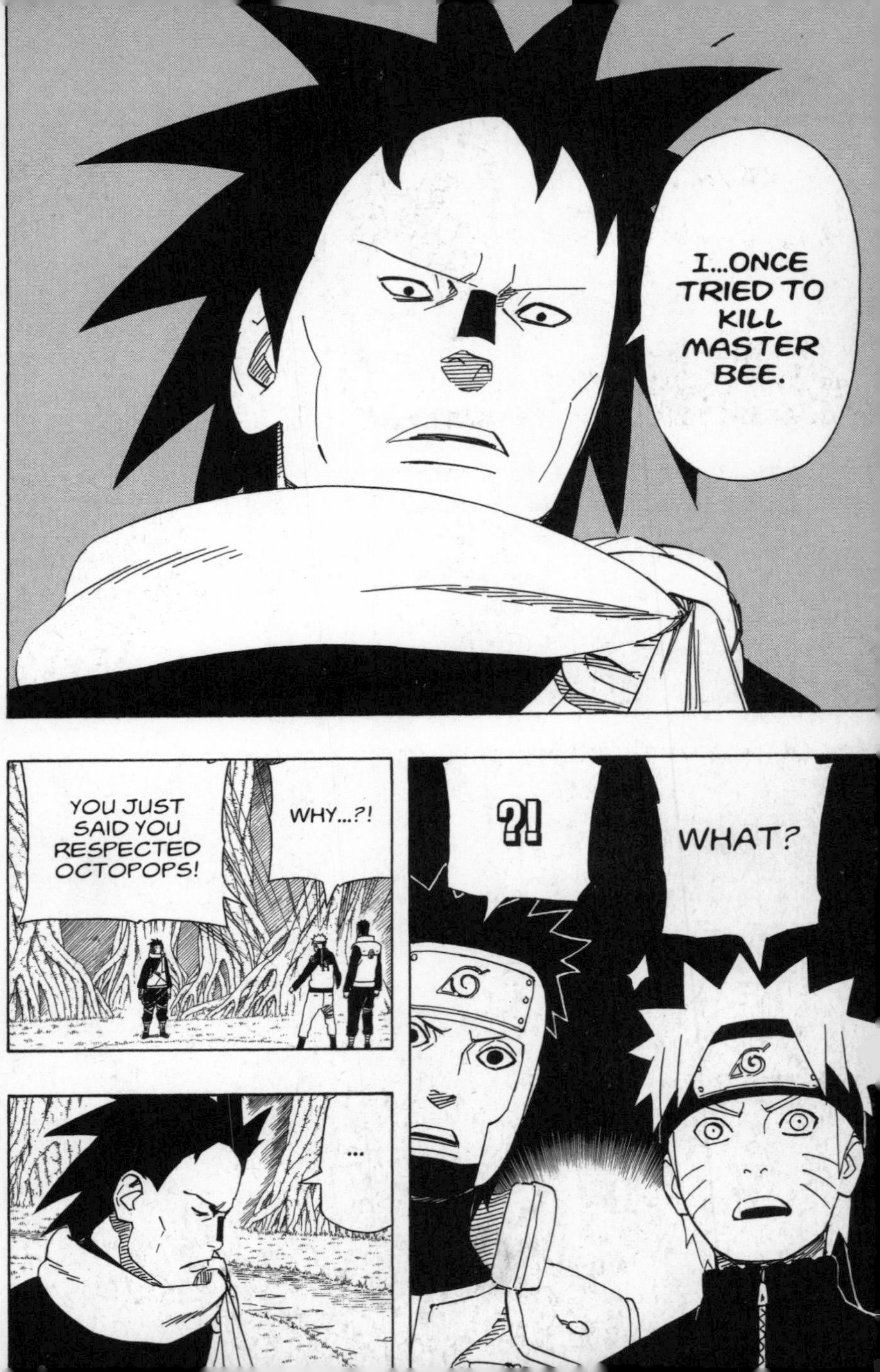
I...ONCE TRIED TO KILL MASTER BEE.
WHAT?
?!
WHY...?!
YOU JUST SAID YOU RESPECTED OCTOPOPS!
...

READ THIS WAY

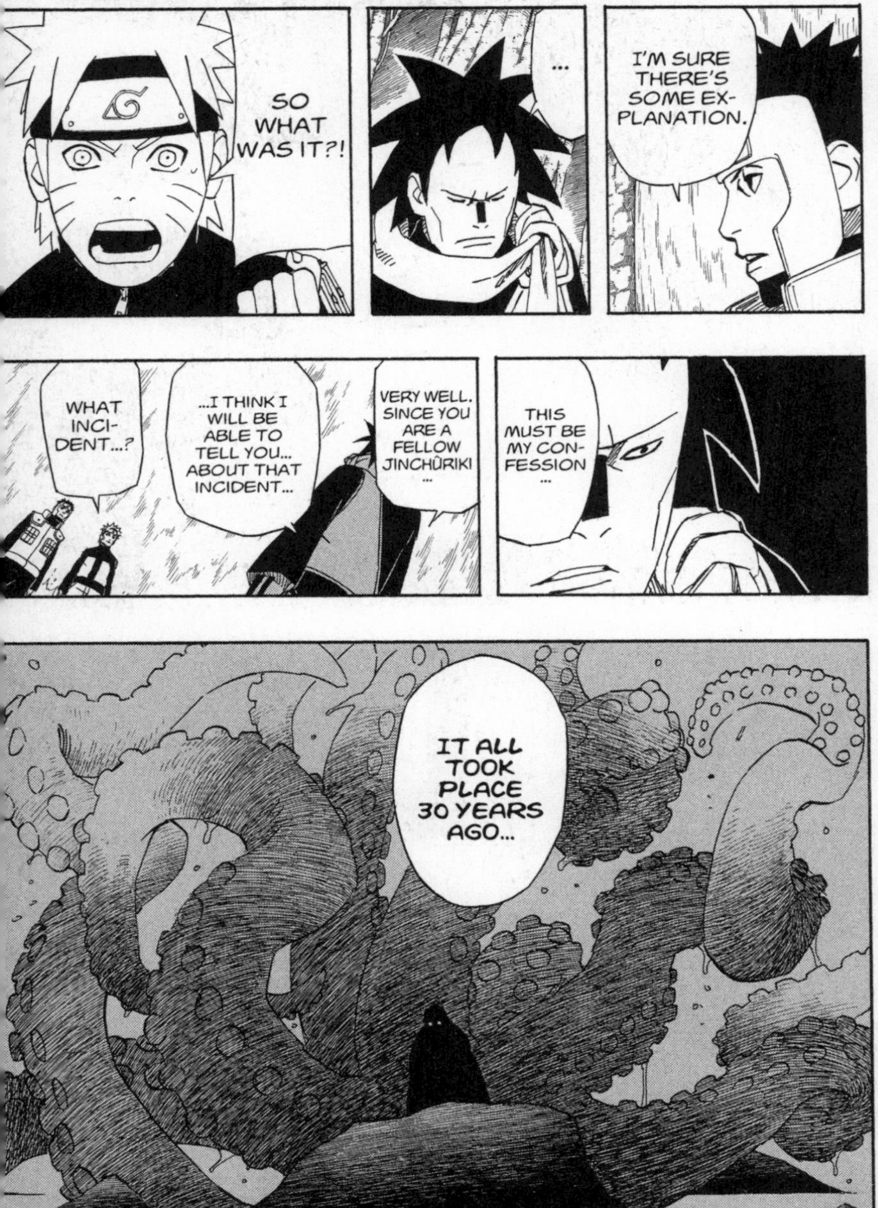
I'M SURE THERE'S SOME EXPLANATION.
...
SO WHAT WAS IT?!
THIS MUST BE MY CONFESSION...
VERY WELL. SINCE YOU ARE A FELLOW JINCHŪRIKI...
...I THINK I WILL BE ABLE TO TELL YOU... ABOUT THAT INCIDENT...
WHAT INCIDENT...?
IT ALL TOOK PLACE 30 YEARS AGO...

NARUTO

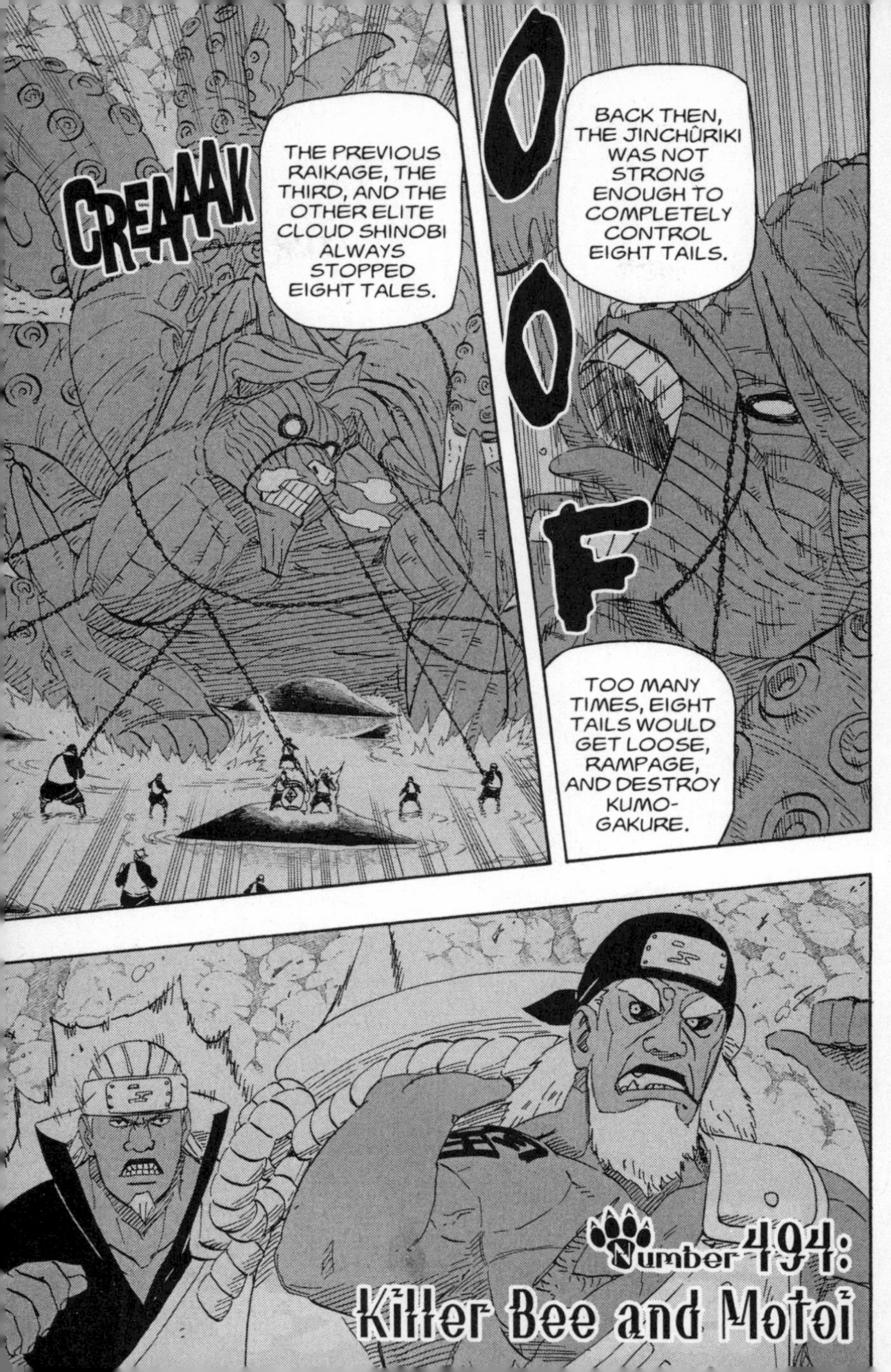
BACK THEN, THE JINCHÛRIKI WAS NOT STRONG ENOUGH TO COMPLETELY CONTROL EIGHT TAILS.
OOOF
TOO MANY TIMES, EIGHT TAILS WOULD GET LOOSE, RAMPAGE, AND DESTROY KUMO-GAKURE.
CREAAAK
THE PREVIOUS RAIKAGE, THE THIRD, AND THE OTHER ELITE CLOUD SHINOBI ALWAYS STOPPED EIGHT TALES.
Number 494:
Killer Bee and Motoi

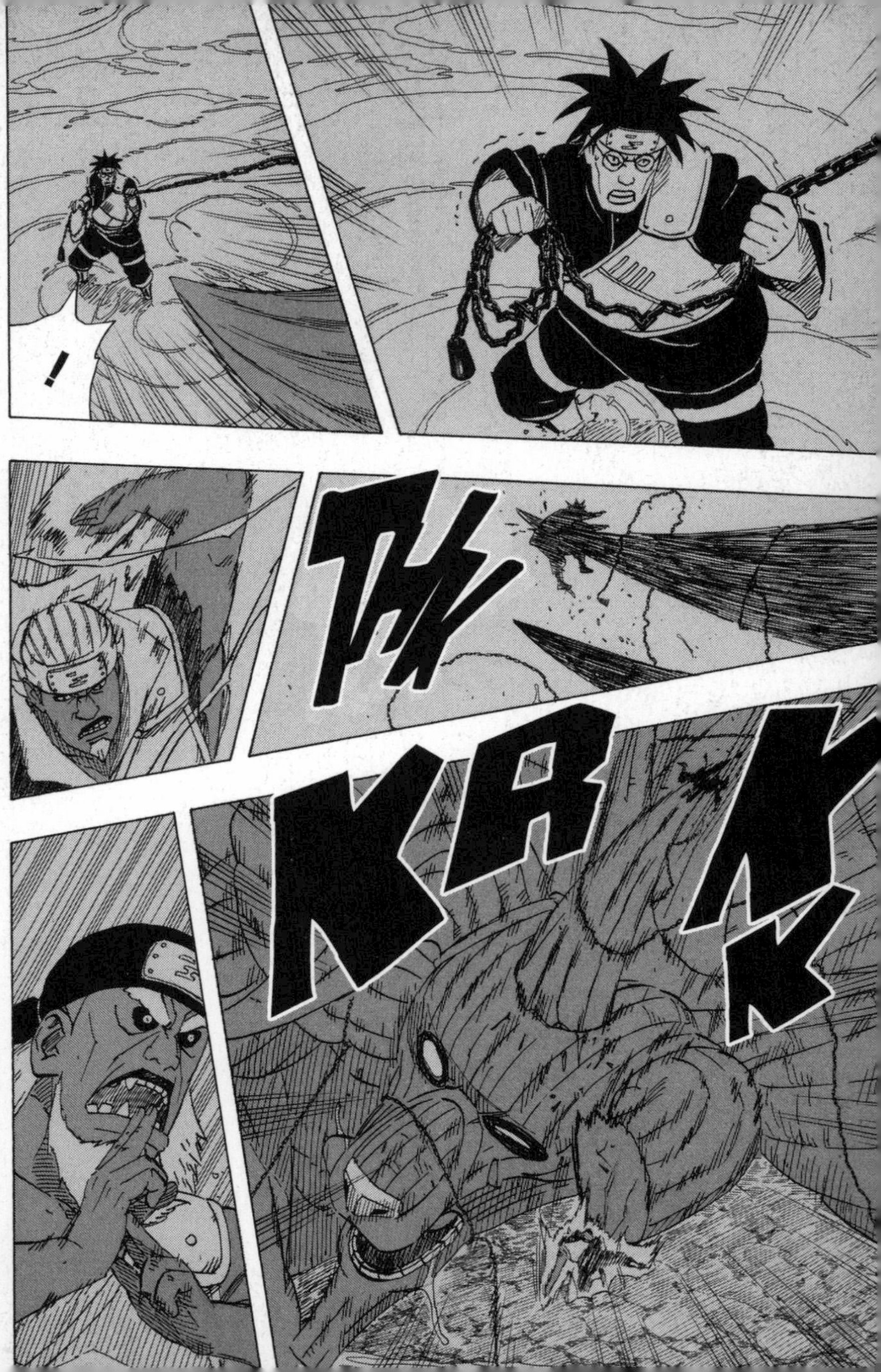
!
THK
KRAK

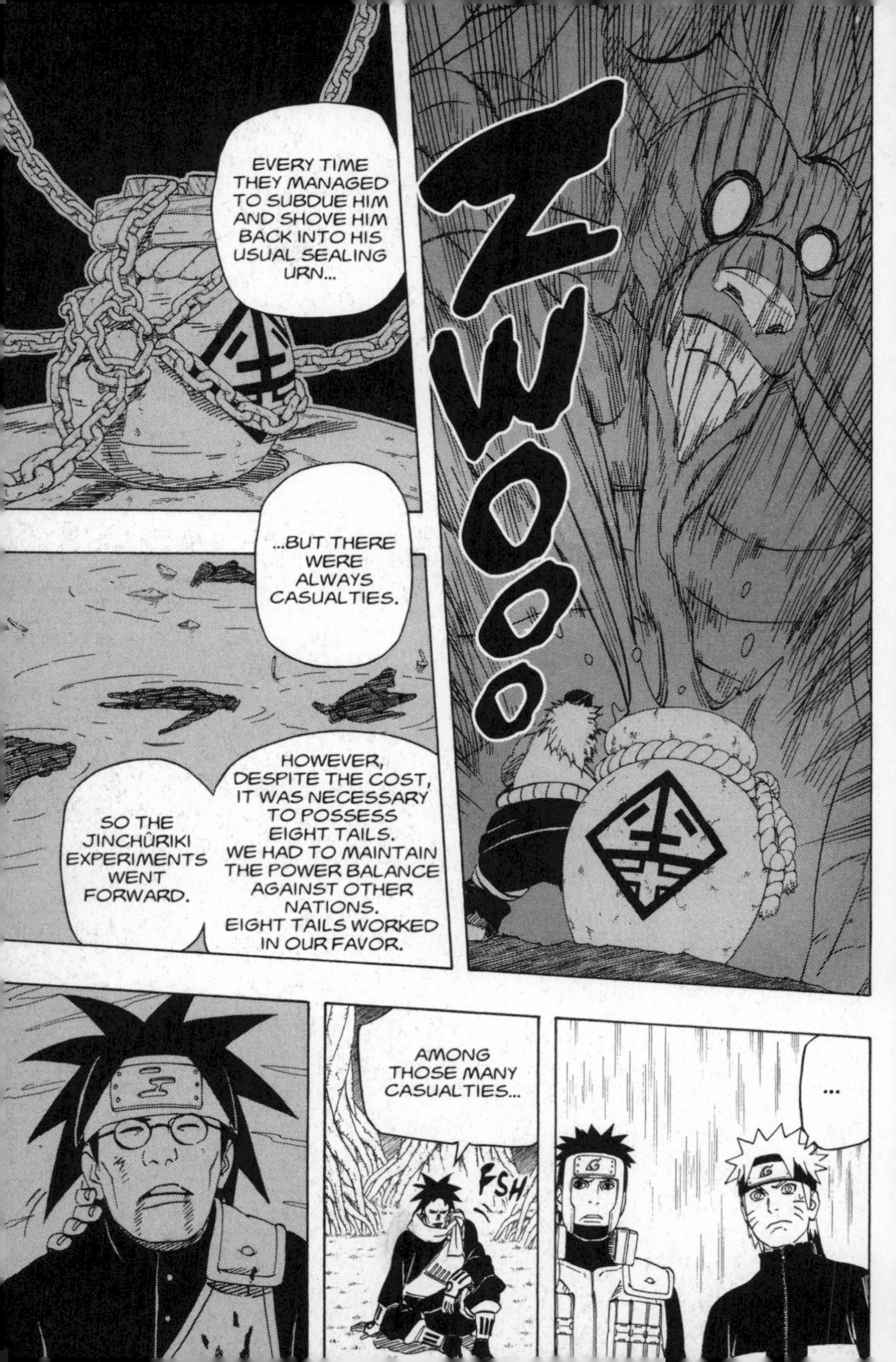
ZWOOO
EVERY TIME THEY MANAGED TO SUBDUE HIM AND SHOVE HIM BACK INTO HIS USUAL SEALING URN...
...BUT THERE WERE ALWAYS CASUALTIES.
HOWEVER, DESPITE THE COST, IT WAS NECESSARY TO POSSESS EIGHT TAILS. WE HAD TO MAINTAIN THE POWER BALANCE AGAINST OTHER NATIONS. EIGHT TAILS WORKED IN OUR FAVOR.
SO THE JINCHÛRIKI EXPERIMENTS WENT FORWARD.
...
AMONG THOSE MANY CASUALTIES...
FSH

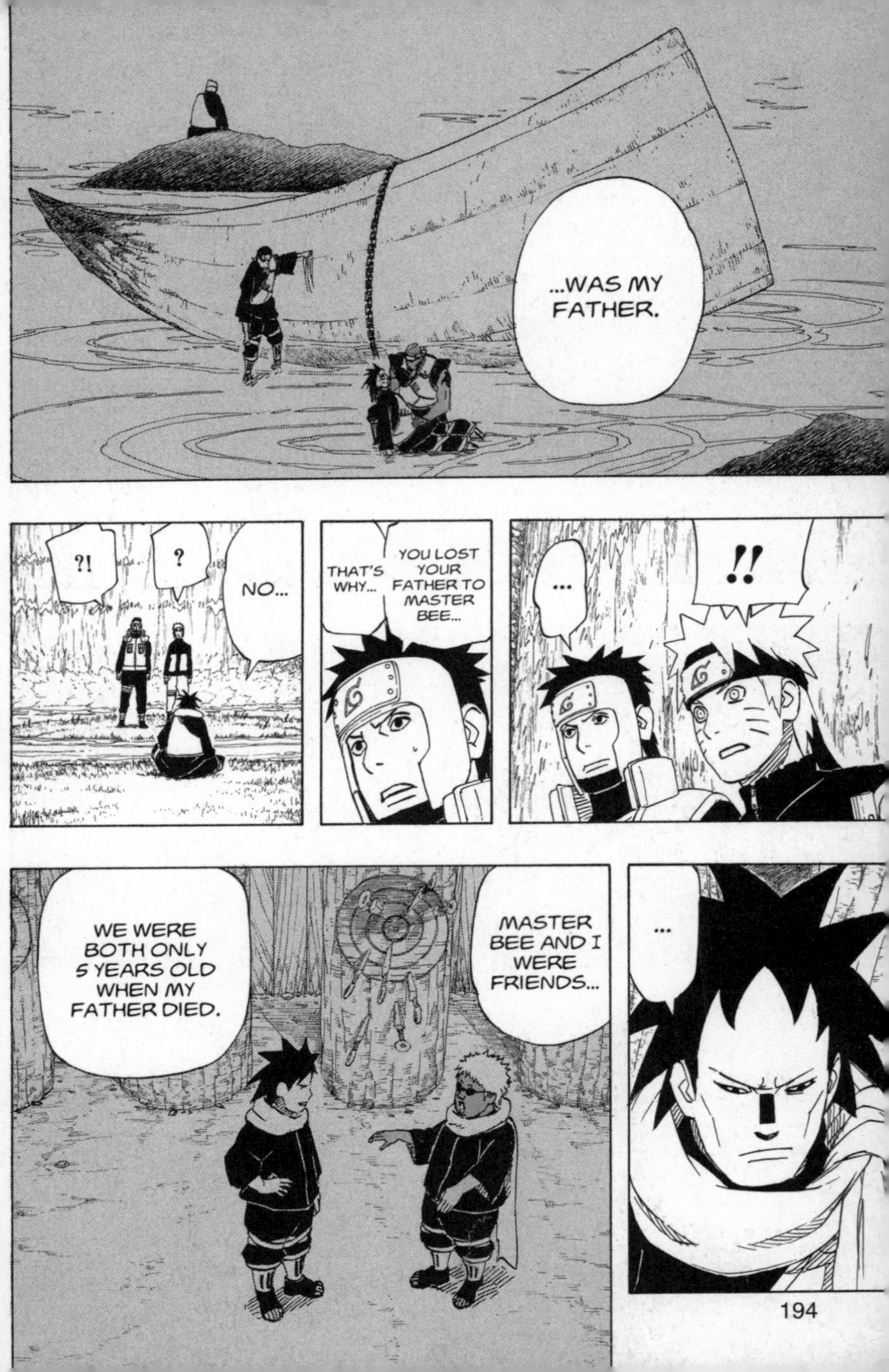
...WAS MY FATHER.
!!
...
YOU LOST YOUR FATHER TO MASTER BEE...
THAT'S WHY...
NO...
?
?!
...
MASTER BEE AND I WERE FRIENDS...
WE WERE BOTH ONLY 5 YEARS OLD WHEN MY FATHER DIED.

READ THIS WAY

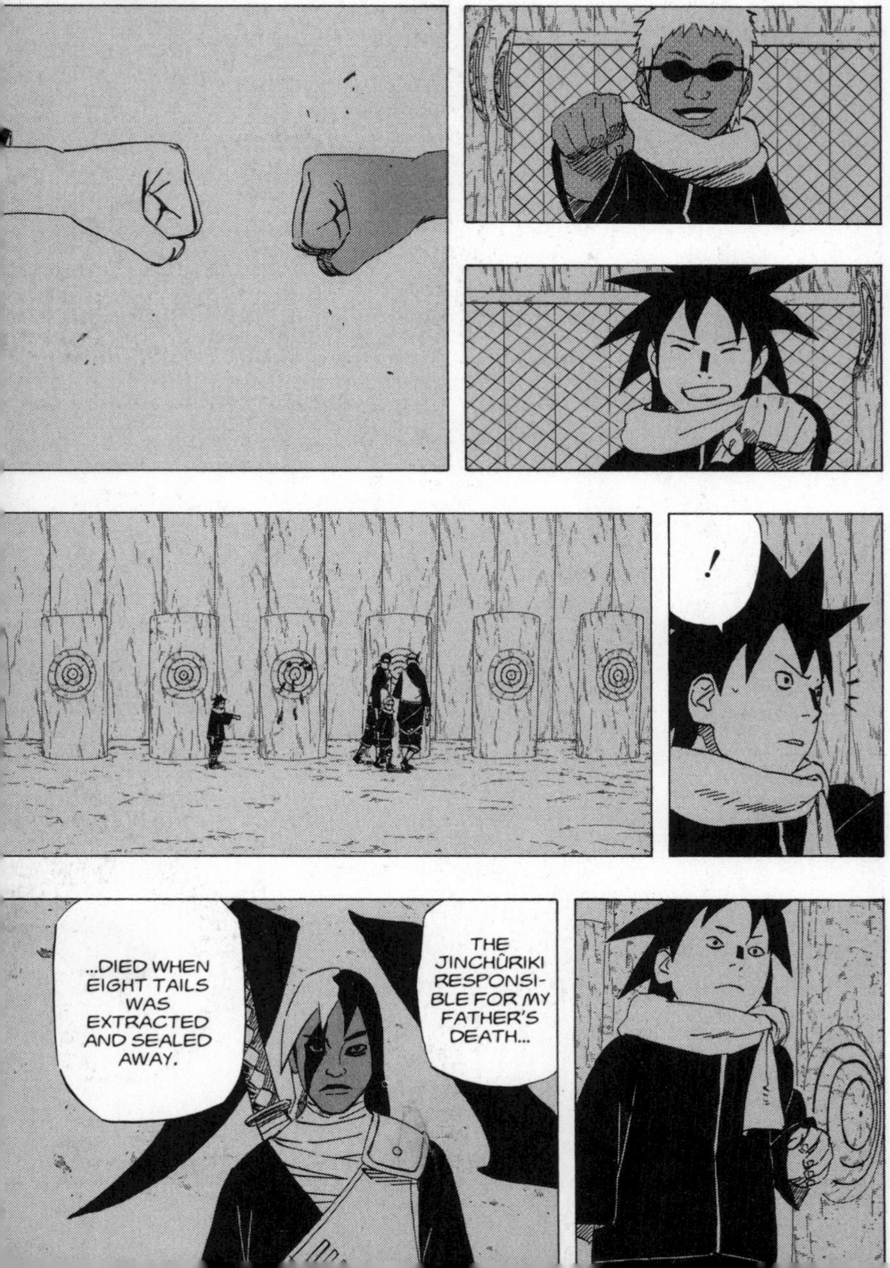
!
THE JINCHÛRIKI RESPONSI-BLE FOR MY FATHER'S DEATH...
...DIED WHEN EIGHT TAILS WAS EXTRACTED AND SEALED AWAY.

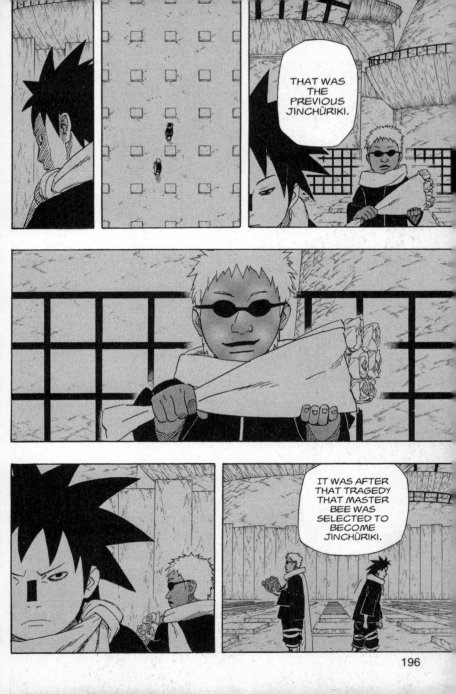

THAT WAS THE PREVIOUS JINCHŪRIKI.

IT WAS AFTER THAT TRAGEDY THAT MASTER BEE WAS SELECTED TO BECOME JINCHŪRIKI.

196

READ THIS WAY

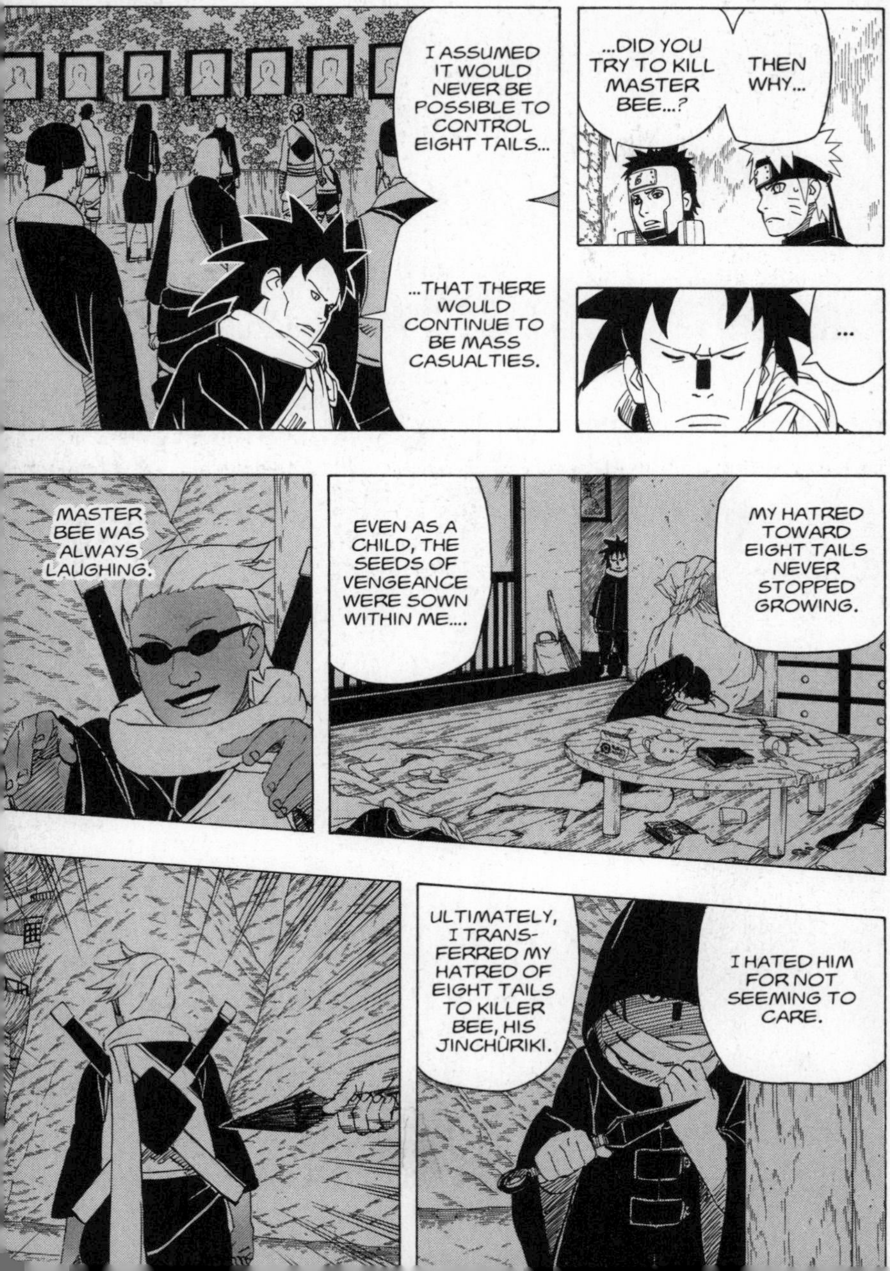
THEN WHY...
...DID YOU TRY TO KILL MASTER BEE...?
...
I ASSUMED IT WOULD NEVER BE POSSIBLE TO CONTROL EIGHT TAILS...
...THAT THERE WOULD CONTINUE TO BE MASS CASUALTIES.
MY HATRED TOWARD EIGHT TAILS NEVER STOPPED GROWING.
EVEN AS A CHILD, THE SEEDS OF VENGEANCE WERE SOWN WITHIN ME....
MASTER BEE WAS ALWAYS LAUGHING.
I HATED HIM FOR NOT SEEMING TO CARE.
ULTIMATELY, I TRANS-FERRED MY HATRED OF EIGHT TAILS TO KILLER BEE, HIS JINCHÛRIKI.

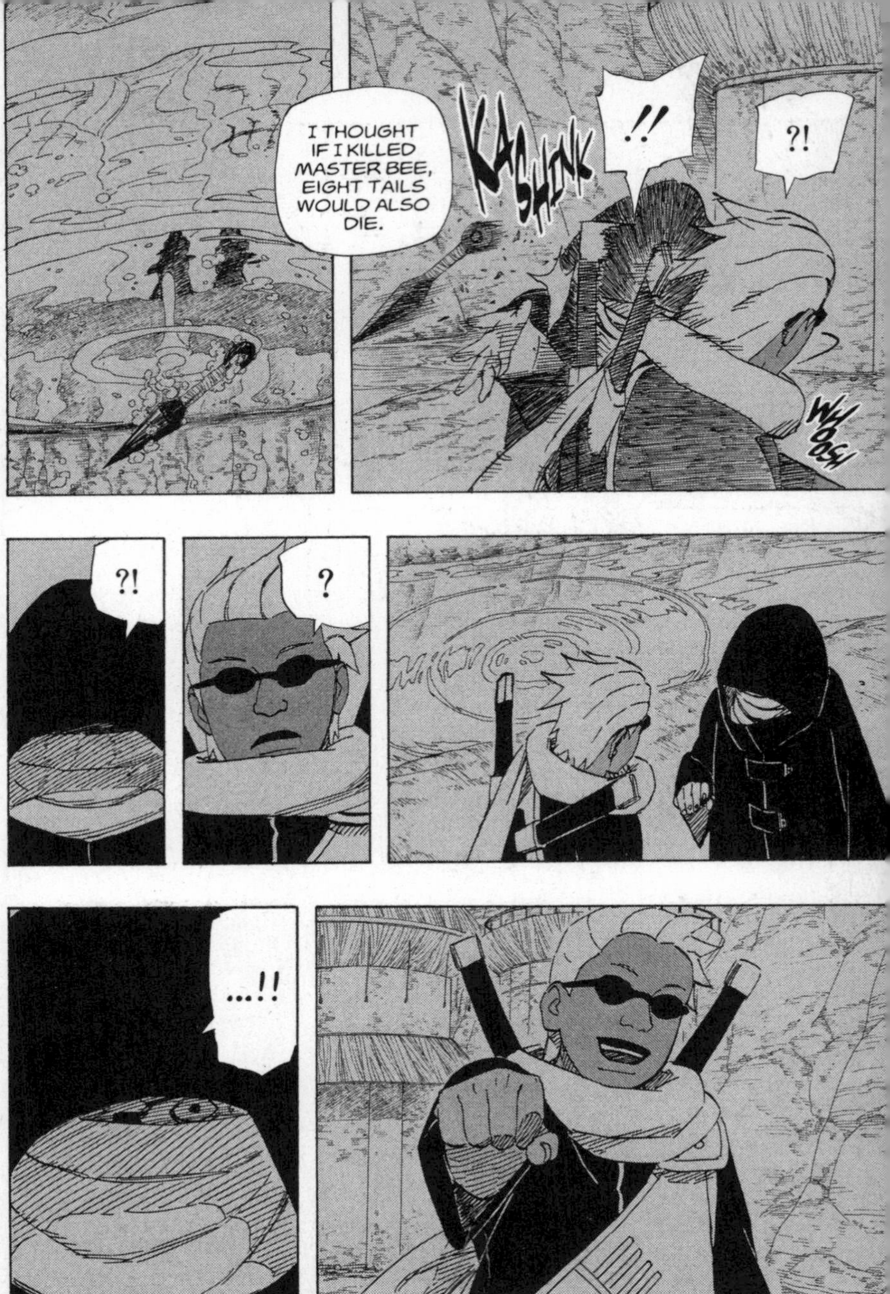
?!
!!
KASHINK
WHOOSH
I THOUGHT IF I KILLED MASTER BEE, EIGHT TAILS WOULD ALSO DIE.
?
?!
...!!

READ THIS WAY

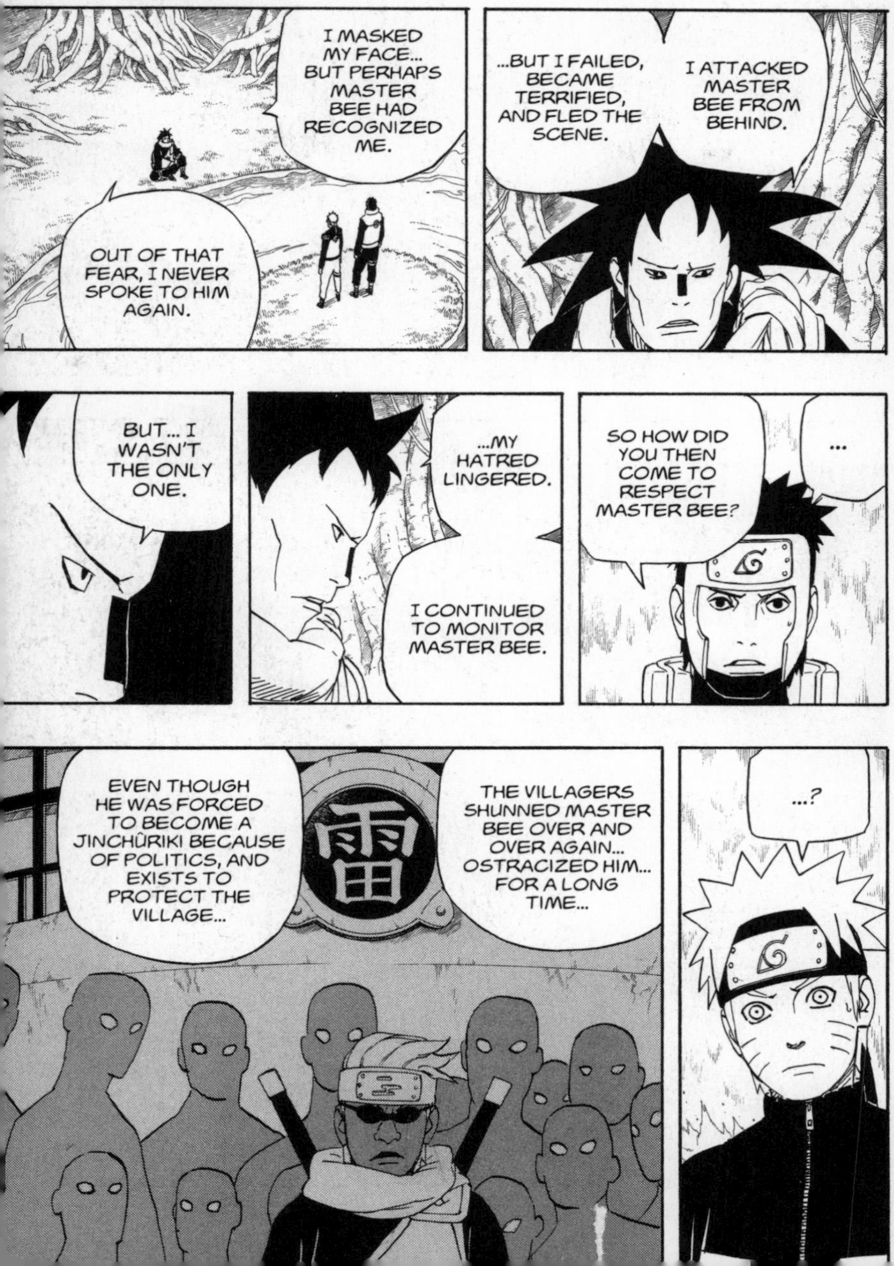
I ATTACKED MASTER BEE FROM BEHIND.
...BUT I FAILED, BECAME TERRIFIED, AND FLED THE SCENE.
I MASKED MY FACE... BUT PERHAPS MASTER BEE HAD RECOGNIZED ME.
OUT OF THAT FEAR, I NEVER SPOKE TO HIM AGAIN.
...
SO HOW DID YOU THEN COME TO RESPECT MASTER BEE?
...MY HATRED LINGERED.
I CONTINUED TO MONITOR MASTER BEE.
BUT... I WASN'T THE ONLY ONE.
...?
THE VILLAGERS SHUNNED MASTER BEE OVER AND OVER AGAIN... OSTRACIZED HIM... FOR A LONG TIME...
EVEN THOUGH HE WAS FORCED TO BECOME A JINCHÛRIKI BECAUSE OF POLITICS, AND EXISTS TO PROTECT THE VILLAGE...
雷

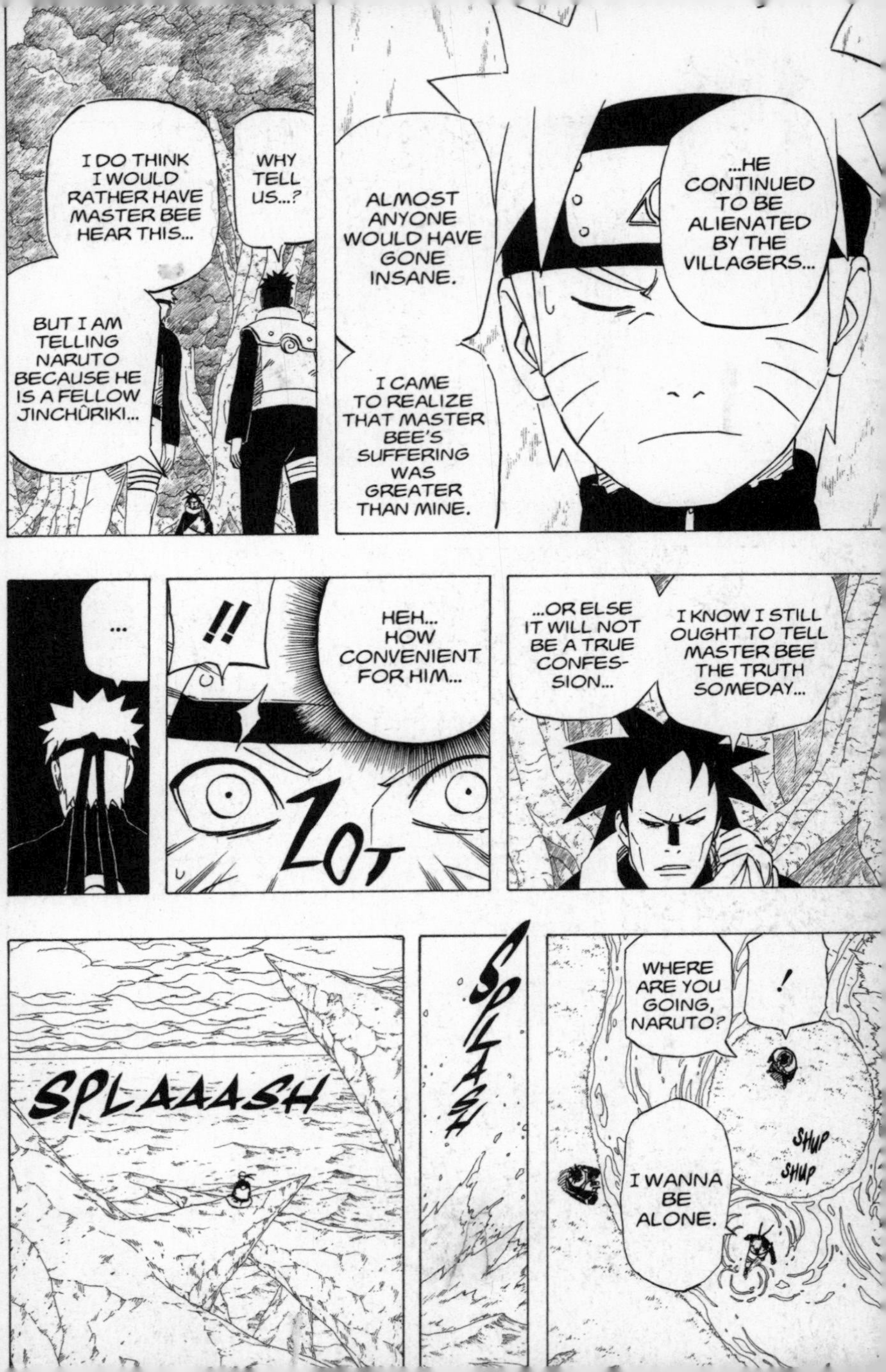
...HE CONTINUED TO BE ALIENATED BY THE VILLAGERS...
ALMOST ANYONE WOULD HAVE GONE INSANE.
I CAME TO REALIZE THAT MASTER BEE'S SUFFERING WAS GREATER THAN MINE.
WHY TELL US...?
I DO THINK I WOULD RATHER HAVE MASTER BEE HEAR THIS...
BUT I AM TELLING NARUTO BECAUSE HE IS A FELLOW JINCHÛRIKI...
I KNOW I STILL OUGHT TO TELL MASTER BEE THE TRUTH SOMEDAY...
...OR ELSE IT WILL NOT BE A TRUE CONFESSION...
HEH... HOW CONVENIENT FOR HIM...
!!
ZOT
...
!
WHERE ARE YOU GOING, NARUTO?
SHUP
SHUP
I WANNA BE ALONE.
SPLASH
SPLAAASH

READ THIS WAY

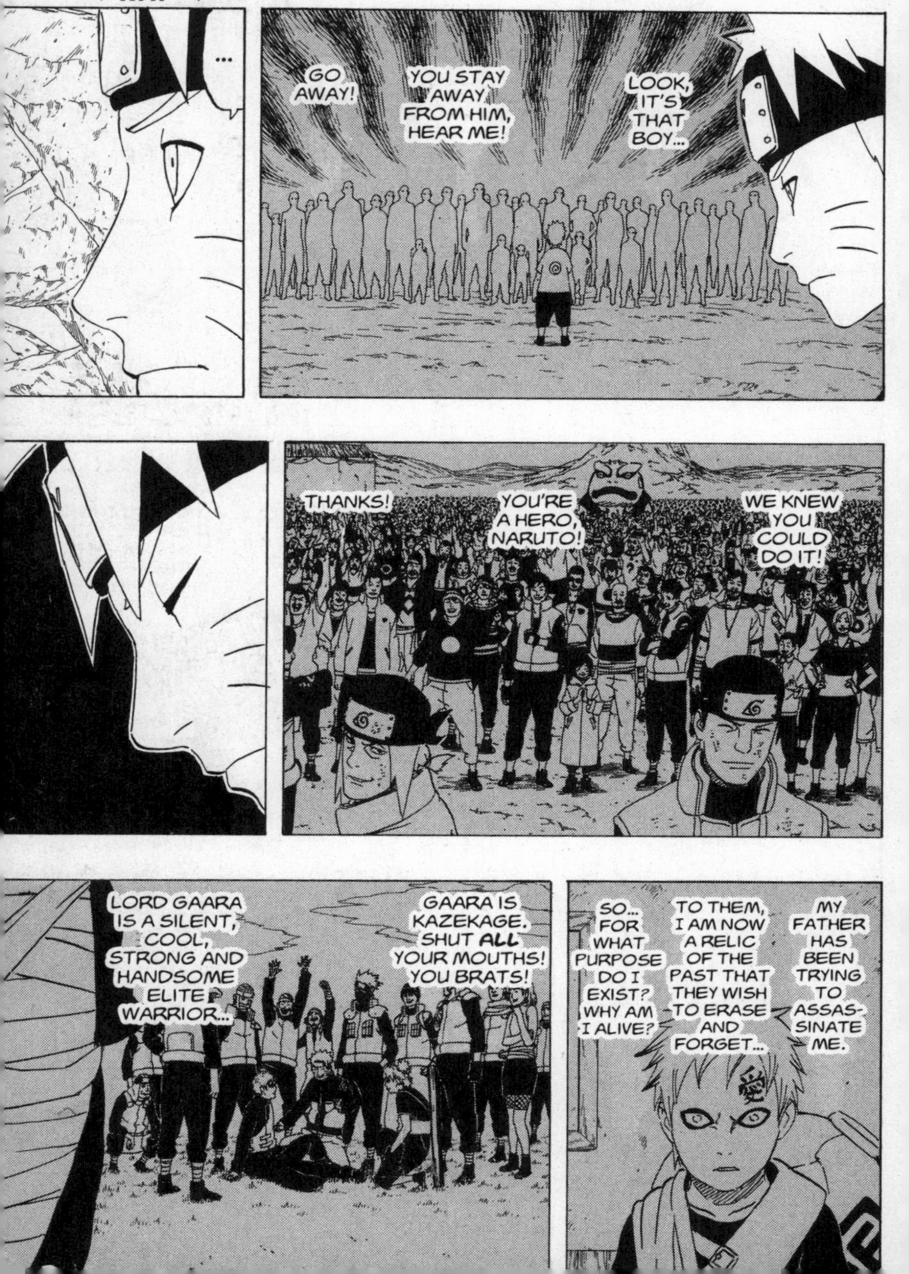
LOOK, IT'S THAT BOY...
YOU STAY AWAY FROM HIM, HEAR ME!
GO AWAY!
...
WE KNEW YOU COULD DO IT!
YOU'RE A HERO, NARUTO!
THANKS!
MY FATHER HAS BEEN TRYING TO ASSAS-SINATE ME.
TO THEM, I AM NOW A RELIC OF THE PAST THAT THEY WISH TO ERASE AND FORGET...
SO... FOR WHAT PURPOSE DO I EXIST? WHY AM I ALIVE?
GAARA IS KAZEKAGE. SHUT **ALL** YOUR MOUTHS! YOU BRATS!
LORD GAARA IS A SILENT, COOL, STRONG AND HANDSOME ELITE WARRIOR...

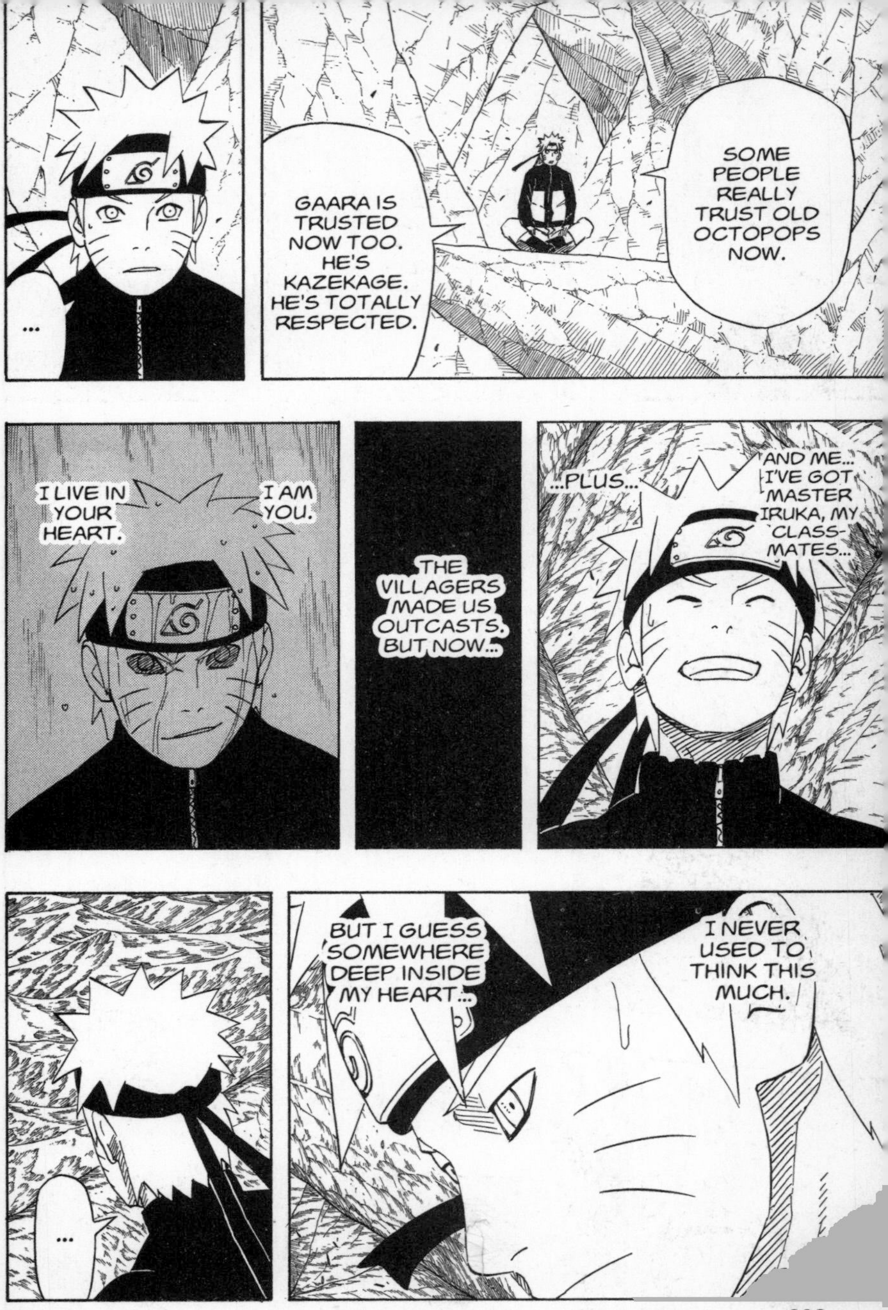
SOME PEOPLE REALLY TRUST OLD OCTOPOPS NOW.
GAARA IS TRUSTED NOW TOO. HE'S KAZEKAGE. HE'S TOTALLY RESPECTED.
...
AND ME... I'VE GOT MASTER IRUKA, MY CLASSMATES...
...PLUS...
THE VILLAGERS MADE US OUTCASTS. BUT NOW...
I AM YOU.
I LIVE IN YOUR HEART.
I NEVER USED TO THINK THIS MUCH.
BUT I GUESS SOMEWHERE DEEP INSIDE MY HEART...
...

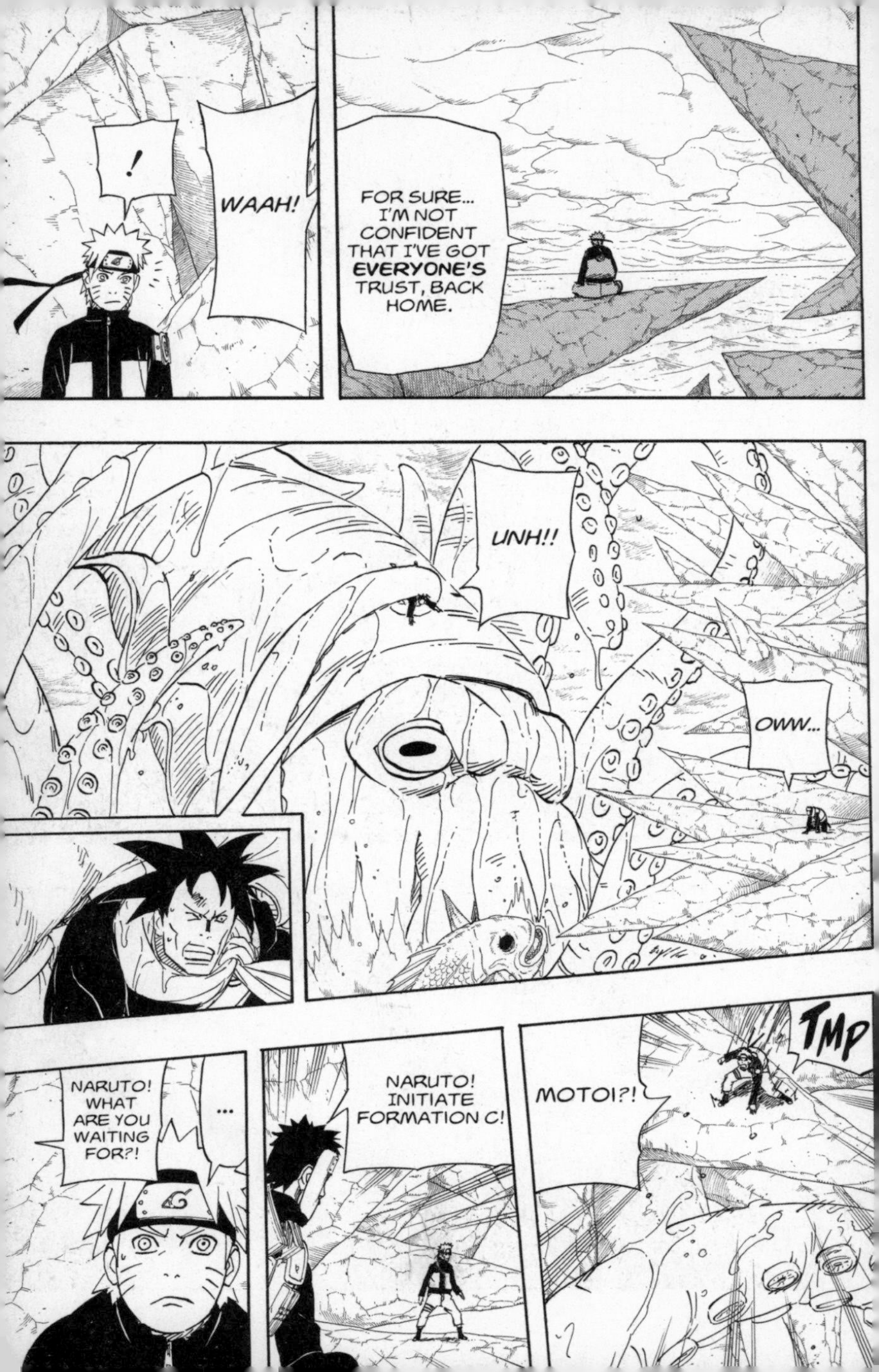
FOR SURE... I'M NOT CONFIDENT THAT I'VE GOT **EVERYONE'S** TRUST, BACK HOME.
WAAH!
!
UNH!!
OWW...
TMP
MOTOI?!
NARUTO! INITIATE FORMATION C!
...
NARUTO! WHAT ARE YOU WAITING FOR?!

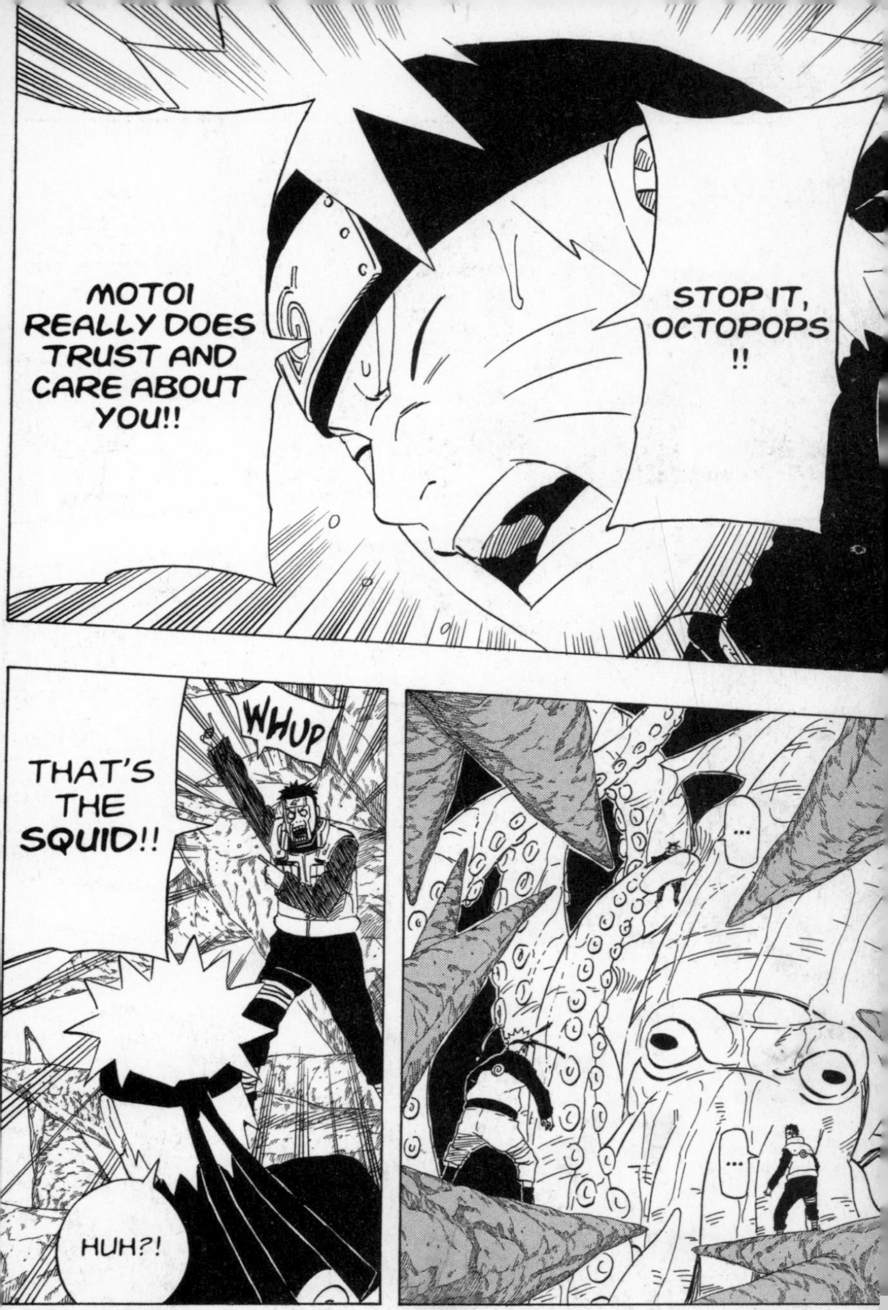
STOP IT, OCTOPOPS!!
MOTOI REALLY DOES TRUST AND CARE ABOUT YOU!!
...
...
WHUP
THAT'S THE SQUID!!
HUH?!

READ THIS WAY

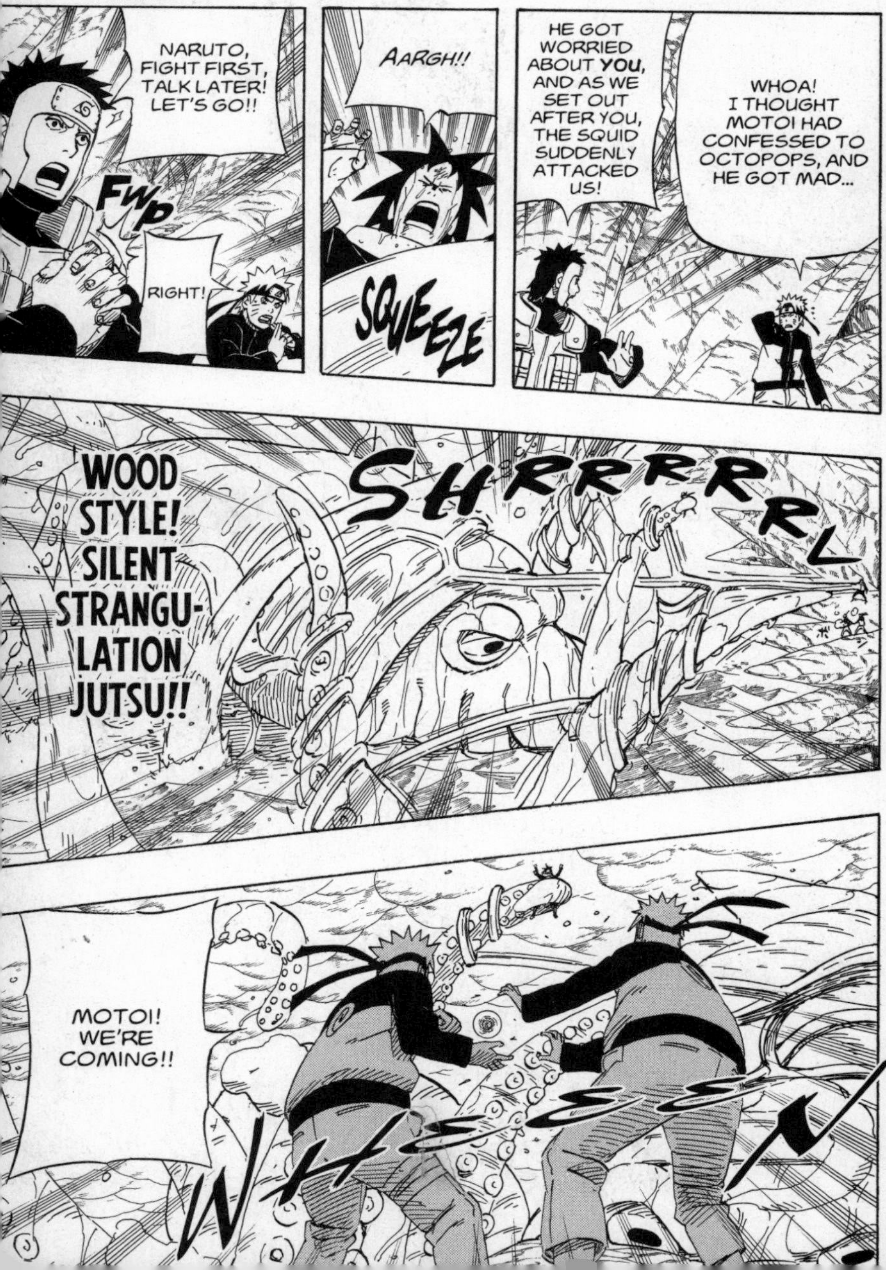
WHOA! I THOUGHT MOTOI HAD CONFESSED TO OCTOPOPS, AND HE GOT MAD...
HE GOT WORRIED ABOUT **YOU**, AND AS WE SET OUT AFTER YOU, THE SQUID SUDDENLY ATTACKED US!
AARGH!!
SQUEEZE
NARUTO, FIGHT FIRST, TALK LATER! LET'S GO!!
FWP
RIGHT!
SHRRRRRL
WOOD STYLE! SILENT STRANGULATION JUTSU!!
WHSSSSN
MOTOI! WE'RE COMING!!

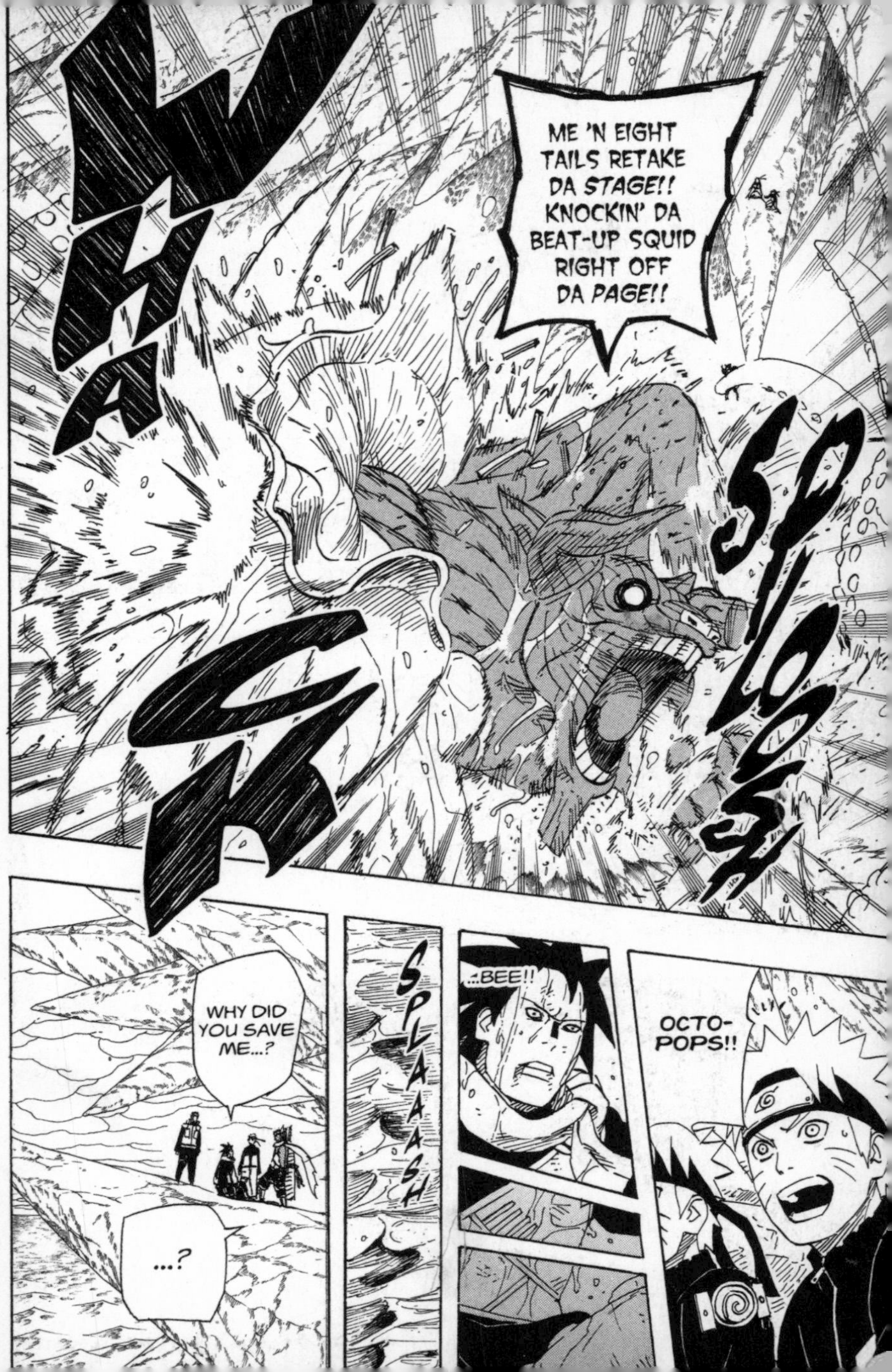
ME 'N EIGHT TAILS RETAKE DA STAGE!! KNOCKIN' DA BEAT-UP SQUID RIGHT OFF DA PAGE!!
SPLOOSH
WHACK
OCTO-POPS!!
...BEE!!
SPLAASH
WHY DID YOU SAVE ME...?
...?

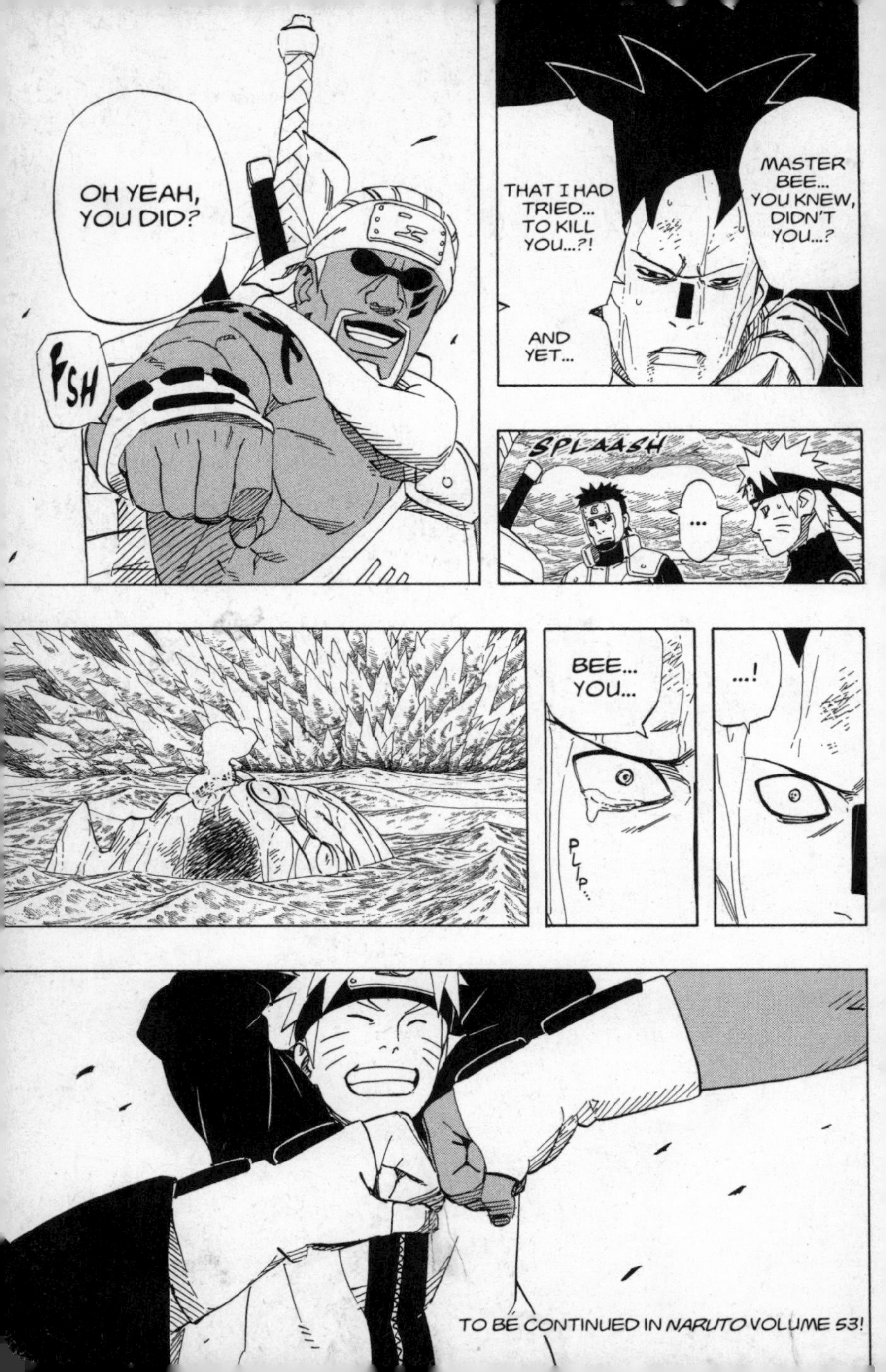
MASTER BEE... YOU KNEW, DIDN'T YOU...?
THAT I HAD TRIED... TO KILL YOU...?!
AND YET...
SPLAASH
...
OH YEAH, YOU DID?
FSH
...!
BEE... YOU...
PLIP...
TO BE CONTINUED IN NARUTO VOLUME 53!

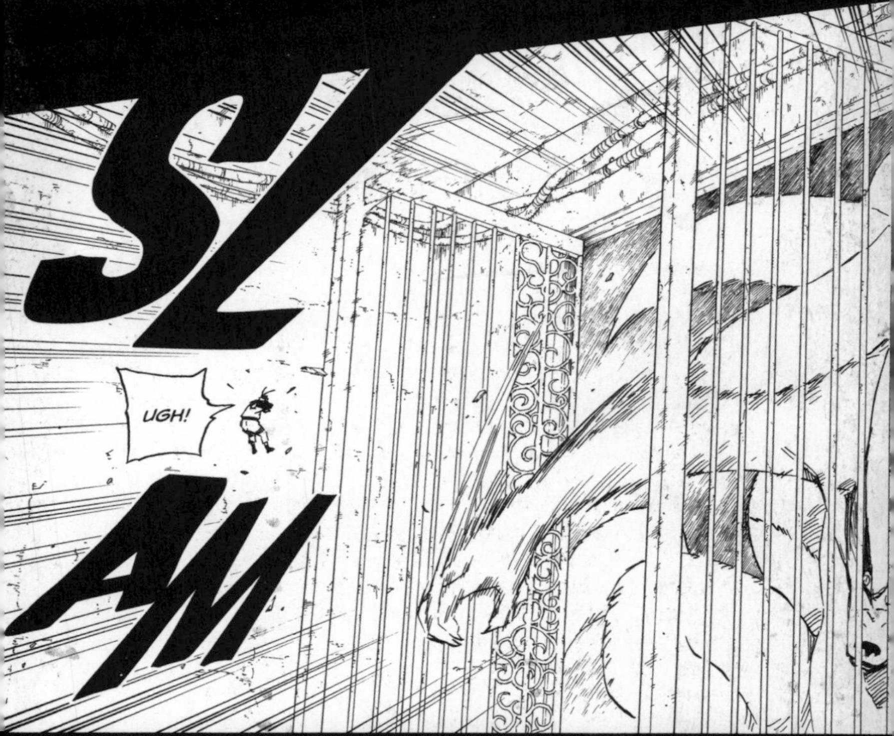
SLAM
UGH!

IN THE NEXT VOLUME...

THE BIRTH OF NARUTO

Naruto faces his inner demons at the Waterfall of Truth! Can he tame the darkness inside himself while still retaining his biju's power? An important figure from his past shows up during the struggle to relate the history of his family and village, revealing astonishing new information about Naruto and Nine Tails!

AVAILABLE DECEMBER 2011!
READ IT FIRST IN SHONEN JUMP MAGAZINE!